EUROPEAN
MYTH & LEGEND

AN A–Z OF PEOPLE AND PLACES

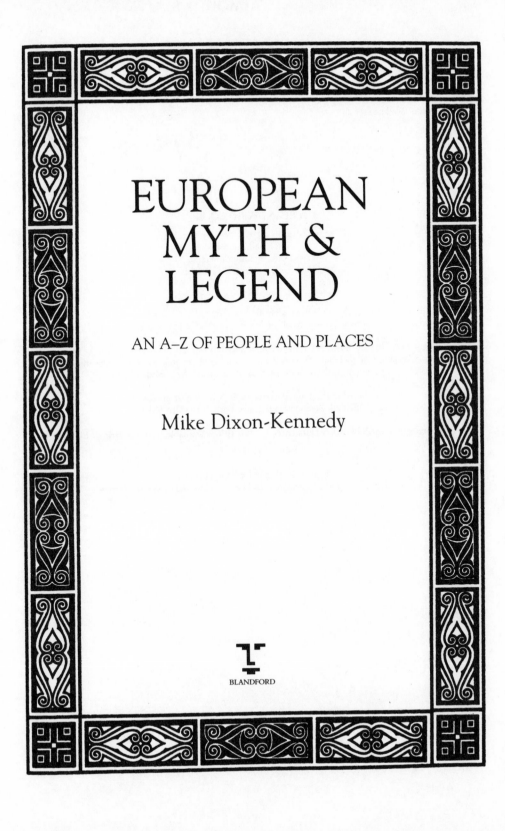

EUROPEAN MYTH & LEGEND

AN A–Z OF PEOPLE AND PLACES

Mike Dixon-Kennedy

BLANDFORD

For Gill, whose tolerance knows no bounds

A BLANDFORD BOOK

First published in the UK 1997 by Blandford
A Cassell Imprint
Cassell Plc, Wellington House
125 Strand, London WC2R OBB

Distributed in the United States by Sterling Publishing Co., Inc.,
387 Park Avenue South, New York, NY 10016-8810

A Cataloguing-in-Publication Data entry for this title is available from the British Library

ISBN 0-7137-2676-8

Typeset by Falcon Oast Graphic Art
Printed and bound in Great Britain by Hartnolls Limited, Bodmin, Cornwall

CONTENTS

PREFACE

Having studied the amazingly complex area of world mythology and legend for more years than I care to remember, there are few stories more stirring than those of ancient Europe, and in particular Russia. Regrettably for us at the end of the twentieth century, very few Russian pre-Christian (pagan) beliefs remain. Those that do have become Christianized, their pagan roots long forgotten.

My first introduction to Russian legend was the story of the witch Baba-Yaga, though I forget who told me about her – I have a feeling it was a Russian sailor whose ship was at Shoreham harbour in Sussex, quite near my childhood home. Many years later, as I came to start my serious research into world mythology, Baba-Yaga came back into the frame. However, apart from that one witch, there seemed to be very little else Russian in my researches. Even now, and even though this book covers Russian mythology and legend, the stories I have managed to collect come mainly from the eastern portion of that vast country – a simple fact that has allowed me to include them in a book about European myth and legend.

I felt that the stories needed telling, for they weave a magical, colourful path that is part fantasy and part embroidered fact. However, due to the paucity of information I managed to collect, I had to look deeper into my research database to see how I could write a book with such meagre pickings. To begin with, I tried conflating Russian with Slavonic, enabling me to look at all the Slavonic-speaking peoples, such as the Poles and Czechs. Disappointment followed, for the Polish and Czech information is even more meagre than the Russian. Southern Slavonic countries provided little more. I needed to look further.

My trusty school atlas now came to the rescue. Studying a map of Europe, I considered the validity of including myths and legends from surrounding countries. The first I looked at were the Baltic countries of Lithuania, Latvia and Estonia. The first two produced a little, but Estonia turned up absolutely nothing. Still, at last I was getting somewhere, even though I did not have anything approaching a book in length.

Next I turned to the Finno-Ugric group, mainly Finland but also any country whose inhabitants spoke one of the Finno-Ugric group of languages. By combining these with the Baltic and Slavonic information I had collected over the years, I came up with nearly enough to compile a single volume. For good measure, I have also included a few of the legends of some Turkic-speaking peoples when they came within the general geographical area being investigated.

Finally, I looked at the remainder of Europe, including the Germanic-speaking lands from the Teutonic heartland up into Scandinavia, as well as some more random myths and legends from across Europe. Having already written books that cover Celtic and Arthurian myth and legend, I omitted all but a very few of those entries. I have also excluded Graeco-Roman myth and legend, as their inclusion would make this book cumbersome and I intend to write a separate volume on that subject. You will find a few small entries on that enigmatic British legendary figure Robin Hood here, but they are few and they are short, my reason being that this is another subject deserving the full treatment (with King Arthur, Robin Hood remains one of the best known, best loved and least studied of all European heroes).

My last problem, having the information to hand, was how to present it clearly and concisely. The dictionary format came out far ahead of any other style, particularly as it brings the book into line with those already published and builds upon the information in those volumes. I hope you will find the stories within this book as enjoyable as I have.

Whenever you sit down to write a book like this, there are obviously many different people who need to be thanked for their help. However, to list all those who have over the years provided me with information, guided me as to where to look and corrected my countless mistakes and assumptions would need a volume of its own. Needless to say, they all know just who they are and to each and every one of them I say a great big 'Thank you'.

My final thanks have to go to my long-suffering wife, Gill, and to Christopher, Charlotte, Thomas and Rebecca, my four often 'fatherless' children. For long periods of time over many years, they have lost me to my research, my passion. Very rarely have they complained and I hope that now they will be able to enjoy the results of their solitude. Whoever thinks writers lead a solitary life should have thought for the writers' partners, for theirs is the true solitude.

Mike Dixon-Kennedy
Cornwall

HOW TO USE THIS BOOK

Although this book is arranged as a simple, straightforward dictionary, several conventions have been adopted to make cross-referencing much easier and the text more decipherable.

i   Where headwords have alternative spellings, these are given under the main entry within the book. If the variant spellings are widely different, then each variant is given its own, shorter entry directing you to the main entry. Where the variant is simply a matter of the omission or addition of a letter or letters, then those letters affected are enclosed in brackets within the headword: for example, the entry **Il`ya Murom(y)ets** gives two versions of the epithet, **Muromets** and **Muromyets**, both of which are acceptable.

Where the variation is a different ending, then the most common is given first: for example, the entry **Svaro~zhich, ~gich** means that the most common variant is **Svarozhich**, the less common **Svarogich**.

Where the addition is 's' for plurals this too is given in brackets.

Where the difference is a complete word, then that word is enclosed in brackets. This occurs when an epithet or surname is part of the full title of the subject but is not commonly used: for example, **Mikula (Selyaninovich)**.

ii   Where words appear in SMALL CAPITALS within an entry, this indicates that there is a separate entry for them.

iii   Where words appear in *italics* within an entry, following standard editorial conventions this indicates that the title of a book or the name of a ship is being referred to or a foreign language used. If these words are also in small capitals, then they have their own separate entry.

Words appearing in italics as subheadings give the origin of the myth or legend.

iv   Where more than one entry appears under a headword, each entry is preceded by a number. Further references to that particular entry within the text of the book are followed by the appropriate superscript number: for example, IVAN[4]. The exceptions to this rule are the elements, such as the wind, or celestial objects, such as the sun and moon, which sometimes have numbers, but at other times are more general.

SPELLING AND PRONUNCIATION GUIDE

All the spellings within this book are literal. This has been particularly necessary when translating from Cyrillic into English. All names are pronounced phonetically in full; every vowel and consonant should be sounded. Accented letters should be stressed. For Russian names an aspirant, indicated by `, has been included where necessary. This means that the consonant preceding the aspirant should be stressed more strongly.

The final 'r' of many Norse and Teutonic names should not be pronounced as a separate syllable. In the past this error has led to many variations, but as far as is humanly possible I used the most correct form. It is pronunciation of the final 'r' in the name Baldr, for example, that commonly though mistakenly leads to its becoming Balder.

Vowels should be pronounced as follows:

á   as *or* in sw*or*d
ø   as the French *eu* in p*eu*r
æ   as *ai* in f*ai*r
au   as *ou* in cl*ou*d

RUSSIAN TITLES

Russian rulers and their families were given titles that may be unfamiliar to the reader. Briefly, they were as follows:

tsar or **czar**   a Russian emperor. The title was first used c. 1482 by Ivan Basilovich, Grand Duke of Muscovy, and then by emperors of Russia until the 1917 revolution. The word is derived from the Latin, Caesar.

tsarevich or **czarevich**   the son of a tsar. Historically the tsarevich was the oldest son, but the name is correctly applied to any son, not just the heir.

tsarevna or **czarevna**   the daughter of a tsar. Like the tsarevich, the tsarevna was usually the oldest daughter of the tsar, but the name is correctly applied to any daughter.

tsarina or **czarina**   the wife of a tsar who, unlike a tsarita, is empress simply by marriage.

tsarita or **czarita**   an unmarried empress.

BRIEF HISTORICAL AND ANTHROPOLOGICAL SURVEY

The Slavs and the Balts

Known to the classical writers of the first and second centuries AD as the Vanedi, a people living beyond the Vistula, the Slavs and the Balts form the northeastern branch of the Indo-European language family spoken in central and eastern Europe, the Balkans and parts of north Asia. During the fifth and sixth centuries AD they expanded considerably, forming several distinct groupings.

The Slavs are usually divided into the Western Slavs, comprising Poles, Czechs, Moravians and Slovaks; the Eastern Slavs, comprising Russians, Ukrainians and Belorussians; and the Southern Slavs, comprising Bulgars, Serbs, Croats and Slovenes. The closely related Balts are also divided into three groups: the Latvians, Lithuanians and Prussians.

There is such a high degree of uniformity among the Slavonic languages that experts speak of a dialect continuum in which the speakers of one variety understand, to a tolerable degree, much of what is said in other varieties. The main difference lies in the fact that some Slavonic languages, such as Polish, are written in the Roman alphabet, while others, like Russian, use the Cyrillic alphabet. By looking at the turbulent history of the Slavs and Balts, it is quite easy to see why very little of their native mythology and legend survives.

Western Slavs

Poles
The various tribes of Poland were first united in the tenth century under one Christian ruler, Mieczyslaw. Mongols devastated the country in 1241, and thereafter German and Jewish refugees settled among the Slav population. Poland became the largest country in Europe when it united with Lithuania between 1569 and 1776. In the mid-seventeenth century Poland was utterly defeated in a war against the combined forces of Russia, Sweden and Brandenburg, a defeat from which it never fully recovered. Further wars with the Ottoman Empire left the country crippled. The country was partitioned by Russia, Prussia and Austria in 1772, and again in 1793 when Russia and Prussia seized further areas, before fully

EUROPEAN CULTURAL DIVISIONS

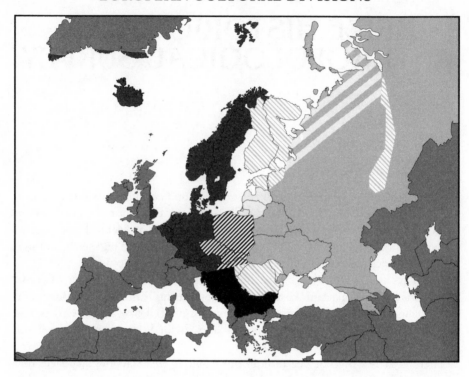

KEY

 Eastern Slavs

 Western Slavs

 Southern Slavs

 Balts

Finno-Ugric

 Norse and Teutonic

Mixed (Finno-Ugric and Eastern Slav)

Outside the scope of this book

 Mixed (Romano-Celtic-Teutonic); Celtic; Graeco-Roman; other cultures

occupying the country in 1795. It was not until 1918 that Poland once again became an independent republic.

Czechs

The indigenous people of the area today recognized as the Czech and Slovak Republics. Czechoslovakia as an independent republic did not come into existence until 1918, after the break-up of the Austro-Hungarian empire at the end of the First World War. It was made up mainly of the Bohemian crownlands – Bohemia, Moravia (see below) and part of Silesia, the three areas in which the Czech language originated – along with Slovakia – that part of Hungary inhabited by Slavonic peoples.

Moravians

Moravia was a part of the Avar territory from the sixth century AD until conquered by the Holy Roman Empire of Charlemagne. In 874 the Slavonic prince Sviatopluk founded the kingdom of Great Moravia, ruling until 894. The Magyars invaded and conquered Great Moravia in 906, the kingdom becoming a fief of Bohemia in 1029. In 1526 it was passed to the Habsburgs and became an Austrian crownland in 1849. Moravia was incorporated into the new republic of Czechoslovakia in 1918, remaining a province of that country until 1949.

Slovaks

Inhabitants of Slovakia and southern Moravia, a region that was settled in the fifth and sixth centuries AD by Slavs. Occupied by the Magyars in the tenth century, it was part of the kingdom of Hungary until 1918, when it became a province of Czechoslovakia.

Eastern Slavs

Russians

The term Russian refers to 'Great Russian', the Slavonic language spoken in Russia, as opposed to 'Little Russian' or Ukrainian, and 'White Russian', as spoken in Belorussia. The entries in this book, however, do not differentiate between the different Russian languages. An entry with the subheading Russian covers all three of the Eastern Slav groups.

The southern steppes of Russia were originally inhabited by nomadic peoples and the northern forests by Slavs, the latter gradually spreading southwards. During the ninth and tenth centuries, Viking chieftains established their own rule in Novgorod, Kiev and other cities. Between the tenth and twelfth centuries, Kiev united the Russian peoples into a single empire, adopting Christianity via Constantinople in 988. The thirteenth century saw the Mongols overrun the southern steppes, while the fourteenth century saw Belorussia and the Ukraine come under Polish rule. Mongol dominance remained until Ivan III, prince of

Moscow, united the northwest against the Mongols between 1462 and 1505, but it was not until 1547 that Ivan IV began a programme of Russian expansion, conquering Kazan and Astrakhan and beginning the colonization of Siberia. Following a Cossack revolt, the eastern part of the Ukraine was reunited with Russia in 1667. Peter the Great wrested the Baltic seaboard from Sweden, and by 1700 the colonization of Siberia had reached the Pacific Ocean. Between 1762 and 1796 Catherine the Great annexed the Crimea and part of Poland, and recovered the western part of the Ukraine and Belorussia, or White Russia.

Ukrainians

Closely related to Russian, the Slavonic language spoken in the Ukraine is referred to by the Russians as 'Little Russian', a term Ukrainians dislike. The Ukraine was a state by the ninth century, coming under Polish rule during the fourteenth century, until Russia absorbed the eastern Ukraine in 1667 and the remainder in 1793 from Austrian rule.

Belorussians

Originally part of the Russian empire, Belorussia or 'White Russia', came under Polish rule during the fourteenth century. This was the situation until 1796, when Catherine the Great recovered Belorussia. The language spoken by Belorussians is closely related to Russian and is sometimes referred to as 'White Russian'.

Southern Slavs

Bulgars

In ancient times Bulgaria comprised Thrace and Moesia, and was the Roman province of Moesia Inferior. Later occupied by Slavs in the seventh century it was conquered by the invading Bulgars. From Asia, they were absorbed into the native population. Khan Boris adopted Eastern Orthodox Christianity in 865, and under his son Simeon (893–927) the country became a leading power. From the eleventh century Bulgaria was ruled by Byzantium and even though a second independent Bulgarian empire was founded in the fourteenth century, Bulgaria was part of the Ottoman Empire for almost 500 years, until it became an independent kingdom in 1908.

Serbs

Settling in the Balkans in the seventh century at the invitation of Emperor Heraclius, in the Roman province of Moesia, Serbs became Christians in the ninth century. United as one kingdom c. 1169, they formed a single empire covering most of the Balkans under Stephen Dushan (1331–55). Defeated at Kosovo in 1389, they came under Turkish domination, the Turks annexing Serbia in 1459. Uprisings between 1804 and 1816 led the Turks to recognize Serbia as an autonomous principality. After a war with Turkey (1876–8), Serbia became an independent kingdom. The two Balkan Wars, 1912–13, greatly enlarged Serbia's territory at the expense of Turkey and Bulgaria. The designs of Serbia on Bosnia-Herzegovina, backed by Russia, led to friction with Austria and the outbreak of the First World War in 1914. Serbia became the nucleus of the new independent republic of Yugoslavia in 1918.

Croats

Part of Pannonia in Roman times, Croatia was settled by Carpathian Croats during the seventh century. For 800 years, from 1102, Croatia was an autonomous kingdom under the Hungarian crown, before becoming an Austrian crownland in 1849. Then in 1868 Croatia became a Hungarian crownland. In 1918 it became part of the new independent republic of Yugoslavia.

Slovenes

Members of the Slavonic people of Slovenia and parts of the Austrian alpine provinces of Styria and Carinthia. Slovenia was settled during the sixth century. Until 1918, when it became a part of Yugoslavia, it was the Austrian province of Carniola. In 1989 Slovenia voted to give itself the right to secede from Yugoslavia.

Balts

Latvians

Latvian is one of the only two remaining languages of the Baltic branch of the Indo-European family, the other being the closely related Lithuanian.

Lithuanians

The Lithuanian language has, through the geographical position of Lithuania, retained many ancient features of the Indo-European family of languages. It did not acquire a written form until the sixteenth century, and is one of the only two Baltic languages to survive, the other being Latvian.

Prussians

Inhabitants of the north German state of Prussia. Formed in 1618 by the union of Brandenburg and the duchy of Prussia (formed 1525), Prussia became a kingdom in 1701 under Frederick I at which time the Baltic language of Prussian became extinct. Silesia, East Frisia and West Prussia were annexed by Frederick II between 1740 and 1786, the lost territory being restored after the Congress of Vienna in 1815, along with lands in the Rhineland and Saxony. A war in 1864 with Denmark resulted in the acquisition of Schleswig-Holstein. After World War I, Prussia became a republic, but lost its independence in 1932 in Hitler's Germany. Prussia ceased to exist in 1946 after World War II when the Allies divided its territories between East and West Germany, Poland and Russia.

Finno-Ugric

Although closely related to both the Balts and Slavs, with whom they became closely assimilated, the Finno-Ugric peoples do not belong to the Indo-European family. Their language grouping, a subfamily of the Ural-Altaic family, contains more than twenty different tongues, from Norway in the west to Siberia in the east and to the Carpathian mountains in the south. Finno-Ugric peoples may be subdivided into four main groups according to their geographical position. The first comprises the Finns, Lapps, Estonians (though Estonia is generally thought of as a Baltic country), Livonians and Karelians. The second comprises the Cheremiss-Mordvin peoples of the middle and upper Volga. The third comprises the Votyaks, Permyaks and Zyrians, who inhabit the Russian provinces of Perm and Vyatka. The fourth comprises the Voguls and Ostyaks of western Siberia. The Magyar people of Hungary are usually included in the fourth grouping as they originated in western Siberia, but they are normally considered a Turkic people.

The Finno-Ugric peoples were widely influenced by their Indo-European neighbours, the Balts, the Slavs and the Norse/Teutons. Many of their legends bear direct comparison with those of the Balts and the Slavs, and again a short look at the histories of the various Finno-Ugric peoples and their countries will give some indication of why the only major source of Finno-Ugric myth and legend is the Finnish epic poem the *Kalevala*.

Group 1

Finns
Inhabitants of Finland who speak Finnish, a member of the Finno-Ugric language family, and closely related to neighbouring Estonian, Livonian, Karelian and Ingrian languages. At the beginning of the nineteenth century Finnish had no official status, Swedish being the language of education, government and literature in Finland. It was not until the publication of the *Kalevala* (see page 132) in 1835 that the Finns' linguistic and nationalistic feelings were aroused.

The Lapps (see below) once inhabited the area now known as Finland, but they were driven by Finnic nomads from Asia into the far northern region they occupy today c. the first century BC. The area was conquered during the twelfth century by Sweden and for most of the following 200 years was the scene of numerous wars between Sweden and Russia. As a duchy of Sweden, Finland was allowed a certain degree of autonomy, becoming a Grand Duchy in 1581. Russia annexed Finland in 1809, during the Napoleonic Wars. The country proclaimed its independence in 1917, during the Russian Revolution, and though Russia initially attempted to regain control, they acknowledged Finland's independence in 1920.

Lapps

Though today the Lapps are very much a minority race – possibly fewer than 20,000 remain – they once occupied the entire area of Finland. They were driven north into what is today known as Lapland by Finnic invaders from Asia c. the first century BC. Though their homeland is known as Lapland, this has no political definition, falling within the Arctic Circle across four countries: Norway, Sweden, Finland and Russia.

Estonians

Estonia, like the other Baltic countries, has had a turbulent history. It was a democratic republic between 1919 and 1934, when the government was overthrown in a Fascist coup, and in 1940 it became a Soviet republic. Unlike the languages of its neighbours, Latvia and Lithuania, Estonian is not a Slavonic language, the Finno-Ugric spoken having been transported from nearby Sweden and Finland.

Livonians

Livonia was a former region of Europe on the eastern coast of the Baltic Sea that covered most of present-day Latvia and Estonia. Conquered in the early part of the thirteenth century and converted to Christianity by the Livonian Knights, a crusading order, it remained independent until 1583, when it was divided between Poland and Sweden. In 1710 it was occupied by Russia and in 1721 was ceded to Peter the Great. The Latvian portion of Livonia was inhabited by Slavonic-speaking peoples, while the Estonian part retained the Finno-Ugric language. Today Livonian is still spoken by a few.

Karelians

Karelia is an Autonomous Soviet Socialist Republic in the northwest of Russia, between the Finnish border and the White Sea. It was occupied in early times by nomadic Finnic settlers, who gave the area its Finno-Ugric language, which has been retained despite the best efforts of the Communist regime to enforce the speaking of the Slavonic Russian.

Group 2

Cheremiss-Mordvin

The indigenous inhabitants of the region comprising the middle and upper Volga that is today the Autonomous Republic of Mordovia or Mordvinia. The region was conquered by Russia during the thirteenth century and did not regain autonomy until 1930. Almost none of the Finno-Ugric-speaking Cheremiss-Mordvin peoples have survived.

17

Group 3

Votyaks, Permyaks and Zyrians
Indigenous peoples from a region to the east of the Ural mountains who have been almost totally absorbed by the Slavonic-speaking Russians. Their Finno-Ugric languages remain only in a few isolated pockets, but virtually nothing remains of their ancient traditions and beliefs.

Group 4

Voguls and Ostyaks
Ancient indigenous peoples from western Siberia. As with many of the early peoples of Asiatic Russia, very little remains of their customs and beliefs as they have been almost totally absorbed by the invading and conquering Slavonic-speaking Russians.

Magyars
The Magyars comprise the largest single ethnic group in Hungary. Of mixed Ugric and Turkic origin, the Magyars arrived in Hungary from western Siberia towards the end of the ninth century. Their place of origin means they are included as a Finno-Ugric-speaking people, although their language today more closely resembles a Turkic language. This is because Hungary was overrun by Turkish invaders during the sixteenth century and remained a Turkish kingdom until the end of the seventeenth century, when the Turks were driven out by the Habsburgs and Hungary came under Austrian rule.

Magyar is still the native tongue of Hungary and is today spoken in pockets within the Czech Republic, Slovakia, the former Yugoslavia, Romania and Moldovia. The Magyar kingdom was first established in the late ninth century, when the ten Magyar tribes overran the country, until then inhabited by Celts and Slavs, under a chief named Arpád. As with most of the region, Hungary's very turbulent history has unfortunately almost totally wiped out the ancient customs and beliefs of the original Siberian Magyar people.

Norse and Teutonic

The terms Norse and Teutonic apply to the Indo-European settlers of northern Europe, particularly Germany and Scandinavia, though the name Germanic, which is also sometimes applied to these people, also includes the British people. Between the fourth and sixth centuries AD these peoples began to move south and west – Angles and Saxons in Britain (hence Anglo-Saxon), Franks into Gaul (hence France) and the Vandals and Goths into the central European heartland – each expansion crushing the Graeco-Roman and Roman-Celtic civilizations they encountered. By the middle of the eighth century the English and most of the continental Germanic peoples had been converted to Christianity, and most of the myths and legends of the indigenous peoples were sadly lost for ever.

As a result, scholars must now rely on place-names and archaeological evidence for information regarding the pagan beliefs of the pre-Christian Anglo-Saxons and continental Germanic peoples. However, this information can be greatly supplemented by the works of various contemporary writers. The Roman Tacitus (c. 55–120) recorded many of the beliefs of the continental Teutons, a race he greatly admired in his *Germania*, while the great Anglo-Saxon epic *Beowulf* provides evidence of pagan cultures. Although this great poem dates from the Christian era, it preserves the tradition of the pagan times before it.

Most of the Norse and Teutonic myths and legends that have survived come from Scandinavia, which did not start the conversion to Christianity until the tenth century. Sweden held on to its pagan beliefs the longest and did not succumb to Christianity until almost two centuries later. However, like the beliefs of other pagan cultures, those of Scandinavia were not written down by believers in the old religions but rather by Christian scribes, and are as a result often 'contaminated'. Some scholars go so far as to say that the Norse sagas were really historical novels rather than records of the pagan society, but whatever is the case they do preserve a great deal of valuable ancient material.

Apart from the various sagas, there is also a small collection of Icelandic poems, the *Codex Regius*, that concern the pagan gods, but this is only forty-five pages in length. Therefore, for the most part we must rely on the work of the Icelandic scholar Snorri Sturluson (1178–1241), who compiled an anthology of heathen stories that is known as the *Prose Edda*. The authenticity of this work can, to a certain degree, be checked, for a number of the poems Snorri quotes as his sources still exist. Research seems to suggest that Snorri was a dedicated, true scholar who did not apply the artistic licence so commonly found in the telling of pagan stories. Equally valuable is the *Gesta Danorum*, written by the Danish chronicler Saxo Grammaticus (c. 1150–c. 1220).

All this leaves the scholar with the quandary of trying to determine just what in these records is true and how much is literary convention. One of the most striking elements of Norse and Teutonic tradition concerns the shaman, although shamanism does not appear to have been an original aspect of their pagan beliefs. It now seems likely that this charismatic form of worship was imported from other cultures, such as the Slavs or even the Finno-Ugric peoples, with whom there would undoubtedly have been contact.

Most people refer to the Norse peoples as Vikings, and while this is not altogether incorrect, it is also not correct, for the Vikings were just one of the Norse and Teutonic peoples. They established themselves in Scandinavia between the eighth and eleventh centuries and were characterized by a mix of barbarism and chivalry, both tenets being taken to extremes. They are famous for their raids on the eastern coast of Britain, killing men and children and raping the women before also putting them to the sword. The Vikings were not, however, mindless thugs, for their mythology shows that they had built up a complex philosophy to explain and justify their behaviour.

The Norse gods decreed that men should be almost superhumanly brave and that death was the greatest reward on offer, for that would confer on them the honour of living out eternity in the presence of and entertained by the gods. And even though the Vikings might not at first appeal to people today, having a culture that was based on war and aggression – looting, pillaging, raping and a host of other barbarous crimes – their civilization was an attempt to explain the hard conditions in which they lived. The day was short, the winters long and hard, and people tried to live in harmony with the harshness and sought to explain, through their mythology, the reasons for everything, from the cracking of a glacier to the need to kill a fellow human being, either as a sacrifice or in battle.

Other Peoples Included

Yakut

A Turkic-speaking people living near the Lena river in northeast Siberia, one of the coldest regions on earth. Today there is an institute in Yakutsk, the coldest point of the Arctic, for studying the permafrost there. Very few of the beliefs of the ancient Yakut people have survived. Turkic is an Ural-Altaic language, and thus closely linked to Finno-Ugric.

Tungus

An ancient people from one of the coldest regions on earth, Siberia. A single major Tungus legend only has survived – which is unfortunate, as the story of Ivan the Mare's son is particularly fine.

Lett

Indigenous inhabitants of Latvia who were closely related to their neighbours the Lithuanians. Their language is Baltic, with characteristics of both Latvian and Lithuanian.

DICTIONARY

Aasa
Norse and Teutonic
According to Snorri STURLUSON, the wife of GUDROD and mother, by him, of HÁLFDAN SVARTI.

acorn
Norse and Teutonic
The symbol of life, fecundity and immortality, the acorn was sacred to THÓRR.

A'Dale, Alan
British
One of the companions of ROBIN HOOD, his so-called MERRY MEN.

Ægir
Norse and Teutonic
Also called HLER. The chief of the sea giants and master of the oceans, Ægir represents the peaceful ocean and was often referred to as 'the Ale-brewer', thus suggesting mastery of the arts of brewing. While not having the status of a god, his relationship with the gods was good. He was welcomed at their feasts and in return they were entertained by him and his consort, RAN, in his marine palace. NORSE and TEUTONIC peoples believed that drowned sailors were also entertained at his undersea palace and that the treasure from sunken ships was stored there. Ægir is said to have had nine daughters, who may have been the nine giantesses who mothered HEIMDALLR.

Aelle
Anglo-Saxon
An ANGLO-SAXON king of Sussex who, along with his sons CISSA, CYMEN and WLENCING, defeated the Britons at Cymenes ora in 477, once again fighting their forces near Mearc rædesburna in 485, and capturing ANDERIDA (modern Pevensey, Sussex) *c.* 491. According to the Venerable BEDE[2], Aelle was BRET-WALDA, a title held by various kings of various Anglo-Saxon countries.

Aesc
Anglo-Saxon
The traditional and eponymous founder of the AESCING tribe that reigned in Kent between 488 and 512, and a son of HENGIST, an association that is supported by those who link Aesc with ASKR and the fact that Hengist claimed descent from WODEN.

Aeschere
Anglo-Saxon
The counsellor to HRODGAR who was seized by GRENDEL's mother in vengeance for the death of her son.

Aescing
Anglo-Saxon
Kentish ANGLO-SAXON tribe that was traditionally founded by and takes its name from AESC, possibly one of the sons of HENGIST.

Æsir

Norse and Teutonic

Generic term applied to the group of gods led by ODÍNN, the 'All Father', others within the grouping being VILLI, VÉ, THÓRR, BALDR, LOKI, FREYJA, TYR, HOENIR, MÍMIR and HEIMDALLR.

Three of the Æsir, Odínn, Villi and Vé, who were sons of BÖRR, the son of BÚRI and BESTLA, the daughter of YMIR, killed Ymir, and from his corpse formed MIDGARDR, the domain of mankind. They made the seas and the lakes from his blood, the earth from his flesh, mountains from his bones, and rocks and pebbles from his teeth, jaws and smaller broken bones. From his skull, they formed the dome of the sky, which was supported at the four corners of the world by four DWARFS, and from his eyebrows they made a wall to protect Midgardr from the FROST GIANTS, the descendants of BERGELMIR, who had survived the bloody deluge caused by the slaying of Ymir that drowned all the original Frost Giants by sailing away in his boat to found a new gigantic race.

Having created the world of men, the Æsir built a home for themselves at the end of one of the three roots of the great ash tree YGGDRASILL which they called ASGARDR. Here Odínn lived in the silver-roofed hall VALASKJÁLF with his wife, FRIGGA, kept his wondrous horse SLEIPNIR, and was brought information by his two ravens, HUGINN and MUNINN, while he sat on his seat HLIDSKJÁLF, from which he could survey all the world at once. The Æsir commissioned one of the giants to build a wall around Asgardr. The giant promised to have the wall completed within a year, his payment to be the SUN[5] and the MOON[5], and the goddess FREYJA as his wife. With the help of his wonderful stallion SVADILFARI, it seemed likely that the giant would complete the enormous task within the allotted time, a situation

that the Æsir feared lest, upon receipt of the due payment, he became too powerful. So the Æsir commissioned LOKI to find some way of preventing the giant completing the work on time, which he did, and the wall was never finished. The incomplete wall was guarded by the silent Heimdallr, who carried a trumpet called GJALLARHORN with which he could warn the Æsir of any approaching danger. Between Midgardr and Asgardr the Æsir built the rainbow bridge BÏFROST.

A great battle was once fought between the Æsir and the VANIR until, at length, a truce was declared and the two sides met to make their peace. The entire assembly spat into a cauldron and so created KVASIR, a being of such wisdom that he could answer any question. However, two dwarfs killed Kvasir and, by mixing his blood with mead, brewed the MEAD OF INSPIRATION, which inspired whoever drank it to speak words of great wisdom and to compose wondrous poetry. Odínn, by way of his magic arts, stole this from the dwarfs and took it to Asgardr, where it was known as either KVASIR'S BLOOD or SHIP OF THE DWARFS.

A variant story says that when the truce was called, the Vanir and the Æsir agreed on an exchange of hostages. The two greatest Vanir, NJÖRDR and FREYR, went to live in Asgardr. The Æsir sent the handsome but silent Hoenir and the wise Mímir. However, because Hoenir never spoke a word, the Vanir felt that they had been cheated and so beheaded Mímir, sending the head back to Asgardr, where Odínn charmed it back to life and gave it the power of speech. Thenceforth Odínn consulted the head in times of crisis.

Snorri STURLUSON thought that the word Æsir was derived from the word ASIA, and made Thórr a grandson of King Priam of Troy, with Odínn his twentieth-generation descendant. Their opponents, the Vanir, were accordingly originally inhabitants of the land on the River DON, 'formerly called VAVAQUISL', from which their name was said to have derived. Although Sturluson's idea receives little or no support today, it is still likely that the Vanir were late arrivals from ASIA MINOR and their initial rivalry with the Æsir most probably represents an accommodation of an earlier mythology.

The mythology of the Æsir clearly demonstrates that even the gods were in the hands of fate, over which they had no control, and that they were inexorably moving towards their doom, the RAGNARØKR. On this day the forces of evil will overcome the gods and their allies, the EINHERJAR, the slain champions that were the beloved of Odínn. Out of the cataclysm two humans, LÍF and LÍFDRASIR will survive to repeople the new earth and worship BALDR, the son of Odínn, in a new heaven.

Afi
Norse and Teutonic
The husband of AMMA, whose son KARL was the progenitor of the race of peasants. Afi assumed that the child was his son, but Karl was in fact the son of HEIMDALLR.

Afron
Russian
The tsar of an unnamed realm and the owner of the HORSE WITH THE GOLDEN MANE. When IVAN[6] was caught trying to steal both the horse and its golden bridle, even though the wolf helping Ivan had warned him not to touch the bridle, Afron gave him a chance to redeem himself. If Ivan could bring him ELENA THE BEAUTIFUL, after whom he had lusted for some time, he would not only forgive Ivan but also give him the Horse with the Golden Mane and its bridle. If he failed, Ivan would be branded a common thief.

Ivan succeeded in abducting Elena the Beautiful with the assistance of the shape-changing wolf who had been helping him throughout his quest, which started as one set by his father, Tsar Vyslav ANDRONOVICH, to capture the FIREBIRD. However, Ivan fell in love with Elena the Beautiful, and she with him, so the wolf assumed her shape when they came back to Afron's palace. Afron kept his word and gave Ivan both the Horse with the Golden Mane and its golden bridle. Ivan and the real Elena the Beautiful rode away on the horse. The wolf resumed its true form and rejoined Ivan, thus leaving Afron with nothing. How he reacted to this trick is not recorded.

Agder
Norse and Teutonic
The domain of HARALDR[1], the father of AASA, and thus grandfather of HÁLFDAN SVARTI. GUDROD, Aasa's husband, died when Hálfdan Svarti was just one year old and travelled to Agder, where Aasa ascended the throne of her father's kingdom. The throne passed to Hálfdan Svarti when he came of age at eighteen.

Agnar(r)
Norse and Teutonic
The elder son of HRAUDINGR and brother of GEIRRØDR. His right to ascendancy was usurped by his brother, who cast him adrift and thus became the sole heir. However, Agnar survived and later sneaked back into his brother's palace, where he worked as a servant. After the death of Geirrødr, Agnar assumed his rightful place. A variant says that Agnar actually perished at sea and it was Geirrødr's own son, in this case also named Agnar, who succeeded to the throne after Geirrødr's death.

Agne
Norse and Teutonic
The son of DAG[1], brother of DAGEID, and father of ALRIC and ERIC.

Aht~i, ~o
Finno-Ugric
1 The god of the waters whose consort was VELLAMO and who was described as having a beard made of moss. He lived in the 'black slime' of an undersea cave at the foot of a cloud-swathed promontory, and was attended by TURSAS, VETEHINEN and all the other water spirits. Ahti was generally bad-tempered and apt to attack human beings.
2 An alternative name for the hero LEMMINKAINEN.

Ai
Norse and Teutonic
The husband of EDDA. Their son THRALL was the progenitor of the race of serfs.

Ainikki
Finno-Ugric
The daughter of KYLLIKKI and sister of LEMMINKAINEN. She reported to her brother that his wife, KYLLI, had broken her marital promise. Lemminkainen then divorced Kylli.

Aino
Finno-Ugric
The sister of the thin LAPLANDER JOUKANAINEN who threw herself into the sea when her brother promised her hand in marriage to the ageing VÄINÄMÖINEN.

Aitvaras
Lithuanian
A mysterious and curious flying creature, sometimes depicted as a cockerel, sometimes with the head of the lucky grass snake ZALTYS and the fiery tail of a comet.

Ajysyt
Siberia – Yakut
The mother goddess of the YAKUTs, a TURKIC people living near the River Lena in Siberia. Literally translated, her name means 'Birth-giver', though she is also referred to as 'Mother of Cradles' and was believed to be present whenever one of her devotees gave birth. In her aspect AJYSYT-IJAKSIT-KHOTAN she was the 'Birth-giving Nourishing Mother'. She brought the souls of the newborn baby down from heaven so that a complete human being could come into existence. Other Siberian tribes thought that the mother goddess dwelt in heaven on a mountain that had seven storeys. There she determined the fate of all people by writing in a golden book at the birth of every child.

The Altai Tartars acknowledged a similar deity known as the 'Milk-lake Mother', and the Yakuts themselves possess a curious myth about a white youth who encounters a calm 'lake of milk' near the cosmic tree, the world pillar of YRYN-AL-TOJON, the 'White Creator Lord'. Having sought the blessing of the tree, this youth felt a warm breeze, heard the tree creak and saw a female divinity, Ajysyt, arise from the roots. She offered him milk from her full breasts and, having satisfied his thirst, the youth felt his strength increase a hundredfold. Thus the milk-breasted mother of life, the mother goddess, and the cosmic TREE OF LIFE[2] are combined into one sustaining and nourishing entity.

Ajysyt-ijaksit-khotan
Siberia – Yakut
'Birth-giving Nourishing Mother', an aspect of the YAKUT mother goddess, AJYSYT.

Akka
Finno-Ugric
The goddess of the harvest and female sexuality. The consort of UKKO, Akka is also known as RAUNI which means 'Mountain Ash'. The rowan, or mountain ash, tree is sacred to her, as her alternative name would indicate. She was called MADER AKKA by the LAPP people.

Akka was often represented by a triangle or a six-sided polygon, and was responsible for the fertility of the fields. She also helped her husband in the act of creation; he created the souls and she created the bodies. In ESTONIA she was called MAAN-ENO.

Alaisiagae
Teutonic

Generic name given to two or four female spirits associated with the god of war, though they were not necessarily war goddesses themselves. Traditionally there were two Alaisiagae, BAUDIHILLIE and FRIAGABI, but after their cult had been imported to BRITAIN by the Romans, they were joined by two others, BEDE[1] and FINNILENE. The Alaisaigae had characteristics similar to the VALKYRJA, and it may be that they were a TEUTONIC version of their NORSE counterparts. In Britain worship of the Alaisiagae appears to have been localized in the area immediately south of Hadrian's Wall, though their original area of worship seems to have been the central Teutonic heartland.

Alans
Russian

A tribe of the barbarian peoples known as the SARMATIANS who inhabited RUSSIA in Roman times. Their descendants, the OSSETES, still inhabit the CAUCASUS. They tell a story very similar to that concerning the passing of King ARTHUR. It is possible that the story of Arthur was carried to the region by the Romans, but when the story of BATRADZ, the Ossete hero, is considered, it would seem that this might actually be the source of the Arthur legend as it appears to be the older of the two.

Alba(ny)
Anglo-Saxon

The post-ANGLO-SAXON name, traditionally Irish in origin, for SCOTLAND.

Alberich
Norse and Teutonic

The ELF[3] King and the guardian of the treasure of the NIBELUNGEN, which was stolen from him by SIGURDR/SIEGFRIED.

Alcis
Norse and Teutonic

The name given to twin deities who were worshipped in forest sanctuaries by priests wearing ornate, effeminate costumes. TACITUS reports that they were worshipped by the NAHARVALI tribe, and remarks on the outstanding similarity between the cult of Alcis and that of the Graeco-Roman twin deities Castor and Polydeuces (Roman Pollux), adding, though, that in his opinion the cult was indigenous rather than imported. Other than this reference by Tacitus, no other evidence has been found of this cult among the NORSE and TEUTONIC peoples.

Alemanni
General

Indigenous Germanic people who once inhabited GERMANY. They were conquered in 496 by Clovis, King of the FRANKS, and from then until the middle of the eighth century the Germanic peoples remained under the control of the Franks.

Alenka
Russian

The daughter of an unnamed witch, though some authorities give her mother as none other than BABA-YAGA. When her mother brought home the young IVASHKO to be her supper, Alenka was ordered to cook him. Having heated up the stove, Ivashko tricked her and pushed Alenka deep into its fire, locking the door, and escaped. When the witch returned, she chided her daughter for having left the meal unattended, but nonetheless sat down with the friends she had invited to dinner and unwittingly ate her daughter, a fact that was brought to her attention by Ivashko a short while later.

Alenushka
Russian

Although of royal lineage, Alenushka and her brother IVANUSHKA were forced to wander like gypsies after their parents had died. During their wanderings the pair came to a pond where a herd of cattle were grazing. Ivanushka rushed to the water to slake his thirst, but Alenushka stopped him, warning him that if he drank he would turn into a calf.

The next water they came to was a lake where a flock of sheep were grazing. Again Ivanushka ran to the water's edge and again Alenushka stopped him from drinking, warning him that if he did he would turn into a lamb. At the next stretch of water there were some pigs nearby. Alenushka stopped Ivanushka from drinking by warning him that he would become a piglet. However, by the time they reached the next pond, near which some goats were grazing, Ivanushka's thirst was so great that he ignored his sister's advice. As soon as he drank, Ivanushka turned into a kid.

Alenushka harnessed her brother and they continued on their way, eventually coming to a royal palace, where Ivanushka ran off and began to eat the well-manicured grass before the palace. The royal guards brought Alenushka and her brother before the tsar, who was immediately taken with Alenushka and asked her to marry him. She consented, and so found a new home for herself and her brother.

Some time later the tsar had to be away on business. While he was absent a sorceress who had designs on the tsar cast a spell on Alenushka and she became ill, growing thinner and weaker each day. All around the palace the flowers and the grass died. Once more the tsar had to go away, and this time the sorceress told Alenushka that she could cure herself if she went to the sea's edge at dusk and drank a little of the water. Alenushka did so, but the sorceress tied a huge boulder around her neck and threw her far out to sea. The sorceress then assumed the likeness of Alenushka and returned to the palace, where the tsar rejoiced to see his wife restored to full health.

Ivanushka remained by the water, where he bleated for his sister. In the palace the sorceress nagged the tsar to kill Ivanushka, for she said, she had grown tired of the way he smelt. At first the tsar would not hear of it, but eventually he reluctantly agreed. Ivanushka, learning of his fate, asked the tsar for permission to go to the seashore. The tsar agreed.

There Ivanushka called for his sister, but Alenushka replied that she could not come because of the boulder tied around her neck. Ivanushka returned to the palace, but at midday once more asked for permission to visit the seashore. When there he yet again called to his sister, and yet again received the same reply. As dusk began to fall, Ivanushka asked permission of the tsar for a third time. Once more he agreed, but, curious about Ivanushka's strange behaviour, he followed the kid to the edge of the water. There Ivanushka called to his sister and this time she came bobbing to the surface.

The tsar immediately swam out to Alenushka, released the boulder and carried her back to the palace. There he ordered his guards to light a huge bonfire. When the sorceress came to see what was happening, the tsar threw her on to it and burned her to death. As the sorceress died, so the gardens around the palace burst back into flower, and Alenushka lived happily with her brother Ivanushka for the rest of their days.

Alesha
Russian

The son of LEONTII, a priest from ROSTOV, Alesha lived in KIEV at the court of Prince VLADIMIR BRIGHT SUN. When Vladimir asked his knights which one would rescue Princess ZABAVA from the clutches of a DRAGON[1] who had carried her away, it was Alesha who told the prince about Dobrynya NIKITICH's pact with the dragon, thus making the prince command that knight to rescue the girl, or be beheaded.

Alesha was not always inept, as the story of his arrival at Kiev proves. Riding from Rostov with his squire EKIM, he decided to come to Kiev, for their other choices, Sezdal and CHERNIGOV, were sure, they thought, to lead them into trouble, either from wine or from women. Arriving in Kiev, they immediately realized that all was not as it should be, for there were no grooms to stable their horses, which they had to leave in the courtyard.

Entering the royal palace, they presented themselves to Vladimir Bright Sun, who had already heard of Alesha and bade him join them that night at a banquet as guest of honour. Alesha chose not to sit at the table but instead to perch himself on the stove in the banqueting hall, a position usually occupied by beggars and serfs. Shortly after the meal had got under way, the door to the hall was thrown open and a giant, brutish creature slithered in. This was TUGARIN, a heathen monster with the girth of two fully grown oak trees, eyes set far apart in his ugly head and ears that were nearly eight inches long. Paying no respect to Vladimir, Tugarin seated himself between the prince and his wife.

Watching these events from his place on the stove, Alesha inquired how serious the argument must have been between the prince and his wife to allow such an ugly creature to sit between them. Ignoring Alesha, Tugarin plunged the blade of his knife into a roast swan that was set before him and ate it whole, spitting out the bones as he swallowed the flesh. Alesha again taunted Tugarin by saying that his father, Leontii, had once had a mongrel dog that choked to death on a swan's bone, and how he hoped Tugarin would do the same. Tugarin ignored the taunts and ate a huge game pie in a single mouthful.

Alesha tried once more, saying that his father had had an old cow that had rooted around in the dirt for food and had choked to death. He hoped that the ill manners of Tugarin would lead him to the same fate. At last Tugarin rose to the bait and asked Vladimir Bright Sun who the ignorant peasant was. When he heard that it was none other than Alesha, for even Tugarin had heard of him, he threw his long knife at him, but Ekim was too quick and caught the knife by its handle. Seeing this, Tugarin pushed the table over and challenged Alesha to meet him out on the steppe.

Alesha was only too happy to oblige and immediately set out on foot. Some way away from Kiev, he came across a pilgrim who carried a heavy staff weighing ninety *poods* (c. 3,240 lb). Exchanging clothes with the pilgrim, Alesha also borrowed the staff. Soon afterwards he caught sight of Tugarin, sat astride a powerful horse, flying overhead on a set of paper wings he had made. Alesha prayed for a heavy shower of rain and his prayer was answered almost immediately. As the rain fell, Tugarin's paper wings fell to pieces and he crashed to the ground. Tugarin realized who the pilgrim was and galloped towards him, fully intending to crush him under his horse's hoofs.

Alesha nimbly sidestepped the rushing horse and hid beneath its flowing mane. As Tugarin searched for Alesha, the knight struck out with the staff, knocking Tugarin's head from his shoulders. Picking up the head, he planted it on the end of the staff and returned to Kiev riding Tugarin's horse.

Alexander the Great
General
Historical ruler of MACEDONIA (356–323 BC), the son of King Philip II and Queen Olympias. At the age of nineteen, he succeeded his father as the King of Macedonia and Olympus. Alexander was educated by the philosopher Aristotle and, immediately after the death of his father, embarked on a campaign of expansion the likes of which had never been seen before. He conquered Greece in 336 BC and in 334 BC crossed the Dardanelles for the campaign against the vast Persian empire, quickly winning his first victory at the River Granicus. In 333 BC he routed Darius at Issus and then set out for Egypt, where he was greeted as Pharaoh. In the meantime, Darius had assembled an army of half a million men for a final battle, but at Arbela on the Tigris he was utterly defeated by Alexander, who had just 47,000 under his command.

He remained in Babylon for a month after his victory and then marched to Susa and Persepolis. In 330 BC he moved on to Ecbatana (modern Hamadán in Iran). Soon after he received news that Darius was dead. In Afghanistan he founded colonies at Herat and Kandahar, and in 328 BC reached the plains of Sogdiana, where he married Roxana, the daughter of King Oxyartes. Alexander then pressed on towards India, but at the river Hyphasis (now Beas) his men refused to go any further and he was forced to turn back. They reached Susa in 324 BC and here Alexander married Darius's daughter. He died in Babylon the following year of malaria.

Alfheimr
Norse and Teutonic
The name given to that region of ASGARDR that is the home of the elves of light (see ELF). It is sometimes, incorrectly, known as ELFHEIMR.

Alfrigg
Norse and Teutonic
One of the four DWARFS who enjoyed a night of carnal knowledge with FREYJA after they had made her the necklace BRÍSINGAMEN. The other three dwarfs so rewarded were BERLING, DVALIN[1] and GRERR.

Alka
Lithuanian
A collective term for sacred fields, springs or groves which could not, respectively, be ploughed, fished or felled. These Alka were specially sacred places for the cremation of the dead, and as sites where votive offerings could be left for the gods.

Alric
Norse and Teutonic
The son of AGNE, brother of ERIC, and thus grandson of DAG[1].

Alsvidr
Norse and Teutonic
The name of the horse that pulled the chariot of the MOON[5].

Alsvin
Norse and Teutonic
One of the horses that draw the chariot of the SUN[5] across the sky every day, the other being ARVAKR.

Alvis
Norse and Teutonic
The DWARF who fell in love with THRUD, the daughter of THÓRR. While she and all of the ÆSIR approved of the match, Thórr did not and, having derided the size of his

prospective son-in-law, spent the rest of the night firing questions at him until the SUN[5] rose and turned the luckless Alvis to stone.

Alvit
Norse and Teutonic
One of the VALKYRJA and sister of OLRUN and SVANHVIT. They were allegedly raped by EGIL, VÖLUNDR and SLAGFIDR, which would seem to identify these three Valkyrja as the SWAN MAIDENS.

Amleth
Danish
The hero of a legend that was recorded in the thirteenth century by the chronicler SAXO GRAMMATICUS and later used by William SHAKESPEARE in his famous tragedy *Hamlet*.

Amma
Norse and Teutonic
The wife of AFI and the mother of KARL, whom she gave birth to nine months after she and her husband had been visited by HEIMDALLR, who slept that night between husband and wife. Afi assumed that the child was his own son, and is thus usually referred to as the father of Karl, though he was actually only assuming the role of foster father.

Anderida
Anglo-Saxon
The Old English name for Pevensey, Sussex, the town having been captured from the Britons by AELLE and his sons CISSA, CYMEN and WLENCING some time *c.* 491.

Andhrimnir
Norse and Teutonic
The cook at VALHALLA, he spent all his time cooking the boar SÆHRIMNIR to feed the dead warriors who lived within Valhalla as ODÍNN's eternal guests.

Andronovich, Vyslav
Russian
The tsar of an unnamed realm and father of three sons, DMITRII, VASILII[2] and IVAN[6]. He coveted the FIREBIRD and sent his sons on a quest to find it for him. Ivan succeeded, also securing ELENA THE BEAUTIFUL and the HORSE WITH THE GOLDEN MANE. However, his brothers killed him and made out that they were the ones who had been successful. Ivan, however, was restored to life by a wolf that had helped him, using the WATER OF LIFE AND DEATH. When Vyslav Andronovich learned of the treachery of Dmitrii and Vasilii, he had them thrown into the deepest dungeon within his palace.

Andvaranaut
Norse and Teutonic
The cursed ring of ANDVARI.

Andvari
Norse and Teutonic
A king of the DWARFS who accidentally killed OTR, HREIDMAR's third son. The ÆSIR, or more accurately LOKI, sought recompense for the death and obliged Andvari to give up his vast hoard of gold. Andvari tried to keep back a ring, ANDVARANAUT, with which he could win new wealth, but Loki insisted on having everything. The ring was cursed and brought great sorrow to its owner, and was ultimately to cause the death of the hero SIGURDR/SIEGFRIED.

Angantyr
Norse and Teutonic
A hero, who once lost to OTR, and father of HERVORR.

Angles
Teutonic
A Germanic tribe that originated in the Schleswig-Holstein region of northern Europe. Along with their neighbours the

SAXONS, they invaded BRITAIN during the fifth century AD, settling in East Anglia (hence its name), Mercia and Northumbria.

Anglo-Saxon(s)
General
The collective name for the ANGLES and SAXONS who, together with the JUTES, conquered much of BRITAIN between the fifth and seventh centuries AD. The Angles settled in East Anglia, Mercia and Northumbria; the Saxons in Essex, Sussex and Wessex; and the Jutes in Kent and southern Hampshire, most notably the Isle of Wight. The Angles and Saxons came from the Schleswig-Holstein region and may have united prior to the invasion; the Jutes are usually said to have originated in JUTLAND. There was probably considerable intermarriage with the Romanized Celts, although the latter's language and culture were almost totally suppressed.

Following the invasion and conquest, a number of independent kingdoms were established, commonly referred to as the Heptarchy ('seven kingdoms'). These survived until the early ninth century, when they were amalgamated and united under the overlordship of Wessex.

Anglo-Saxon Chronicle
British
A history of England from the time of the Roman invasion to the eleventh century. Begun in the ninth century, during the reign of King Alfred, and written as a series of chronicles in Old English by monks, the work was still being executed in the twelfth century.

The *Chronicle*, which comprises seven different manuscripts, forms a unique record of early English history, and of the development of Old English prose up to its final stages in the year 1154, by which time it had been superseded by Middle English.

Angrboda
Norse and Teutonic
The giantess consort of LOKI whose name roughly translates as 'Boder of Grief' and the mother by him of FENRIR, MIDGARD-SORMR and possibly HEL.

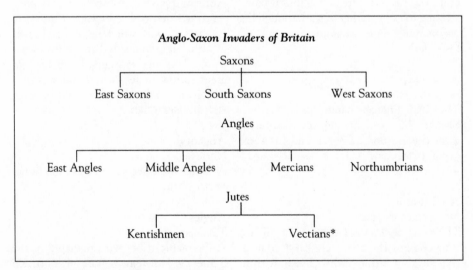

Anglo-Saxon Invaders of Britain

Saxons

East Saxons   South Saxons   West Saxons

Angles

East Angles   Middle Angles   Mercians   Northumbrians

Jutes

Kentishmen   Vectians*

* Inhabitants of the Isle of Wight.

Angurvadel
Norse and Teutonic
The magic sword that was owned by VIKING.

Anna
Russian
The sister of BASIL II, the Byzantine emperor, and wife of VLADIMIR I. In 987 or 988 Vladimir had made the political decision to accept Christianity as part of a pact with Basil which included marrying his sister.

Annar
Norse and Teutonic
The second husband of NIGHT[2] and father by her of a daughter, EARTH.

Antero Vipunen
Finno-Ugric
A giant who lay beneath the earth, a poplar tree growing from his shoulders, birch from his temples, fir from his forehead, alder from his cheeks, willow from his beard and a wild pine from between his teeth. While the hero VÄINÄMÖINEN was building his ship, he forgot the spell required to bind his work. Väinämöinen felled all of the trees that grew from Anterro Vipunen and then thrust an iron staff into the giant's throat. Antero Vipunen gagged and swallowed Väinämöinen, staff and all.

Once inside the giant, Väinämöinen, proving ever resourceful, turned his shirt into a forge, his shirt sleeves and coat into a pair of bellows, created a hammer from his elbow and an anvil from his knee, and then set to work hammering so fiercely that the anvil sank into the giant's heart. At length, unable to endure the suffering any longer, Antero Vipunen regurgitated Väinämöinen and unhappily promised to repeat the charm that would enable the hero to finish building his ship.

Apples of Youth
Norse and Teutonic
The golden apples of the goddess IDUNN which preserved the youth and vigour of the gods. The giant THJÁZI blackmailed LOKI into helping him steal the apples and kidnap Idunn. Soon afterwards the ÆSIR began to age, and when Loki's part in the theft and kidnap was discovered he was threatened with death if he failed to recover both the goddess and her apples. Disguising himself as a falcon, Loki managed to penetrate the home of Thjázi while the giant was away fishing. There he turned Idunn into a nut, carrying her and the apples safely back to ASGARDR.

Archangel(sk)
Russian
The home of Ivan SAVEL`EVICH. Surrounded by dense forests, Archangelsk lies on the flatlands of the northern Dvina, about thirty miles from the point where the river flows into the White Sea. English merchants were the first to settle around the mouth of the River Dvina during the sixteenth century. Ivan II founded the city, which has survived since then on its wood, fur and leather industries. It is the centre of the Russian wood industry because of the forests nearby.

Arcona
Baltic Coast
Location on the BALTIC coastline where SVANTOVIT had his chief temple. Here the god was depicted in four aspects on a wooden carved pillar holding a bull's-horn cup in his right hand. A white stallion, sacred to the god, was kept either in the temple itself or in the temple precincts, along with its saddle and bridle, accompanied by Svantovit's sword and battle-flag.

Ar(k)vakr
Norse and Teutonic
One of the horses that every day pulled the chariot of the SUN[5] across the sky.

Arthur
British
Semi-legendary, mythologized King of BRITAIN whose name is possibly a form of Artorius, a Roman *gens* name, though it might have Celtic origins, coming from *artos viros*, meaning 'bear man', or from Artaios, or even from Artos, an obscure deity who also has connections with a bear cult. He clearly dominates late Celtic mythology, though the legends that surround him undoubtedly come from the post-Christian era and draw on a multitude of different sources. The period immediately after the withdrawal of the Roman legions early in the fifth century AD is known as the Dark Ages since there is so little information about it. It is thought that this is when a powerful leader, chieftain or even a series of such leaders or chieftains commanded the Celtic troops of the West Country and held the invading SAXONS at bay. However, the truth of the matter is that no one knows for certain.

The Arthur whose legends concern the Knights of the Round Table, Queen Guinevere and the Holy Grail is almost certainly a composite figure who combines the attributes and achievements of more than a single person. One hypothesis says that he is to be identified with the Celtic king Riothamus, but the more contemporary view is that Arthur was a professional soldier, never a king, in the service of the British kings during the period between the departure of the Roman legions and the influx of the Saxon invaders.

True Celtic references to Arthur do not exist. Indeed, there are no contemporary references to him, either historical or legendary. Those sources that have a Celtic connection – that is, those that make him the cousin of Culhwch – date from a period far removed from the final days of Celtic influence in Britain. The *Mabinogion* remains the nearest source of reference to a Celtic Arthur, but traditionally even that carries no Arthurian references.

Many people claim that Arthur was a Celtic king, but it seems more likely that he was a powerful general whose ability in battle won him the respect of his peers. Time and the imagination of later writers then elevated him in rank, but even then the exploits of those surrounding him surpass his own.

Arthur will always remain a fascinating area of study, but to consider him as a Celtic king, or even deity, would be wrong until some concrete evidence has been uncovered that inextricably links him with the Celtic period. He most likely originated in the dying days of the Celtic peoples in Britain, the stories surrounding him growing as the people were forced further and further away from their native lands. Eventually Arthur will rise again, or so the legends say, and restore their lands to the dispossessed Celtic people – a legend that raises Arthur way above the level of mere king and places him among the élite race of gods. Perhaps that is the truth behind the stories of Arthur. In essence he seems a godlike figure, so, as the Celtic people were driven from their lands, maybe a long-forgotten god was brought out, dusted down and given a new name and persona, a persona that would allow the defeated Celts to retain pride in their own race, together with the hope that one day they would return.

Asabrú
Norse and Teutonic
Alternative name for the rainbow bridge BÏFROST.

Asaheim
Norse and Teutonic
One of the names given by Snorri STURLUSON to the land immediately to the east of TANAKVISL, identified with ASIA, in which ASGAARD (ASGARDR) lay. He also calls this region ASALAND, both names possibly deriving from Asia.

Asaland
Norse and Teutonic
Snorri STURLUSON says that ASGAARD (Sturluson's spelling of ASGARDR) lay within the land immediately to the east of TANAKVISL, that area being identified with ASIA, which Sturluson calls Asaland or ASAHEIM, from which he says the name Æsir is also derived.

Asegeir
Norse and Teutonic
Generic name given to the twelve wise men who decided that they should unify the VIKINGS. They set sail in a small ship and soon found themselves in the midst of a great storm, at which point they offered their prayers to FORSETTI. They then noticed that there was a thirteenth passenger on the ship. This mysterious stowaway steered them to an island, where he created a spring and revealed himself to be none other than Forsetti. He gave the Asegeir instructions to keep that island immune from attack and then promptly disappeared. The island, HELIGOLAND, was from that day forth safe from attack.

Asgaard
Norse and Teutonic
The name used by Snorri STURLUSON to refer to ASGARDR, which he said lay within a land known as either ASALAND or ASAHEIM.

Asgard(r)
Norse and Teutonic
The home of the gods whose variant name Asgard is a mistake caused by the fact that the last 'r' is silent. Asgardr, which is described as lying at the centre of the universe, was built by the ÆSIR after they had formed MIDGARDR. Within its bounds they resided in splendid palaces, of which the chief was VAL-HALLA, the palace of ODÍNN, to which heroes who had fallen in battle were carried in triumph by the VALKYRJA.

The Æsir sought to protect their home by commissioning a giant to build a wall around it, a task which he said he would complete within a year and for which he required payment in the form of the SUN[5], the MOON[5] and the goddess FREYJA as his wife. The Æsir readily agreed to the terms, as they thought the job could not possibly be completed within the contracted time, but the giant had the help of his stallion SVADILFARI and looked likely to finish the job ahead of schedule. This frightened the Æsir, because they thought the giant would become too powerful if rewarded as agreed, and so they had LOKI prevent him from finishing on time. The wall was never finished and the giant was eventually killed by THÓRR.

With the wall unfinished and Asgardr open to attack, the Æsir set the silent HEIMDALLR as the guard. He carried a trumpet called GJALLARHORN which he would blow to warn the Æsir of any impending danger, thus giving them advance warning. With their home completed, the Æsir built a rainbow bridge between it and the earth which was called BÍFROST. Asgardr finally fell following the death of the beloved BALDR.

Asia
Norse and Teutonic
The vast geographical region from which

Snorri STURLUSON says the name ÆSIR derives and which lay to the east of TANAKVISL. The ancient legends refer to this region as SWITHIOD THE GREAT, the land of the gods, which is also known as ASGARDR, ASALAND or ASAHEIM.

Technically Asia is the largest of the continents, encompassing a third of the total landmass of the earth, forming the eastern part of Eurasia to the east of the Ural Mountains, and includes eastern RUSSIA, India, Japan and China as well as many smaller countries.

Asia Minor
Norse and Teutonic
The historical name for Anatolia, the Asian part of Turkey.

Askr
Norse and Teutonic
The man, whose name means 'Ash', who was made from one of the two trees that the gods ODÍNN, HOENIR and LÓDURR came across while walking on the shore. From the other tree the gods made the woman EMBLA, whose name possibly means 'Elm'. Odínn gave them their spirit, Hoenir gave them their intelligence and Lódurr gave them their bodies and senses. Askr and Embla were thus the first people to be created.

Aslaug
Norse and Teutonic
The daughter of SIGURDR and BRYNHILDR. At the age of just three the girl was orphaned and Brynhildr's father hid her within a harp. A peasant couple broke open the harp and found the girl, whom they assumed was a mute. Many years later, however, she willingly spoke to RAGNAR LODBRÓKR, who made her his wife.

Athlis
Norse
A king of SWEDEN who won a battle-helmet called HILDIGOLTR ('Battle-swine'), which was named after HILDSVÍN, the golden pig owned by FREYJA, FREYR's sister. To the NORSE and TEUTONIC peoples, the boar appears to have been both a fertility and a protective symbol, and such helmets were often decorated with images of boars and other swine-like animals or effigies.

Athos, Mount
Serbian
Serbian mountain where legend records that the body of Prince MARKO was buried by a priest who came across the corpse beside the burial place of SARAC, the prince's horse.

Atla
Norse and Teutonic
One of the nine WAVE MAIDENS, the daughters of ÆGIR.

Atlé
Norse and Teutonic
A warrior who once challenged FRITHIOF.

Atli
Norse and Teutonic
King of the HUNS and brother of BRYN-HILDR who is better known by his historical TEUTONIC name of ATTILA THE HUN. He appears as Atli in the VÖLSUNGA SAGA and the poems of the EDDA, while in the NIBELUNGENLIED he appears as ETZEL. Atli became the third husband of GUDRUNN after the death of SIGURDR, when the gold he owned was taken away and hidden at the bottom of the River RHINE by GUN-NARR, HÖGNI and GUTTORMR. Atli killed the thieves in his attempt to repossess the gold, but he failed to discover its hiding place. To avenge the death of her brothers, Gudrunn then killed Atli before

fleeing the country. The marriage between Atli and Gudrunn produced two sons, ERP and EITEL, but both were killed by their mother.

Attila the Hun
Teutonic
Historical king of the HUNS who lived *c.* 406–53. In the NIBELUNGENLIED he appears as the legendary King ETZEL, while in the VÖLSUNGA SAGA and the heroic poems of the EDDA he appears as ATLI.

Attila the Hun became king at the age of twenty-eight in 434, and soon had VANDALS, OSTROGOTHS, GEPIDS and FRANKS fighting under his banner. As a result, his domain extended over GERMANY and SCYTHIA, from the RHINE to the frontiers of China. In 447 he devastated all the countries between the BLACK SEA and the Mediterranean. In 451 he invaded GAUL, but was utterly defeated after the siege of Orléans. He died in 453 in a pool of blood following a haemorrhage in bed, a fact that gave rise to fanciful stories of vengeance and murder by his wife.

Aud
Norse and Teutonic
The son of NIGHT[2] and her first husband, NAGLFARI.

Aud-humla, ~umulla
Norse and Teutonic
'Rich, hornless cow', the primordial cow who fed the giant YMIR, who had either been found in the ice or created from drops of water. Like all cattle, she enjoyed licking salt, and from the salt-encrusted rocks by the sea her lapping freed the man BÚRI, whose son BÖRR married Ymir's daughter BESTLA and became the father of the ÆSIR. A slight variant to this story says that Audhumla licked the salt from stones and these stones became the man

Búri. Yet another variant says that Búri was enclosed within an iceberg that Audhumla licked and so released him.

Augeia
Norse and Teutonic
One of the daughters of ÆGIR, thus one of the nine WAVE MAIDENS. This name appears slightly suspicious as it is distinctly Latin in structure, so it may be a Latinization of an earlier, no longer recorded name.

Aurgelmir
Norse and Teutonic
Alternative name for YMIR.

Aurgiafa
Norse and Teutonic
One of the nine WAVE MAIDENS, the giant daughters of ÆGIR.

Aurora(s)
Russian
The two ZVEZDA, the MORNING STAR[3] and the EVENING STAR, the daughters and attendants of DAZHBOG[1], and sisters to the two, some say three, ZORYA. Their names are ZVEZDA DENNITSA and ZVEZDA VECHERNYAYA.

Aurora Borealis
1 *Norse and Teutonic*
  The so-called Northern Lights, a phenomenon the name of which is a complete misnomer as 'aurora' means 'dawn'. Legend says that this event is a reflection of the beauty of GERDR, as well as being a display put on by ULLR to emphasize his prowess to gods and mortals alike. Technically the lights in the night sky (though they occur in the day as well, but then it is too bright to view them) are caused by streams of charged particles from the sun striking the atmosphere in the region of the northern magnetic pole. The particles

become excited and expel energy as light in much the same way as a neon bulb does.

2 *Russian*

Called NAINAS, the personification of the familiar and spectacular phenomenon, he was betrothed to NIEKIA, but they were never married, because of the intervention of PEIVALKÉ and his father, the SUN[1].

Aurvandill

Norse and Teutonic

Also ORVANDIL. The husband, or brother, of GRÓA, a VOLVA (seer), whom THÓRR had brought out of the FROST GIANTS' kingdom in a basket. When the man suffered a frost-bitten toe, Thórr amputated it and hurled it into the sky, where it became the star known as AURVANDILL'S TOE.

Aurvandill's Toe

Norse and Teutonic

The name given to a star that was said to have been formed from the frost-bitten toe that THÓRR had amputated from AURVANDILL and then hurled into the sky.

Auseklis

Latvian

The goddess MORNING STAR[1], who is known in LITHUANIA as AUSRINE. Auseklis is the deification of the planet VENUS when seen in the morning sky shortly before sunrise.

Ausrine

Lithuanian

In LITHUANIA, the name for AUSEKLIS, the MORNING STAR[2], a deification of the planet VENUS when seen in the dawn sky.

Austri

Norse and Teutonic

The name of the DWARF who was placed in the east by ODÍNN, VILLI and VÉ as one of the four whose job it was to support the skull of YMIR that formed the vault of the sky. The north was supported by NORDRI, the south by SUDRI and the west by WESTRI.

Authumia

Norse and Teutonic

A variant of AUDHUMLA.

Autrimpas

Prussian

The god of the sea and lakes, though not, it appears, of rivers and streams.

Avdot`ya

Russian

The wife of Mikhail POTYK, with whom she made a pact that if one of them died, then the other would join them in the tomb. Avdot`ya died first and, as good as his word, her husband was lowered into the tomb beside her, but he took with him a rope that was connected to the church bell so that, if he changed his mind, he could summon assistance and be released.

Lighting a candle, Mikhail Potyk settled down beside the body of his dead wife. Around midnight many snakes entered the tomb, one of which turned out to be a fire-breathing DRAGON[1]. Unafraid, Mikhail Potyk cut off its head, which he rubbed on to the body of his dead wife, who came back to life. Then pulling on the rope, he rang the church bell and both he and Avdot`ya were released, living on for many more happy years.

Baba-Yaga
Russian

Possibly the best known of all the Russian legendary characters is Baba-Yaga. She is usually portrayed as a malevolent witch, though she can, in fact, also be benevolent if she feels so disposed.

Although unnamed in the story of IVAN THE PEA, the old crone who lives in the forest in a strange house which revolves in the wind is none other than Baba-Yaga. In that story she is far from malevolent, but maybe Baba-Yaga realized that even she was no match for Ivan the Pea.

In almost every story that concerns Baba-Yaga she lives in a cottage in the most remote and inaccessible part of a deep forest. This cottage sits on four sets of chicken's legs, one at each corner, and revolves, either freely in the wind or when some unheard word is spoken. Any hero looking inside the cottage was likely to find Baba-Yaga crammed into every corner of the house, with her nose pressed hard against the roof.

Descriptions of Baba-Yaga vary widely. In some she is simply said to be an old crone, leaving the rest to the imagination. In others she is an aged, ugly crone who is so emaciated that she is little more than skin and bone. Her teeth are long and very sharp, sometimes protruding over her lips. Her teeth need to be sharp, for she is a cannibal, the bones of her victims forming the gate and fence that surround her home.

Some commentators insist that the bones around Baba-Yaga's house indicate that she has a very strong connection with the spirit world, even going so far as to say that her house guards the point where the two worlds - the world of the living and the world of the dead - meet. This may explain why in certain cases she is benevolent to humans, for her aim is not to send people into the afterlife but rather, like the Greek Cerberus, to stop the dead escaping.

Baba-Yaga possesses truly awesome power, for time itself is in her hands; the SUN[1], DAY[1] and NIGHT[1] obey her implicitly. She also has connections with the LESHII, for like him she kidnaps small children, and she has power over the forest and the animals that live there. In another aspect she is regarded as the guardian of the fountain that supplies the WATER OF LIFE AND DEATH.

The story of VASILISA THE BEAUTIFUL clearly demonstrates both the malevolent and benevolent sides of Baba-Yaga, as well as her powers, for here she sets the poor girl impossible tasks, threatening her that she will be eaten if she fails in any of them, but when Vasilisa has completed them all, Baba-Yaga gives her a magical skull that rids her of her cruel stepmother and stepsisters. Another story concerning a Vasilisa, VASILISA THE WISE, demonstrates the compassionate nature of Baba-Yaga, for in this story she tells IVAN[5] how he might regain his wife, Vasilisa the Wise, and hold on to her for ever.

Bagputys

Lithuanian

A sea god who is particularly associated with storms, riding the choppy seas in a boat with a golden anchor.

Bald Mountains

Russian

A range of mountains near KIEV. They were said, in the legend of IVAN THE PEA, to have marked the boundary of the kingdom of the DRAGON[1] that carried off his sister, VASILISA OF THE GOLDEN BRAID, and killed her two other brothers.

Bald(e)r

Norse and Teutonic

The handsome son of ODÍNN and FRIGGA (though some sources erroneously name his mother as FREYJA) and husband of NANNA whose variant, Balder, comes from the fact that though the 'r' is silent it is sometimes mistakenly pronounced.

The god of light, beauty, brightness and wisdom whose name means 'lord', Baldr was the wisest and best loved of all the gods – loved, that is, by everyone except the jealous LOKI. Described as a cheerful youth who was outstandingly beautiful, Baldr had premonitions in the form of ominous dreams of terror and gloom, so to cheer him up his mother made everything on the earth – animals, metal, stones, trees, water, etc. – swear that they would never harm him, though some versions of the myth say that the ÆSIR had to persuade Frigga to do this. However, Frigga overlooked one thing, mistletoe, and this omission came to the attention of LOKI, who had disguised himself as an old woman so that he might watch Frigga exacting her promises. From that day on, the other gods enjoyed pelting whatever came to hand at Baldr, simply for the amusement they gained from seeing how their missiles shied away from his inviolate skin at the very last instant. On one such occasion Loki sharpened a twig of mistletoe, which he gave to Baldr's blind brother HÖDR, guiding the blind god's aim. The mistletoe struck home, much to everyone's horror, and Baldr fell to the ground dead.

Nanna, his wife, died of grief the moment she heard the news. The gods built a great funeral pyre on Baldr's ship, *HRINGHORNI*, and in it they reverently laid the bodies of Baldr and his wife. They also placed Baldr's horse and many treasures on the pyre, including Odínn's great ring DRAUPNIR. As the pyre was lit, a giantess pushed *Hringhorni* off its rollers and it floated away from the shore on the outgoing tide. All the world mourned the passing of the god, and this mourning is repeated every spring when, it is said, the melting of the frost, ice and snow represents the tears of the world for Baldr.

However, the gods were not about to give up one they loved without a fight and, at Frigga's request, Odínn's son HERMÓDR[1] mounted his father's great stallion SLEIPNIR and rode down to NIFLHEIMR, the UNDERWORLD[4], land of the dead, in an attempt to rescue his dead brother. After riding for nine days Hermódr came to the River GJALL, which circles the Underworld. There MODGUDR, the guardian of its golden bridge, GJALLARBRÚ, told Hermódr that Baldr had crossed the bridge the previous night in the company of five troops of dead horsemen. Hermódr rode Sleipnir over the bridge until they came to the gates of the Underworld, HELGRIND, which Sleipnir easily leapt over.

Hermódr dismounted and entered the palace of the goddess HEL, and there in the great hall of her palace he found both the goddess and his brother, who had the seat of honour beside her. He explained to Hel that he had come to recover the spirit of his dead brother and she decreed that he could return to the land of the living if everything on the earth shed tears at the loss of Baldr, but if not Baldr would remain with her. Having listened to the judgement of Hel, the two brothers took leave of each other, each giving the other gifts, those from Baldr to Hermódr including the ring Draupnir, which was to be returned to Odínn.

When he had returned, Hermódr explained the conditions set by Hel and at this the gods beseeched everything, animate and inanimate, to weep for the loss of Baldr. At first it seemed that all had complied, for even the stones and metal wept tears, but unfortunately for the gods one ill-tempered giantess named THOKK refused, exclaiming that she saw no point in crying for someone who had been no use for her, either dead or alive, and he might just as well stay where he was. So for the time being Baldr had to remain in the Underworld.

The Æsir were understandably furious, for they believed that Thokk was none other than Loki in yet another of his disguises, and took after Loki, who had fled in terror. Even though Loki changed himself into a salmon, the Æsir caught him and bound him across three stones with the entrails of his own sons. Above him they placed a serpent, from whose open mouth venom dripped into his face. SIGYN, the wife of Loki, tried to catch the venom in a bowl, but every time she went to empty the container the venom once again dripped into Loki's face, so that he writhed in agony, his torment making the earth tremble. There Loki will remain until the RAGNARØKR. The death of Baldr marked the start of the fall of ASGARDR, the home of the gods, but he will duly return to lead the new order following the Ragnarøkr.

While Baldr roughly falls into both NORSE and TEUTONIC mythology, no myths about the god are known among the Teutons other than a reference to

him in association with the god WODAN in the second MERSEBURG CHARM, a ninth-century pagan spell. Snorri STURLUSON calls him Odínn's blond son, beloved of the gods, a description which gives rise to the popular conception of Baldr as a radiant sky god, while SAXO GRAMMATICUS describes him as 'sprung secretly from celestial seed', and talks of him as a hero, thus suggesting a parthenogenetically born deity, a celestially born warrior like SKJOLDR, a guise in which early Skaldic lays refer to Baldr.

The picture of Loki as the murderer of Baldr is possibly a late addition to the field of Norse and Teutonic mythology, for it is supported only by the LOKASENNA, a relatively late work. The VOLUSPÁ and the BALDRS DRAUMAR support the view of Saxo Grammaticus, who attributes the death of Loki to Hödr alone. This version is given below. Other points worth noting from the story above are the inclusion of the mistletoe, a plant that is not native to ICELAND, the home of Snorri Sturluson. The inclusion of the plant may be a misunderstanding by Sturluson of his sources, for Norse tradition says that there once was a wonderful sword called MISTILLTEINN ('Mistletoe'), and Saxo Grammaticus alludes to Baldr being killed with just such a magical weapon. However, further confusion possibly arises from the shaping of the mistletoe into a dart, for this may derive from a version of the story of Baldr which says that he was killed by a charmed stick being pointed at him, a common and well-known feature of the art of the SHAMAN, which is referred to several times in association with Odínn, Baldr's father.

Saxo Grammaticus, in what is possibly the older of the two versions of the story, describes the warrior Baldr (note he is not described as a god) in his GESTA DANORUM as being attended by a group of minor goddesses whom he considers resemble the VALKYRJA. These attendants feed the warrior on food steeped in venom to protect him from all weapons and ills.

Baldr contended for the hand of the beautiful Nanna with Hödr and fought several battles over her. On one occasion Baldr's fleet and army were thoroughly routed, even though the gods had supported them, but on another Baldr was victorious, although he still did not win the hand of Nanna, whom Hödr married. As a result Baldr pined so badly and became so weak that he had to be transported in a cart, but even though Baldr was weak, Hödr knew that he could not kill his adversary without the magical sword that was guarded by MIMINGUS, a SATYR. Hödr set out on the long and perilous journey, through cold and dark nether regions, to reach the OTHERWORLD land in which Mimingus lived. There he took the satyr by surprise and managed to steal the sword without any resistance.

Hödr retraced his steps and, coming upon the cart carrying the weakened Baldr, managed to inflict a wound on his invincible foe. The very next day their two armies met in a final battle, though Baldr was already so weak, both from his anguish at the marriage of Nanna to his enemy and from the wound, that he had to be carried on to the field of combat. Three days later he died. Odínn was furious and swore that he would have his revenge. With this in mind, Odínn fathered BOUS on the Princess RINDA, planning that Bous should grow into a mighty warrior, meet Hödr on the field of combat and kill him, thus avenging the death of Baldr. Each of these ambitions came to pass exactly as Odínn had intended.

Baldrs Draumar
Norse and Teutonic

An early work that, along with the VOLUSPÁ, supports the later works of SAXO GRAMMATICUS in which the death of BALDR is attributed to HÖDR alone.

Balkan(s)
General

The name given to a peninsula of south-eastern Europe that stretches into the Mediterranean Sea between the Adriatic and Aegean Seas and comprises Albania, Bulgaria, Greece, ROMANIA, Turkey (the European part) and the former Yugoslavia. It is traversed by the River DANUBE, which drains into the BLACK SEA on the east.

Balmung
Norse and Teutonic

The name of the sword that was made by VÖLUNDR and subsequently owned by SIGMUNDR.

Baltic
General

Name given to a large shallow arm of the North Sea, as well as being collectively applied to the countries LITHUANIA, LATVIA and ESTONIA.

Bannik
Slavonic

The spirit of the bath-house who was seen as a wizened little man with wild white hair and a long, straggly beard. He was invoked to give some impression of the future by exposing a naked back out of the bath-house into the fresh air. If the future was to be pleasant, then Bannik could be felt stroking the back. However, if the future was to be unpleasant, Bannik would run his nails down the exposed spine. Every fourth bathing session belonged to Bannik, who would entertain his spirit friends in the bath-house. If a human was foolish enough to enter while Bannik and his guests were there, he would be extremely lucky to get off with a simple drenching in boiling water. More likely he would emerge badly beaten, or would be found lying in the bath-house with his neck broken.

Bardoyats
Prussian
The god of ships and patron of sailors.

Barri
Norse and Teutonic
The grove sacred to FREYR where GERDR agreed to meet the god after his proposal of marriage had been accepted, following threats from his emissary SKÍRNIR.

barstukai
Lithuanian
Also known as PARSTUKAI. An UNDER-WORLD[3] being, sometimes described as a FAIRY, who was believed to influence the harvest and also to perform household chores for those who had made offerings to PUSKAITIS. Offerings were left to them by farmers, who would lay out tables of food in barns, where the *barstukai* were believed to gather and feast at midnight.

Basil II
Russian
A historical Byzantine emperor (*c.* 958–1025). The son of Romanus II and brother of ANNA, Basil became sole ruler in 976, but just a few years later his reign was endangered by an uprising of nobles led by Bardas Sclerus, who was assisted by General Bardas Phocas. Basil put down this revolt, only for the same men to lead a similar one almost a decade later, this revolt seriously threatening to topple Basil. He was saved when he entered into an alliance with VLADIMIR I, who, as part of his pact with Basil, converted to Christianity and married Anna. Vladimir sent 6,000 troops to help Basil and thus tipped the scales in his favour. He successfully put down the uprising in 989. Basil II later became known as Basil Bulgaroctonus ('Bulgar-slayer') after a fifteen-year-long war against Bulgaria.

Batradz
Russian
A hero of the ALANS, SARMATIAN ancestors of the OSSETES, the story of his death is remarkably similar to that of King ARTHUR. Having received a mortal wound, Batradz called upon his two companions to throw his sword into the water. Twice they pretended to carry out his instructions and twice their lies were uncovered. When they finally complied, the waters turned blood-red and the surface was whipped into a frenzy though no wind blew. Some have sought to suggest that this is the origin of the return of Arthur's sword Excalibur to the Lady of the Lake, a theory that is not entirely impossible, as it is known that Sarmatian soldiers served in the Roman army in BRITAIN under Lucius Artorius Castus.

Baudihillie
Teutonic
'Giver of Freedom' or 'Ruler of Battle', the name of one of the ALAISIAGAE, minor war spirits who were worshipped in the TEUTONIC heartland and whose worship was later taken to northern BRITAIN, presumably by the Romans, though this has never been proved. Some sources name two Alaisiagae, while others name four. Her companions were BEDE[1], FINNILENE and FRIAGABI. Only one site of worship has been definitely associated with the Alaisiagae and that is an altar at Housesteads Roman fort on Hadrian's Wall.

Baugi
Norse and Teutonic
The giant brother of the equally gigantic SUTTUNGR, from whom he helped OÐÍNN to steal the MEAD OF INSPIRATION, his payment to the god whom he had employed as a labourer.

Bede

1 *Teutonic*

The name of one of the ALAISIAGAE, minor war spirits who were worshipped in the TEUTONIC heartland and whose worship was later taken to northern BRITAIN, presumably by the Romans, though this has never been proved. Some sources name two Alaisiagae, while others name four. Her companions were BAUDIHILLIE, FINNILENE and FRIAGABI. Only one site of worship has been definitely associated with the Alaisiagae and that is an altar at Housesteads Roman fort on Hadrian's Wall.

2 *British*

ANGLO-SAXON scholar, theologian and historian (*c.* 673–735). Born near Monkwearmouth, Durham, at the age of seven he was placed in the care of Benedict Biscop at the monastery of Wearmouth, and in 682 moved to the new monastery at Jarrow, Northumberland. He was ordained priest there in 703 and remained a monk for the rest of his life. He was a prolific writer, producing homilies, works on grammar and physical science, as well as commentaries on the Old and New Testaments. His greatest work was his *Historia Ecclesiastica Gentis Anglorum* (*Ecclesiastical History of the English People*), which he completed in 731 and which remains the single most valuable source for early English history.

Belaye

Teutonic

Princess who became the second wife of LOHENGRIN. After her husband had been killed by her parents, who thought that their daughter was being held under an enchantment, Belaye died of grief.

Beldegg

Norse and Teutonic

Son of ODÍNN who became the King of West Saxony.

Belé

Norse and Teutonic

The heir to the kingdom of SOGN whose throne was usurped.

Beli

Norse and Teutonic

One of the giant descendants of KARI. He may be the same as the Beli, brother of GERDR, who lost his life after he had unwisely attacked FREYR, who killed him using an antler as he had forgotten his sword.

Belt of Strength

Norse and Teutonic

The unimaginative name of the belt that was worn by THÓRR which gave him his tremendous strength.

Belyanin, Bel

Russian

The tsar of an unnamed kingdom, husband of NASTAS`YA OF THE GOLDEN BRAID and father of three sons, PETER, VASILII[1] and IVAN[1]. One day, while the children were still quite young, a huge gust of wind blew Nastas`ya away. Many years later Bel Belyanin's sons set off to find their mother, a quest which Ivan completed.

Be~ow, ~aw

Teutonic

Very little is known about this deity, who possibly has a fertility role, as his name is known only from a few ANGLO-SAXON genealogies.

Beowulf

Norse, Teutonic and Anglo-Saxon

The eponymous hero of BEOWULF. Beowulf sailed to DENMARK with fourteen companions and there killed the monster GRENDEL, as well as Grendel's mother, in an underwater duel. This episode is almost certainly a version of THÓRR's fight with the monstrous MIDGARDSORMR. Beowulf succeeded his uncle HYGELAC as King of the GEATS and ruled for fifty years. At the end of his reign a DRAGON[2] whose treasure had been stolen by a runaway slave (most likely a variant of the story of FÁFNIR) attacked Beowulf's kingdom. The elderly monarch set out to fight the monster, but his sword was soon broken in the fray and all his companions save one fled, his kinsman WIGLAF. Between them they managed to kill the dragon, but not until after Beowulf had received a mortal wound. A huge barrow was built above the ashes of Beowulf's funeral pyre, around which the dragon's hoard had been piled.

Beowulf
Norse, Teutonic and Anglo-Saxon
Epic ANGLO-SAXON poem that was composed *c.* 700 and is today the only complete surviving example of the Germanic folk-epic, the oldest epic English poem known, and the most important example of Anglo-Saxon versification. It exists as a single manuscript that was copied in about 1000 and forms part of the Cottonian collection in the British Museum.

Bergelmir
Norse and Teutonic
Also FARBAUTI. A FROST GIANT who survived the cataclysmic flood caused by the blood of the murdered YMIR by sailing away over it in his boat. He then founded a new race of Frost Giants. It is now thought that this story is a post-Christian invention based on the story of Noah and the biblical deluge. Some sources name Bergelmir as the father of LOKI by LAUFEIA.

Berling
Norse and Teutonic
One of the four DWARFS who made the necklace BRÍSINGAMEN, his partners being ALFRIGG, DVALIN[1] and GRERR. All four were rewarded by FREYJA, who spent a night with each of them.

berserk~ir(s), ~er(s)
Norse and Teutonic
Name given to legendary warriors dedicated to the god ODÍNN. They were so called because they wore bearskin shirts into battle rather than armour and drove themselves into a martial frenzy, fighting ferociously with little or no conscious awareness of any danger. Later legends built on the frenzy aspect of these warriors and said that this state brought about a transformation that turned the warriors into bears or wolves, howling and foaming at the mouth (hence the modern usage of the word 'berserk'), which rendered them immune to sword and flame. This later exaggeration undoubtedly contributed to many of the European WEREWOLF legends.

Bertha
Norse and Teutonic
One of the variant names applied to FRIGGA. She was also known as HOLDA, NERTHUS and WODE.

Bestla
Norse and Teutonic
The giant daughter of YMIR who married BÖRR, the son of BÚRI, and by him became the mother of the ÆSIR gods ODÍNN, VILLI and VÉ.

Beyggvir
Norse and Teutonic
Variant of BYGGVIR.

Beyla

Norse and Teutonic

A minor god whose name appears to mean 'Bee'. She was a companion of FREYR, along with another minor god, BYGGVIR, her husband.

Biarki

Danish

A legendary warrior, also called BODVAR-BIARKI, who was a henchman of HROLF, King of DENMARK. He was given the name 'Little Bear' as he had the ability to assume the form of a bear at will.

Bïfrost

Norse and Teutonic

Also ASABRÚ. The rainbow bridge that the ÆSIR constructed between ASGARDR and MIDGARDR using fire, air and water. During the RAGNARØKR it is stated that SURTR will lead his forces from MÚSPELL-HEIMR and shatter Bïfrost, before joining the giants and monsters congregating on the plain of VÍGRÍDR in front of VALHALLA.

Bil

Norse and Teutonic

The personification of the waning MOON[5], a sister of HIUKI and the companion of MANI. Some sources say that Bil and Hiuki were originally mortal children whom Mani took up to the heavens to escape the cruelty of their father, after which he made them water-bearers. They carry between them a pole named SIMUL and a pail called SOEG.

Billingr

Norse and Teutonic

The King of the RUTHENES and the father of RINDA.

Bilskirnir

Norse and Teutonic

The name given to THÓRR's hall in ASGARDR.

Bird's Way

Lithuanian

Alternative name for the MILKY WAY[2], the heavenly bridge across which the spirits of the dead cross to reach their eternal home, the MOON[2].

Bjarg

Norse and Teutonic

According to the ORKNEYINGA SAGA, the kingdom of King HROLF, son of SVADI. It was within this kingdom, in a region known as HEIDEMARK, that NOR and GOR found their sister GOI, who had been abducted three years previously and had married her abductor, Hrolf.

Björn

Norse and Teutonic

A friend and attendant of FRITHIOF.

Black God

Slavonic

The name given to CHERNOBOG, Black God being the literal translation (*chernyi*, black, and *bog*, god). The personification of all things evil, he is opposed by BYELOBOG, his exact opposite, the personification of all things good, the WHITE GOD.

Black Forest

General

Mountainous region of coniferous forests in Baden-Württemberg, GERMANY. Bounded to the west and the south by the River RHINE, it covers an area of 1,800 square miles and rises to some 5,000 feet.

Black Sea
General
An inland sea in southeastern Europe that is linked with the Sea of Azov and Sea of Marmara, and with the Mediterranean via the Dardanelles.

Black Shuck
British – East Anglia
A dog the size of a calf with saucer-shaped eyes that blaze green in the dark. He is alleged to stride along the country lanes as an omen of coming ill-fortune.

Black Stream
Russian
A small river that flowed into Lake IL`MEN` from the west. At some time a miller built his mill on that stream, all but damming up its waters and, more importantly for this legend, stopping the fish of the river from gaining access to the lake – a fact they bitterly resented, as they told the river.

Appearing as a man dressed from head to foot in black, Black Stream came to a man from NOVGOROD who was fishing in his waters and, offering to show him a place where the water teemed with fish, asked the man to do him a favour. The man readily agreed and, having been led to the spot where the fish filled the water almost completely, Black Stream gave the man a message which he told him to pass on to a peasant he would meet in Novgorod who would be dressed in a blue kaftan, blue trousers and a blue hat.

Returning to Novgorod, the man duly found the peasant and passed on the message, not realizing that the peasant was none other than the personification of Lake Il`men`. That night, in response to Black Stream's plea, Lake Il`men` sent a huge wave thundering up Black Stream which washed the mill away.

This story seems to refer to an ancient custom of making a human sacrifice whenever a new mill was built, warning of the likely consequences if that sacrifice was forgotten.

Blodughofi
Norse and Teutonic
The name of FREYR's horse.

Blondel
French
Originally known as Blondel de Nesle, this French minstrel lived in the late twelfth century and was generally associated with King Richard I (Richard Coeur de Lion). He later passed into legend when, it is said, he located the king, who had been imprisoned, by singing a song that they had composed together under a window, and rescued him.

Bluebeard
French
A legendary rich nobleman whose story was popularized by the writer Charles Perrault in France *c*. 1697. He has been historically identified as Gilles de Rais, who was said to have murdered six wives for disobeying his order that they should not enter a permanently locked room in his home. His seventh wife, having opened the door and seen inside the bodies of her husband's previous wives, was saved from a similar fate only by the arrival of her brothers, who killed Bluebeard.

Boden
Norse and Teutonic
One of the two bowls into which FJALR and GALR drained the blood of KVASIR, whom they had murdered, this blood being mixed with honey to form the MEAD OF INSPIRATION.

Bodvar-Biarki
Danish
Alternative name sometimes given to BIARKI.

Bodvildr
Norse and Teutonic
The daughter of NIDUDR. She was raped by VÖLUNDR in revenge for her father's theft of all his property.

Boe
Norse and Teutonic
A variant sometimes used to refer to BOUS.

bogatyr
Russian
The Russian name for a knight of Holy Russia (plural *bogatyri*). These knights usually appeared in the wonder tales, the VOLSHEBNYE SHAZKA, but are not unknown as the heroes in the other categories of Russian legends, the BYLINA and the BYLICHKA. The *bogatyri* kept alive pagan beliefs under Christianity.

Boggart
British
Alternative name sometimes used to refer to PUCK.

Bolthor(n)
Norse and Teutonic
The giant father of BESTLA, though her father is usually named as YMIR, leading some to theorize that Bolthorn was simply a title of that giant.

Bolwerk
Norse and Teutonic
One of the many pseudonyms used by ODÍNN so that he could pass unrecognized among mortals. It was in this guise that he seduced GUNNLOD in order to steal the MEAD OF INSPIRATION.

Borghildr
Norse and Teutonic
A princess who bore the boys HAMOND and HELGI to SIGMUNDR. Sigmundr's son SINFIOTLI, by SIGNY, killed Borghildr's

brother in a brawl, so Borghildr poisoned him, after which Sigmundr divorced her.

Boris, Saint
Russian
Russian Orthodox saint who, according to some legends, was, along with Saint GLEB, a smith who forged the first plough. This plough was of enormous proportions and was forged with implements of like size. The two smiths were reported to have used twelve golden hammers and tongs that weighed almost twelve *poods* (c. 430 lb). Other versions of this legend name the two saintly smiths as Saint KUZ`MA and Saint DEM`YAN.

Bornholm
Norse and Teutonic
The legendary birthplace of VIKING, a Danish island in the BALTIC Sea lying some twenty-two miles southeast of the nearest point of the coast of SWEDEN.

Bör(r)
Norse and Teutonic
The son of BÚRI who married BESTLA, the daughter of YMIR, and fathered the three principal gods of the ÆSIR: ODÍNN, VILLI and VÉ – the murderers of Börr's father-in-law.

Bous
Norse and Teutonic
Sometimes called BOE and VÁLI, Bous was the son ODÍNN fathered on the Princess RINDA with the single purpose in mind that, once he had grown to manhood, he should kill HÖDR and thus avenge the death of BALDR.

boyars
Russian
Name given to landowners within the Russian aristocracy. These nobles wrested power in NOVGOROD from the merchant guilds in 1416 and remained in control

until 1476, when the city came under the control of IVAN THE GREAT. During the sixteenth century the boyars formed such a powerful group that they began to threaten the authority of the tsar. However, their influence was decisively broken by IVAN THE TERRIBLE in 1565, when he confiscated most of their land.

Brabant
General
Former duchy of western Europe that comprised the Dutch province of North Brabant and the Belgian provinces of Brabant and Antwerp. They were divided when Belgium gained independence in 1830. It was within this realm that ELSA OF BRABANT was besieged by Frederick de TELRAMUND and subsequently rescued by LOHENGRIN.

Bragafull
Norse and Teutonic
According to Snorri STURLUSON in the YNGLINGA SAGA from HEIMSKRINGLA, the Bragafull was the 'cup of BRAGE', from which a drink would be taken to underline the solemnity of a vow made in the god's name. This, however, is a confusion with BRAGARFULL.

Bragarfull
Norse and Teutonic
The chieftain's toast which Snorri STURLUSON confuses with a solemn vow made in the name of the god BRAGE which he calls the BRAGAFULL.

Brag~i, ~e
Norse and Teutonic
The god of poetry, music and eloquence, the son of ODÍNN and GUNNLOD, a giantess the god had seduced. It seems that Bragi may simply be an aspect of Odínn, as one of his names, 'Long-bearded One', is also used to refer to that god. The husband of IDUNN, he is said to have killed his brother-in-law, though the legend of their fight sadly no longer exists. Late sagas depict Bragi as welcoming dead warriors to VALHALLA. In this role he was said to have had runes carved on his tongue by his father so that he could compose songs and poems to honour the gods and fallen warriors. Snorri STURLUSON in his YNGLINGA SAGA from HEIMSKRINGLA calls the god Brage and says that a solemn vow would be taken to the god from a cup known as BRAGAFULL, 'the cup of Brage'. This vow was in fact the chieftain's toast, the BRAGARFULL, which further demonstrates the confusion Sturluson has brought to the relating of NORSE mythology and legend.

Branstokk
Norse and Teutonic
The name given to the oak tree that stood in the midst of the hall of VOLSUNGR. During the wedding feast of SIGGEIR and SIGNY a stranger appeared and thrust a sword into the tree, saying that whoever could remove it might keep it, whereupon it would bring them victory in every battle. The stranger then disappeared. Siggeir was the first to try, but he could not remove it. Likewise Volsungr's nine older sons tried and failed. Finally, when the turn of SIGMUNDR came, he slid the blade easily from the trunk. The ownership of this sword, and the consummate ease with which Sigmundr removed it from Branstokk, are cited as the reasons for a feud between Siggeir and the VOLSUNGS.

Breid(h)ablik
Norse and Teutonic
'Great Brilliance', the name given to the hall in ASGARDR that BALDR shared with his brother HÖDR and his wife, NANNA.

Brennu Njáals Saga
Norse

'The Saga of Njáll's Burning', the saga from ICELAND that tells the story of NJÁL.

Bretwalda
Anglo-Saxon

'Britain-ruler', a title assumed by the ANGLO-SAXON kings in rotation to signify that, for their allotted time, they and their kingdom held supremacy within the Heptarchy ('seven kingdoms'). The use of the title, and its significance to the Anglo-Saxon peoples, appear to have marked the first attempt made to unify BRITAIN under a sole sovereign – something that did not finally occur until the various Anglo-Saxon kingdoms were united under the overlordship of Wessex.

Bright Sun
Russian

Epithet applied to the historical prince VLADIMIR I of KIEV and later used in the amalgamation of Vladimir I and VLAD-IMIR II to form the legendary prince of Kiev VLADIMIR BRIGHT SUN.

Brim~ir, ~er
Norse and Teutonic

Also OKOLN~IR, ~UR. The name of one of the halls of the gods that will exist after the RAGNARØKR, in which the inhabitants will enjoy warmth and drink nothing but the strongest drink.

Brísingamen
Norse and Teutonic

A great treasure, believed to have been a necklace, that was owned by FREYJA. It was her most beloved possession and had been given to her by the DWARFS ALFRIGG, BERLING, DVALIN[1] and GRERR in return for her sleeping with them, after having stumbled on their smithy while wandering in SVARTALFHEIMR. LOKI told ODÍNN of Freyja's behaviour, whereupon

Odínn decreed that she must give up the necklace unless, along with her role as goddess of sex, she also took on the portfolios of war and death as well, roles she reluctantly assumed in order to be allowed to keep the jewel (cf. BROSINGAMENE).

Brisings
Norse and Teutonic

Sometimes erroneously called the Brosings, wherein lies the confusion between the BRÍSINGAMEN and the BROSINGAMENE, the Brisings were the four smith DWARFS ALFRIGG, BERLING, DVALIN[1] and GRERR who slept with FREYJA in return for the Brísingamen.

Britain
General

Island in northwest Europe which is thought to take its name from Priteni, the name the PICTS used for themselves. It comprises the countries of England, Scotland and Wales. The invasions and conquest that took place in the first millennium AD all but destroyed the Celtic tradition in England, though it remains in fragmentary form in the West Country, mainly in Cornwall and in Wales. Scotland was never a true Celtic domain, though a number of Celtic stories involve that country.

In legend the island was first ruled over by a giant, Albion, whose name was subsequently poetically applied to the island and whose career was outlined in Holinshed's *Chronicles* of 1577. Surprisingly, Geoffrey of Monmouth (d. 1155) does not mention Albion, instead simply saying that giants predated men in Britain. He reports that Britain was colonized by Brutus, a descendant of Aeneas, and the island then maintained its independence until the Roman invasion.

The *White Book of Rhydderch*, which dates from the fourteenth century, gives an entirely different, and decidedly Welsh, early history, saying that the country was first called Myrddin's Precinct, Myrddin being Latinized to his more famous variant Merlin in the text. It was then known as the Isle of Honey, before becoming Britain, the country allegedly being named after Prydein, son of Aedd (who may be cognate with the Irish sun god Aedh), had conquered it.

Unsurprisingly Geoffrey of Monmouth makes no mention of this concept. Other traditions say that Prydein came from Cornwall and conquered Britain after the death of Porrex, the latter appearing as one of the successors of Brutus in Geoffrey of Monmouth. Irish tradition says that the country was named after Britain, the son of Nemedius, who settled on the island. Others still say that Britain simply derives from the Latin name for the island, *Britannia*.

The history of Britain prior to the Roman invasion and occupation is little more than legendary concepts. Archaeology is perhaps the best alternative guide. Before 2800 BC the inhabitants were Neolithic hill farmers. They were followed by people who worked both copper and gold, and were in all probability true Celts. At some stage Celts who were able to work iron became the dominant people, but even archaeologists find it difficult to put a date on the start of their pre-eminence. Julius Caesar made exploratory expeditions to Britain, but it was not until AD 43, in the reign of Claudius, that the Roman occupation began. Eventually Rome abandoned Britain and left it to fend for itself against the Picts from the north, the Irish from the west, and the ANGLES, SAXONS and JUTES from the east.

Brokk
Norse and Teutonic
A DWARF who once won a bet with LOKI.

Brosingamene
Norse and Teutonic
A great treasure that is perhaps cognate with BRÍSINGAMEN. Like that treasure, it is thought to have been either a necklace or a jewelled collar. The ANGLO-SAXON poem BEOWULF says that it was stolen from EORMANRIC HAMA.

Brünhild(e)
Teutonic
The TEUTONIC form of BRYNHILDR.

Brynhildr
Norse and Teutonic
BRÜNHILDE is the TEUTONIC form of this NORSE name. Both versions of the story relating to this character are given below.

ODÍNN, for some unknown reason, condemned Brynhildr, who is described as the most beautiful of the VALKYRJA, to fall into an enchanted sleep within a circle of fire, where she was to remain until someone brave enough to penetrate the wall of flames would wake her. It was in this state, on the crown of a hill, that SIGURDR found her, broke through the fiery circle, woke the sleeping maiden and gave her ANDVARI's cursed ring as a token of his love. Sigurdr then journeyed to the land of the NIBELUNGEN, where he won many admirers through his courage and feats of derring-do. However, Sigurdr was given an enchanted drink that made him forget his love for Brynhildr and fall in love with the Nibelung GUDRUNN, whom he married. But he obviously did not forget all about Brynhildr, as he later persuaded his brother-in-law GUNNARR to seek her hand.

Gunnarr accepted the challenge but failed to penetrate the fiery circle that surrounded Brynhildr, so Sigurdr assumed the guise of Gunnarr and plighted his troth in his brother-in-law's stead. The couple exchanged rings, which led to Sigurdr once again becoming the owner of Andvari's ring, which he subsequently passed on to Gunnarr.

Brynhildr, it seems, was aware of the trick and yet she decided to play along. Unfortunately, during the wedding feast of Brynhildr and Gunnarr, the potion that had been given to Sigurdr wore off and he was once again overcome with love. As the feelings of Sigurdr became apparent to the assembled company, Gudrunn mocked the way in which Brynhildr had been so easily tricked, mockery which led Brynhildr to commission Gudrunn's brother GUTTORMR to kill Sigurdr while he lay sleeping. Then, overcome by remorse, Brynhildr killed herself, the unfortunate pair sharing the same funeral pyre.

The Teutonic version of events, as recorded in the NIBELUNGENLIED, says that SIEGFRIED (the Teutonic form of Sigurdr) was made invulnerable after bathing in the blood of FÁFNIR, the DRAGON[2] – invulnerable, that is, except for a spot between his shoulders where a falling leaf had masked his skin from the blood. The furious BRÜNHILDE thus persuaded Siegfried's wife KRIEMHILD (Gudrunn) to make a shirt for her husband that was marked with a cross lying exactly over his one vulnerable spot. This information was passed on to HAGEN, who, guided by the cross, stabbed and killed Siegfried before stealing the treasure of the DWARFS.

Apart from the difference in the death of Sigurdr/Siegfried, the story of Brynhildr is virtually identical in both Norse and Teutonic traditions.

Bulat the Brave
Russian

IVAN[4] found Bulat being flogged in a market-square for owing a large sum of money to a merchant and paid his debt to save him from his torment. Thinking nothing of this, Ivan then began to walk away, but Bulat ran up to him, thanked him and told him that if he had not helped him, Ivan would never have found the girl, VASILISA KIRBIT`EVNA, who was fated to become his wife.

Ivan followed Bulat the Brave's instructions implicitly, and the pair rode a great distance until they came to the land of the Tsar KIRBIT. There, in a tower, just as had been foretold, they found the maiden. Purchasing some chickens, ducks and geese, Bulat told Ivan to have them roasted and to hand him a wing whenever he returned from trying to capture the girl. Bulat then went to the tower and threw a stone to attract the attention of the girl, cracking the gilded roof of the tower in the process. Running back to Ivan, Bulat received a chicken wing and then returned to the tower, where he offered it to Vasilisa Kirbit`evna.

Three times Bulat did this, on each occasion offering the girl the wing he carried, first of chicken, then of duck and finally of goose. As the maiden leaned out of the window to take the last wing offered, Bulat grabbed her and the three made away as fast as their horses would carry them. The following morning, when Tsar Kirbit saw the damage to the tower and found his daughter missing, he and a number of his men gave chase.

Sensing their approach, Bulat pretended to have lost his ring and told his companions to continue while he returned to look for it. Vasilisa Kirbit`evna tried to dissuade him by giving him her own ring, but although Bulat accepted it, he still returned along the route they had followed. Coming across his pursuers, he killed all but the tsar before returning to his companions.

The Tsar Kirbit returned home and

gathered together twice as many men. Bulat the Brave once again sensed their approach and, this time pretending to have lost his scarf, returned and dispatched them all, apart from the tsar, once again. Knowing that his daughter was lost to him for ever, Tsar Kirbit returned home and mourned his daughter, but no longer gave chase.

As night fell Bulat, Ivan and Vasilisa Kirbit`evna made their camp, Bulat telling Ivan that he would scout the area and ordering Ivan to stay awake and watch over the maiden. Ivan managed to stay awake for half the night, but fell asleep soon after midnight. When Bulat awoke him in the morning, the girl was nowhere to be seen. Bulat scolded Ivan, telling him that KOSHCHEI THE DEATHLESS had taken her and that they would have to go in search of her.

After several days' ride they came across a herd of cattle being tended by two men. Having discovered from one of the herdsmen that the cattle belonged to Koshchei, they killed the men and dressed in their clothes before driving the cattle back to where Koshchei lived.

In order to maintain her beauty in such a dreary place, Vasilisa Kirbi`evna had taken to washing her face in goat's milk morning and night. As Bulat and Ivan drove the cattle into the yard a maid was just filling a cup with the goat's milk to take into Vasilisa Kirbit`evna. Bulat slipped the girl's ring off his finger and slyly dropped it into the milk. When Vasilisa Kirbit`evna found the ring she immediately knew who the two herdsmen were and rushed out to greet them. Bulat told the girl that she must discover where Koshchei kept his soul, for without it they could not kill him, and then quickly told her to hide them. Scarcely had they been secreted when Koshchei flew in.

Pretending to have missed him very much, Vasilisa Kirbit`evna snuggled up to Koshchei, telling him that she had been scared for him. He replied that she had no need to be frightened for him as he did not carry his soul with him but kept it in a broom in the kitchen. When Vasilisa Kirbit`evna told Bulat this he knew that Koshchei had been lying, so told the girl to be even more cunning.

That evening, when Koshchei returned, Vasilisa Kirbit`evna presented him with the broom, finely decorated, as a gift, telling him that his soul was too precious to leave lying around. Koshchei laughed, telling her that his soul was in fact in the goat that provided the milk she washed in. Again Bulat knew he was lying, so Vasilisa Kirbit`evna presented Koshchei with the goat, elaborately decorated. Koshchei once again laughed and told her that his soul was not in the goat, but rather in an egg, inside a duck, inside a hare, under a huge oak on a remote island in the middle of an endless ocean.

When Vasilisa Kirbit`evna relayed this to Bulat, he knew that at last Koshchei had been telling the truth. Immediately he and Ivan set off to find the island. *En route* they grew dangerously short of food, so, coming across a dog, they made to kill it. The dog pleaded for mercy, saying that he would be of use to them, and Bulat let the dog go free. Next they came to an eagle and the same thing happened. On the shore of the ocean they met a lobster and exactly the same thing happened again.

Crossing the ocean took many days, but finally they came to the island on which a single, huge oak tree grew. Bulat unearthed the tree with ease and the hare jumped out and ran away. Instantly the dog they had spared appeared and caught the hare. Out of the hare the duck flew high into the sky, where it was pounced upon by the eagle Bulat and Ivan had spared. Out of the duck fell the egg, which rolled into the sea, from where it was recovered by the lobster. Having Koshchei's soul in their possession, Bulat and Ivan returned to Vasilisa Kirbit`evna and that evening, when Koshchei returned, they confronted him and, smashing the egg on his forehead, killed him.

Ivan returned to his homeland, where he married Vasilisa Kirbit`evna in fulfilment of the prophecy, and made Bulat the Brave his most trusted friend and adviser.

Bulgar
General
Term used to refer to an inhabitant of Bulgaria, though the name is correctly used to refer to invaders from ASIA who entered the region in the seventh century and conquered and subjugated the Slav population.

Búri
Norse and Teutonic
The father of BÖRR, and thus grandfather of ODÍNN, who was born of the ice that was licked into shape by AUDHUMLA, the primordial cow, though some sources say that Búri was simply released when Audhumla lapped at the salt-encrusted rocks that lay beside the vast primordial ocean while nourishing YMIR, the first being, who had been created from drops of water.

busi-urt
Finno-Ugric – Votyak
One of the classes of URT. The soul of the cornfield that protects the D'U-URT, the soul of the corn, and ensures a good harvest.

Buyan
Slavonic
An oceanic island that was the home of the North, East and West Winds.

Byelobog
Slavonic
The WHITE GOD, known as BYELUN in RUSSIA (*byeli*, white, and *bog*, god). He represents the forces of good, light and life, and is opposed by CHERNOBOG, the BLACK GOD, who represents the forces of evil, and is the cause of all misfortune. Byelobog, which is the name of the White God in the BALKAN states, was usually represented as a venerable old man with a flowing white beard, dressed in white clothes. He roamed around the country, seen only by day, doing works of kindness such as curing sick animals, helping hunters make a good kill, finding lost items and ensuring a good crop.

Byelun
Russian
The Russian name for BYELOBOG, the WHITE GOD, the personification of good, light and life. Represented as an old man, dressed all in white with a flowing white beard, Byelun was seen only during daylight hours and carried out all manner of acts to the benefit of mankind. He would be particularly important in a country where large parts of the year were spent in virtual darkness.

Byggvir
Norse and Teutonic
A minor god who, along with BEYLA, was attendant on FREYR. His name which appears to derive from *bygg*, may mean 'Barley'.

bylichka
Russian
One of the main types of Russian legend, along with the BYLINA and the SHAZKA. The *bylichkas* deal with the supernatural world and with beings that come from the land of the dead, the UNDERWORLD[1]. When pagan beliefs were at their

strongest, the common peasants of ancient Russia half-believed the *bylichkas*, which tend to be short and told in the first person, being related from father to son down through the generations.

bylina
Russian

One of the categories of Russian legend (plural *byliny*), as opposed to the SHAZKA and the BYLICHKA. The *byliny* deal with the heroes of old, such as IL`YA MUROMETS and Dobrynya NIKITICH, and were intended to be sung or chanted. As such they are regarded as poetry rather than prose. They all have a distinctive style and deal with deeds of great daring. A mixture of pure fantasy and historical fact, the *byliny* recount stories of the ancient battles against the enemies of ancient Russia.

Byrgir
Norse and Teutonic

A well that HIUKI and BIL were made to fetch water from all night long, every night, in their pail SOEG by their cruel father. MANI saw their plight and took the two children up to the MOON[5], where they were made Mani's water-bearers.

Caedmon
British
Legendary seventh-century singer, poet and minstrel who was said to have received his musical gifts from heaven in a dream, possibly suggesting a SHAMANistic trait.

Cancer
Finno-Ugric
One of the nine monstrous offspring of LOVIATAR and WIND². The other monsters are named as PLEURISY, COLIC, GOUT, TUBERCULOSIS, ULCER, SCABIES, PLAGUE and ENVY.

Canterbury
General
Cathedral city in Kent which was called *Durovernum* by the Romans and was the SAXON capital of Kent. The Celtic Church was established at Canterbury in Roman times, but in the fifth century, when the Romans left and the heathen Saxons and JUTES replaced them as the rulers of southeast England, Christianity was extinguished in the city.

Around 580 the local king, Aethelbert, married Bertha, a Christian princess. She brought a chaplain with her and, though Aethelbert retained his pagan beliefs, he allowed his queen to restore an ancient Christian church to the east of the city. This church, Saint Martin's, is still there and claims to be the oldest Christian church in England.

Canterbury became the home of British Christianity after 597, when Pope Gregory sent Saint Augustine to England. Bertha welcomed the missionary to Canterbury and before long her husband had accepted Christianity and was baptized in the church of Saint Martin. In 598 Augustine built an abbey to the east of the city wall, around Aethelbert's pagan temple, which became the Church of Saint Pancras. A former Celtic Christian church was remodelled as a cathedral and on his death Augustine was buried in his abbey.

Caucasus
General
Name given to a series of mountain ranges that run for 750 miles between the Caspian Sea and the BLACK SEA. The highest peak within this series is Elbruz, which rises to 18,480 feet.

Celt(s)
General
The Celts originated, so it is widely accepted today, in central Europe *c.* 1200 BC in the basin of the upper DANUBE, the Alps, and parts of France and south GERMANY. Classical legend accounts for the naming of the people thus: Celtina, daughter of Britannus, had a son by Hercules named Celtus, who became the progenitor of the Celtic people.

The Celts developed a transitional culture between the Bronze and Iron Ages (ninth to fifth centuries BC) known as the Halstatt, from excavations carried out at a site of that name to the southwest of Salzburg. They farmed and raised cattle and were pioneers of iron-working, reaching their peak in the period from the fifth century BC to the Roman conquest (known as La Tène, from the archae ological site of that name in Switzerland).

In the sixth century BC they spread into Spain and Portugal and were known as the Celtiberi ('Iberian Celts'). Over the next 300 years they also spread into the British Isles, north Italy (sacking Rome in 390 BC), Greece and the BALKANS, though they never established a united empire, probably because they were divided into numerous tribes. Their various conquests were made by emigrant bands which established permanent settlements in these areas, as well as in that part of Asia Minor that was later to be known as Galatia. In the first century BC the Celts were defeated by the forces of the Roman Empire and by Germanic tribes, and were confined to western Europe, especially England, Wales and Ireland. Even here they were not safe, for the Romans invaded BRITAIN in AD 43 and sought to annihilate Celtic beliefs. This they failed to do, and it was not until the arrival of the ANGLES and SAXONS in the fifth century AD that the Celts were pushed into the furthest corners of Britain. By that time the continental Celts had all but disappeared, and those left as true Celts were confined to the southwest of England, parts of Wales and almost all of Ireland. The advent of Christianity was the final nail in the Celtic coffin, though Ireland has managed to retain most of its Celtic beliefs, customs and traditions right up to modern times.

Cheremiss
Finno-Ugric
The indigenous inhabitants of the region comprising the middle and upper Volga that is today the Autonomous Republic of Mordovia or Mordvinia. The region was conquered by RUSSIA during the thirteenth century and did not regain autonomy until 1930. Almost none of the FINNO-UGRIC-speaking Cheremiss-Mordvin peoples have survived.

Chernava
Russian
Daughter of the SEA TSAR. When SADKO had been detained beneath the oceans by her father, she was to be his bride and if they consummated their marriage, Sadko would be forever under the spell of the Sea Tsar. However, Sadko had the help of Saint NIKOLAI OF MOZHAISK and, following his instructions, did not lie with the girl, so was released. Chernava is also the spirit of the river of the same name, for all rivers were the children of the Sea Tsar, even those that sprang from the blood of fallen heroes, and it was to the banks of her river, which flows near NOVGOROD, that Sadko was transported when the Sea Tsar was forced to release him.

Chernigov
Russian
Town and port on the River DESNA in northern UKRAINE which has an eleventh-century cathedral. In the legend of IL`YA MUROMETS, that hero frees the inhabitants of the town, who are under siege. They ask him to become their tsar, but Il`ya refuses, as he is *en route* to the court of VLADIMIR BRIGHT SUN at KIEV.

Chernobog
Slavonic
The BLACK GOD (*cherni*, black, and *bog*, god). He was the epitome and personification of evil, darkness and death. Usually represented as a dark figure, dressed all in black, he was seen only during the hours of darkness and was opposed by BYELOBOG, the WHITE GOD, the person-

ification of all things good. Chernobog was particularly feared in northern RUS-SIA, where long periods of each year would be spent in virtual darkness.

Cissa
Anglo-Saxon

A son of AELLE who accompanied his father when his SAXON forces defeated the Britons.

Clovis
General

Merovingian ruler of the FRANKS (465–511), the grandson of Merovich. In 481 he succeeded his father, Childeric I, as king of the Salian Franks and spent his entire life expanding the Frankish kingdom. When he died in his capital, Paris, the kingdom was divided between his four sons, who continued the expansion he had started.

Cockaigne
British

Medieval English legend saw Cockaigne as a mythical country of leisure and indolence where no one ever worked, and fine food and drink were plentiful and there to be had for the asking.

Cold
Finno-Ugric

The unnamed son of LOUHI, the ruler of the northernmost land of POHJOLA.

Colic
Finno-Ugric

One of the nine monstrous offspring of LOVIATAR and WIND[2]. The other monsters are named as PLEURISY, GOUT, TUBERCU-LOSIS, ULCER, SCABIES, PLAGUE, CANCER and ENVY.

Copper Kingdom
Russian

One of the three kingdoms of WHIRLWIND that were located on a plateau at the top of some tremendously high mountains. The tsarita of this kingdom, a prisoner of Whirlwind, lived in a copper palace that was guarded by DRAGONS[1]. She was set free by IVAN[1], along with her sisters, the tsaritas of the SILVER KINGDOM and the GOLDEN KINGDOM, when he killed Whirlwind and released his mother, NAS-TAS`YA OF THE GOLDEN BRAID. She married VASILII[1], one of the two brothers of Ivan. Her sister the tsarita of the Silver Kingdom married PETER, while ELENA THE FAIR, the tsarita of the Golden Kingdom, married Ivan.

Croatia
General

A constituent republic within the former Yugoslavia. Part of Pannonia in Roman times, the country was settled by Carpathian Croats in the seventh century. From 1102 Croatia was an autonomous kingdom under the Hungarian Crown, an Austrian crownland from 1849 and a Hungarian crownland from 1868; it was included in the kingdom of Serbs, Croats and Slovenes which became Yugoslavia in 1931.

Crnojevic, Ivan
Serbian

Heroic enemy of the invading Turks who is believed to sleep in a cave near Obod in southern MONTENEGRO, at the northern tip of Lake Skadar. There he lies in the arms of the mountain nymphs (see VILA) awaiting the time when he will arise and defend his people. This story bears direct comparison with that of Prince MARKO, and may have been influenced by stories of King ARTHUR taken to the area by the Romans.

Thunder is, to this day, interpreted as the anger of Ivan Crnojevic, and the river named after him, the Rijeka Crnojevica, which flows into Lake Skadar a few miles from the cave, was said to have been formed by the tears he shed over the misfortunes of his people.

Crucifixion of Odínn
Norse and Teutonic
The name given to the story of ODÍNN, stabbed and hanged from YGGDRASILL, which appears in the poem HÁVAMÁL. Originally it was thought that this story was a post-Christian adaptation of the crucifixion of Christ, though now it is considered to reflect the symbolic death of the SHAMAN, by means of which he was said to comprehend and find hidden wisdom. The poem relates that for nine days Odínn hung stabbed, and without food and water, sacrificed to himself from Yggdrasill. Then the god peered down and took the runes of knowledge and was thus set free.

Cymen
Anglo-Saxon
Son of the SAXON leader AELLE and brother to CISSA. He accompanied his father when his forces defeated the Britons.

Czech
General
Name given to an inhabitant of the former Czechoslovakia, and still in use to refer to an inhabitant of the Czech Republic.

Dag

Norse and Teutonic

1 The god of day, the son of NOTT by DELLINGR. He was escorted by a marvellous white horse with a shining mane named SKINFAXI. Dag appears to have originated as a wise man who, like ODÍNN, understood the language of the birds; he had a sparrow which brought him news from far and wide in much the same way as Odínn's ravens brought him news. However, a peasant killed the sparrow after it had stolen some grain and Dag then took revenge on the domain in which the bird had been killed. Dag was himself killed on the way home again, though by whom is not recorded. It seems that after he had been killed he was elevated from being a specially gifted, almost blessed mortal to the ranks of the gods. Dag had a daughter named DAGEID and a son named AGNE, whose own sons were ALRIC and ERIC.

2 The sole survivor of the family of HUNDINGR after they had made the mistake of fighting SIGMUNDR's sons SINFIOTLI and HELGI. Dag was allowed to live only after he had promised never to avenge the death of his kinsfolk, a promise he later broke when he killed Helgi.

Dageid

Norse and Teutonic

Daughter of DAG[1] and brother of AGNE.

Dain

Norse and Teutonic

1 A DWARF who was a master smith.

2 The name of one of the four stags that live on YGGDRASILL.

Dalmat

Russian

The tsar of an unnamed realm who owned the FIREBIRD that was the purpose of a quest by the sons of Tsar Vyslav ANDRONOVICH: DMITRII, VASILII[2] and IVAN[6]. When Ivan was caught trying to steal the Firebird and its gilded cage, Dalmat gave him a chance to redeem himself. If he could steal for him the HORSE WITH THE GOLDEN MANE, which belonged to Tsar AFRON, he would not only forgive Ivan but also give him the Firebird and its cage. Ivan tricked Dalmat with the help of a shape-changing wolf, who became the Horse with the Golden Mane, and then, once Ivan had ridden away with the real one, resumed his shape as a wolf and disappeared. Dalmat's reaction to this deception is not known.

Danube, River

General

The second longest European river, some 1,776 miles in length. It rises on the eastern slopes of the BLACK FOREST and flows across Europe to enter the BLACK SEA in ROMANIA through a swampy delta. Russian legend calls the Danube the River DUNAI.

Datan

Polish

One of the three gods of the field, the others being LAWKAPATIM and TAWALS. All three were invoked to ensure a good harvest; if they were not thus called upon, they could become malevolent and ruin the crop.

Dausos

Lithuanian

A mysterious realm of the dead, governed by DIEVAS, which may have been the MOON[2]. It was not simply a heaven, or a paradise, but a realm of that nature. It lies beyond the slippery high hill of the sky, up which the dead have to climb. To stop them from slipping down again, the dead needed strong fingernails, or claws like those of an animal. As the journey was believed to be very long, spirits were also said to have made the trip on horseback, or in the smoke of cremation fires, or by travelling along the BIRD'S WAY (the MILKY WAY[2]), or in a boat such as that used by the SUN[2] at night as he travels the dark sky back to the east ready for the next day's journey.

Day

1 *Russian*

Though Day does not have any specific legends surrounding him as a character, the legends of BABA-YAGA the witch say that he, along with the SUN[1] and NIGHT[1], are under the command of the witch. In these tales he is described as a horseman with a white face, dressed from head to foot in white, who rides a brilliant white horse which has a white saddle and harness. He is the brother of Night, who is his complete opposite, though his relationship to the Sun is never revealed. Some say that the Sun may be the father of both Day and Night, but this is never revealed in any of the stories in which Day makes an appearance.

2 *Norse and Teutonic*

The literal translation of DAG[1].

Dazhbog

In all three sections below the basic elements of Dazhbog as listed under the Russian heading apply equally.

1 *Russian*

The son of SVAROG, god of the sky, brother to SVAROZHICH, the god of fire, and himself god of the SUN[1], happiness, destiny and justice. The giver of warmth and light, he was much revered by the early Russians, especially as much of RUSSIA is usually covered by snow and ice, and the winter nights were almost unendurably long. The disappearance of Dazhbog was always greeted with dismay, and occurrences such as eclipses, when Dazhbog was said to have been devoured by wolves, were taken to be a warning of terrible times to come, such as plague, famine or the start of war. The Russians believed that Dazhbog ruled over the twelve kingdoms of the zodiac, where he was served by two beautiful maidens, the two ZVEZDA, the personifications of the AURORAS, and the seven planets, while comets acted as his messengers. Daily he drove his golden chariot, drawn by a pair of fire-breathing white horses, across the sky from his golden palace in the east, while his balding old uncle, MYESYATS, the MOON[1], awaited his arrival in the evening. Some stories, however, say that Dazhbog married Myesyats, who is in this case female, and thus became the father of the stars. Occasionally the genders of Dazhbog and Myesyats are reversed, making Dazhbog the sun goddess and Myesyats the moon god.

2 *Polish*

According to Polish belief, Dazhbog

lived in the east in a paradise of milk and honey, a land of eternal sunlight, from which he rode out each new morning in a golden chariot with diamond wheels that was drawn by twelve white fire-breathing horses, although some accounts say that his chariot was drawn by three horses, one of gold, one of silver and one of diamond.

3 *Serbian*

The Serbs saw Dazhbog as an upright young man who grew steadily older as the day wore on, to die each evening as a red-faced, bloated elderly gentleman.

Dellingr
Norse and Teutonic
The god of dawn who was the third husband of NIGHT[2] and the father of DAG[1].

Dem`yan, Saint
Russian
Russian Orthodox saint who, according to some legends, was, along with Saint KUZ`MA, a smith who forged the first plough, although other versions of this legend name the two saintly smiths as Saint BORIS and Saint GLEB. Kuz`ma and Dem`yan, however, had nothing at all to do with smithing; they were brothers who had been doctors and were martyred. Their connection with the legends surrounding smiths stems simply from the fact that Kuz`ma sounds similar to the Russian word for a smithy, *kuznya*. As a result they became, in the Russian Orthodox calendar of saints, the patrons of smiths and craftsmen. Churches dedicated to them were often to be found in the part of a town in which smiths and craftsmen carried out their business.

The plough reputedly forged by Kuz`ma and Dem`yan was of enormous proportions and was forged with implements of like size. The two smiths were reported to have used twelve golden hammers and

tongs that weighed almost twelve *poods* (*c*. 430 lb). One particular story, apparently of Ukranian origin (related under Kuz`ma), tells how this plough was first used.

As Kuz`ma and Dem`yan were called upon during the marriage ceremony to forge a strong and lasting marriage, they also came to be regarded as the patron saints of marriage in Russia.

Denmark
General
Country in northern Europe that consists of a peninsula and a great number of islands. It is bounded to the north by the Skagerrak, to the east by the Kattegat, to the south by GERMANY and to the west by the North Sea. The early history of Denmark is highly confused as there is scant evidence extant. However, what is certain is that the Danes originated in SWEDEN, from where they migrated during the fifth and sixth centuries. Ruled by local chieftains, the Danes terrorized much of Europe with their piratical raids from the eighth to the tenth centuries until Haraldr Bluetooth (*c*. 940–85) unified Denmark and established Christianity as the official religion. Perhaps the most famous Danish king was Canute, whose empire embraced Denmark, NORWAY and England, but on his death in 1035 the empire fragmented.

Dennitsa
Slavonic
The shortened, popularized version of ZVEZDA DENNITSA, the MORNING STAR[3].

Desna
Russian
River that flows through the UKRAINE and at whose confluence with the River DNEPR lies the city of KIEV, the third largest city of RUSSIA.

Devana
Czech

The goddess of the hunt, whose name is cognate with the Roman Diana. Among the Serbs she was known as DIIWICA, while among the Poles she was DZIEWONA.

Devil
Russian

Though the devil as known in other cultures does not appear widely in the Russian legends, he is said to reside in the UNDERWORLD[1], where he is the lord of the dead, bringer of misfortune and ruler of demons, witches and serpents. Some authorities claim that the witch BABA-YAGA is the servant of the devil, but there is no evidence to support this. One particular legend shows that the devil could also have a compassionate nature, provided he was given the respect he thought he deserved.

An unnamed smith once saw a frightening image of the devil in a local church. Returning to his smithy, he had a painter re-create the likeness on the doors to his workshop. For ten years he always gave the devil a cordial greeting as he came to work and bade him goodnight every evening as he left. After he had died, his son inherited the smithy, but he swore never to show something so hideous the respect his father had. Instead he used to hit the image with a large hammer squarely between the eyes every time he passed it. For three years the devil withstood the insults until finally he could bear them no longer.

Transforming himself into a young man, he went to the smithy, where he asked to be made the smith's apprentice. Having been taken on, the devil soon proved his worth and so was often left to mind the forge. On one such occasion the ageing wife of a local landowner came to the smithy to have her horse shod. The devil told her that they had just started a new line of business, the rejuvenation of old people. The vanity of the woman got the better of her and she paid the devil.

Gathering two pails of milk, the devil took hold of the woman in his tongs and cast her into the middle of the furnace. When all that was left were her bones, the devil removed these from the fire and placed them in a tub. He then poured the milk over the still-crackling bones and within a few minutes a young woman stepped forth. Returning to her husband, she persuaded him to go for the same treatment.

When the old man arrived at the smithy the devil had gone and the smith was back at the forge. Threatening the smith with all kinds of punishment if he did not do for him what he had done for his wife, the landowner obliged the smith to do as he asked. Throwing the landowner into the fire, the smith burned him until only his bones were left. These he placed in the tub and poured milk over them. Several hours passed and nothing happened. Anxious for her husband, the recently rejuvenated woman came to the smithy, but when she found only the charred bones of her husband she ran to have the young smith arrested for murder.

As she left, the devil reappeared and the smith explained his predicament. The devil then revealed who he was and told the smith that, provided he promised from that moment forth to always be civil to him and never hit his image again, he would restore the man. The smith agreed and by the time the woman had returned to have the smith arrested she was greeted by her young husband.

Diar
Norse and Teutonic

A little-used, rare name for the old gods that is believed to be a term imported in the ninth or tenth century from Ireland.

Its meaning seems rather ambiguous, as it was used by Snorri STURLUSON to refer to the priests of ODÍNN, and it may be for this very reason that it was not a popular term.

Diev(a)s
Lithuanian and Lett

The high god of the sky whose name is cognate with the Sanskrit *dyut*, to shine, and *deiuos*, of the sky. He was depicted as a handsome king dressed in a silver robe, wearing a cap, belt and sword. He lives beyond the slippery high hill of the sky, far beyond the realm of DAUSOS, in an enclosed kingdom that may be entered only through three silver gates. Within the walls of his kingdom are his manor house, farms, sauna and garden, the entire realm being surrounded by an impenetrable forest.

Every day Dievas leaves his home and drives, very carefully, down the slippery high hill of the sky in a chariot of gold or on a copper sledge. He takes great care not to make the earth tremble or to disturb so much as a single dewdrop, for Dievas is primarily concerned with the promotion of the earth's fertility. Dievas stimulates the growth of crops while he tramples weeds underfoot. In association with LAIMA, Dievas is also responsible for the determination of man's fate. He was attended on by his unnamed sons, the DIEVO SUNELIAI, and the MOON[2] god MENUO.

Although the most powerful of the Baltic deities, he is not the king or ruler of the gods but rather *primus inter pares*. His variant name, Dievs, was almost exclusively used by the Letts.

Dievo suneliai
Lithuanian

Collective name given to the unnamed sons of DIEVAS. They were attendant on their father, along with the MOON[2] god MENUO.

Diiwica
Serbian

The Serbian name for DEVANA, the goddess of the hunt.

Dimstipatis
Lithuanian

Alternative name for ZEMEPATIS, the god of the homestead. This variant is cognate with *dimstis*, home, and *patis*, father.

Dísir
Norse and Teutonic

A generic name given to a group of female deities who were especially connected with fertility rites celebrated in the autumn. The chief of the Dísir was FREYJA, whose temple was sometimes referred to as the 'Disa Hall'. In SWEDEN the sacral kingship was closely connected with the worship of the Dísir, and with a ritual sacrifice carried out in the 'Disa Hall' known, unsurprisingly, as the 'Disa sacrifice'.

Dmitrii
Russian

One of the sons of Tsar Vyslav ANDRONOVICH and brother to VASILII[2] and IVAN[6]. When their father sent them on a quest to locate and capture the FIREBIRD, Dmitrii travelled with Vasilii, while Ivan travelled alone. When Ivan was on his way home, having successfully completed the task, as well as bringing with him the HORSE WITH THE GOLDEN MANE and the maiden ELENA THE BEAUTIFUL, his brothers ambushed and killed him. Returning to the palace, they claimed the success as their own, casting lots to share the spoils; Vasilii won Elena the Beautiful and Dmitrii won the Horse with the Golden Mane. Both brothers were thrown into the tsar's deepest dungeon after Ivan, miraculously brought back to life by the wolf that had helped him on his quest with the WATER OF LIFE AND

DEATH, returned to the royal palace to reveal his brothers' treachery.

Dne(i)pr, River
Russian
River, total length 1,400 miles, that rises in the Smolensk region of WHITE RUSSIA and flows south past KIEV, Dnepropetrovzk and Zaporozhe, to enter the BLACK SEA east of Odessa. The river has many lakes along its length and features in many of the Russian legends that developed around the court of VLADIMIR BRIGHT SUN, which was situated at Kiev. In the legend of SUKHMAN, the river is reported to have told that hero of the TARTAR army that was attempting to cross her to reach Kiev.

Dobie
British
One of the various names applied to the uniquely British PUCK.

Dogoda
Slavonic
The god of the west wind, he was perceived as the most gentle of the deities that personified the winds.

Dojran, Lake
Serbian
Lake that straddles the border between MACEDONIA (in the southern part of former Yugoslavia) and northern Greece to the east of the border town of Gevgelija. Serbian legend says that the lake was originally a shallow hollow in the centre of which there was a deep well safeguarded by no less than thirteen locks. A local girl, DOJRANA, was in love with a local boy, but the Turks had other plans for her. Preferring death to concubinage, Dojrana ran to the well and jumped down it. Thereafter the locks could never be closed again and the water gushed over the plain, forming the shallow lake that lies there today.

Dojrana
Serbian
A girl who lived in southern MACEDONIA and fell deeply in love with a local boy. Unluckily for her, the Turks had other ideas about her future, but, preferring death to concubinage, Dojrana threw herself down a deep well that was protected by thirteen locks. The locks could not be closed after her suicide and the water from the well gushed forth to form Lake DOJRAN, so named in her honour.

Domovikha
Slavonic
The wife of the DOMOVOI, she lived in the cellars of houses, while her mate lived in the household stove.

Domovoi
Slavonic
The spirit of a family's founding ancestor who lived right in the heart of the huge stove that was the focal point of the home. The Domovoi looked after the welfare of the family and was sometimes affectionately referred to as 'grandad' (or *chelovek*, 'fellow'). According to legend, the Domovoi (like many Slav spirits of this type, at once singular and plural) staged a revolt against SVAROG when the universe was created. Svarog drove them from his realm, whereupon they fell to earth, some landing in backyards, some coming down chimneys into the family stove, some into forests and some on to the plains. Each group were Domovoi and each had the same characteristics, but over the years those outside the home disappeared, or were assimilated with other spirits, to leave but a single race of Domovoi. His wife, the DOMOVIKHA, lived in the cellars of houses.

Very few people have ever managed to catch a glimpse of the Domovoi, though everyone heard him in the creakings and groanings of the house. Those who have, describe him as a dwarfish, ageing man covered with soft fur, even on the palms of his hands and the soles of his feet. The only visible parts of his body through this downy covering were his piercing eyes and his pointed nose. Sometimes he would also be given horns and a tail, but he was usually conceived, according to peasant lore, as an animated stock of hay. Less approachable and much shyer than the Domovoi were the DVOROVOI, the spirit of the household yard, and possibly a derivation of the Domovoi expelled by Svarog that fell into household yards.

Although mischievous, the Domovoi would never harm the family with whom he lived unless he was offended in some way. One such story tells of two peasants who lived next door to each other. One owned horses that were well fed and well groomed, while the horses of his neighbour were sickly and thin. Wishing to find out why his horses were so much finer than those of his neighbour, the peasant hid at night and caught the Domovoi grooming and feeding his horses, finally watering them from the large butt in the yard. The following day, not wanting the water he drank himself contaminated by an ugly spirit, he asked his jealous neighbour what he should do. The neighbour knew that a Domovoi was surely helping and so, keen to have his neighbour reduced to the same level as himself, he suggested that the man drill a large hole in the butt. He could then bung it up during the day, but let all the water out at night. Foolishly, the man followed this advice and when the Domovoi came to water the horses he found what had happened. In his rage he smashed the stables to pieces and killed all the horses.

The importance of the Domovoi was reflected by the fact that every time the master of the house left, his wife would ensure that the mouth of the stove was covered so that the Domovoi did not leave as well. Later traditions said that the Domovoi lived not only in the stove but also in the cattle sheds and stables, for he was particularly fond of farm animals. At night he would feed the horses and then comb and groom them, neatly plaiting their manes and their tails. Every time the peasant bought a new animal, he would lead it around the yard to make sure that the Domovoi approved of his purchase, and ask the Domovoi to welcome the newcomer to his home. However, the spirit of the yard, including the stables and sheds, was usually referred to as the Dvorovoi.

Don, River
General
River that rises to the south of MOSCOW and runs 1,180 miles to enter the extreme northeastern end of the Sea of Azov. In its lower reaches the river is a mile wide and for almost four months of every year it is closed by ice. Its upper navigable reaches are connected to the VOLGA by means of a canal.

Donar
Teutonic
The TEUTONIC name for the god of thunder, who was particularly associated with oak trees, he is perhaps better known by his NORSE name, THÓRR.

Dovre
Norse and Teutonic
According to the ORKNEYINGA SAGA, Dovre was the mountain home of SVADI, the father of HROLF of BJARG, King of HEIDEMARK.

Dragon(s)
1 Russian
   Dragons abound in Russian legends. Some have the more usual serpentine form, such as the twelve-headed one dispatched by Dobrynya NIKITICH,

while others, usually from the time of the BYLINY, have the head of a serpent, the body of a man and fly on a winged horse, such as that killed by IVAN THE PEA when he rescued his sister VASILISA OF THE GOLDEN BRAID from its clutches.

Although dragons date from the pagan age of RUSSIA, they continued to be associated with Christian knights and legends, and in popular belief are still held to be the cause of many natural phenomena. Eclipses of the sun and moon were taken to be caused by dragons, their reappearance showing that even dragons could not withstand their power - a sign to reassure people that, although malevolent, dragons could always be defeated by the good and the righteous.

Dragons were not the most intelligent of creatures and were easily tricked. One story that particularly illustrates this point tells of a gypsy who wandered into a village the day after all but one man living there had been devoured by a particularly ferocious dragon. This man pleaded with the gypsy to leave before the dragon reappeared, but as they spoke a huge shadow fell over them both, and the dragon landed right in front of them.

When the monster made towards the gypsy, he held his hand up and told the dragon that if it tried to eat him he would choke, for the man boasted that he was far stronger than the dragon. The dragon scoffed at this and suggested a test. Picking up a millstone, he proceeded to crush it into a fine powder. The gypsy applauded, but asked the dragon if it could make water run from a stone. Before the dragon realized what was going on, the gypsy had picked up a muslin bag full of cream cheese and begun to squeeze the liquid from it.

Impressed, the dragon thought that it might be better to befriend the gypsy and so asked him to bring back the fattest oxen he could find in the field for their dinner. The gypsy knew that he was not strong enough to do that, so he herded the cattle into one end of the field and began to tie their tails together. When the dragon came to see why the gypsy was taking so long, the gypsy told him that he had thought it better to drag back the whole herd, for then they would not need to fetch any more food for a long time. Impatiently, the dragon skinned a large ox, threw it over his back and carried it to the village.

Having filled two cooking pots with fresh meat, the dragon gave the ox skin to the gypsy and told him to go to the well, fill it with water and then bring it back to cook the meat in. The gypsy had trouble carrying the skin to the well, but once there he started to dig a channel around it. Once again the dragon grew impatient and came to see what the delay was. The gypsy explained that he thought it better to bring back the whole well, for then they would never run out of water. The dragon, anxious to eat, filled the ox skin himself, carried it back and poured the water into the cooking pots.

Now they needed firewood. The dragon sent the gypsy into the forest to collect a large oak tree. There the gypsy began to make a rope from the bark of the trees and had wound this around twenty trunks by the time the dragon came to see what was taking so long. Again the gypsy explained that he thought it far better to bring twenty trees than a single one, for then they would never run out of firewood. The dragon laughed, tore up a huge tree and strode back to the village, broke it up and built a huge fire under the cooking pots. Soon the dragon began to eat, but the gypsy pretended to sulk and refused to eat.

When asked why he was sulking, the gypsy replied that the only way he would know that they were true friends was if the dragon came to meet his family. The dragon agreed and hitched three fine horses to a large cart, and the pair drove back to the gypsy camp. There they were greeted by the gypsy's naked children, who ran noisily around the cart. When the dragon asked who they were, the gypsy replied that they were his children, hungry as usual and what a fine meal they would make of the dragon.

With that the dragon leapt down from the cart and hurried away, never again to attack a human. The gypsy sold the horses and the cart, and he and his family lived on the proceeds, in comfort, for many years.

For other Slavonic legends concerning dragons see ALESHA, Ivan the Pea, Dobrynya Nikitich, IL`YA MUROMETS.

2 *Norse and Teutonic*

While dragons are quite common in both NORSE and TEUTONIC tradition (see, for example, FÁFNIR and BEOWULF), they differ quite markedly from dragons as perceived in other parts of Europe, and indeed further afield. Rarely depicted as either winged or fire-breathing, these dragons were usually huge serpents and were generally referred to as the guardians of a grave or, more particularly, of treasure. Later sagas developed the theme of the dragon further and made such animals the metamorphosis of a corpse.

draugr
Norse and Teutonic

The name given to the restless occupant of a grave, though little more is known. It is thought that the term referred to the spirit of the deceased which would visit the living, rather than to the corpse which would, like the zombie of Voodoo tradition, rise from the grave.

Draupnir
Norse and Teutonic

The fabulous gold ring of ODÍNN from which all other rings are said to have derived as, every ninth night, Draupnir spawned eight identical rings. FREYR borrowed the ring when he wanted to woo GERDR, but it was rejected by her when SKÍRNIR offered it to her as a token of Freyr's love and devotion. The ring is perhaps best known from its appearance in the myth of BALDR, when it was placed by the grieving Odínn on the funeral pyre of Baldr and his wife, NANNA, that had been built on Baldr's ship HRINGHORNI. After HERMÓDR[1] had travelled down to NIFLHEIMR and met with the goddess HEL in his attempt to restore Baldr to life, he brought the ring back from the UNDERWORLD[4] when he delivered Hel's terms.

Driva
Norse and Teutonic

According to Snorri STURLUSON in HEIMSKRINGLA, DRIVA, the wife of VANLANDE (a son of SWEGDE) beseeched the witch HULD to either cast a spell over her husband so that he would return to FINLAND or kill him. Vanlande immediately felt the desire to return to Finland, but his friends and counsellors advised him not to, so he simply lay down to sleep. After a short while Vanlande awoke and called out to his advisers that the MARA (the nightmare was the way the NORSE witch or succubus often chose to haunt male victims) was trampling him. His men hastened to his side, but they were too late and he died. In this story the Mara is said to have been the power of

GRIMHILDR's daughter. Huld also arranged for GISL and UNDUR, the sons of VISBUR, Vanlande's son, to kill their father without being either detected in or suspected of the crime.

Droma
Norse and Teutonic
The name of the second chain that the ÆSIR used in their attempt to bind FENRIR.

Drotn(e)r
Norse and Teutonic
According to Snorri STURLUSON, one of the names given to the priests of ODÍNN, whom he also calls DIAR. Drotnr means 'lord', but does not appear to have any direct relevance to the ancient, pagan gods, and was later used widely to refer to both God and Christ.

Dunai, River
Russian
The ancient Russian name for the River DANUBE, which formed, so legend tells us, from the blood of Dunai IVANOVICH after he had thrown himself on his upturned spear for shooting his wife, Princess NASTAS`YA, through the heart with a poisoned arrow.

Duneyr
Norse and Teutonic
The name of one of the four stags that live in the branches of YGGDRASILL.

Durnir
Norse and Teutonic
A DWARF whose name perhaps means 'Doorkeeper'. Durnir appears in the YNGLINGA SAGA in the section concerning King SWEGDE. Having married VANA, a VANAHEIMR maiden, by whom he had a son named VANLANDE, Swegde set out to seek GODHEIM, the appropriately named kingdom of the gods. After a while he came to a mansion called STEIN, to the

east of SWITHIOD THE GREAT. Near the entrance, under a huge boulder, sat Durnir, who beckoned Swegde to enter within the stone portal (or beneath it), for there he would meet ODÍNN. Without a moment's hesitation, Swegde entered the stone, which instantly closed behind him. The *Ynglinga Saga* says that Swegde entered the hall of a giant named SÖKMIME and was never seen again.

d'u-urt
Finno-Ugric – Votyak
The soul of corn which is protected, while growing in the field, by BUSI-URT, the soul of the cornfield.

Dvalin
Norse and Teutonic
1 One of the four DWARFS who manufactured the necklace BRÍSINGAMEN for FREYJA and were rewarded with a night of unbridled lust with the goddess. His three compatriots were ALFRIGG, BERLING and GRERR. Dvalin also appears to have been the dwarf who was ordered to make a new head of hair for SÍF by LOKI after he had cut it off. He is also reputed to have made the spear GUNGNIR and the wonderful, collapsible ship SKIDBLADNIR.
2 The name of one of the four stags that live on YGGDRASILL.

Dvorovoi
Slavonic
The spirit of the household yard. Closely related to the DOMOVOI, the Dvorovoi lives in the sheds and stables of a house and tends the animals. New animals brought to the house are introduced to him so the Dvorovoi might welcome them to their new home. However, the Dvorovoi was hostile to animals with white fur, though he would tolerate chickens that had white feathers, for they had their own god.

The Dvorovoi could be influenced in two ways: bribery and punishment. If a piece of bread and some bits of sheep's wool were left out, then the Dvorovoi would do man's bidding. He could also be made to obey by taking a long stick and a thread from the shroud of a dead man, tying this thread to the stick and then using it to whip the yard, for in the process the Dvorovoi was sure to be lashed. Those who could see the Dvorovoi would pin him to a fence with a pitchfork. However, as the story of KATYA shows, the Dvorovoi was a jealous character who could exact his own revenge if he so desired.

dwarf(s)
Norse and Teutonic
Small, ugly, evil but clever supernatural creatures who hide from the light of day in caves and rocks, for if the rays of the SUN[5] catch a dwarf, it will instantly turn to stone. They mostly lived underground, where they were considered the guardians of mines and minerals, and were skilled in metal-working, particularly as armourers. Dwarfs abound in both NORSE and TEUTONIC tradition.

Four dwarfs named AUSTRI, NORDRI, SUDRI and WESTRI are said to support the dome of the sky, formed out of YMIR's skull; the dwarfs themselves were said to have been created by the gods like maggots in Ymir's flesh. As masters of metal-working they made FREYR a golden boar named GULLINBURSTI ('Golden-bristled') that shone even in the dark and was so swift it could easily outrun a horse. The dwarfs were also responsible for making a fabulous piece of jewellery, possibly a necklace, for FREYJA which was known as BRÍSINGAMEN, her reward for sleeping with each of them in turn.

Dwarfs are known by any number of different names in the myths and legends, although not all the names really apply to dwarfs. They are called dark elves, GNOMES, KOBOLDS and TROLLS, but of these only dark elves can accurately be applied to dwarfs, the other three being entirely separate races of supernatural creatures. Dark elves, as dwarfs are commonly called in Norse tradition, lived in SVARTALFHEIMR, while light elves – dwarfs who were benevolent rather than malevolent – lived in ALFHEIMR.

Dziewona
Polish
The name by which the goddess of the hunt, DEVANA, was known to the Poles.

Dzuli
Siberia – Tungus
Also MUXDI. The name given to a statuette of a revered ancestor who was thought to have gone to live with the gods and could thus be relied upon, if treated with respect, to bring good fortune to the household.

Earth
Norse and Teutonic
The daughter of NIGHT[2] and ANNAR.

Ebissa
Anglo-Saxon
Son of HENGIST and brother to OCTA, AESC, HARTWAKER, SARDOINE and RENWEIN.

Eckhardt
Teutonic
The inseparable friend of TANNHÄUSER.

Edda
Norse and Teutonic
The wife of AI and the mortal mother of THRALL, by HEIMDALLR.

Edda
Norse and Teutonic
Name that has been given to two collections of early literature which together make up the main source of Old NORSE mythology. The term strictly applies to the *Prose Edda*, which was compiled by Snorri STURLUSON, an Icelandic priest, *c.* 1230 as a manual of instruction for professional poets. It includes a section on myth and a section called 'Skalde', which explains the use of diction, metre, alliteration, etc. The *Poetic Edda* is a collection of poems that was discovered by Brynjólfr SVEINSSON *c.* 1643. It had been written by a group of anonymous Norwegian poets between the ninth and twelfth centuries, and contains epic poetic narrative featuring the traditional TEUTONIC heroes and mythological subjects.

Egia
Norse and Teutonic
The name of one of the nine WAVE MAIDENS, the giantess daughters of ÆGIR.

Egil
Norse and Teutonic
One of the sons of WADA, King of the Finns, his brothers being VÖLUNDR and SLAGFIDR. The three brothers took the SWAN MAIDENS as their wives. After their wives had flown away, Egil and Slagfidr went in search of them, while Völundr remained at home in WOLFDALES, where he worked as a smith.

Egils Saha ok Asumndar
Norse and Teutonic
A late work which tells the story of ODÍNN leading a giantess down into the UNDERWORLD[4].

Eglimi
Norse and Teutonic
King of ORKNEY and the father of HIORDIS, who became the last wife of SIGMUNDR.

Einherjar
Norse and Teutonic
Generic name applied to the dead warriors who spend all day in battle and feast all night, every night, on roast boar in VALHALLA.

Einmyria
Norse and Teutonic
The daughter of LOKI and GLUT, her sister being EISA.

Eira
Norse and Teutonic
Also EYRA. One of the attendants of FRIGGA who latterly became the goddess of medicine. The NORSE people were unusual among Indo-Europeans in that the deity of medicine was female – a trait reflecting the fact that in their society only women were allowed to practise that art.

Eiríkr inn Sigrsaeli
Swedish
'Eric the Victorious', a historical and famous tenth-century king of SWEDEN. Prior to the battle of FYRISVELLIR in 960, the king dedicated himself to ODÍNN, solemnly vowing to sacrifice himself to the god after ten years had passed. A tall figure wearing a hooded cloak appeared before him and handed him a stick, telling him to shoot it over the heads of the army of his enemy, STYRBJÖRN. Eiríkr followed the instructions and as the stick flew over the army, the entire company was struck blind and shortly afterwards an avalanche totally engulfed it.

Eisa
Norse and Teutonic
One of the two daughters of LOKI and GLUT, her sister being EINMYRIA.

Eitel
Norse and Teutonic
A son of ATLI (ETZEL) and GUDRUNN.

Ekim
Russian
The squire of ALESHA, whom he accompanied from ROSTOV to the court of Prince VLADIMIR BRIGHT SUN at KIEV. There he caught the knife thrown at his master and friend by the vile monster TUGARIN.

Elb
Norse and Teutonic
Alternative name for ELF[1] which has given its name to the River Elbe.

Eldhrimnir
Norse and Teutonic
The name of the cauldron in VALHALLA in which the boar SÆHRIMNIR was cooked each day.

Eld~ir, ~e
Norse and Teutonic
One of the two main servants of ÆGIR, the other being FUNFENGR.

Elena the Beautiful
Russian
A princess from an unnamed kingdom who was abducted by IVAN[6] and the shape-changing wolf that was helping him. Ivan had been set the task of abducting Elena by Tsar AFRON after he had been caught trying to steal the HORSE WITH THE GOLDEN MANE and its bridle, itself a task set by Tsar DALMAT, who had caught Ivan trying to steal the FIREBIRD and its cage for his father. Elena was carried away by the wolf in recompense for killing his horse. By the time they arrived at the kingdom of Tsar Afron, Ivan and Elena had fallen in love. The wolf assumed Elena's form and was left in her stead. Ivan and Elena then rode away on the Horse with the Golden Mane and were later rejoined by the wolf.

Having completed all his allotted tasks, Ivan, Elena and the Horse with the Golden Mane were on their way to the home of Tsar Vyslav ANDRONOVICH, Ivan's father, when they were ambushed by DMITRII and VASILII[2], Ivan's jealous brothers. Ivan was killed and Elena fell by lot to Vasilii. The treachery of the two brothers was revealed after Ivan had been restored to life by the wolf, using some of the WATER OF LIFE AND DEATH. Dmitrii and Vasilii were thrown into a deep dungeon, and Elena the Beautiful married Ivan.

Elena the Fair
Russian

The tsarita of the GOLDEN KINGDOM, one of the three kingdoms within the realm of WHIRLWIND. She and her sisters, the tsaritas of the COPPER KINGDOM and the SILVER KINGDOM, were the prisoners of Whirlwind. When IVAN[1] came to rescue his mother, NASTAS`YA OF THE GOLDEN BRAID, Elena told him where he might find her, making him promise to return and free her as well. This he did, though his brothers PETER and VASILII[1] tried to claim the success for themselves and stranded Ivan in Whirlwind's realm. After Ivan had returned home with the help of LAME and ONE-EYE, servants of Whirlwind, it was Elena who first realized that someone with magic powers from the realm of Whirlwind had returned, and set the three tasks which uncovered the treachery of Peter and Vasilii[1]. She married Ivan, while her sister the tsarita of the Copper Kingdom married Vasilii, and her other sister, the tsarita of the Silver Kingdom, married Peter.

Elf
Norse and Teutonic

1 Also ELB, HELFERICH and HELFRAT. A water sprite whose name was later given to the River Elbe in GERMANY.

2 One of the VIKINGS, he married HIORDIS after the death of SIGMUNDR and thus became the foster father of SIGURDR.

3 The name given to a supernatural being that possibly owes its naming to ELF[1]. Although elves abound in the mythology and folklore of countless civilizations, they are regarded as being very much NORSE in origin. Here they were regarded as a class of supernatural being, DWARFish in form, with formidable magical powers which they exercised malevolently or benevolently at will. They were therefore seen as highly mischievous creatures. In Norse tradition the King of the Elves was ALBERICH.

Malevolent elves were said to milk farmers' cows dry, ride their horses all night, snuff out candles and prevent bread rising. Superstition also attributed to elves the practice of stealing children and leaving a deformed or unpleasant changeling in their place. Benevolent elves love the woods and the fields, where they dance and sing to the music of magic harps. They help farmers to make butter and brew beer successfully.

Elfheim(r)
Norse and Teutonic

A simple variant of ALFHEIMR, the land of the elves (*heimr* signifies 'the land of').

Eljudnir
Norse and Teutonic

The hall of HEL that lay within her realm of NIFLHEIMR. It was to this hall that HERMÓDR[1] travelled on his quest to restore BALDR and NANNA to life, and where he was to see his brother for the last time.

Elk of Hiisi
Finno-Ugric

A camel-like animal that was owned by HIISI, along with another fabulous beast, an unnamed fire-breathing horse. Both beasts were captured by LEMMINKAINEN as the first two of the three tasks set him by LOUHI, the ruler of POHJOLA.

Elli
Norse and Teutonic

'Old Age'. Disguised as an old crone, Elli was introduced to THÓRR as the foster mother of UTGARDR-LOKI, who suggested that the pair should wrestle. No matter how hard he tried, Thórr could not throw the crone, but she easily forced the god on to one knee and might well have thrown him had Utgardr-loki not intervened and stopped the contest. It was only as Thórr took his leave the following day that the deception was revealed to him.

Ellida
Norse and Teutonic
The name of the magical ship that was given to VIKING by ÆGIR.

Elsa of Brabant
Teutonic
The daughter of the Duke of BRABANT. During the siege of her castle by Frederick de TELRAMUND, the hero LOHENGRIN was summoned from the GRAIL temple and came to her aid in a swan-boat. He duly defeated her assailant and then married Elsa, but cautioned her that she must never ask him his name. Having borne him two children, Elsa at length asked the forbidden question, whereupon Lohengrin was immediately carried away again in the swan-boat.

Elvidnr
Norse and Teutonic
The name given to the hall of the goddess HEL.

Embla
Norse and Teutonic
The first woman, her name possibly means 'Elm'. She and the first man, ASKR ('Ash'), were created from the two trees that ODÍNN, HOENIR and LÓDURR found as they were walking along the seashore. Odínn gave them their spirit, Hoenir gave them their intelligence and Lódurr bestowed on them their senses and their bodies.

Envy
Finno-Ugric
One of the nine monstrous offspring of LOVIATAR and the WIND[2]. The other monsters are named as PLEURISY, COLIC, GOUT, TUBERCULOSIS, ULCER, SCABIES, PLAGUE and CANCER.

Eormanric Hama
Norse, Teutonic and Anglo-Saxon
According to the ANGLO-SAXON poem BEOWULF, Eormanric Hama was the owner of the BROSINGAMENE. It was then stolen from him.

Eostre
Anglo-Saxon
A spring goddess who is believed to have given her name to the Christian festival of Easter.

Equus Bipes
Norse
The Latin antiquarian name given to the HAVHEST, signifying that this particular creature was regarded as a form of sea-horse.

Erda
Norse and Teutonic
Alternative name for FJORGYNN, along with JÖRD.

Eric
Norse and Teutonic
The son of AGNE and brother of ALRIC. His aunt was DAGEID and his grandfather DAG[1].

Erisvorsh
Slavonic
The god of storms. To the CZECH peoples he was VARPULIS, the god of storm winds and an attendant of PERUN.

Erlkönig
Teutonic
A GOBLIN king who haunted the BLACK FOREST and exercised a fatal and malignant influence on people, especially children, by offering them alluring promises that would ultimately lead to their destruction.

Ermenrich
Norse and Teutonic
The King of GOTHLAND who married SWANHILDR the VALKYRJA.

Erna
Norse and Teutonic
The wife of JARL.

Erp
Norse and Teutonic
A son of ATLI (ETZAL) and GUDRUNN.

Esbern Snar~e, ~i
Norse and Teutonic
A lover of HELVA, whom he wanted to marry, and thus struck a bargain with a TROLL to build him a church. The troll agreed, adding that in payment he would ask Esbern Snare to name him or lose his eyes and his heart. Helva came to the aid of her lover, and when the church was complete Esbern Snare was able to tell the troll that his name was FINE.

Eskeri
Siberia – Tungus
The creator who plunged into the primeval waters and brought back a clump of mud from which he fashioned the earth.

Estonia
General
Former republic of RUSSIA, Estonia is now one of the independent BALTIC countries, along with its neighbours LATVIA and LITHUANIA. Having suffered much turmoil and suppression, very little now remains of Estonian mythology and legend.

Etzel
Teutonic
The legendary TEUTONIC name for the historical ATTILA THE HUN. The NORSE name for the same character is ATLI. The third husband of KRIEMHILD (Norse GUDRUNN), whom he shunned after hearing how she had arranged for HAGEN to kill SIEGFRIED and then herself killed Hagen after he had refused to tell her where he had hidden the treasure of the DWARFS. She eventually met her death at the hands of one HILDEBRAND[2].

Evening Star
Slavonic
The personification of the planet VENUS when seen in the early evening sky. In Slavonic mythology the Evening Star is ZVEZDA DENNITSA, the sister to ZVEZDA VECHERNYAYA, the MORNING STAR[3]. Together the sisters are referred to as the ZVEZDA, the daughters of DAZHBOG, and sisters to the two, or three, ZORYA.

Evpraksiya, Princess
Russian
Daughter of the King of LITHUANIA and sister to Princess NASTAS`YA. She was brought from Lithuania to KIEV to become the bride of VLADIMIR BRIGHT SUN by Dunai IVANOVICH, who married her sister, and Dobrynya NIKITICH. She and her sister were married at the same service, by their marriage becoming Christians.

Eyra
Norse and Teutonic
Variant of EIRA.

Eyrbyggja Saga
Norse and Teutonic
Saga recounting stories surrounding THÓRR's temples and the ritual rekindling of the sacred fire within it.

Eystein
Norse and Teutonic
King of RAUMARIKE whose kingdom was subdued by HÁLFDAN SVARTI. Eystein resubjugated Raumarike as soon as Hálfdan Svarti had returned to WEST-FOLD, but once again lost his kingdom, after which he fled to HEIDEMARK. Hálfdan Svarti followed him and the two once again joined battle. Eventually peace prevailed and Hálfdan Svarti gave Eystein half of the domain of Heidemark.

Eyvindr Kelda
Norse and Teutonic
Legendary descendant of HARALDR INN HÁRFARGI. A wizard, or SHAMAN, of some renown, he was drowned by OLÁFR TRYGGVASON.

Ezerinis
Lithuanian
The god of lakes, but not, so it would appear, of rivers and streams.

Fadir
Norse and Teutonic
The husband of MODIR. They were visited by the god HEIMDALLR, who slept with Modir, the son born of the union being JARL, the ancestor and progenitor of the race of warriors through his marriage to the aristocratic ERNA.

Fáfn~ir, ~er
Norse and Teutonic
Son of HREIDMAR and brother of REGINN and OTR. Reginn and Fáfnir killed their father to take possession of the gold of the NIBELUNGEN, which they had forced the ÆSIR to steal from ANDVARI the DWARF after LOKI had unwittingly killed Otr. However, Fáfnir made off with the booty and changed himself into a monstrous DRAGON[2] to guard it. Reginn fostered SIGURDR, the posthumously born son of SIGMUNDR, and when that hero was old enough he gave him instructions to kill Fáfnir. This Sigurdr did, but when he ate the dragon's heart he learned the speech of the birds, who told him that Reginn intended to kill him and keep the hoard for himself. As a result, Sigurdr killed Reginn, but as the gold contained the cursed ring of Andvari, ownership of the gold meant that Sigurdr was destined for a life of sorrow. The TEUTONIC version of this story says that SIEGFRIED (the Teutonic form of Sigurdr) killed Fáfnir with the NOTHUNG SWORD and that the golden hoard was hidden in the depths of the River RHINE, becoming known as the 'Rhinegold'.

Fáfnisbani
Norse and Teutonic
A title given to SIGURDR that means 'Scourge of FÁFNIR'.

fairy
General
Abounding throughout the mythologies of the world, a fairy is usually a magical, often mischievous being who is normally depicted as a tiny human with wings. Originally fairies were genuinely feared, being capable of taking the most frightening revenge on anyone who offended them. However, in more recent times they have become pretty and gentle things. Still, in fairy stories, such as *Sleeping Beauty*, both sides of the fairy are shown with good fairies often being pitted against a single, far more powerful, evil one.

Farbauti
Norse and Teutonic
Variant name for BERGELMIR.

Faust
Teutonic
Legendary wandering astrologer, magician and necromancer who lived in GERMANY during the late fifteenth and early sixteenth centuries and made a pact with MEPHISTOPHELES, the DEVIL or the devil's advocate, to forfeit his soul in return for one moment of complete and utter contentment. Only finally, after the devil had constantly tried to tempt Faust,

does Faust realize that true happiness comes from helping others, eventually announcing that he is perfectly content. However, even though he had sold his soul to the devil, and should thus have endured eternity in purgatory, his soul was taken up to heaven.

The legend is thought to have been based around the life of Dr Johann Faustus (c. 1488–1541), though the wandering scholar and conjurer Georg Faust, who lived in the early sixteenth century, has also been connected with the story. Earlier figures, such as the first-century Middle Eastern magician Simon Magus, seem to have given much to the story. In 1587 the first of a series of books recounting the legends appeared. In BRITAIN, Marlowe's tragedy *Dr Faustus* was first performed in 1594. During the eighteenth century the legend became a major subject for pantomime in England and puppet plays in Germany. The definitive work on the legend, however, remains the play *Faust* by Goethe (1749–1832), a masterpiece in which Faust is presented as a symbol of humanity striving for the infinite. This play includes the love affair with, and seduction and death of, GRETCHEN, a village maiden.

Fenia
Norse and Teutonic
According to Snorri STURLUSON in *HEIMSKRINGLA*, FENIA, along with MENIA, were enormously strong giantesses who were brought to SWEDEN by FRODE to grind gold and bring good luck to both him and his domain. Other sources say that the giantesses were taken to DENMARK by King FODI for the same purpose, the variation apparently being a confusion. It seems most likely that Fenia and Menia were captured and enslaved by Frodi, King of Denmark.

Fenri(~r, ~s)
Norse and Teutonic
One of the evil offspring of LOKI and ANGRBODA, a wolf, who was fettered and chained to a rock, with a sword jammed between his jaws, by TYR. The gods had to use three chains, LÆDINGR, DROMA and GLEIPNIR, in their attempts to fetter Fenrir, the last of the three being the one with which they at last succeeded. There he will remain until the RAGNARØKR, when he will escape and devour the SUN[5] and the MOON[5], following which, for three long years, the FIMBULVETR will shroud the earth. During the epic battle between the ÆSIR and the monster, Fenrir will be pitted against Tyr, each killing the other, though some sources erroneously refer to THÓRR and Fenrir being pitted against each other.

Fensalir
Norse and Teutonic
The name of FRIGGA's hall in ASGARDR.

Fimbulvetr
Norse and Teutonic
The name given to the bitter shroud of total darkness and cold that will envelop the earth for three years following the swallowing of the SUN[5] and the MOON[5] by FENRIR, an event that will herald the start of the RAGNARØKR. At the end of this time, the gods and the monsters will assemble on the plain of VÍGRÍDR to fight the final battle that will lead to the total destruction of the old order but from whose ashes, like the mighty phoenix, a new order will rise, led by the reborn BALDR.

Fine
Norse and Teutonic
The name of the TROLL who hoped to ensnare ESBERN SNARE, who had commissioned the troll to build him a church, payment being Esbern Snare's eyes and

heart if he could not name the troll once the church had been finished. HELVA, Esbern Snare's lover, came to his aid and told him the name of the troll, who was thus denied his payment.

Finland
General
Country of Scandinavia that is bounded to the north by NORWAY, to the east by RUSSIA, to the south and west by the BALTIC Sea and to the northwest by SWEDEN. The country was originally inhabited by LAPPS, but they were driven northwards by Finnic invaders from Asia around the first century BC into the area they occupy to this day. During the twelfth century the country was conquered by Sweden, and for the following two centuries the area was the scene of a great many wars between Sweden and Russia. As a duchy of Sweden, Finland was allowed an increasing measure of autonomy, becoming a Grand Duchy in 1581. In 1809, during the Napoleonic Wars, Finland was annexed by Russia, under whose rule it remained until 1917, when it declared its independence. Russia tried to regain its lost territory, but finally recognized the independence of Finland in 1920.

Finn Focwalding
Anglo-Saxon
According to the ANGLO-SAXON poem *The Fight at Finn's Burg*, Finn Focwalding was the brother-in-law of HNÆF. During a visit by Hnæf and HENGIST a fight broke out during which Hnæf was killed. Hengist became the leader of Hnæf's followers and entered the service of Finn Focwalding, but later killed him.

Finnilene
Teutonic
The name of one of the ALAISIAGAE, minor war spirits who were worshipped in the TEUTONIC heartland and whose worship was later taken to northern BRITAIN, presumably by the Romans, though this has never been proved. Some sources name two Alaisiagae, while others name four. Her companions were BEDE[1], FRIAGABI and BAUDIHILLIE. Only one site of worship has been definitely associated with the Alaisiagae and that is an altar at Housesteads Roman fort on Hadrian's Wall.

Finno-Ugric
General
Name given to a language grouping of twenty or more tongues that are spoken by in excess of 22 million people in scattered communities from NORWAY in the west, SIBERIA in the east, and the Carpathian Mountains in the south. For further information, see pages 15–17.

Firebird
Russian
A fabulous bird, described as having eyes that sparkled like crystal and feathers of gold that shone as bright as day itself. Owned by Tsar DALMAT, the bird used to steal the golden apples that grew in the garden of Tsar Vyslav ANDRONOVICH. He set his three sons, DMITRII, VASILII[2] and IVAN[6], the task of locating and obtaining the bird for him. Ivan succeeded, but his brothers ambushed and killed him, claiming that they had completed the quest when they presented the bird to their father. Their false claim was exposed when Ivan was restored to life thanks to the WATER OF LIFE AND DEATH, which was sprinkled on him by the shape-changing wolf that had been helping him. The Firebird remained in the ownership of Vyslav Andronovich, for Dalmat had given the bird to Ivan after the completion of a task that he had set the young man, while Dmitrii and Vasilii were thrown into their father's deepest dungeon for their treachery.

Fjal(a)r
Norse and Teutonic
One of the two DWARFS who killed
KVASIR, GILLINGR and Gillingr's wife, his
partner in crime being GALR. They then
brewed the MEAD OF INSPIRATION by mixing Kvasir's blood with honey to make
the inspiring brew.

Fjöln~e, ~ir
Norse and Teutonic
The son of FREYR and GERDR.

Fjorgyn(n)
Norse and Teutonic
Also ERDA, JÖRD. A fertility goddess, one
of the three wives of ODÍNN and the
mother of THÓRR.

Flateyjarbók
Norse and Teutonic
An ancient text that tells the story of the
Norwegian GUNNARR HELMINGR, his flight
from King OLÁFR TRYGGVASON, his
marriage to the priestess of FREYR
(Gunnarr Helmingr actually taking the
place of the god for a while) and his secret
return to SWEDEN.

Fodi
Norse and Teutonic
Variant of FRODI that is to be found in
some sources, though, as so much is confused, it is quite possible that Fodi and
Frodi were two separate characters around
whom a similar mythology has arisen.

Folkvang
Norse and Teutonic
The hall of FREYJA in ASGARDR to which
half of those warriors slain in battle go,
the remainder, possibly the more valiant
or respected half, going to VALHALLA, the
hall of ODÍNN.

Fornjot
Norse and Teutonic
According to the ORKNEYINGA SAGA,
Fornjot was the King of FINLAND and
KVENLAND. He had three sons: HLER (also
known as ÆGIR), LOGI (also called LOKI)
and KARI.

Fornjotnr
Norse and Teutonic
Variant name for YMIR.

Forset(t)i
Norse and Teutonic
The son of BALDR and NANNA, the god of
justice and truth and the law-maker of
the gods. The other gods of the ÆSIR held
Forsetti in great esteem and gave him the
hall GLITNIR, with a silver roof supported
on pillars of gold, in which to reside.
Forsetti was particularly worshipped by
the FRISIANS. He was said to speak so elo-
quently that opposing factions would
instantly make peace - and if they didn't,
he would simply strike them all dead.

Franks
General
Germanic people influential in Europe
between the third and eighth centuries.
Believed to have originated in Pomerania
on the BLACK SEA, they had settled on the
RHINE by the third century, spread into
the Roman Empire by the fourth, and
gradually conquered most of GAUL and
GERMANY under the Merovingian
(481–751) and Carolingian (768–987)
dynasties. The kingdom of the Western
Franks became France, to which they
gave their name, while that of the Eastern
Franks became Germany.

Freawaru
Norse, Teutonic and Anglo-Saxon
Daughter of HRODGAR who was married
to INGELD, the leader of the HEATHO-
BARDS, in an attempt to put an end to the

bloody feud between the Heathobards and the Danes.

Freki
Norse and Teutonic
The name of one of the two wolves owned by ODÍNN, the other being GERI.

Freya
Norse and Teutonic
Simple variant of FREYJA that has sometimes been confused as a separate deity, that confusion stemming from Snorri STURLUSON in the YNGLINGA SAGA from HEIMSKRINGLA, as well as from other ancient texts.

Freyfaxi
Norse and Teutonic
Legendary horse mentioned in the HRAFNSKELS SAGA FREYSGODA, and also in the *Vatnsdoela Saga*. In these texts the horse was either dedicated to or owned by the god FREYR. She is also sometimes confused with FRIGGA, the wife of ODÍNN, but this again stems from the multiplicity of variations in the ancient texts so heavily relied upon to give the modern picture of ancient NORSE and TEUTONIC beliefs.

Freygerdr
Norse and Teutonic
A mortal woman who married FREYR in his guise as FRIDLEEF after he had rescued her from the clutches of a DRAGON[2]. Their son was FRODI.

Frey(j)a
Norse and Teutonic
The leading goddess of the VANIR, the daughter of NJÖRDR and SKADI and twin sister of FREYR, Freyja is often erroneously included among the VALKYRJA. One of the most ancient of all NORSE and TEUTONIC deities, truly one of the DIAR, Freyja was a fertility and mother goddess whose name means 'lady'. She became so celebrated that all women of distinction were given the title FRUE in her honour. In origin she may have been a moon goddess, or the goddess of the night who was drawn across the skies by two cats or boars. Eventually, however, she became the goddess of love and was often identified with the planet VENUS. The wife of ODR and mother of HNOSS and GERSEMI, she was soon abandoned by her husband, after which she spent her time weeping tears of gold, or lowering herself further and further into the realms of debauchery.

Living in the hall FOLKVANG within ASGARDR, Freyja welcomed half of the warriors who had been slain in battle, the others going to spend their eternal lives with ODÍNN in VALHALLA. This idea, found in the GRÍMNISMÁL, appears to connect Freyja with the UNDERWORLD[4], though this side of her is the one that is least known. Some sources say that Freyja lived in a hall named SESSRYMNIR, which lay within the realm of Folkvang, a hall that was so impregnable that it could be entered only if Freyja herself were to open the gates. Freyja was so beautiful that all who saw her immediately lusted after her, and more often than not, whether god or mortal, they succeeded in bedding her. Her lasciviousness is well illustrated by the story of the BRÍSINGAMEN, a wondrous jewel that had been made by four DWARFS known collectively as the BRISINGS. No sooner had Freyja seen the gem, usually described as a necklace, than she agreed to spend a night of carnal lust with each of the four dwarfs that had made it in return for ownership. She also owned a magnificent golden boar, HILDSVÍN, that was also made for her by some dwarfs.

Freyja's chronology is a little confused. She is a Vanir goddess but is usually cited as having lived at Asgardr from the very first days of its construction – that is, before the war between the ÆSIR and the

Vanir, and so before her brother and father came to live in Asgardr, as the terms of the truce demanded. She was, however, evidently of great importance to the Æsir, as well as to the FROST GIANTS, who seem always to have been trying to find a way to obtain her for themselves. During the construction of Asgardr the Æsir commissioned one of the Frost Giants to build the wall around their home. He asked for and was promised Freyja as his wife, along with the SUN[5] and MOON[5], as payment, because the Æsir thought he would never complete the job within the time agreed. However, when it began to look likely that he would, thanks to the help he was being given by his horse SVADILFARI, the Æsir had LOKI find some way of preventing him. Loki led out a beautiful filly, which diverted the attention of Svadilfari, the result of their subsequent union being SLEIPNIR, and so the wall remained incomplete.

On another occasion the Frost Giant THRYMR stole MJOLLNIR, the great hammer of THÓRR, and held it to ransom, demanding the hand of Freyja as payment. On this occasion HEIMDALLR, who appears here to have found his voice, suggested that Thórr should dress as Freyja and travel to JÖTUNHEIMR to recover his lost weapon. At first reluctant to put on woman's attire, Thórr finally agreed and set off, accompanied by the ever resource-ful LOKI. During the wedding feast Loki twice came to the rescue of Thórr when it seemed that the subterfuge would be discovered, until finally Thrymr placed Mjollnir in 'Freyja's' lap as his wedding gift, whereupon Thórr threw off his disguise and quickly dispatched Thrymr and all the assembled wedding guests.

On yet another occasion the drunken HRUNGNIR threatened to sink Asgardr and carry off both SÍF, Thórr's blonde-haired wife, and Freyja. Hrungnir's threat came to nothing as he was easily defeated and killed by Thórr, but the story further illustrates the length that the Frost Giants, whether drunk or sober, would go to in order to obtain the services of Freyja in her role as one of the most potent of all fertility goddesses.

Freyja's association with cats possibly stems from the link between cats and the VOLVA, who practised a sort of trance divination known as SEIDR that Freyja was said to have invented and then taught them. These volva, a form of SHAMANKA, wore animal costumes, often those of cats and always, so far as records can tell us, wore gloves made from the skin of cats. Freyja has additional connections with the arts of the SHAMAN as she was a shape-shifter, often assuming the shape of a falcon, in which form she would fly from Asgardr to all the corners of the NINE WORLDS.

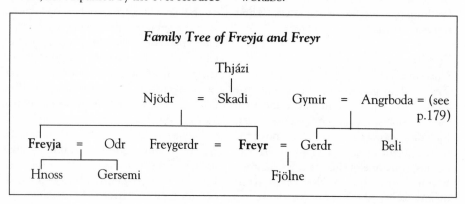

Family Tree of Freyja and Freyr

Freyja had several names, one of which, GEFN, seems to connect her with GEFJUN, a goddess of the VIKINGS who, like Freyja, was promiscuous and had a fabulous jewel that had been given to her by a lover.

Frey(r)
Norse and Teutonic
Also FRO. The son of NJÖRDR and SKADI and twin brother of FREYJA, to whom he was, at one stage, married. God of fertility and summer, the dispenser of rain and sunshine, Freyr became one of the most popular of all the NORSE and TEUTONIC deities, with grand temples and a widespread cult. His popularity does not seem to have been diminished by the fact that his worship called for human sacrifice. One of the leading VANIR deities, he and his father came to ASGARDR following the war between the ÆSIR and his people as the hostages called for by the truce. He drove a chariot drawn by a golden boar, GULLINBURSTI ('Golden-bristled'), made for him by the DWARFS SINDRI and BROKK, and owned a magical ship, SKÍDBLADNIR, that was made for him by the dwarf DVALIN[1], both commissions at the request of LOKI. The ship was large enough to carry all the Æsir, always had a following wind and was able to fly through the air, but when not in use it could be folded down and carried in a pocket. Freyr owned a horse called BLODUGHOFI and lived in a hall in the realm of ALFHEIMR.

Freyr fell in love with GERDR, the daughter of the giant GYMIR and the giantess ANGRBODA, after catching sight of her while sitting on the HLIDSKJÁLF. Freyr, however, did not travel down to the UNDERWORLD[4] kingdom of her father, but instead sent his servant and friend SKÍRNIR to woo Gerdr on his behalf, offering her gifts that included ODÍNN's wonderful ring DRAUPNIR, as well as some golden apples. Gerdr refused the gifts and rejected the suit as Freyr had killed her brother BELI, so Skirnir turned nasty and threatened to abduct her to a cave at the edge of the world, where she would be left to wither and die. Gerdr finally consented, but rather than travel back to Asgardr with Skírnir, she agreed to meet her husband-to-be in his sacred grove some nine days later. Their son was FJÖLNE. This marriage is thought to represent the union of the earth and the sky, the references to apples and a sacred grove indicating a fertility rite that was echoed in the ritual union that played an important part in the cult of Freyr.

Snorri STURLUSON in the YNGLINGA SAGA from HEIMSKRINGLA says that the god incarnate built a great temple at UPPSALA and made it his chief seat, thus becoming readily accessible to the people and able to help with their desires and prayers.

A good example of the cult of Freyr is to be found in the FLATEYJARBÓK, which tells the story of the Norwegian GUNNARR HELMINGR, who, having offended King OLÁFR TRYGGVASON, fled to SWEDEN. There, in the temple of Freyr, he was attracted to the god's wife, the beautiful young priestess. Later that year, when it came round to the time for Freyr's autumn progress from his temple to bless the land, Gunnarr Helmingr was invited to accompany it, even though the priestess felt that Freyr might not be pleased. Soon after their departure from the temple the party found themselves in the midst of a severe blizzard and all those in the party, except Gunnarr Helmingr and the priestess, abandoned the god. Gunnarr Helmingr led the wagon on for a while and then stopped to rest, even though the priestess said that Freyr would attack them.

In desperation, Gunnarr Helmingr called on the god of Oláfr Tryggvason – that is, the Christian God – and with his help overcame Freyr, who then departed and left the couple alone. Gunnarr Helmingr destroyed the image of Freyr, dressed himself in the god's finery and took his place. The couple then continued their journey and were greeted with delight at the feast to be held in Freyr's honour when the people saw that their god had assumed human form and could thus join them. They were delighted when the god demanded rich clothes and gifts in place of the normal human sacrifice and they were overjoyed when they learned that the priestess was pregnant. Shortly afterwards, when Oláfr Tryggvason sent word that he commanded his return, Gunnarr Helmingr stole away secretly, taking with him all his godly gifts and the priestess.

Freyr's fertility cult was also connected with horses and boars, both well-known ancient fertility symbols. These animals are mentioned several times, particularly the golden boar Gullinbursti that pulled his chariot and could easily outrun even the fleetest of horses, as well as a horse named FREYFAXI that was either owned by or dedicated to the god. The boar, which seems particularly closely associated with the cult of Freyr, seemed to have a protective role to both Norse and Teutonic peoples, as well as being a fertility symbol. For this reason, helmets were often decorated with their image. King ATHLIS of Sweden won just such a battle-helmet, named HILDIGOLTR ('Battle-swine'), which also happens to be the name of a golden pig owned by Freyr's sister Freyja.

When Freyr died, his death was concealed for three years. Shortly before, as he lay on his deathbed, Freyr commanded his priests to build a tumulus in which they were to lay him after death. Then for three years the priests perpetuated the image of the living god by offering Freyr gold, silver and copper through a door in the tumulus which had three holes in it.

During these three years the land knew wonderful prosperity.

Like his sister Freyja, Freyr was given another name: YNGVE. This was long considered a name of honour, so all descendants of Freyr have, since that time, been referred to as YNGLING.

Friagabi
Teutonic

The name of one of the ALAISIAGAE, minor war spirits who were worshipped in the TEUTONIC heartland and whose worship was later taken to northern BRITAIN, presumably by the Romans, though this has never been proved. Some sources name two Alaisiagae, while others name four. Her companions were BEDE[1], FINNILENE and BAUDIHILLIE. Only one site of worship has been definitely associated with the Alaisiagae and that is an altar at Housesteads Roman fort on Hadrian's Wall.

Friar Tuck
British

Portly monk with a liking for strong ale who joined the outlaws in SHERWOOD FOREST led by ROBIN HOOD (his MERRY MEN). He not only provided them with spiritual guidance but could also hold his own in the numerous fights against the rich and corrupt, and particularly against the men of the SHERIFF OF NOTTINGHAM.

Fridleef
Norse and Teutonic

One of the aliases used by FREYR so that he could travel incognito among mankind.

Frigg(a)
Norse and Teutonic

Also BERTHA, HOLDA, NERTHUS and WODE. The protectress of marriage, bringer of children and goddess of the hearth, the supreme ÆSIR goddess and the second wife of ODÍNN. As she was not always his staunchest supporter, she was frequently depicted as an argumentative and deceitful wife who, while Odínn was once away for an extended period, was said to have slept with both VILLI and VÉ. She is also alleged to have once slept with ULLR. Frigga is often confused with FREYJA as both are fertility deities and have strong associations, Frigga being the maternal aspect and Freyja the promiscuous. Not much is known about Frigga's origins. Some sources say that she is the daughter of Odínn and JÖRD, while others say that she was Jörd's sister. Frigga lived in the hall FENSALIR, where she spent much of her time spinning thread from gold or brightly coloured clouds. Following her son Baldr's dreams of doom and foreboding, she was sent by the Æsir to ask all things on the earth, animate and inanimate, to swear that they would never harm the beloved god. All things complied, but unfortunately Frigga forgot to ask the mistletoe, an omission that was to lead to the death of Baldr at the hands of LOKI and HÖDR.

Frija
Teutonic
The wife of WODAN, and thus the purely TEUTONIC variant of FRIGGA.

Frisian(s)
General
A Germanic people who have given their name to the low-lying islands off the coast of GERMANY and the Netherlands that were formed when the sea inundated the land. They were numbered among the barbarian invaders of BRITAIN by the Byzantine historian Procopius, whose writings date from the late fifth and early sixth centuries. The language was closely akin to ANGLO-SAXON, with which it formed the Anglo-Frisian branch of the West Germanic language family.

Frithiof
Norse and Teutonic
The son of THORSTEN and INGEBORG. Frithiof was fostered by HILDINGR, whose other charge was the Princess INGEBORG, the daughter of BELÉ. (In the legends there is much confusion between the two Ingeborgs.) The two fell in love, but Hildingr forbade their marriage on the grounds that they came from different backgrounds. The marriage was also refused by HELGÉ, the brother of Ingeborg and HÁLFDAN, and he even commissioned the witches HAM and HEIDR to shipwreck Frithiof. This plan backfired when Frithiof cut up a golden torque into sufficient pieces for all his men, who invoked RAN with them and were thus able to run down the witches and the whale they were riding.

Frithiof travelled far and wide during his voyages, helped with the conquest of the ORKNEYS and eventually came to the court of SIGURDR RINGR, whom Ingeborg had been forced to marry. There he became the friend and confidant of Sigurdr Ringr, after whose death he finally married Ingeborg.

Fro
Norse and Teutonic
Variant name sometimes applied to FREYR.

Frod~i, ~e
Norse and Teutonic
The son of FREYR and the mortal FREYGERDR, whom he saved from the attentions of a DRAGON[2] while in his guise of FRIDLEEF. Frodi is recorded in NORSE mythology as a pacifist king of DENMARK who ruled at about the time of Christ. He was said to have taken the giantesses FENIA and MENIA to his kingdom, where he set them to spinning gold to ensure the prosperity of his kingdom and his subjects. Snorri STURLUSON IN *HEIMSKRINGLA*

uses the variant Frode and makes him a king of SWEDEN, while other sources refer to him as FODI.

Frost

1 *Russian*

In most Russian folk-tales and legends, Frost appears as a nameless demon, although in a story concerning the fate of MARFUSHA Frost is given the name MOROZKO. In another story, where he remains nameless, he appears to a peasant as a thin and hunched man with grey hair and bushy white eyebrows. He is usually a malevolent spirit, but, as the story of Marfusha illustrates, he can show compassion when he is so disposed.

2 *Finno-Ugric*

The frost spirit of FINNO-UGRIC mythology is named as METSOLA, who, it appears, might also have been the goddess of the woodlands.

Frost Giant(s)

Norse and Teutonic

The name given to two breeds of giants. The first grew from between the toes of YMIR, but all except BERGELMIR and his mate were drowned in the deluge of blood that flooded the world when Ymir was killed by ODÍNN, VILLI and VÉ. Bergelmir sailed away across the floods to found the second race of Frost Giants, who lived in JÖTUNHEIMR, the land that lay beneath the second root of YGGDRASILL.

So afraid of the Frost Giants were the gods of the ÆSIR that they actually commissioned one of their number to build a wall around ASGARDR within a year. The payment demanded by the unnamed giant was the SUN[5], the MOON[5] and the goddess FREYJA. When, with the help of his wonderful horse SVADILFARI, it looked likely that the giant would complete the task within the contracted time, the Æsir had LOKI find a way of preventing this,

lest the Frost Giants should become too powerful once they got their hands on Freyja. Loki produced a filly which distracted Svadilfari, leaving the giant unable to complete the work on his own. The result of the union between the filly and Svadilfari was SLEIPNIR. As the wall was never finished, Asgardr remained open to attack, an attack that will come at the start of the RAGNARØKR.

The attempts of the Frost Giants to lay their hands on Freyja, possibly due to her lascivious nature, did not stop there. Once the giant THRYMR stole MJOLLNIR and held it to ransom, demanding Freyja in return. This attempt to obtain Freyja did not work, as THÓRR travelled to Jötunheimr in disguise, regained his hammer and then killed Thrymr and all his assembled guests. Even less successful was the threat by the drunken HRUNGNIR to sink Asgardr and to steal away both SÍF, Thórr's golden-haired wife, and Freyja. Thórr challenged the giant to a fight, so the Frost Giants made a man of clay, MOKKURKALFI ('Mist-calf'), to support their champion, but to no avail as both Mokkurkalfi and Hrungnir were quickly disposed of in the fight.

Frosti

Norse and Teutonic

According to the ORKNEYINGA SAGA, the son of KARI, and thus the grandson of FORNJOT, the father of SNÆR THE OLD, grandfather of THORRI, and great-grandfather of NOR, GOR and GOI.

Frue

Norse and Teutonic

Honorific applied to all women of distinction in honour of FREYJA.

Fulla

Norse and Teutonic

One of the many attendants of FRIGGA, she acted as that goddess's messenger.

Snorri STURLUSON in *HEIMSKRINGLA* describes her as a fertility goddess in her own right who wears a golden headband.

Funfengr
Norse and Teutonic
One of the two main servants of ÆGIR, the other being ELDIR.

Fyrisvellir
Norse and Teutonic
Battle fought in 960, prior to which King EIRÍKR INN SIGRSAELI dedicated himself to ODÍNN, solemnly vowing to sacrifice himself to the god after ten years had passed. A tall figure wearing a hooded cloak appeared before him and handed him a stick which he told the king to shoot over the heads of the army of his enemy, STYRBJÖRN. Eiríkr followed the instructions. As the stick flew over the army, all of them were struck blind and shortly afterwards an avalanche totally engulfed them.

Gabija
Lithuanian

The goddess of fire and the domestic hearth. Some accounts say that she was brought to earth by PERKUNAS, while others say that she was carried by a swallow that was badly burned in the process.

Gal(a)r
Norse and Teutonic

One of the two DWARFS who killed KVASIR, GILLINGR and Gillingr's wife, his partner in crime being FJALR.

Gambantein
Norse and Teutonic

The name of the magical staff or wand of HERMÓDR[1].

Gandalf
Norse and Teutonic

The King of VINGULMARK. He fought an inconclusive war against HÁLFDAN SVARTI, after which it was decided that Vingulmark should be equally divided between them.

Gangleri
Norse and Teutonic

According to the *Prose EDDA* of Snorri STURLUSON, Gangleri was the name used by King GYLFI of SWEDEN when he travelled incognito to ASGARDR to test the wisdom of the ÆSIR. This story appears in the GYLFAGINNING, the first section of the *Prose Edda*.

Gangrad
Norse and Teutonic

One of the many aliases adopted by ODÍNN for his frequent trips among mankind.

Gardarike
Norse and Teutonic

The name used by Snorri STURLUSON to refer to RUSSIA in his version of the life of ODÍNN.

Garmr
Norse and Teutonic

The hound of HEL who is chained in the cave GNIPA beside the entrance to NIFLHEMIR. It appears that he might have been another form of FENRIR. During the RAGNARØKR the god TYR will be pitted against Garmr, his mortal enemy, by whom he will be defeated, though he will succeed in killing Garmr too.

Gaul
General

Roman province in western Europe that stretched from what is now northern Italy to the southern part of the Netherlands. The name is most commonly used today to refer to France, but this is not strictly accurate. The Gauls themselves were divided into several distinct groups but united under a common religion that was controlled by the Druids. One group of Gauls invaded Italy c. 400 BC, sacked Rome and settled between the Alps and the Apennines. This region, known as Cisalpine Gaul, was conquered by Rome *c*. 225 BC. The Romans conquered southern Gaul between the Mediterranean and the Cevennes *c*. 125 BC. The remaining Gauls as far as the RHINE were conquered by Julius Caesar between 58 and 51 BC.

Gautreks Saga
Norse and Teutonic
Relatively late saga that tells the story of VIKARR, King of the VIKINGS, who prayed to ODÍNN for a favourable wind. He and his men then drew lots to find out who should be sacrificed to the god in payment. The lot fell to Vikarr, who quickly suggested that they should hold a symbolic hanging. However, as the king stood with entrails wound around his neck like a noose and the man STARKADR uttered the ritual dedication and struck the king with a stick, that stick turned into a sword and impaled the king, while the entrails turned into a rope and Vikarr was hanged.

Geats
Norse, Teutonic and Anglo-Saxon
According to the poem BEOWULF, the Geats were a race ruled over by HÆDCYN until he was killed by his brother. BEOWULF himself was said to have succeeded HYGELAC as the king of the Geats and ruled for fifty years.

Gefj~un, ~on
Norse and Teutonic
With a name so similar, it is quite possible that Gefjun, talked of by the VIKINGS as a goddess to whom unmarried girls went after death, is cognate with GEFN, and thus an aspect of FREYJA, like whom she was said to own a wonderful item of jewellery that had been a gift to her from a lover. However, Gefjun is usually referred to as an attendant of FRIGGA.

She is particularly associated with agriculture. It is said that ODÍNN sent her to find some land and she approached GYLFI, the King of SWEDEN, sleeping with him

and thus winning from him the right to take as much land as she could plough in a day. Gefjun went away and became the mistress of a giant, by whom she conceived and bore four giant sons. These sons she transformed into oxen, and with them pulling her plough she tilled the whole of SJÆLLAND, thus isolating it from the Swedish mainland, her four sons towing the land out to sea. The resulting hole in Sweden quickly filled with water to form Lake MALAREN. Gefjun then went to live at LEIRE with SKJOLDR, Odínn's son and the first king of DENMARK. Since the shapes of Lake Malaren and Sjælland bear no relation to each other, there is no possibility that the island once filled the hole that became the lake.

Gefn
Norse and Teutonic
An aspect of FREYJA, though little else is known of this goddess, except that she is perhaps cognate with GEFJUN.

Geirrødr
Norse and Teutonic
One of the FROST GIANTS who decided that he was going to kill THÓRR. To help him, he captured LOKI while that god was disguised as a falcon and made him promise to deliver Thórr to him. Loki kept his end of the bargain, but warned Thórr, who killed Geirrødr.

Gelgia
Norse and Teutonic
The name given to the end of the chain GLEIPNIR with which the ÆSIR finally succeeded in fettering FENRIR.

Gepids
General
Ancient TEUTONIC people who were united, along with the VANDALS, OSTROGOTHS and FRANKS, under the banner of ATTILA THE HUN shortly after he became

king in 434 at the age of twenty-eight. In this way the kingdom of Attila the Hun was extended greatly.

Gerd~r, ~a
Norse and Teutonic

The beautiful giantess daughter of the giant GYMIR and ANGRBODA, the sister of BELI, whom FREYR caught sight of while sitting on ODÍNN's HLIDSKJÁLF seat and instantly fell in love with. Freyr sent his servant and friend SKÍRNIR down to the UNDERWORLD[4] kingdom of Gymir to woo Gerdr on his behalf, with gifts of golden apples and the wonderful ring DRAUPNIR. At first Gerdr rejected Freyr's suit, but quickly changed her mind after Skírnir had threatened to cast a spell over her which would imprison her in a cave on the very edge of the world where she would be left to 'wither like a thistle'.

Skírnir returned to ASGARDR with the good news, though Gerdr did not accompany him as she had consented only if they met nine days later in Freyr's sacred grove, a reference that possibly refers to a fertility rite, a mystical union between earth and sky, that, so the records show, played an important role in the cult of Freyr. Gerdr and Freyr became the parents of FJÖLNE. Gerdr is often connected with the spectacular display of the AURORA BOREALIS[1], which is said to be the reflection of her beauty.

Geri
Norse and Teutonic

One of the wolves that constantly accompanied ODÍNN.

Germany
General

Nation of central Europe that has had a long and chequered history, its boundaries having changed countless times over the centuries. Prior to the fourth century AD, Germany was settled by West Germanic peoples who originated in Scandinavia and moved into the region between the rivers RHINE, Elbe and DANUBE, where they were confined by the Roman Empire. In 496 Clovis, King of the FRANKS, conquered the ALEMANNI, the dominion of the Germanic peoples remaining under the control of the Franks until the middle of the eighth century, when the Holy Roman Emperor Charlemagne extended his authority over Germany and imposed Christianity as the state religion, a move that all but destroyed the traditions and pagan religious beliefs of the SAXONS.

The term TEUTONIC is used widely throughout this book to refer to peoples who inhabited Germany, along with the Scandinavian countries they originated from, and whose beliefs became an integral part of Germanic or Teutonic belief. The term Germanic can be a little confusing, as it is applied to a branch of the Indo-European family of languages, and as such covers the now extinct Gothic, as well as Danish, Faroese, Icelandic, Norwegian, Swedish, Afrikaans, Dutch, English, Flemish, FRISIAN, German and Yiddish. Thus to use the term Germanic would infer that the legend or myth could come from anywhere between Iceland in the north and South Africa in the south, an inference that is not simply inaccurate but so way off the mark as to make a nonsense of the use of the term in the context of myths and legends.

Gersemi
Norse and Teutonic

One of the two daughters of FREYJA and ODR.

Gessler
Teutonic

A fourteenth-century Austrian bailiff to whose hat William TELL refused to pay due respect. As a result, Gessler ordered William Tell to shoot an apple from the head of his son with an arrow. William Tell successfully accomplished the task and with a second arrow killed Gessler.

Gesta Danorum
Norse and Teutonic

A collection of NORSE and TEUTONIC stories that was compiled by the twelfth-century Danish chronicler SAXO GRAMMATICUS. It remains one of the most important of all sources of Norse and Teutonic tradition.

Gillingr
Norse and Teutonic

The father of SUTTUNGR, Gillingr was the giant responsible for brewing the MEAD OF INSPIRATION, for the ownership of which he was killed by the DWARFS FJALR and GALR. Gillingr was drowned, but accounts vary as to how the two dwarfs managed to do this. One says that they came across the giant while he slept on a river bank and simply rolled him in. Another says that they sent him fishing in a leaky vessel, while yet another says that the tricky pair took the giant fishing, capsized the boat in full knowledge that Gillingr could not swim and then merrily rowed back to shore again.

Gimli
Norse and Teutonic

The golden-roofed hall of FORSETTI in ASGARDR that was the home, after death, of all good and virtuous men. After the RAGNARØKR it will become the home of the new order of gods.

Ginnungagap
Norse and Teutonic

The primordial abyss that lay between the southern MÚSPELLHEIMR, a region of fire and light, the NIFLHEIMR, the northern land of ice and snow. In the void of Ginnungagap sparks from Múspellheimr met the icy discharges of Niflheimr and slowly melted them. Beneath the melting ice there appeared the giant YMIR, from whose armpit the first man and the first woman grew, and from whose feet came the FROST GIANTS.

Gioll
Norse and Teutonic

The name of the rock to which the ÆSIR chained FENRIR.

Giraitis
Lithuanian

God of the forests. He is referred to in seventeenth- and eighteenth-century manuscripts, thus suggesting that he is a deity of comparatively modern invention.

Gisl
Norse and Teutonic

Son of VISBUR and brother of UNDUR, thus grandsons of VANLANDE. They killed their father under the influence of the witch HULDR, who caused them to be neither detected nor suspected of the crime.

Giuki
Norse and Teutonic

King of the NIBELUNGEN, husband of GRIMHILDR and father of GUNNARR, GUTTORMR, HÖGNI and GUDRUNN.

Gjall
Norse and Teutonic

'Resounding River', the river that encompassed the UNDERWORLD[4] of NIFLHEIMR.

Gjallar(brú)
Norse and Teutonic

'Resounding Bridge', the golden bridge that crossed the River GJALL and allowed entry to the UNDERWORLD[4] of NIFLHEIMR, and which was guarded by MODGUDR.

Gjallarhorn
Norse and Teutonic
'Resounding Horn', the great trumpet that was carried by the silent HEIMDALLR as he kept watch over the incomplete wall that surrounded ASGARDR and on which he would blow to warn the ÆSIR of impending danger. During the RAGNAR-ØKR it is said that Heimdallr will sound Gjallarhorn, and ODÍNN will lead forth the forces of the Æsir. The name of the horn, having the stem *Gjall* seems to suggest that it has an UNDERWORLD[4] origin (see GJALL).

Gjalp
Norse and Teutonic
1 The name of one of the WAVE MAID-ENS, the daughters of ÆGIR.
2 A daughter of GEIRRØDR.

Gjolp
Norse and Teutonic
'Howler', one of the nine daughters of ÆGIR.

Gladsheimr
Norse and Teutonic
The name of one of ODÍNN's halls in ASGARDR. It contained the twelve golden thrones where the ÆSIR met in council.

Glaumvor(r)
Norse and Teutonic
The second wife of GUNNARR.

Gleb, Saint
Russian
Russian Orthodox saint who, according to some legends, was, along with Saint BORIS, a smith who forged the first plough. This plough was of gigantic pro-portions and was forged with implements of like size. The two smiths were recorded as having used twelve golden hammers and tongs that weighed almost twelve *poods* (c. 430 lb). Other versions of this legend name the two saintly smiths as Saint KUZ`MA and Saint DEM`YAN.

Gleipnir
Norse and Teutonic
The third chain that was used by the ÆSIR to fetter FENRIR, the one with which they finally succeeded.

Glen
Norse and Teutonic
The husband of SOL.

Glitn(i)r
Norse and Teutonic
The hall of FORSETTI in ASGARDR.

Glúm
Norse and Teutonic
A minor goddess who was an attendant of FRIGGA.

Glut
Norse and Teutonic
The first wife of LOKI and the mother, by him, of EINMYRIA and EISA.

Gna
Norse and Teutonic
A minor goddess who, like GLÚM, was attendant on FRIGGA and acted as that great goddess's messenger. Her most important assignment in this role was to take an apple of fertility to the mortal RERIR. She rode the horse HOFVARPNIR.

Gnipa
Norse and Teutonic
Also GNIPPAHELLR. The cave at the entrance to NIFLHEIMR in which the hell-hound GARMR is chained and from where he will escape at the start of the RAGNAR-ØKR to do battle with TYR.

Gnippahellr
Norse and Teutonic
Variant of GNIPA.

gnome(s)
General

Found in many traditions, gnomes are traditionally thought of as supernatural subterranean beings who guard the treasures of the world. Sometimes confused with DWARFS or GOBLINS, gnomes are always depicted as small, deformed – often hunchbacked – creatures who resemble wizened old men. They are seen by some as the guardians of mines, though they are usually said to guard all the hidden wealth of the earth, not just that being torn out through the greed of mankind. The traditional king of the gnomes was GOB, who ruled with a magical sword, and it is quite possible that it is the naming of their ruler that has led to confusion between gnomes and goblins.

Gob
General

Traditionally named as King of the GNOMES, he ruled with a magical sword. Some believe that Gob may be NORSE in origin, but this is not certain.

goblin(s)
General

SPRITES of uncertain origin who live in a grotto but aim their mischief at human beings and their households. Traditionally goblins create noise and disturbance, and move objects and furniture at night, only to run away unseen if disturbed, or at morning light. They may have been invented as an early explanation of poltergeists. Goblins are generally depicted as small figures with pointed ears and mischievous smiles. Goblins and GNOMES are often confused, a problem compounded by the fact that GOB, King of the Gnomes, is sometimes incorrectly called King of the Goblins.

Godheim(r)
Norse and Teutonic

Post-Christian name sometimes applied to ASGARDR, the home of the gods, though in this variant it was most often used to refer to SWITHIOD THE GREAT.

godi
Icelandic

The name given to a cult priest in ICELAND.

Goi
Norse and Teutonic

The daughter of THORRI and sister of NOR and GOR, according to the ORKNEYINGA SAGA. She was abducted by King HROLF of BJARG and taken to HEIDEMARK, where King Hrolf made her his wife. Three years after her abduction her brothers came to look for her, only finding her after an extensive search of the mainland by Nor and all the islands by Gor.

Golden Kingdom
Russian

One of the three kingdoms of WHIRLWIND that were located on a plateau at the top of some tremendously high mountains. The tsarita of this kingdom, ELENA THE FAIR, a prisoner of Whirlwind, lived in a golden palace that was guarded by DRAGONS. She was set free by IVAN[1], along with her sisters, the tsaritas of the SILVER KINGDOM and the COPPER KINGDOM, when he killed Whirlwind and released his mother, NASTAS`YA OF THE GOLDEN BRAID. She married Ivan, and her sisters married PETER and VASILII[1], Ivan's brothers.

Göll
Norse and Teutonic

One of the VALKYRJA, a sorceress whose name appears to suggest that she made herself known to her victims by her awful screeching wail.

Göndul
Norse and Teutonic
According to Snorri STURLUSON in HEIM-SKRINGLA, Göndul was one of the VALKYRJA and had the particular job of selecting from among the slain those who would spend eternity in the company of ODÍNN.

Gor
Norse and Teutonic
The son of THORRI and brother of NOR and GOI, according to the ORKNEYINGA SAGA. Three years after Goi had mysteriously disappeared, the two brothers set out to find her, Nor searching the mainland and Gor all the islands. They were unsuccessful until they came to HEIDE-MARK, where they found their sister, whom King HROLF of BJARG had abducted and made his wife.

Gothland
General
Not the land of the GOTHS, as might be expected, but rather an island, today known as Gotland, under the sovereignty of SWEDEN that lies in the BALTIC Sea. Originally disputed between Sweden and DENMARK, the island was ceded to Sweden in 1645.

Goths
General
Generic name for an East Germanic people who settled near the BLACK SEA some time around the second century AD. They actually consist of two distinct groupings: the OSTROGOTHS to the east and the VISIGOTHS to the west.

Götterdämmerung
Teutonic
'Twilight of the Gods', the TEUTONIC name for the RAGNARØKR.

Götterdämmerung
Teutonic
The epic musical masterpiece written by Richard WAGNER concerning the exploits of SIEGFRIED, the destruction of the gods and the world in conflict with the powers of evil.

Gout
Finno-Ugric
One of the nine monstrous offspring of LOVIATAR and WIND[2]. The other monsters are named as PLEURISY, COLIC, TUBERCU-LOSIS, ULCER, SCABIES, PLAGUE, CANCER and ENVY.

Grail
General
The Holy Grail, that divine object sought by King ARTHUR and his band of noble knights, does not really have a place in general European myth and legend, since its appearance relates to the spread of the Arthurian romances, particularly through French and German authors. The most notable European reference to the Grail is in the TEUTONIC story of LOHENGRIN and ELSA OF BRABANT. Here Lohengrin was said to be a guardian of the Grail at the Grail Temple. However, even this reference appears to be a later addition to a much older story, and so has to be treated with a little caution.

Great Bear
Finno-Ugric
The constellation Ursa Major of the northern celestial hemisphere. This star formation appears in the story of VÄINÄMÖINEN, the son of ILMATER LUON-NOTAR. For thirty years Väinämöinen gestated within his mother and pleaded with the SUN[3] god, PAIVA, and the MOON[3] god, KUU, to deliver him from his gloomy home. Neither replied, so he also called on the spirit of the Great Bear, OTAVA, asking to learn how he might escape.

Again he received no reply, so finally Väinämöinen made his own way out of his mother, only to fall into the sea, already an old man.

Greenland
General
Called *Kalaalit Nunaat* in Greenlandic, Greenland is the world's largest island, lying between the North Atlantic and the Arctic Oceans. The first European to land on the island was Eric the Red (940–1010), who had, according to a thirteenth-century saga, been banished from ICELAND, sailed westwards and came across a large island which he called Greenland in *c.* 982. Explorers from Greenland were said to have established a settlement on the eastern seaboard of North America which they called VINLAND.

Greip
Norse and Teutonic
1 'Grasper', one of the WAVE MAIDENS, the nine daughters of ÆGIR.
2 A daughter of GEIRRØDR.

Grendel
Norse, Teutonic and Anglo-Saxon
A mythical sea giant, a man-eating monster, half-man and half-fish, who was allegedly descended from YMIR (some sources even make Grendel a direct descendant of the biblical Cain). Grendel is perhaps best known from the epic ANGLO-SAXON poem in which he is killed by the eponymous hero, BEOWULF.

Grerr
Norse and Teutonic
One of the four DWARFS who made the necklace BRÍSINGAMEN for FREYJA and were recompensed by a night of lust with the goddess. The other three are named as ALFRIGG, BERLING and DVALIN[1].

Gretchen
Teutonic
The name of the village maiden who appears in Goethe's *Faust*. In this work, following the pact made between FAUST and MEPHISTOPHELES, the DEVIL causes the love affair, seduction and death of Gretchen in order to obtain one moment's sublime happiness for Faust in return for his soul.

Greyfellr
Norse and Teutonic
The horse of SIGURDR and a direct descendant of SLEIPNIR.

Grid
Norse and Teutonic
A giantess who welcomed THÓRR and LOKI to her home as they travelled to meet GEIRRØDR. Once Loki had fallen asleep, Grid told the drunken Thórr that Geirrødr was planning to kill him. Since he had foolishly set out with none of his weapons, Grid supplied him with new gloves made of iron, a replacement BELT OF STRENGTH and an unbreakable staff named GRIDSTAV in place of MJOLLNIR. On another occasion she gave her son VÍDAR, whose father was ODÍNN, a massive shoe that was made out of either leather or iron.

Gridstav
Norse and Teutonic
The unbreakable staff that GRID gave to THÓRR.

Grim
Anglo-Saxon
ANGLO-SAXON name for WODAN that today survives in such English place-names as Grim's Dyke. His name is an Anglo-Saxon term that denotes someone wearing a hood that covers their face and is cognate with the Old Norse GRIMR, a title applied to Odínn.

Grimhildr
Norse and Teutonic

The wife of GIUKI, thus Queen of the NIBELUNGEN. It would appear that this name is in fact a corruption of KRIEMHILD.

Grímnir
Norse and Teutonic

The name given to the hooded, disguised figure of ODÍNN, one of the many pseudonyms adopted by the god on his journeys down from ASGARDR to MIDGARDR.

Grímnismál
Norse and Teutonic

Text stating that half of those warriors slain in battle go to VALHALLA, the hall of ODÍNN, while FREYJA receives the rest in FOLKVANG.

Grimr
Norse and Teutonic

Old NORSE name, sometimes applied to ODÍNN, which appears to have been the origin of GRIM, one of the ANGLO-SAXON names used to refer to WODAN.

Griottunagardr
Norse and Teutonic

The location of the duel between THÓRR and the giant HRUNGNIR.

Gripir
Norse and Teutonic

The stable master or ostler of ELF[2]. He once prophesied all that was to pass in SIGURDR's life.

Gróa
Norse and Teutonic

A VOLVA (seer) who attempted to charm a fragment of the whetstone of HRUNGNIR out of THÓRR's forehead, where it had lodged after Thórr had smashed it. While Gróa was doing this, the god began to talk of the time he had brought her husband, AURVANDILL, out of the kingdom of the

FROST GIANTS in a basket, and how he had amputated one of Aurvandill's toes after it had become frost-bitten, the toe being hurled into the sky, where it became the star AURVANDILL'S TOE. So interested was Gróa in the story that she forgot to complete her incantation and the fragment of whetstone stayed lodged in Thórr's forehead.

Gruagach
British

One of the various names applied to PUCK.

Grundel
Norse, Teutonic and Anglo-Saxon

Variant of GRENDEL.

Gudr
Norse and Teutonic

'Battle', one of the VALKRYJA.

Gudrod
Norse and Teutonic

According to Snorri STURLUSON in HEIM-SKRINGLA, Gudrod was the husband of AASA and father, by her, of HÁLFDAN SVARTI and OLÁFR. He died when Hálfdan Svarti was just one year old.

Gudrunn
Norse and Teutonic

One of the NIBELUNGEN whose TEUTONIC name was KRIEMHILD. Some sources make Gudrunn one of the VALKYRJA, but this is mistaken. She fell in love with HELGI after seeing his prowess in battle and married him. Her marriage was short-lived, as Helgi was murdered by DAG[2], so next she married SIGURDR while he was under the influence of a magical potion that caused him to forget he was already married to BRYNHILDR, whose hand he later, while still charmed, persuaded Gudrunn's brother GUNNARR to seek. As Gunnarr was unable to penetrate the fiery circle that protected Brynhildr, Sigurdr assumed his likeness and plighted Gunnarr's troth.

Brynhildr, well aware of the trick, resolved to play along. However, during the wedding feast the effects of the potion wore off and once again Sigurdr was filled with love for her. Gudrunn mocked the Valkyrja for the ease with which she had been tricked and Brynhildr, driven into a fury by this mockery, vowed to have her revenge. She persuaded her brother-in-law GUTTORMR to kill Sigurdr while he slept, but then, overcome with remorse, she killed herself and shared Sigurdr's funeral pyre. Gudrunn, far from showing any grief or signs of remorse at her actions, immediately remarried, her next husband being ATLI (Teutonic ETZEL, the legendary name for ATTILA THE HUN), King of the HUNS. Atli later killed GUTTORMR, after which Gudrunn killed Atli and then fled the country.

Gullifaxi
Norse and Teutonic
'Golden-mane', the name of HRUNGNIR's horse. The horse was given to MAGNI by THÓRR after he had freed his father from beneath Hrungnir's corpse.

Gullinbursti
Norse and Teutonic
'Golden-bristled', the name of the golden boar that was made for FREYR by the DWARFS BROKK and SINDRI. It shone in the dark and was so fleet of foot that it could easily outrun the fastest horse.

Gullinkambi
Norse and Teutonic
The name of a cockerel living in VALHALLA, where its crowing each morning awoke the EINHERJAR so that they might sally forth to resume their eternal battling. Gullinkambi will also crow at the sound of HEIMDALLR's horn to warn the ÆSIR of the onset of the RAGNARØKR.

Gull-topr
Norse and Teutonic
The name of HEIMDALLR's horse.

Gullveig
Norse and Teutonic
A witch, one of the VANIR who came to ASGARDR and explained to the ÆSIR that she had an insatiable lust for gold. Her lust revolted the Æsir, who determined that she should be burned, but after having tried three times the witch was still alive. The Æsir then relented and allowed her to live in Asgardr, her name now becoming HEIDR. However, her treatment did not go unnoticed by the Vanir, and some cite this as the reason for their war with the Æsir.

Gungnir
Norse and Teutonic
The name given to the great spear owned by ODÍNN with which he stirred up discord. The spear was commissioned by LOKI from DVALIN[1] the DWARF as a peace offering to placate Odínn and SÍF.

Gungthiof
Norse and Teutonic
A son of FRITHIOF and brother of HUNTHIOF.

Gunn
Norse and Teutonic
One of the VALKYRJA.

Gunnarr
Norse and Teutonic
The eldest son of GIUKI and GRIMHILDR, and brother of GUDRUNN. After SIGURDR had married Gudrunn, Gunnarr was persuaded by his brother-in-law to seek the hand of BRYNHILDR, to whom Sigurdr had been married. However, unlike Sigurdr, Gunnarr was unable to penetrate the wall of fire that encircled the VALKRYJA, so Sigurdr adopted his guise and plighted

Gunnarr's troth in his stead. However, by so doing Sigurdr once again took possession of the cursed ring of ANDVARI, which he duly passed on to Gunnarr.

Following the wedding feast, Brynhildr swore her revenge and had GUTTORMR kill Sigurdr, after which she took her own life, thus leaving the unfortunate Gunnarr as a widower, once again proving that whoever owned the cursed ring of Andvari would suffer great sorrow.

Gunnarr Helmingr
Norse and Teutonic

The FLATEYJARBÓK tells the story of the Norwegian Gunnarr Helmingr, who, having offended King OLÁFR TRYGGVASON, fled to SWEDEN. There, in the temple of FREYR, he was attracted to the god's wife, the beautiful young priestess. Later that year, when it came to the time for Freyr's autumn progress from his temple to bless the land, Gunnarr Helmingr was invited to accompany it, even though the priestess felt that Freyr might not be pleased. Soon after their departure from the temple, the party found themselves in the midst of a severe blizzard and everyone except Gunnarr Helmingr and the priestess abandoned the god. Gunnarr Helmingr led the wagon on for a while and then stopped to rest, even though the priestess said that Freyr would attack them.

In desperation Gunnarr Helmingr called on the god of Oláfr Tryggvason – that is, the Christian God – and with his help overcame Freyr, who then departed and left the couple alone. Gunnarr Helmingr destroyed the image of Freyr, dressed himself in the god's finery and took his place. The couple then continued their journey and were greeted with delight at the feast to be held in honour of Freyr when the people saw that their god had assumed human form and could thus join them. They were delighted when the god demanded rich clothes and gifts in place of the normal human sacrifice and they were overjoyed when they learned that the priestess was pregnant. Shortly afterwards, when Oláfr Tryggvason sent word that he commanded his return, Gunnarr Helmingr stole away secretly, taking with him all his godly gifts and the priestess.

Gunnlod
Norse and Teutonic

The giantess daughter of SUTTUNGR who was mercilessly seduced by ODÍNN so that he might steal the MEAD OF INSPIRATION, the child resulting from their union being BRAGI.

Gunther
Teutonic

The TEUTONIC name for GUNNARR.

Guttormr
Norse and Teutonic

The brother of GUDRUNN. Following the marriage of BRYNHILDR and GUNNARR at the connivance of Gudrunn, Guttormr was persuaded by Brynhildr to kill Sigurdr while he slept. Later, after Gudrunn had remarried, Guttormr was killed by his new brother-in-law, ATLI.

Gwyligi
British – Wales

The 'Dog of Darkness' that had the ability to paralyse anyone who heard his strange, supernatural howl, as well as pole-axing them with a single glance from his fiery eyes.

Gylfaginning
Norse and Teutonic

The first section of the *Prose* EDDA that contains the story of GANGLERI.

Gylfi
Norse and Teutonic

King of SWEDEN who disguised himself as

a vagrant, in which guise he used the name GANGLERI, and travelled to ASGARDR to test the wisdom of the ÆSIR. While there he conversed with three mysterious creatures named HAR, JAFN-HAR and THRIDI who are alleged to have told him all the fundamentals of NORSE mythology. King Gylfi is also recorded as having given SJÆLLAND to GEFJUN after she had slept with him and he had promised her all the land she could plough in a day.

Gylve
Norse and Teutonic
The name used by Snorri STURLUSON to refer to King GYLFI.

Gymir
Norse and Teutonic
The giant father of GERDR who lived in an UNDERWORLD[4] kingdom. It is thought by some that Gymir may in fact be another name for ÆGIR, or one of Ægir's sons.

Háar
Norse and Teutonic
According to Snorri STURLUSON in *HEIMSKRINGLA*, Háar was one of ODÍNN's names. It originally seems to have meant 'armour' and only later came to be associated with the god.

Haddingr
Danish
Famous hero, a firm favourite of ODÍNN, by whom he was taught the stratagem of arranging his troops in a wedge formation. During one battle the god descended in the guise of an old man and stood directly behind Haddingr, shooting arrows over his head to drive away the magical storm that had been created by his enemies.

Hadubrand
Teutonic
According to the early-ninth-century *HILDEBRANDSLIED*, Hadubrand was the son of HILDEBRAND[1], a young knight who remained unknown to his father, who had been away fighting abroad for a number of years, when the two fought.

Hædcyn
Norse, Teutonic and Anglo-Saxon
A character from the poem *BEOWULF*. The son of HREDEL, King of the GEATS, and thus BEOWULF's uncle. He was said to have killed his brother.

Hagal
Norse and Teutonic
The foster father of HELGI, SIGMUNDR's son.

Hagbarthus
Norse and Teutonic
The name by which SAXO GRAMMATICUS refers to HARBARDR.

Hagen
Teutonic
According to the *NIBELUNGENLIED*, Hagen was the Burgundian retainer of King GUNTHER. SIEGFRIED had been made invulnerable by bathing in the blood of the DRAGON[2] FÁFNIR – invulnerable, that is, except for a single spot between his shoulders, where a leaf had masked him from the blood. BRÜNHILDE, furious at being tricked into marriage, persuaded Siegfried's wife, KRIEMHILD, to make the hero a shirt marked with a cross that fell over his one vulnerable spot, which Kriemhild had mentioned in confidence to Hagen. Guided by this, and incited by Brünhilde, Hagen stabbed and killed Siegfried, and then took the treasure of the DWARFS and hid it. Kriemhild demanded to be given the treasure, and when Hagen refused to reveal his hiding place she killed him.

Hake
Norse and Teutonic
Son of GANDALF and brother of HELSING and HYSING. He survived the battle with HÁLFDAN SVARTI and fled to ALFHEIMR.

Haki
Norse
Legendary early king of NORWAY who was

placed in a burning boat that was then allowed to drift out to sea as he lay dying.

Hakon
Norse and Teutonic
The father of THORA.

Hálfdan
Norse and Teutonic
The son of BELÉ and a close friend and confidant of VIKING. His brother was HELGÉ.

Hálfdan Svarti
Norse and Teutonic
According to Snorri STURLUSON in HEIM-SKRINGLA, Hálfdan Svarti (whose epithet means 'the Black'), so named because of his jet-black hair, was the son of GUDROD and AASA. Gudrod died when Hálfdan was just one year old and Aasa immediately travelled with her infant westwards to AGDER where she established herself as ruler of the kingdom that her father, HAR-ALDR[1], had reigned over. At the age of eighteen Hálfdan Svarti succeeded her. He travelled to WESTFOLD and there divided the kingdom between himself and his brother OLÁFR. He then fought against King GANDALF in VINGULMARK. As neither gained a conclusive victory, they agreed that Hálfdan should have dominion over half the kingdom, just as his father had before. From Vingulmark,

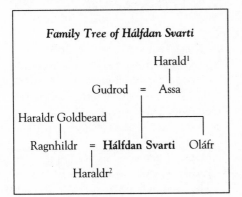

Family Tree of Hálfdan Svarti

Harald[1]
|
Gudrod = Assa

Haraldr Goldbeard
|
Ragnhildr = **Hálfdan Svarti**   Oláfr
|
Haraldr[2]

Hálfdan proceeded to RAUMARIKE and subdued it. However, no sooner had Hálfdan returned to Westfold than King EYSTEIN resubjugated Raumarike.

Hálfdan immediately set off and retook Raumarike, and then pursued the defeated Eystein to HEIDEMARK, where he once again defeated him. However, the pair eventually made peace, after which Hálfdan gave Eystein half of the domain of Heidemark.

Hálfdan married RAGNHILDR, a daughter of HARALDR GOLDBEARD, who was the king in SOGN. They had a son named HARALDR[2], who was raised in Sogn by Haraldr Goldbeard. When Haraldr Goldbeard died, the kingdom passed to the young Haraldr, but he died when he was just ten years old. Hálfdan immediately rode north to Sogn when he learned of his son's death, and there claimed the heritage and dominion of his son without opposition.

Hálfdan then fought against HYSING and HELSING, the sons of Gandalf whom he had left as regents to govern Sogn in his stead. The battle took place in Vingulmark and, having defeated the brothers, Hálfdan took possession of that land. HAKE, brother of Hysing and Helsing, survived the battle and fled to ALFHEIMR.

Hálfdan Svarti was a historical character, though the legends that have sprung up around him are of a dubious nature. King of NORWAY, he lived some time during the ninth century. After his death, his body was quartered, four different districts keeping a piece each – which suggests the ritual dismemberment of a sacrificial victim as part of a fertility rite.

Halogaland
Norse and Teutonic
Region of northern NORWAY where the fertility goddess THORGERDR HOLGAR-BRUDR was particularly worshipped.

Haloge
Norse and Teutonic
King of NORWAY and the father of VIKING, though some sources say that Haloge was none other than LOKI in disguise.

haltija
Finno-Ugric
The name given to the concept of the spirit or soul which all things possess. It had different names among different Finno-Ugric peoples: URT among the Votyak (see also BUSI-URT, D`U-URT) and ORT among the CHEREMISS, for example.

Ham
Norse and Teutonic
One of the two witches, the other being HEIDR, who were summoned by HELGÉ to interfere with a voyage being undertaken by FRITHIOF. The two witches attacked ELLIDA on the backs of two whales, but Frithiof dealt with their magic by cutting up a golden armlet into sufficient pieces for all his men and, using these, propitiating the goddess RAN. With her assistance, they were able to regain control of the ship and run down the witches and the whales they were riding.

Hamd(i)r
Norse and Teutonic
A son of GUDRUNN by JONAKUR, her fourth husband.

Hamel(i)n
Teutonic
Town in Lower Saxony, GERMANY, Hamelin being the English form of the German Hameln. Famous for the legend of the PIED PIPER, the town lies on the River WESER and numbers among its fine old buildings the Rattenhaus, the rat-catcher's house.

Hammond(r)
Norse and Teutonic
A son of SIGMUNDR and BORGHILDR.

Hanseatic League
General
Taking its name from *Hanse*, the German for 'group' or 'society', the Hanseatic League was a confederation of northern European trading cities from the twelfth century until 1669. At its height in the late fourteenth century, it consisted of over 160 towns and cities, among them Lübeck, Hamburg, Cologne, Cracow and Breslau. The basis of the league's power was its monopoly of the BALTIC trade and its relations with Flanders and England. Its gradual decline from the fifteenth century was due to the movement of trade routes and the formation and development of national states.

The earliest confederation had its headquarters at Visby, SWEDEN, and included over thirty cities. However, this was quickly eclipsed by a similar league based at Lübeck. Both Hamburg and Lübeck established offices in London, in 1266 and 1267 respectively, and they amalgamated with the office in Cologne in 1282 to form the so-called 'Steelyard'. There were three other such offices, at Bruges, Bergen and NOVGOROD. The last general assembly of 1669 marked the end of the Hanseatic League, a forerunner of the modern European Union.

Har
Norse and Teutonic
One of the three mysterious creatures that GYLFI, in his disguise as GANGLERI, consulted in ASGARDR, the other two being named as JAFNHAR and THRIDI.

Haraldr
Norse and Teutonic
1 Father of AASA and ruler of AGDER.
2 The son of HÁLFDAN SVARTI and

RAGNHILDR who was raised in SOGN by HARALDR GOLDBEARD. He ascended to the throne of Sogn on the death of Haraldr Goldbeard, but himself died when he was just ten years old, after which his father claimed the kingdom without opposition.

Haraldr Goldbeard
Norse and Teutonic
King of SOGN, father of RAGNHILDR and foster father of HARALDR[2]. When he died, the kingdom passed to his young grandson, but as he died when he was only ten years old, Sogn was then included within the kingdom of HÁLFDAN SVARTI, Haraldr's father.

Haraldr Hilditonn
Danish
'Harald Wartooth', a legendary king of DENMARK. Haraldr Hilditonn was promised divine protection by ODÍNN in return for the souls of all those the king killed. However, in a display of the treacherous side of his nature, Odínn stirred up discord between Haraldr and his friend King RINGR. Odínn then taught Ringr how to draw up his troops in the invincible wedge formation and, in the ensuing conflict, took the place of Haraldr Hilditonn's charioteer, threw the king from the chariot and stabbed him to death.

Haraldr inn Hárfargi
Norway
'Harald Fairhair', a legendary ninth-century king of NORWAY.

Harbardr
Norse and Teutonic
The lover of SIGNY, whose father killed him. SAXO GRAMMATICUS refers to him as HAGBARTHUS.

Hardur Saga
Norse and Teutonic
Saga from ICELAND concerning the exploits of HÖDR.

Har~fe, ~ke
Teutonic
A variant of HOLDA.

Harkon, Jarl
Norse and Teutonic
Devotee of THORGERDR HOLGARBRUDR who referred to the goddess as his wife, though SAXO GRAMMATICUS says that the goddess was married to one of FREYR's relatives and, along with all her companions, became a prostitute – a reference that undoubtedly suggests that the cult of Freyr involved temple prostitution.

Hartwaker
Anglo-Saxon
Son of HENGIST and brother to EBISSA, OCTA, AESC, SARDOINE and RENWEIN. It is thought that Hartwaker succeeded his father as the ruler of German Saxony after Hengist left for BRITAIN, and ruled from 448 to 480.

Hati (Hrodvitnisson)
Norse and Teutonic
'Hatred', one of the wolves that chase the SUN[5] and the MOON[5] across the sky. The companion of SKÖLL, some sources say that Hati will devour the Moon and Sköll the Sun, an event heralding the start of the RAGNARØKR.

Hávamál
Norse and Teutonic
'High Song', an epic poem in which the story of the self-sacrifice of ODÍNN on YGGDRASILL is to be found. Some sources claim that the epic was written by the god himself as a code of practice for his devotees.

Havhest
Norway

The sea-horse that is probably a transformation of the EQUUS BIPES of antiquarian Scandinavian folklore. Often represented as a horse–fish hybrid with a stylized fish's tail, the Havhest was originally perceived as a denizen of the sea and the inveterate enemy of the sea serpent in all its forms, the LINDORMR, a land snake blown to gargantuan proportions becoming the sea serpent in the final stages of the mutation.

The Havhest is described as having teeth that are about six feet long in a double row both top and bottom. Its eyes, small and yellow, glitter and spit fire. It exhales steam from its nose and throat and has breath that is so bad it could make people nauseous at a great distance. A long, wavy mane flows right down its back, while its thick forefeet resemble the forelimbs of a seal. Its long, slippery tail, usually forked like that of a fish, is used to whip the sea into a frenzy and is reputed to have sunk more than a few passing ships.

Havman
Norway

A merman, this creature may be related to the HAVHEST, though the two are quite distinct. The Havman has a blue skin and swims using only its fish's tail, its body remaining erect above the waves while it brandishes a fish as its weapon.

Heardred
Norse, Teutonic and Anglo-Saxon

A historical figure, the son of HYGELAC, King of the GEATS. Both he and his father were killed in a war against the FRANKS in c. 521.

Heathobards
Norse, Teutonic and Anglo-Saxon

The name of a TEUTONIC tribe with whom the Danes had a long-standing, bloody feud. HRODGAR attempted to quell it by marrying his daughter FREAWARU to INGELD, the leader of the Heathobards.

Heidemark
Norse and Teutonic

Ancient kingdom which HÁLFDAN SVARTI ruled, though after his battles with EYSTEIN and the subsequent peace between them he gave half of Heidemark to Eystein.

Heidr
Norse and Teutonic

One of the two witches, the other being HAM, summoned by HELGÉ to interfere with a voyage being undertaken by FRITHIOF. The two witches attacked ELLIDA on the backs of two whales, but Frithiof dealt with their magic by cutting up a golden armlet into sufficient pieces for all his men and, using these, propitiated the goddess RAN. With her assistance, they were able to regain control of the ship and run down the witches and the whales they were riding.

Heidrún
Norse and Teutonic

A goat that was said to have nourished YGGDRASILL and to have supplied the occupants of VALHALLA with an endless supply of mead, which she produced instead of milk.

Heimdal(l)(r)
Norse and Teutonic

A sun god, or god of light, who was sometimes called 'Gold-toothed', as he had teeth that were made of pure gold. Heimdallr needed to sleep only as long as a bird, could see in the dark and had ears so sharp that he could hear the grass or the wool on a sheep's back grow. However, for all these gifts Heimdallr was mute. The ÆSIR gave him the job of keep-

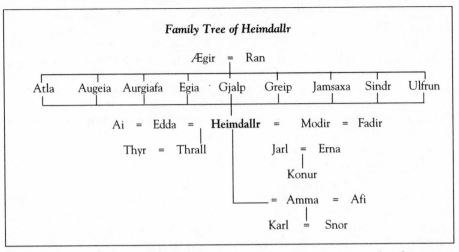

Family Tree of Heimdallr

Ægir = Ran

Atla   Augeia   Aurgiafa   Egia · Gjalp   Greip   Jamsaxa   Sindr   Ulfrun

Ai = Edda = **Heimdallr** = Modir = Fadir

Thyr = Thrall   Jarl = Erna

Konur

= Amma = Afi

Karl = Snor

ing watch over the incomplete wall that surrounded ASGARDR, and he was to blow on his great trumpet, GJALLARHORN, to warn them of any approaching danger. According to some sources, rather than watching over the wall, Heimdallr was guardian of the rainbow bridge, BÏFROST. In the guise of RIGER he would wander around MIDGARDR, sleeping with mortal women to found the races of serfs, peasants and warriors, thus allowing all social classes to claim descent from the gods.

Heimdallr is a complex character whose precise function remains unclear. As some sources refer to him as the 'White God', this has led to his association with the Slavonic BYELOBOG, and with the Finnish YAKUT stories of the father of mankind, who was simply known as the WHITE YOUTH and who was fed by the spirit of the WORLD TREE[2]. In the *Rígspula*, Heimdallr is identified with RÍG. Heimdallr was said to have been raised by nine giantesses, who are usually taken to be marine beings and were possibly the nine daughters of ÆGIR, though some sources talk of the god being miraculously born simultaneously to these nine giantesses. Heimdallr is also associated with FREYJA, but no evidence has yet been found to support a cult in his honour. The majority of references to this deity seem to suggest some association with the VANIR, but even this connection remains tenuous.

Summoned by Gjallarhorn, the gods will ride out of ASGARDR at the start of the RAGNARØKR, during which time Heimdallr will be pitted against his greatest enemy, LOKI. Heimdallr also appears in the story of the theft of MJOLLNIR by THRYMR. In this it is Heimdallr who suggests that THÓRR should adopt the guise of FREYJA in order to recover his great hammer from the FROST GIANT, though whether Heimdallr found his voice to make this suggestion, or wrote it down, is not recorded.

Heime
Norse and Teutonic
The son of VÖLUNDR and the owner of the sword MIMMINGR, made for him by his father, though some sources say that this sword had originally been manufactured by MIMINGUS.

Heimskringla
Norse and Teutonic
History of the kings of NORWAY that was written between *c*. 1223 and 1235 by Snorri STURLUSON, the culmination of a

century of historical research and composition in ICELAND.

Hel(a)
Norse and Teutonic

Goddess and guardian of the UNDERWORLD[4]. She was possibly a daughter of LOKI and ANGRBODA, as she was raised with the terrible wolf FENRIR and the great serpent MIDGARDSORMR, who would have been her brothers in this case. She is described as having one half of her face human, the other half being completely blank. Some sources say that the Underworld was named Hel after her, but it is more usual to refer to the domain as NIFLHEIMR. However, the goddess did lend her name to HELGRIND, the gates which led into the land of the dead.

Hel was visited by HERMÓDR[1] when he came to ask for the return of BALDR from her kingdom. Her condition for his return was that everything must weep for the loss of the god – a condition that was met by all except the giantess THOKK, so Baldr had to remain where he was. Hel was also unsympathetic when BRAGI came to her to attempt to reclaim IDUNN.

In his role as the god of winter, ULLR was said to spend a couple of months each winter in Niflheimr, while some accounts say that Hel and SKULDR, one of the three NORNS, were in fact the same. She and her spirit army will support the other gods during the RAGNARØKR, after which Niflheimr will be consumed, along with everything else, by the fire started by SURTR.

Helf~erich, ~rat
Norse and Teutonic

Variant name(s) for ELF[1].

Helfgi Hundingsbani
Norse and Teutonic

The alleged lover of SIGRÚN, one of the VALKYRJA.

Helgé
Norse and Teutonic

Son of BELÉ and brother of HÁLFDAN. He refused to allow his sister INGEBORG to marry FRITHIOF, commissioning the witches HAM and HEIDR to shipwreck Frithiof. He eventually agreed to Ingeborg becoming engaged to SIGURDR RINGR.

Helgi
Norse and Teutonic

A son of SIGMUNDR and BORGHILDR who was fostered by HAGAL. He became the husband of GUDRUNN, but was killed by HUNDINGR DAG.

Helgrind
Norse and Teutonic

Also called NÁGRIND and VALGRIND. The gates that separated the land of the living from NIFLHEIMR. The gates could be reached only by first crossing the River GJALL, which encircles the UNDERWORLD[4], over the golden bridge GJALLARBRÚ, which was guarded by MODGUDR.

Heligoland
General

One of the north FRISIAN islands in the North Sea that is administered by the state of Schleswig-Holstein, GERMANY, having been ceded by BRITAIN in 1890 in exchange for Zanzibar.

Helsing
Norse and Teutonic

Son of GANDALF and brother of HYSING and HAKE. He and his brother Hysing were placed as regents over SOGN by HÁLFDAN SVARTI, but Hálfdan Svarti was forced to do battle with the usurping brothers at VINGULMARK in order to regain control over his kingdom. Helsing and Hysing were killed and Hake fled to ALFHEIMR.

Helva
Norse and Teutonic
The lover of ESBERN SNARE who told him that the name of the TROLL he had made a bargain with was FINE, and by so doing saved his life.

Hengist
Anglo-Saxon
Semi-legendary leader of the JUTES who, along with his brother HORSA, was among the first wave of invaders to reach BRITAIN after the Roman Legions left, settling in Kent c. 450. The ANGLO-SAXON CHRON-ICLE says that Hengist died in 488, but sadly does not record the manner of his death. Some of his earlier history may be gleaned from BEOWULF and the ANGLO-SAXON poem *The Fight at Finn's Burg.* These mention a Hengist, thought to be the same one, who was a follower of HNÆF, King of the Danes. During a visit to Hnæf's brother-in-law FINN FOCWALD-ING, a fight broke out during which Hnæf was killed. Hengist became the leader of Hnæf's followers and entered the service of Finn Focwalding, but later killed him.

Hengist is credited with sons named EBISSA, OCTA, AESC and HARTWAKER, and daughters SARDOINE and RENWEIN. Today Hengist is generally, if not universally, accepted as a historical character.

Heorot
Norse, Teutonic and Anglo-Saxon
The name given to the hall of HRODGAR, King of DENMARK, in the poem BEOWULF.

Herfjoturr
Norse and Teutonic
'War-fetter', one of the VALKRYJA.

Hermódr
1 *Norse and Teutonic*
The son of ODÍNN and FRIGGA who welcomed dead warriors to the home of the gods and acted as a messenger between ASGARDR and MIDGARDR. At his mother's request, Hermódr rode his father's great eight-legged stallion SLEIPNIR down to NIFLHEIMR to rescue the spirit of his dead brother BALDR. After riding hard for nine days, Hermódr came to the River GJALL. There MODGUDR, guardian of the bridge GJALLARBRÚ, told him that Baldr had crossed the bridge only the previous night in the company of five troops of dead horsemen.

Hermódr crossed the bridge and came to the HELGRIND, the gates to the UNDERWORLD[4], which Sleipnir easily bounded over. Dismounting, Hermódr entered the palace of HEL. He soon stood before the goddess in her great

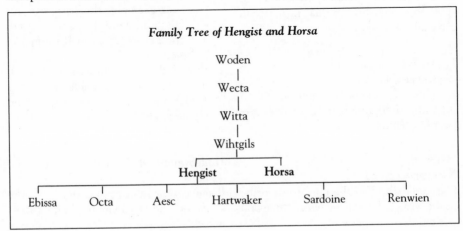

Family Tree of Hengist and Horsa

Woden
|
Wecta
|
Witta
|
Wihtgils
|
Hengist   **Horsa**

Ebissa   Octa   Aesc   Hartwaker   Sardoine   Renwien

hall and there he saw Baldr, seated in the place of honour. Quickly Hermódr explained the purpose of his journey. Hel considered the request and duly said that she would release Baldr from the land of the dead if all things on earth, animate and inanimate, shed tears at his loss. Baldr and Hermódr then exchanged gifts, Hermódr being asked to return the ring DRAUPNIR to their father, before the brothers bade farewell, and Hermódr rode back to ASGARDR to relate Hel's conditions. Unfortunately for Baldr, the giantess THOKK refused to weep at his death and so, until the RAGNARØKR, Baldr remains in the Underworld.

2 *Anglo-Saxon*

King of the Danes, a notorious and legendary king who was both miserly and bloodthirsty. Possibly owing his origins to HERMÓDR[1], he was compared unfavourably with the hero BEOWULF.

Herne the Hunter
British

The leader of the WILD HUNT, an antlered giant still said to be living in Windsor Great Park. It seems quite likely that Herne the Hunter is a memory of the Celtic cult of Cernunnos, though he has, in relatively late times, been mooted as the father (possibly spiritual rather than physical) of ROBIN HOOD.

Hervor(r)
Norse and Teutonic

Daughter of ANGANTYR, whom she raised from the dead in order to recover the sword TYRFINGR.

Hialli
Norse and Teutonic

Character who had the misfortune to be in the wrong place at the wrong time and was murdered in place of HÖGNI.

Hiisi
Finno-Ugric

One of the three evil spirits, the others being LEMPO and PAHA, who directed the axe of VÄINÄMÖINEN while he was carrying out his last task of carving a boat from the fragments of the spindle and shuttle that had belonged to the Maid of POHJA. The three spirits caused Väinämöinen's axe to slip so that he drove it hard into his knee. Hiisi was reputed to have been the owner of two fabulous beasts, a fire-breathing horse and a camel-like animal that was known as the ELK OF HIISI. Both beasts were captured by LEMMINKAINEN as the first two of the three tasks set him by LOUHI, the ruler of POHJOLA.

Hildebrand
Teutonic

1 The hero of the HILDEBRANDSLIED, a poem that dates from c. 800. In this Hildebrand returns home after fighting abroad for many years, only to be challenged and forced into a fight with a young knight who will not reveal his name but later turns out to be his son HADUBRAND. The poem exists only in a fragmentary form now, but would seem to be a version of a fairly common Indo-European story: compare, for example, the Irish story of Cú Chulainn and his son Conlaí, and the Persian story of Rustam and Sohrab.

2 The killer of KRIEMHILD. Though uncertain, it is possible that this Hildebrand is none other than Hildebrand[1].

Hildebrandslied
Teutonic

Poem dating from c. 800 that tells the story of the eponymous hero HILDE-BRAND[1].

Hildigoltr

Norse and Teutonic

'Battle-swine', the name of a helmet owned by King ATHLIS.

Hildingr

Norse and Teutonic

The foster father of both FRITHIOF, the son of THORSTEN and INGEBORG, and the Princess INGEBORG, the daughter of BELÉ. His two charges fell in love, but Hildingr forbade their marriage because of class differences.

Hildr

Norse and Teutonic

'Battle', the name of one of the VALKRYJA.

Hildsvin

Norse and Teutonic

'Battle-swine', the golden pig that was owned by FREYJA, as well as being an alternative name for HILDIGOLTR, the battle-helmet of King ATHLIS that was decorated with images of boars.

Himinbergs

Norse and Teutonic

The name used by Snorri STURLUSON to refer to HIMINBJORG.

Himinbjorg

Norse and Teutonic

The hall of HEIMDALLR within ASGARDR.

Himinhrjotr

Norse and Teutonic

The name of the huge ox, owned by HYMIR, that was killed by THÓRR, who used its head in his attempt to catch MIDGARDSORMR.

Hiordis

Norse and Teutonic

Daughter of EGLIMI and wife of SIGMUNDR in his autumn years. So incensed was LYGNI that Hiordis should have chosen the aged Sigmundr instead of him that he raised an army against Sigmundr in order to take his revenge.

Hiuki

Norse and Teutonic

The personification of the waxing MOON[5], the brother of BIL and one of the companions of MANI. Tradition ascribes the markings on the surface of the Moon to the children who carry a pole called SIMUL and a pail named SOEG. One version says that they were originally earthbound children who were made to carry water all night long in Soeg from the well BYRGIR by their cruel father, until Mani rescued them and took them to the Moon. Some authorities believe that the story of Hiuki and Bil may be the origin of the popular children's rhyme Jack and Jill.

Hladgunnr

Norse and Teutonic

One of the VALKYRJA, she used to set traps for her victims.

Hler

Norse and Teutonic

Usually taken as a variant name for ÆGIR, some sources say that Hler was one of the first gods to be created, a son of the giant YMIR. As such he is named as the god of the sea, a role that was later assumed by Ægir, thus leading to the confusion and the association.

Hlesey

Norse and Teutonic

The island near where ÆGIR and his consort RAN lived. It is this island that has given rise to the variant of HLER for Ægir (or vice versa).

Hlidskjálf

Norse and Teutonic

The seat of ODÍNN that was located in the silver-roofed hall VALASKJÁLF, the god's home within the confines of VALHALLA. From this seat he could survey the entire world. It is also the position from which FREYR is said to have first set eyes on, and immediately fallen in love with, GERDR, the daughter of the giant GYMIR.

Hlin
Norse and Teutonic

One of the goddesses attendant on FRIGGA. The goddess of consolation, she was very beautiful and kissed away the tears of those mourning the passing of a loved one, as well as relieving grief and listening to the prayers of mankind, which she relayed to the appropriate deity with her recommendations for an answer.

Hlodin
Norse and Teutonic

Variant for NERTHUS.

Hlokk
Norse and Teutonic

One of the VALKYRJA.

Hlora
Norse and Teutonic

One of the foster parents of THÓRR, along with VINGNIR. Together, these foster parents constitute sheet lightning, an attribute of their ward, who was so grateful to them that he used the alternative names of HLORRIDI and VINGTHÓRR in their honour.

Hlorridi
Norse and Teutonic

Alternative name used by THÓRR in honour of HLORA, one of his foster parents.

Hnæf
Anglo-Saxon

King of the Danes who numbered HENGIST among his followers. According to the ANGLO-SAXON poem *The Fight at Finn's Burg*, during a visit to Hnæf's

brother-in-law FINN FOCWALDING, a fight broke out, during which Hnæf was killed. Hengist became the leader of Hnæf's followers and entered the service of Finn Focwalding, but later killed him.

Hnoss
Norse and Teutonic

One of the two daughters of FREYJA and ODR, her sister being GERSEMI.

Hob(goblin)
British

Variant name(s) applied to PUCK.

Höd(r)
Norse and Teutonic

Sometimes incorrectly spelt Hodur because of the silent 'r' at the end of the name. Hödr was the blind god who unwittingly threw the dart made from a sharpened sprig of mistletoe, his arm being guided by LOKI, that killed BALDR. Hödr is also the hero of HARDUR SAGA.

In his GESTA DANORUM, SAXO GRAMMATICUS gives a different version of the death of Baldr. In this he and Hödr were rivals for the hand of the beautiful NANNA and fought several battles over her. On one occasion Baldr's fleet and army were utterly routed, even though they had the support of the ÆSIR, while on another Baldr was victorious, though Hödr still went ahead and married Nanna anyway.

Pining with grief, Baldr became so weak that he had to be carried in a cart, but even though his foe was now severely weakened, Hödr still knew that he could not kill him without using the magical sword that was guarded by MIMINGUS. Hödr set out on the long and arduous journey, through darkness and cold, until he came to the OTHERWORLD land where Mimingus lived. There, taking the SATYR by surprise, he managed to steal the sword and make his way home again.

With the sword Hödr managed to

inflict a wound on Baldr. The following day their armies met for the last time on the field of battle, even though Baldr was still so weak that he had to be carried and supported wherever he went. Three days later he died. To avenge the death of his son, ODÍNN fathered BOUS or VÁLI on the Princess RINDA with the single aim that, when his son had grown to manhood, he would avenge his dead brother by killing Hödr, plans which eventually came to fruition.

Hoenir
Norse and Teutonic
One of the three gods, the other two being ODÍNN and LÓDURR, who came upon two trees that had grown from the armpits of the giant YMIR as they were walking along the seashore. From these the three created the first man, ASKR ('Ash'), and the first woman, EMBLA (possibly 'Elm'). Odínn gave these first people their spirit, Hoenir gave them their intelligence, while Lódurr gave them their senses and their bodies. In another version of this creation myth, Hoenir was the brother of Odínn and LOKI, and this time gave mankind the gifts of movement and their senses.

They also created the DWARFS 'like maggots in Ymir's flesh'. They ordered NIGHT[2] and DAY[2] to drive across the sky in their chariots, and two blond children, the girl SUN[5] and the boy MOON[5], also to drive across the skies. These two children are pursued by two wolves that will one day catch and swallow them, thus bringing about the end of the world, the RAGNARØKR.

Like HEIMDALLR Hoenir appears to have been mute – a trait that is demonstrated in the story of the hostage exchange that followed the war between the ÆSIR and the VANIR. After a truce had been agreed, the two sides decided to exchange hostages. The two most notable Vanir, NJÖRDR and FREYR went to live in ASGARDR. The Æsir responded by sending Hoenir and the wise MÍMIR. However, as Hoenir never spoke the Vanir felt that they had been cheated and so decapitated Mimir, sending his head back to Asgardr. There Odínn sang a charm over it which brought it back to life, and from thenceforth he consulted the head in any crisis.

Hofvarpnir
Norse and Teutonic
The horse of the goddess GNA.

Högni
Norse and Teutonic
A son of GIUKI and GRIMHILDR, and brother to GUNNARR, GUTTORMR and GUDRUNN. He was killed, along with his brothers by ATLI, who desired possession of the gold of the NIBELUNGEN they had hidden. Though Högni does not feature in all versions of the story, when he does it is said that Gunnarr, having been tortured by Atli, announced that he would reveal the information only if he was brought the heart of his brother Högni. The first heart to be shown to Gunnarr was that of an unfortunate named HIALLI who just happened to be in the wrong place at the wrong time. Gunnarr recognized that the heart was not his brother's. Atli then sent his men out to kill Högni and bring back his heart. This they did, and Gunnarr immediately recognized it for it was. He turned to Atli and said that as his brother was dead and as he was now the only person alive who knew the hiding place of the gold, he wasn't going to give up that information. Furious, Atli had Gunnarr thrown into a pit of serpents and the secret of the hiding place died with him.

Holda
Teutonic
A minor moon goddess whose progress

across the skies is followed by hares that act as a train of torch-bearers. Holda appears to have been a TEUTONIC name for FRIGGA.

Hollr
Norse and Teutonic
Variant of ULLR.

Höne
Norse and Teutonic
The name used by Snorri STURLUSON to refer to HOENIR.

Hood, Robin
British
See ROBIN HOOD.

Horsa
Anglo-Saxon
Brother of HENGIST, whom he accompanied to BRITAIN. After his death, a memorial was said to have been built in his honour, and this has often been linked with a flint heap near Horsted in Kent.

Horse with the Golden Mane
Russian
Fabulous horse owned by Tsar AFRON. When IVAN[6] attempted to steal it for Tsar DALMAT, who had set him the task after he had been caught trying to steal the FIREBIRD and its gilded cage, he was caught yet again because he did not follow the advice of the shape-changing wolf that was helping him, and also tried to make off with the horse's golden bridle.

Afron offered Ivan a chance to redeem himself, telling him to bring him the maiden ELENA THE BEAUTIFUL. If he did then Afron would give him both the horse and the bridle, but if he failed he would be branded a common thief. Ivan succeeded with the help of the wolf, but fell in love with Elena the Beautiful *en route* back to Afron's palace. The wolf assumed Elena the Beautiful's form and

was presented to Afron, who kept his word and gave Ivan both the horse and its bridle. Ivan rode away on the horse and met up with the real Elena the Beautiful, who had been waiting in a forest nearby. The wolf then resumed his true form and disappeared from Afron's palace to rejoin Ivan and Elena the Beautiful.

After Ivan had been killed by his treacherous brothers DMITRII and VASILII[2], the horse fell by lot to Dmitrii. It was, however, restored to Ivan after he had been brought back to life by the wolf, using two small bottles of the WATER OF LIFE AND DEATH. The two murderous brothers were incarcerated by their father when all was revealed.

Horsel
Slavonic
Variant name for URSULA.

Hræsvelgr
Norse and Teutonic
'Corpse-eater', a giant who sat in the far north in the form of an eagle, the flapping of his wings being held responsible for the biting North Wind.

Hrafnkell
Norse
The hero of HRAFNSKELS SAGA FREYSGODA, from ICELAND.

Hrafnskels Saga Freysgoda
Norse
Saga that concerns the exploits of HRAFNKELL and mentions the legendary horse FREYFAXI, suggesting that it was either dedicated to FREYR or owned by that god.

Hraudingr
Norse and Teutonic
The father of AGNAR and GEIRRØDR.

Hredel
Norse, Teutonic and Anglo-Saxon
King of the GEATS and grandfather of
BEOWULF.

Hreidmar
Norse and Teutonic
The father of FÁFNIR and REGINN, by
whom he was murdered. He was also the
father of OTR, who was accidentally killed
by ANDVARI, an act that led Reginn,
Fáfnir and Hreidmar to insist that the
ÆSIR should recompense them by stealing
the hoard of gold that the DWARF owned.

Hrimfaxi
Norse and Teutonic
The horse owned by NOTT.

Hringhorni
Norse and Teutonic
The ship on which BALDR's funeral pyre
was built by the gods of the ÆSIR. The
pyre was shared by Baldr's wife NANNA,
who had died of grief when news of
Baldr's death at the hands of LOKI and
HÖDR reached her. The gods also placed
Baldr's horse on the pyre, as well as a
great number of treasures, including
ODÍNN's great ring DRAUPNIR. With all the
preparations complete, the pyre was lit, a
giantess pushed *Hringhorni* off its rollers
and it floated out to sea on the tide.

Hringr
Norse
According to SAXO GRAMMATICUS, a
nickname of King Sigurdr of SWEDEN,
who described his conquest of HARALDR
HILDITONN, King of DENMARK. It is also
sometimes rendered as RINGR.

Hrist
Norse and Teutonic
One of the VALKYRJA.

Hrodgar
Norse, Teutonic and Anglo-Saxon
Legendary King of DENMARK, a direct
descendant of SCYLD SCEFING. Hrodgar
built a great hall which he called HEOROT
but, according to BEOWULF, was unable to
defend it from the ravages of the monster
GRENDEL.

Hrolf
Norse and Teutonic
King of DENMARK whose henchmen
included the legendary BIARKI. In the
story of NOR, GOR and GOI that appears in
the ORKNEYINGA SAGA, Hrolf is called
Hrolf of BJARG, King of HEIDEMARK, who
has abducted Goi. Nor and Gor later
came to seek their sister. Nor and Hrolf
fought for a long time without any result,
so it was finally decided that Nor should
marry Hrolf's sister, while Hrolf himself
kept Goi.

Hromund(r) Greipson
Norse and Teutonic
Hero who was once said to have owned
the sword MISTILLTEINN.

Hrothwina
Anglo-Saxon
Alternative name for RENWEIN, one of the
two daughters of HENGIST. This version
appears in several sources that seem to
adhere to accepted ANGLO-SAXON
spellings, so it seems quite likely that
RENWEIN is actually a Latinization.

Hrungnir
Norse and Teutonic
One of the FROST GIANTS who, in a
drunken stupor, wildly boasted that he
would abduct both FREYJA and THÓRR's
golden-haired wife SÍF, and then sink
ASGARDR beneath the sea. When Thórr
retaliated, Hrungnir challenged the god
to a duel.

To assist their kinsman in the coming

battle, the Frost Giants created MOKKURKALFI ('Mist-calf'), a man of clay, to support and assist Hrungnir, who advanced against the furious Thórr brandishing a whetstone and guarding himself with a great stone shield. Thórr appeared on the field of combat wearing his iron gloves and his BELT OF STRENGTH and brandishing his hammer, MJOLLNIR. He was attended by his servant THJÁLFI. Hrungnir launched his whetstone directly at Thórr, who immediately retaliated by hurling Mjollnir at his foe. The hammer smashed the whetstone, a piece of which embedded itself in Thórr's forehead (see GRÓA), before continuing on its path of destruction to smash Hrungnir's skull.

Hrymr

Norse and Teutonic

The steersman of the ship NAGLFARI, which will bring the FROST GIANTS across the turbulent waters at the start of the RAGNARØKR.

Hugi

Norse and Teutonic

The personification of Thought who, incarnate and in disguise, ran a race against THJÁLFI in the kingdom of UTGARDR and beat him easily, the deception being one of the tests devised by the giant King UTGARDR-LOKI for LOKI, THÓRR and Thjálfi.

Huginn

Norse and Teutonic

'Thought', one of the two ravens that brought ODÍNN news from every corner of the world, the other being MUNINN, 'Memory'.

Huld(r)

Norse and Teutonic

According to Snorri STURLUSON in HEIM-SKRINGLA, Huld was a witch who was beseeched by DRIVA, the wife of VAN-LANDE (a son of SWEGDE), to either cast a spell over her husband so that he would return to FINLAND or kill him. Vanlande immediately felt the desire to return to Finland, but his friends and counsellors advised him not to, so he simply lay down to sleep. After a short while Vanlande awoke and called out to his advisers that the MARA (the nightmare was the way the NORSE witch or succubus often chose to haunt male victims) was trampling him. His men hastened to his side, but they were too late and he died. In this story the Mara is said to have been the power of GRIMHILDR's daughter. Huld also arranged for GISL and UNDUR, the sons of VISBUR, Vanlande's son, to kill their father without being either detected or suspected of the crime.

Hundingr (Dag)

Norse and Teutonic

A noble who went to war against HELGI due to the impertinence of the latter.

Huns

General

Though used as a derogatory term to refer to the German people during the First World War, the term Huns actually applies to any of a number of Mongoloid peoples who first appeared in history in the second century BC, raiding China across the Great Wall. They entered Europe c. AD 372, settled in Hungary and imposed their authority on the OSTROGOTHS and other Germanic peoples. Under the leadership of ATTILA THE HUN, they raided the Byzantine Empire, invaded GAUL and threatened Rome, but after his death in 453 their supremacy was broken by revolts among their subject peoples.

Hunthiof

Norse and Teutonic

A son of FRITHIOF and brother of GUNGTHIOF.

Hunvor(r)
Norse and Teutonic
A princess from SWEDEN who was rescued by and subsequently married VIKING.

Hvergelmir
Norse and Teutonic
The spring that gushes forth from below the third root of YGGDRASILL in the kingdom of NIFLHEIMR and is the source of all rivers.

Hygelac
Norse, Teutonic and Anglo-Saxon
King of the GEATS and the uncle of BEOWULF. A historical figure, he and his son HEARDRED were killed *c.* 521 during a war against the FRANKS.

Hymir
Norse and Teutonic
A giant who accompanied THÓRR, who assumed the guise of a youth, on a fishing expedition. While Hymir went to fetch some bait, Thórr cut off the head of Hymir's largest ox. Once in the boat, Thórr rowed so swiftly that Hymir began to fear that they might wake the serpent MIDGARDSORMR. Hymir grew even more afraid when the youth rowed straight past the usual fishing ground and instead rowed straight out to sea, finally stopping when he cast his line baited with the ox head into the sea.

After a short while Midgardsormr took the bait. Thórr exerted all his strength and tried to pull the serpent up to the surface, a feat that even he was able to do only after he had stamped holes in the bottom of the boat and braced himself against the sea-bed. Thórr and Midgardsormr stared at each other while Thórr prepared to strike the serpent with MJOLLNIR. As the blow descended, the frightened Hymir cut the line and the serpent slid back beneath the waves. Furious, Thórr struck Hymir on the side of the head so hard that Hymir fell into the water, and then the god waded back to the shore, leaving the giant floundering.

Hymiskvida
Norse and Teutonic
One of the poems that makes up the EDDA, and which tells the story of HYMIR and his fishing trip in the company of THÓRR, who intended to use the trip to catch and kill MIDGARDSORMR.

Hyndia
Norse and Teutonic
The giantess rival of FREYJA who revealed the ancestry of OTTAR HEIMSKI, Freyja's lover, when Ottar was in dispute with ANGANTYR. The THINGR decreed that the dispute should be settled by deciding who had the most distinguished lineage. Freyja took her love to visit Hyndla, an enchantress, who determined Ottar's lineage and then gave him a draft that enabled him to remember and subsequently recite his lineage in full. Angantyr had no such help and so lost the dispute.

Hyrrokin
Norse and Teutonic
The name sometimes given to the giantess who was responsible for slipping BALDR's boat HRINGHORNI off its rollers after his funeral pyre had been lit. She is described as riding on the back of a wolf, using serpents for the reins.

Hysing
Norse and Teutonic
Son of GANDALF and brother of HELSING and HAKE. He and his brother Helsing were placed as regents over SOGN by HÁLFDAN SVARTI, but Hálfdan Svarti was forced to do battle with the usurping brothers at VINGULMARK in order to regain control over his domain. Helsing and Hysing were killed and Hake fled to ALFHEIMR.

I

Iafnhar
Norse and Teutonic
Variant of JAFNHAR.

Iarngreiper
Norse and Teutonic
Variant of JARNGREIPR.

Iarnsaxa
Norse and Teutonic
Variant of JARNSAXA.

Iarovit
Baltic Coast
'Wrath', an alternative name for SVAN-TOVIT.

Iceland
General
Island country in the North Atlantic lying between GREENLAND and NORWAY to the south of the Arctic Circle. The island was first colonized in 874 by NORSE settlers who founded a republic and a parliament in 930. In 1000 the inhabitants adopted Christianity and *c.* 1263 submitted to the authority of the King of Norway. In 1380 Norway and Iceland came under the rule of DENMARK. When Norway became independent in 1814, Iceland remained attached to Denmark, continuing to recognize the Danish monarch even after independence in 1918, although full independence did not come until after a referendum in 1944.

Idavol~l, ~d
Norse and Teutonic
The plain in front of ASGARDR on which the monsters, giants and fiends will congregate, thus signalling the start of the RAGNARØKR.

Idisi
Teutonic
Generic term for women who, like the VALKRYJA, controlled the consequence of battles by aiding some men but binding others. Their name seems to make them cognate with the DÍSIR of NORSE tradition.

Idun(n)(a)
Norse and Teutonic
The goddess of spring and immortal youth, the daughter of IVALD, a DWARF, and the wife of BRAGI. She kept the APPLES OF YOUTH, with which the youth and vigour of the ÆSIR were maintained.

Ifingr
Norse and Teutonic
The river that runs around the plain of IDAVOLL and whose waters never freeze.

Ilma
Finno-Ugric
The god of air and, as the father of the goddess ILMATER LUONNOTAR, the god of creation.

Ilmarinen
Finno-Ugric
The divine smith and brother of VÄINÄMÖINEN. Born on a heap of cinders

in KALEVALA, his destiny was to tame the evil iron. When his brother returned from POHJOLA, he sent Ilmarinen back, as he had promised he would, to forge the SAMPO for the Lady LOUHI.

Ilmarinen set to work. Taking the feathers from a swan, the milk from a barren heifer, a small amount of barley grain and the finest sheep's wool he could find, he cast them into his furnace and summoned a huge number of slaves to stoke the fire. Every day he checked the forge to see what had been created in the flames. Many marvellous objects came from within the furnace: a golden bowl, a red-copper ship, a golden-horned heifer and a plough with silver-tipped handles, golden share and copper frame. Recognizing them as evil, Ilmarinen broke each of these into pieces and threw them back into the inferno. At last, among the flames, the wonderful sampo, with a beautifully decorated cover, appeared. One side of the sampo was a flour mill, one side a slate mill and the third a coin mill.

Ilmarinen presented the sampo to the Lady Louhi, whose daughter, the Maid of POHJA, said she preferred Ilmarinen to his older brother, Väinämöinen. Betrothed to the girl, Ilmarinen returned to Kalevala. During his time away Väinämöinen had been building a ship, aided finally by ANTERO VIPUNEN. He set sail for Pohjola shortly before Ilmarinen returned.

When Ilmarinen found that Väinämöinen had left for Pohjola, and learned of his intention to woo the Maid of Pohja, the girl to whom he was betrothed, he set off in pursuit on the fastest horse he could find. Väinämöinen still arrived first, but even though her mother advised the Maid of Pohja to marry Väinämöinen, she refused, saying that she preferred to marry Ilmarinen. Väinämöinen gave way to his younger brother, concluding that old men should not compete with youths in affairs of the heart. When Ilmarinen arrived, he and the Maid of Pohja were married.

Some years later, after the death of the Maid of Pohja, who had been killed by bears, Ilmarinen returned to Pohjola, hoping to marry his dead wife's sister. When the Lady Louhi refused, Ilmarinen simply abducted the girl. However, she was untrue to him and he turned her into a seagull.

It was on this visit to Pohjola that Ilmarinen realized the true worth of the sampo he had forged, for the whole land of Pohjola had prospered. He brought news of this prosperity to Väinämöinen, and the two brothers, in the company of the hero LEMMINKAINEN returned to Pohjola to steal it. En route their boat rammed a huge pike, from whose jaw Väinämöinen fashioned a wonderful KANTELE, a kind of five-stringed lute. At the sound of its marvellous music, all the people of Pohjola fell asleep, enabling Väinämöinen to snatch up the sampo easily. However, seeing their success, Lemminkainen burst into a triumphant song and woke up the sleeping people.

Seeing that the sampo had gone, the Lady Louhi pursued the fleeing boat with a terrible storm, during which the kantele was washed overboard and the sampo smashed into tiny pieces. Väinämöinen managed to salvage some fragments of the sampo and their magic was so powerful that they alone managed to make the land of Kalevala wondrously prosperous. Although the Lady Louhi attacked the country with plague, and even stole the SUN[3] and the MOON[3], the magic of the fragments of the sampo and the power of Väinämöinen were too strong for her, and finally she was forced to concede defeat.

Ilmater Luonnotar
Finno-Ugric
The daughter of ILMA, the god of air and,

through her birth, the god of creation. Tiring of her lonely existence in the wastelands of air, Ilmater Luonnotar descended into the sea, where she floated on its waves. Even though the WIND[2] that played across the surface of the sea and the water itself awakened life within her, she bore no offspring, and in bodily torment she floated alone for 700 years. Then a teal, seeking somewhere to lay its eggs, spotted Ilmater Luonnotar's knee protruding above the surface and built its nest in the crook. Three days later Ilmater Luonnotar's knee became scorched by the heat of the brooding duck and she shuddered at the pain. The duck flew off the nest and the eggs rolled into the sea. Sinking into the abyss, they became the substance of the universe.

From the lower halves of the shells came the earth, from the upper halves the skies. The yolks formed the SUN[3], PAIVA, and the whites the MOON[3], KUU. The stars came from white spots within the eggs and the clouds from dark spots. Seeing the creation she had caused, Ilmater Luonnotar shaped the coastline and placed rock pillars to secure the sky.

Ilmater Luonnotar's son VÄINÄMÖINEN gestated within her for thirty years, pondering on how he might exist in his gloomy home. He called upon the Sun and the Moon to deliver him from it. Neither replied. He then called to the spirit of the GREAT BEAR, OTAVA, to teach him how he might escape, but still he received no reply. Finally he made his way out and fell, already an old man, from his mother into the sea.

Il`men`, Lake
Russian

Lake to the south of NOVGOROD. Personified as a venerable, bearded old man, the lake was respectfully referred to as Granddad Lake Il`men`. Both benevolent and malevolent, the lake was more likely to respond to the wishes of other water spirits and fish than to those of man. On one occasion he sent a huge surge of water up a river known as BLACK STREAM simply because a mill had been built on that river and was blocking the fish's access to the lake. On this occasion a human carried a message from Black Stream and Lake Il`men` appeared as a well-built peasant dressed in a blue kaftan, blue trousers and a blue hat.

Il`ya
Russian

The Russian name for the Old Testament prophet Elijah, who, following the adoption of Christianity by RUSSIA, replaced the god of thunder, PYERUN. Elijah, or Il`ya, shared many of Pyerun's powers and attributes, such as being able to call down rain and fire from heaven.

Il`ya Murom(y)ets
Russian

A Russian knight, or BOGATYR, who was a hero of the Russian epic tales, or BYLINY. His surname is actually an epithet that simply means he came from the city of MUROM, not far from MOSCOW, though he was actually born in the village of KARACHAROVO, the son of a peasant named IVAN[3]. Born a cripple, too weak even to move, he was miraculously cured by pilgrims who gave him a draught of honey at the age of thirty-three. Shortly after his cure, Il`ya vowed to travel to KIEV, where he would offer his services to Prince VLADIMIR BRIGHT SUN and his wife, EVPRAKSIYA. Attending mass in Murom before setting out, he vowed that he would neither fight nor spill blood before he reached Kiev that evening, where he would once again attend mass.

This vow meant that Il`ya intended to travel over 500 miles in a single day, a feat that would have been impossible had it not been for his wondrous horse, which could gallop like the wind and clear mountains in a single leap. Arming himself with his sabre, his bow and arrows, his massive mace and a long, very sharp lance, Il`ya set out on the most direct route to Kiev, which would take him past CHERNIGOV.

As he approached the city he saw that it was under siege. Praying to God to release him from his vow, he charged the heathen hordes and killed the entire army. The people of Chernigov welcomed him as a hero and offered to make him their tsar. Il`ya refused and instead asked them to point him to the most direct road to Kiev. This they did, but warned him that on that route he would be ambushed by a terrible brigand, half-man and half-bird, known as NIGHTIN-GALE. Unafraid, Il`ya set out along the overgrown road, overgrown because for the last thirty years Nightingale had let no one pass, killing all who attempted the journey by whistling.

Eventually Il`ya came to the stream called SMORODINKA, beside which, in a nest in a tree, lived Nightingale. As Nightingale saw the knight approach, he whistled with all his might. All around trees and grass were flattened, and so strong was the blast that even Il`ya's horse stumbled. Chiding it to regain its feet, Il`ya fired an arrow at Nightingale, striking him on the temple and knocking him from his perch.

Il`ya leapt down from his horse and quickly tied Nightingale up before he regained his senses. Then he tied him to the stirrup of his horse and continued on his way. A short distance down the road, they were to pass the house in which lived Nightingale's daughters and sons-in-law. As they saw Nightingale tied to the stirrup of Il`ya Muromets's horse, they rushed out of the house ready to attack. However, Nightingale made them put down their weapons and had them invite Il`ya into the house to be their guest. Il`ya guessed that as soon as he was inside the house he would be set upon, so, wasting no time, he quickly killed all of Nightingale's children and their husbands.

Finally Il`ya came to Kiev and presented himself to Vladimir Bright Sun, though he arrived slightly too late to attend mass, as had been his intention. When he told Vladimir of all that had befallen him that day, the prince did not believe him. Il`ya led the prince out into the courtyard, where Nightingale was still tied to his horse. Vladimir commanded Nightingale to whistle, but he refused, saying that, as Il`ya had fairly defeated him, only Il`ya could command him now. When Il`ya ordered him to whistle but only at half-strength, Nightingale put his fingers to his lips and whistled at full strength. All around them the guards and courtiers fell dead. Vladimir was himself blown around the courtyard.

Having been accepted by Vladimir Bright Sun as a great knight, worthy of being called a member of his court, Il`ya took Nightingale out on to the steppe and beheaded him. The human half of his body he fed to the wolves and the bird half to the carrion crows. Il`ya served his prince faithfully for many years until he knew his time was coming to an end. His last act was to build Kiev Cathedral. Immediately it was completed, he died and his body turned to stone.

India
Russian
Having no connection with the real country, India is a fantasy land often mentioned in the Russian legends. In the story of Volkh VSESLAV`EVICH, for example, India is ruled over by King SALTYK, whom Volkh kills and so becomes ruler in his stead.

Ing

Norse, Teutonic and Anglo-Saxon

A hero or god of DENMARK who is said to have been an ancestor of the Kings of Bernicia.

Ingeborg

Norse and Teutonic

The daughter of BELÉ whom FRITHIOF married, though this name is also used for a wife of HÁLFDAN and a wife of THORSTEN. Some sources suggest that they are the same character, while others say that they are individuals with the same name.

Ingeld

Norse, Teutonic and Anglo-Saxon

The leader of the HEATHOBARDS.

Ioann the Long Suffering, Saint

Russian

According to a medieval tale this Russian saint buried himself up to the chest for thirty years in order to discipline his body. The DEVIL lit underground fires in an attempt to move him, but to no avail. Finally the devil assumed the guise of an awesome DRAGON[1] which threatened to burn the saint to death. One Easter night the dragon took the saint's head in his jaws and scorched his hair and his beard, but even this did not deflect the saint from his purpose. After this the devil gave up.

Irminsul

Teutonic

The world pillar whose NORSE equivalent seems to be YGGDRASILL, the WORLD TREE[2].

Ivald

Norse and Teutonic

The father of DVALIN[1], the DWARF, and the goddess IDUNN. An excellent smith, he seems to have passed on many of his skills to Dvalin.

Ivan

Russian

1 The youngest son of Tsar Bel BELYANIN and his wife, NASTAS`YA OF THE GOLDEN BRAID. Brother to VASILII[1] and PETER. Many years after Nastas`ya had been blown away by a huge gust of wind the two eldest boys, Vasilii and Peter, set out on a quest to find her. Some time later Ivan also set out on this quest.

Riding through the forest he met with his unnamed uncle, who lived in a splendid palace and gave him a magic ball to follow. This ball, Ivan was told, would lead him to where his mother was being held captive. Following the ball, Ivan caught up with his brothers, whom he persuaded to join him. Together they followed the ball until it came to a stop outside a cave at the foot of some very steep, almost insurmountable mountains. Not wanting to risk their own lives, Vasilii and Peter sent Ivan on alone, stating that they would wait for him at the foot of the mountains.

Ivan entered the cave, where he found a huge iron door barring his entry. Placing his shoulder against the door, he found that it swung open easily. Inside, just as his uncle had told him, Ivan found some metal claws, which he fixed on to his hands and feet, and started to climb. After a month he reached the top – a vast plateau that stretched as far as the eye could see. Following a faint path, he first came to a palace made of copper, the gates of which were guarded by DRAGONS[1] fettered with copper collars and chains. Nearby there was a well with a copper cup on a copper chain. Filling the cup with water, he gave it to the dragons and they immediately fell asleep, thus allowing him to pass in safety.

Once inside, he was greeted by the tsarita of the COPPER KINGDOM. She did not know where Nastas`ya of the Golden Braid was, but suggested that Ivan should journey on to the SILVER KINGDOM, for the tsarita, her middle sister, might know the whereabouts of Ivan's mother. The tsarita gave Ivan a copper ball to follow and bade him farewell.

Outside, Ivan placed the ball on the ground and followed it all the way to the Silver Kingdom. There he placated the dragons that guarded the gates in the same way as before and, entering, was greeted by the tsarita of the Silver Kingdom. She, like her sister, did not know the whereabouts of Ivan's mother, but gave him a silver ball to follow.

This Ivan did until he came to the GOLDEN KINGDOM. Once more he quietened the dragons that stood guard and entered the gleaming palace. Inside, he was greeted by the tsarita of the Golden Kingdom, whose name was ELENA THE FAIR. She knew exactly where Nastas`ya of the Golden Braid was being held. Like her two sisters, she gave Ivan a ball to follow, this time made of gold, which would lead him to where his mother was being held by WHIRLWIND.

Ivan duly followed the ball until he came to a palace that was even more impressive than those he had already visited, this one shining with diamonds and other precious stones. Pacifying the six-headed dragons that guarded the gates, he entered the great hall of the palace, where he found his mother seated upon a magnificent throne, dressed in the most wondrous clothes he had ever seen.

Amazed to see her son, Nastas`ya explained that the secret of Whirlwind's strength lay in a barrel in the wine cellars of the palace that contained a magical water bestowing tremendous strength on whoever drank from it. She then told her son how he might defeat Whirlwind, who was due to return at any minute. First drinking from the barrel his mother had shown him, Ivan switched it with a barrel full of water which sapped the strength of any who drank from it and then hid beneath his mother's cloak.

As Whirlwind returned and leaned over Nastas`ya, Ivan reached out and grasped the mace which Whirlwind always carried. Carrying Ivan high into the air, Whirlwind tried, without success, to shake him free. Returning to the palace, Whirlwind drank from the barrel which normally held the strength-giving water, but because of Ivan's deception his strength was completely sapped. Drinking from the correct barrel, Ivan felt himself filled with tremendous power and, with a single blow from his sword, he decapitated Whirlwind, burned his body and scattered the ashes.

Having released his mother, Ivan made his way back through the three kingdoms, freeing each tsarita as he went. Finally all five came to the top of the mountain at the bottom of which Vasilii and Peter were still waiting. Jealous of their brother's success, they stranded him on the top of the mountain after he had lowered the three maidens and their mother down to them and rode off home to claim the success for themselves.

Ivan wandered back to the palace of Whirlwind, where he found a small whistle which he blew. Instantly two servants appeared, LAME and ONE-EYE, for that is what they were. Ivan requested food and these servants, who had originally served Whirlwind, magically made a magnificent banquet appear. Having eaten and then slept, Ivan asked them if they could return him to his own land. The next moment Ivan found himself standing in the middle of the market-place outside his father's palace.

Rather than returning straight home, for he wanted to find out what had happened to his two brothers, Ivan hired himself out as an apprentice to a shoemaker. That night, as Ivan and the shoemaker slept, Lame and One-Eye made a wonderful pair of shoes and the shoemaker took them to the market to sell the very next morning. As Elena was soon to be married, having been brought back from the mountains by Vasilii and Peter, she needed some new shoes for her wedding. Seeing those that Lame and One-Eye had made, she knew they could have been made only by someone who had come from the kingdoms at the top of the mountains. She bought them and instructed the shoemaker that he was to make her wedding dress, the most magnificent dress anyone had seen, by the very next morning or he would be hanged.

That night, having drunk himself into a stupor, the shoemaker slept and dreamed of his impending death as Lame and One-Eye made the dress. The following day Elena collected the dress and again knew who had made it, so she set the shoemaker a final, impossible task. By the very next morning he was to have made for her a palace out of gold that was to stand in the middle of the sea, connected to dry land by a golden bridge covered with a fine velvet carpet with a garden to either side filled with trees.

That night the shoemaker became so drunk that he had to be carried to his bed and when he rose he continued to drink, for he did not want to be

sober when they came to hang him. However, Lame and One-Eye had once more completed the task, so Elena asked him how he had managed to do so. Not knowing, he asked Ivan and the truth finally came out. Tsar Bel Belyanin was so furious with Vasilii and Peter that he wanted to have them executed, but Ivan interceded. Finally Ivan married Elena, Peter married the tsarita of the Silver Kingdom and Vasilii married the tsarita of the Copper Kingdom. The shoemaker was made into a general and no land was every bothered by Whirlwind again.

2   A young tsarevich who had been born dumb. At the age of twelve he was told by his favourite groom that he was about to have a sister but was warned by the same groom that the girl would be a fearsome witch who would eat her family and everyone who came near her. The groom advised him to ask his father for a swift horse, the swiftest of all those his father owned, so that he might escape before it was too late.

The tsar, delighted to hear his son speak for the first time, personally picked out the horse for him. Having travelled for quite a distance, the young tsarevich started to look for a place to live. First he came across two old seamstresses. They told him that they would have been glad to have taken him in but they did not have long to live, for once they had finished the work they were currently doing, it would be time for them to die.

Broken-hearted, Ivan left and travelled on, next meeting a man whose task in life was to uproot massive trees. Called UPROOT OAK, this man too would have been happy to take Ivan in but he also had only a short time to live, for, as he told the youth, when he had uprooted all the oaks in the forest he was clearing, then it would be his time to die.

Once more overcome with grief, Ivan journeyed on until he met a giant of a man who was busy tipping a range of mountains on to their sides. This man, whose name was OVERTURN MOUNTAIN, once more told Ivan that he would have gladly taken him in had it not been for the fact that his days would be at an end after he had over-turned the entire mountain range.

Down at heart, Ivan rode on until he came to the home of the SUN'S SISTER. She took the youth in and treated him as her own. After a while, Ivan began to think about his family, so, climbing a mountain, he looked far into the distance in the direction of his home and cried. Returning down the mountain, he said that the tears in his eyes were due to the wind. Twice more this happened, but each time Sun's Sister had forbidden the WIND[1] to blow, so Ivan finally told her what was the matter.

As Ivan prepared to leave, Sun's Sister gave him three items to help him on his journey: a comb, a brush and two apples which had the power to rejuvenate whoever ate them. On his way Ivan met his friends once more. Overturn Mountain had only two mountains left to topple before he died. Ivan threw down the brush and a massive mountain range sprang from the earth. Uproot Oak had only two trees left to uproot. Ivan threw down his comb and a huge forest of oak trees appeared. Finally Ivan came to the two seamstresses who were stitching the last seam of their piece. Ivan gave each of them an apple and they were instantly young upon the very first bite. In return they gave Ivan a kerchief which they told him had magical properties.

At last Ivan came to his home and was welcomed by his sister, who asked him to play on the psaltery while she prepared a meal. After she had left a mouse warned Ivan that his sister had really gone to sharpen her teeth, and offered to run up and down the strings of the psaltery to enable Ivan to make his escape.

When Ivan's sister discovered how she had been tricked, she set off in hot pursuit and was soon catching Ivan up. Seeing her riding like the wind after him, Ivan threw down the kerchief, which immediately became a huge, deep lake. Swimming across it slowed Ivan's sister down and allowed him to increase his lead over her. Again she started to close the gap just as Ivan rode past Uproot Oak, who blocked the road with a huge pile of oak trees which Ivan's sister had to gnaw her way through. Again she closed in on her brother just as he passed Overturn Mountain, who blocked the road with a pile of towering mountains. Finally Ivan made it safely back to the home of Sun's Sister, who locked him safely inside, but still his sister would not give up.

Finally she suggested that they should be weighed on a huge pair of scales, the heavier having the right to destroy the other. Ivan sat on the scales first, then the witch, his sister, sat down. She was so heavy that Ivan shot off into the heavens, straight into the Sun's Sister's palace, where he remained safe from the cannibalistic desires of his sister.

3 A peasant from the village of KARACHAROVO, near MUROM, and the father of IL'YA MUROMETS.

4 A young tsarevich from an unnamed kingdom. As a youth he set out to find Princess Vasilisa KIRBIT'EVNA, whom he had been told he would marry. *En*

route he paid the debt of BULAT THE BRAVE, who, indebted to the tsarevich, told him that, had he not helped him, he would never have found the maiden. Together they travelled to the kingdom of Tsar KIRBIT, and there found the girl in a tower with a gilded roof. Bulat the Brave captured the girl and the three of them made their getaway at full speed. When they were chased by Kirbit and his men, Bulat twice dealt with things, on each occasion leaving only the tsar alive.

One night, as Ivan lay asleep, Vasilisa Kirbit`evna was stolen from them by KOSHCHEI THE DEATHLESS. Locating the home of Koshchei in the guise of two of Koshchei's herdsmen, Ivan and Bulat the Brave were told where Koshchei kept his soul after Vasilisa Kirbit`evna had tricked the information out of him.

After a long journey they came to the island on which the soul was hidden inside an egg which was inside a duck which was inside a hare. The three were hidden under a huge oak tree. With the help of three animals whose lives they had previously spared, Ivan and Bulat the Brave returned to the home of Koshchei with the egg that held his soul. Smashing it against his forehead, they killed him and rescued the girl. Ivan married Vasilisa Kirbit`evna and made Bulat his most trusted friend and adviser.

5 The youngest son of an unnamed tsar by one of that tsar's three concubines. As his father could not decide which son should be his heir, he told them each to go out into a field and fire an arrow on which they had written their name in different directions. Wherever the arrow landed, they would rule, marrying the daughter of the house in which the arrow landed. Ivan's arrow landed in a swamp, where he found it in the possession of a shape-changing frog who was, in reality, VASILISA THE WISE. Ivan agreed to marry the frog, which then revealed to him her full beauty, telling him that she would be a frog by day and a beautiful maiden at night.

Ivan fulfilled his promise and married the frog, and for some time they lived happily. However, the tsar devised three tests for the wives of his sons. Each time the frog won, even though the wives of Ivan's two brothers tried to cheat by spying on her. Finally the tsar threw a banquet in the honour of his three daughters-in-law at which the frog appeared in her human form. Grabbing the opportunity to keep his wife in all her beauty, Ivan rushed home before her and burned her frog skin. When she returned, she told Ivan her name for the first time, said he should seek her in the land of the eternal sun and promptly vanished.

Ivan left his home and travelled until he came to the home of the witch BABA-YAGA, who, though at first annoyed to have been disturbed, told him how he might capture Vasilisa the Wise, who flew in every day to visit the witch. Hiding until Vasilisa the Wise had made herself comfortable, Ivan pounced on her, but allowed her to wriggle free as she rapidly changed her shape. Ivan then travelled to Vasilisa the Wise's middle sister, and exactly the same thing happened. Finally, Ivan journeyed to the home of Vasilisa the Wise's youngest sister, and this time he managed to hold on to his wife as she changed her shape. When she changed into an arrow, Ivan broke it across his knee and Vasilisa the Wise resumed her human form, telling him that she would be his for ever.

Together Ivan and Vasilisa the

Wise returned home. There the tsar made Ivan his heir and eventually he ruled in his father's stead.

6   The son of Tsar Vyslav ANDRONOVICH, hence known as Ivan Vyslavovich, and brother of DMITRII and VASILII[2]. Their father owned a wonderful garden in which there was an apple tree on which golden fruit grew. All was well until a FIREBIRD took to visiting the garden and stealing the apples. Perplexed, the tsar promised half his kingdom to whichever of his three sons could catch the thief.

On the first night Dmitrii kept watch, but he had fallen asleep by the time the Firebird landed. On the-second night Vasilii took his turn, but the same fate befell him. However, on the third night it was Ivan's turn. After three hours the garden was filled with a wondrous light and the Firebird settled on the tree. Ivan crept up behind it and took hold of it by the tail. The Firebird struggled so hard that it managed to escape from Ivan, but Ivan managed to pluck out one of her tail feathers. The following morning he presented that feather to his father, who treasured it above any of his other possessions.

As time passed the tsar began to long for the Firebird itself rather than just one of its feathers. Once again he promised one half of his kingdom to whichever of his sons could bring the Firebird back for him. All three set out on the quest, though none knew where they should look.

Ivan rode aimlessly for several days until he came to a crossroads that warned of death for anyone who took anything but the right-hand road, though this road would lead to the death of the rider's horse. Ivan took the right-hand road and on the third day came across a huge grey wolf

which tore his horse in half. Saddened by this loss, Ivan continued on foot until he was almost totally exhausted.

Just then the wolf that had attacked his horse rushed up, apologized for having killed the horse and offered to take Ivan wherever he wanted to go. Ivan explained his quest to the wolf, which immediately sped off with Ivan on his back much faster than any horse could have travelled. Shortly they came to a walled garden within which, so the wolf informed Ivan, the Firebird was kept in a gilded cage. The wolf warned Ivan to take only the Firebird and not to touch the cage, but when Ivan saw the beauty of the cage he forgot the advice and took it down from its place in a tree. Immediately he was surrounded by guards, who hauled him off in front of the Firebird's owner, Tsar DALMAT.

The tsar was understandably furious, but gave Ivan a chance to redeem himself, telling him to ride to the kingdom of Tsar AFRON, and from there acquire for him the HORSE WITH THE GOLDEN MANE. If Ivan could achieve this he would be rewarded with the Firebird. If not he would be branded a common thief. Outside the palace Ivan apologized to the wolf for ignoring its advice and asked for its help in acquiring the Horse with the Golden Mane. The wolf told Ivan to jump on his back and soon they were standing outside the stables of Tsar Afron.

The wolf told Ivan how he might bring the horse out unchallenged, but warned him not to touch the horse's golden bridle. Once inside the stables, Ivan could not resist the bridle, and was immediately arrested by the palace guards and dragged before Tsar Afron. Like Dalmat, Afron was furious, but he too gave Ivan a chance to save his good name. He told Ivan to bring to him Princess ELENA THE BEAUTIFUL. If he did he would be rewarded with the Horse with the Golden Mane and its bridle.

Once more Ivan apologized to the wolf and asked for its help. Jumping on to the wolf's back, the two soon found themselves in the land of Elena the Beautiful. Leaving Ivan on the edge of the plain, the wolf continued to the railings that surrounded the palace gardens. That evening, as Elena the Beautiful strolled in the garden, the wolf captured her and ran off to where Ivan was waiting. Ivan leapt on to the wolf's back and they sped off back towards the land of Tsar Afron. Elena the Beautiful's servants were in hot pursuit, but the wolf easily outran them.

By the time they reached the palace walls of Tsar Afron, Ivan had fallen deeply in love with Elena the Beautiful, and she with him. Ivan asked if the wolf could help them, and the wolf said it could. The wolf would become the image of Elena the Beautiful and would remain in her place, but Ivan had only to think of it and it would be by his side.

Tsar Afron was delighted when the false Elena the Beautiful was presented to him by Ivan and he kept his promise, giving Ivan the Horse with the Golden Mane and its bridle. Ivan rode off on the horse and met up with the real Elena the Beautiful, who was waiting for him in the forest. After travelling a short distance, Ivan thought of the wolf, which immediately appeared by his side.

Coming to the palace of Tsar Dalmat, Ivan once again asked the wolf for its help, for he had grown very attached to the Horse with the Golden Mane. Once again the wolf transformed itself into the horse and was

left in its stead when Ivan left with the Firebird in its gilded cage. A short distance down the road, he thought of the wolf, which was instantly by his side.

Riding back towards Ivan's home, they came to the spot where the wolf had first attacked Ivan, killing his horse. Telling Ivan and Elena the Beautiful that it could go no further, the wolf left them to continue their journey on the Horse with the Golden Mane. At the border of Ivan's homeland, they passed his brothers Dmitrii and Vasilii. Jealous at their brother's success, they ambushed and killed him, dividing the booty by lot. Dmitrii won the Horse with the Golden Mane while Vasilii won Elena the Beautiful, whom the brothers swore to silence at sword's point.

For thirty days Ivan's body lay where he had been killed, until it was discovered by the wolf. Thinking of a way in which he could revive his young friend, it caught a young raven and threatened to tear it in half. The mother raven pleaded for mercy, to which the wolf replied that it would spare the young bird if the mother would bring him some of the WATER OF LIFE AND DEATH. The raven agreed and flew off. Three days later the bird returned with two little bottles of the Water of Life and Death. To test the water the wolf tore the raven in half and then sprinkled the water from one bottle over the carcass. Immediately the bird flew up into the sky fully restored. The second bottle the wolf sprinkled over Ivan, who came back to life.

Ivan returned to the royal palace during the wedding feast of Vasilii. When Elena the Beautiful saw Ivan, she told the tsar the truth, upon which Dmitrii and Vasilii were cast into the palace dungeons, and Elena the Beautiful married Ivan, to whom ownership of the Horse with the Golden Mane was restored.

Ivan the Great
Russian

Properly Ivan III (1440–1505), the ruler and Grand Duke of RUSSIA from 1462 to 1505. He shook off the yoke of the TARTARS and subjected a number of the Russian principalities to his authority. He married Sophia, a niece of Constantine XI Palaeolgus, in 1472, assumed the title 'Ruler of all Russia' and adopted the two-headed-eagle emblem of the Byzantine Empire.

Ivan the Mare's Son
Siberia – Tungus

The hero of a story that comes from the TUNGUS people of SIBERIA. His mother was a mare who had escaped from a peasant couple who intended to eat her. As she ran through the forest, she came upon the corpse of a Tungus warrior and, licking the body, she instantly conceived a son, whom she called Ivan. Raising the boy, she finally told him that the time had come when he must fend for himself, adding that he should leave his arrow standing upright in the ground every night so that she would know he was alive. If she found it lying on the ground then she would know that he was dead.

Ivan promised his mother that he would do that and left her. Several days later he came to a clearing in the forest. In the middle of this clearing was a young man on his hands and knees. When Ivan asked him what he was doing, the youth replied that he was looking for his arrow. Ivan found the arrow, which he returned to the young man, who told him his name was IVAN THE SUN'S SON. The two agreed that from that day forth they would live as brothers.

A few days later the two Ivans returned to the clearing, where they found another youth searching on the ground. He too had lost his arrow and again Ivan the Mare's Son found it. This youth's name was IVAN THE MOON'S SON and he too agreed to live as their brother. In the middle of the clearing they built themselves a home of wooden poles covered with the skins of the animals they had hunted. Every night each Ivan placed his arrow upright in the ground outside their home.

One morning, to their surprise, they found that, during the night, their arrows had been richly decorated. Ivan the Moon's Son said that he would keep watch that night and catch the culprit, but he fell asleep and in the morning their arrows had been decorated once again. Exactly the same thing happened when Ivan the Sun's Son stayed on guard, so the third night Ivan the Mare's Son said he would stand watch.

On the stroke of midnight three herons flew down into the clearing, smashed themselves against the ground and instantly became three beautiful maidens. Each plucked the arrow of the man they professed to love from the ground and set about decorating it. Ivan crept from his hiding place and hid their heron's wings and feathers. When the three maidens had finished the arrows, they could not find their heron skins. The eldest maiden called out for whoever had hidden them to come forward, saying that if he were older than they then he would be their father, if he were younger he would be their brother, but if he were the same age then he would become her husband.

Ivan crept from his place of concealment and revealed himself to the oldest of the three maidens, who told him that her name was MARFIDA. The other maidens were Marfida's sisters, and the three agreed to become the wives of the three

Ivans. All six lived happily in their home in the clearing.

However, one day, when Ivan and his brothers returned from their day's hunting, they noticed that their wives were very pale and thin. On investigation they discovered that some holes had appeared in the ground beneath their home. Puzzled, Ivan and his brothers decided that, instead of hunting the following day, they would stand guard. The following day, while his brothers dozed in the warmth of the sun, Ivan the Mare's Son saw a huge serpent crawl out of one of the holes beneath their home and, wrapping itself around the three wives, start to suck their blood. Ivan drew his bow and shot at the serpent, which quickly slithered back down the hole, warning Ivan as it went that it would return in three days, riding on a cloud of fire.

For three days the three Ivans made as many arrows as they could before taking turns to watch for the approach of the cloud that would bring the serpent. Ivan the Moon's Son saw it first. Ivan the Sun's Son watched it approach. By the time Ivan the Mare's Son came to see, it was directly overhead, the serpent in the middle surrounded by his army of demons.

A mighty battle ensued. Ivan the Moon's Son was killed first. Some time later Ivan the Sun's Son was killed too. Ivan the Mare's Son fought on alone until he had reduced the army of demons to a third of its original size. Then he too was killed, his head cut clean from his body. The serpent gathered up the three maidens and disappeared with them down one of the holes beneath the house.

Ivan the Mare's Son's mother later found his arrow lying on the ground amidst the bodies of the demons. She located his body and his head, licked the body all over and kicked it with her hind legs. The body became whole again. She licked and kicked the body again and it

stirred. Once more she licked and kicked her son and he jumped to his feet fully revived. Next they sought out and found the bodies of the other two Ivans, whom the mare also brought back to life. She left the three brothers discussing how they might rescue their wives.

After hunting for three days, they stitched a long rope from the hides they had collected. To one end of this rope they attached a leather cradle. Climbing into the cradle, Ivan the Mare's Son was lowered down the hole through which the serpent had originally appeared. At the bottom he found himself in the UNDERWORLD[1], the home of the serpent. Following a barren track, Ivan came to a lake. There he saw three women, Marfida and her sisters, coming to draw water. Ivan fired an arrow in front of his wife to tell her that he was there. As Marfida lagged behind her sisters, having collected the water, she and Ivan were reunited.

Marfida told Ivan that he was to kill the serpent at exactly midday, when it slept in its hammock. Ivan did as instructed, and he and the three maidens made their way back to the leather cradle. The wives of Ivan the Moon's Son and Ivan the Sun's Son were hoisted up first. When it came to Marfida's turn, she beseeched Ivan the Mare's Son to go first, but he refused. Having raised Marfida, Ivan the Moon's Son and Ivan the Son's Son cut the rope and threw the cradle back down the hole, thus trapping Ivan the Mare's Son in the Underworld.

Once more his mother came to the rescue. Fearing for her son, she discovered him, dead, at the bottom of the hole. Restoring him to life as she had done before, she told him to hunt until they had enough meat for the journey back to the land of the living. Ivan did as instructed and finally they set off. Each time the mare turned her head Ivan fed her some meat. As they neared the exit he ran out of meat, so he cut off a toe from his right foot and fed that to his mother. Next he cut off his calf and then an ear. Having finally made it out of the Underworld, Ivan's mother coughed up the pieces of her son that she had been fed and, licking his wounds, made him whole again.

Three days later, Ivan came across Marfida, who was being made to drag a heavy load for remaining faithful to her husband. Ivan lifted her on to his shoulders before running after his two false brothers, whom he killed. Taking the three heron skins from his pocket, he plucked some feathers from each of them and made himself a pair of wings, on which he flew, with the three maidens, to their homeland, where they lived out their days in peace and happiness.

Ivan the Moon's Son
Siberia – Tungus
Youth whose lost arrow was found by IVAN THE MARE'S SON and whom he joined as his brother, along with IVAN THE SUN'S SON. During a battle with a huge serpent which had been feeding off the blood of his wife, and that of his brothers' wives, all three Ivans were killed, their wives being carried off to the UNDERWORLD[1] lair of the serpent. All three were restored to life, after which Ivan the Mare's Son was lowered into the Underworld to rescue the maidens. Ivan the Mare's Son was left for dead by his false brothers, who made off with all three women, but he was rescued by his mother and killed both Ivan the Moon's Son and Ivan the Sun's Son.

Ivan the Pea
Russian
The youngest son of Tsar SVETOZAR and his wife, he had two other brothers, both unnamed, and a sister, VASILISA OF THE GOLDEN BRAID. Ivan the Pea was miraculously conceived when his mother swallowed a small pea which grew inside her until she gave birth. Ivan the Pea grew at a very fast rate and by the age of ten was the strongest knight in all the kingdom. Learning of the fate of his sister, who had been carried away by a DRAGON[1], and his two brothers, who had gone in search of her, Ivan the Pea vowed to return them to their home.

He rode for three days until he came to a small wooden house on chicken's legs in the forest that rotated in the wind. The old crone who lived in the house gave him directions to the land of the dragon, in return for which Ivan the Pea promised to bring her some of the life-restoring water that the dragon owned.

Finally coming to the golden palace, which stood on one silver pillar, inside which his sister was being held captive, Ivan the Pea ignored his sister's pleas to run and save his own life, for his two brothers already lay dead in the vaults below. Instead, Ivan the Pea had the court smith make him a huge mace that weighed 500 *poods* (18,000 lb). This mace took forty hours to make and needed fifty men to lift it, but Ivan the Pea lifted it easily with one hand and tossed it high into the air. So high did it fly that it was three hours before it came down again. Ivan the Pea easily caught it with one hand, the impact not harming him in the least, although the mace did bend slightly. Ivan the Pea simply laid it across his knees and straightened it out again.

Shortly after the dragon arrived back at his palace and leapt at Ivan the Pea, but he simply sidestepped and killed the dragon with one throw of the mace, which flew through the palace walls and landed many hundreds of miles away. Ivan the Pea then found the WATER OF LIFE AND DEATH, filled a flask with it for the old crone in the forest, restored his brothers to life by sprinkling some of the water over them and then returned to his homeland with his sister and their brothers, stopping *en route* to deliver the flask to the old crone. After the death of his father, Ivan the Pea became the tsar.

Although the old crone living in the forest is not named in this story, it is generally agreed that she is none other than the witch BABA-YAGA.

Ivan the Sun's Son
Siberia – Tungus
Youth whose lost arrow was found by IVAN THE MARE'S SON, whom he agreed to live with as a brother. They were later joined by IVAN THE MOON'S SON. All three lived happily in a clearing in the forest, marrying magical maidens who used to fly down in heron skins and decorate the arrow of the Ivan they loved. However, a serpent came and started to feed on the blood of the wives. In an epic battle, all three Ivans were killed and their wives carried off to the UNDERWORLD[1] by the serpent.

Ivan the Mare's Son's mother restored all three of them to life, her son being lowered into the Underworld to rescue the three wives. Having killed the serpent and rescued the maidens, Ivan the Mare's Son was left for dead by his false brothers, who made off with all three women. Restored to life once more by his mother, Ivan the Mare's Son escaped from the Underworld, killed both Ivan the Moon's Son and Ivan the Sun's Son, and flew away with the three maidens to their homeland, where they lived their remaining days in peace and happiness.

Ivan the Terrible
Russian
Properly Ivan IV (1530–84), tsar of RUSSIA from 1533. His epithet comes from the Russian word *groznyi*, which signifies 'awe-inspiring' rather than

'terrible'. The grandson of IVAN THE GREAT, he was just three years old when his father, Grand Prince Vasily, died. Authority was at first in the hands of his mother, Elena, but she was murdered in 1537, after which time power fell into the hands of the BOYARS. Ivan assumed power in 1547 and became the first ruler of Russia to use the title 'tsar'. He progressively reduced the power of the nobility in favour of the minor gentry. From 1552 he embarked on a programme of expansion and subjugation. In 1581, in a fit of anger, he accidentally killed his oldest son, which meant that on his death three years later the throne passed to his sickly, feeble-minded second son, Fedor.

Ivanovich, Dunai
Russian
A knight, or BOGATYR, who, at a feast given by Prince VLADIMIR BRIGHT SUN, offered to travel to LITHUANIA, taking only his friend Dobrynya NIKITICH with him, to bring back the Princess EVPRAKSIYA, the daughter of the King of Lithuania, to be Vladimir's wife. When asked by Vladimir what he and his companion would need, he asked simply for an unbroken stallion for each of them, with bridles and whips that had never been used, and a letter stating their mission. So equipped, the two rode from KIEV to MOSCOW and then on to Lithuania. Arriving at the court of the King of Lithuania, Dunai Ivanovich left Dobrynya Nikitich in charge of the horses and entered the great hall, where he was cordially greeted.

However, when Dunai explained the purpose of their visit, the mood very quickly changed, for the King of Lithuania held Vladimir Bright Sun in very poor esteem. Just as Dunai Ivanovich was about to be dragged off to the dungeons, one of the king's men rushed into the hall to tell the King that

Dobrynya Nikitich was bludgeoning his men to death. Taking this as a divine sign, the King agreed and bade the three of them a safe journey.

That night, as they slept, they heard the sounds of a bandit nearby, but not once were they attacked. The following morning Dobrynya Nikitich and Princess Evpraksiya rode off towards Kiev, while Dunai Ivanovich tracked down the bandit that had been stalking them the previous night. When he finally caught 'him' up he knocked the stranger from 'his' mount and demanded to know where 'he' was going. Looking down, Dunai Ivanovich saw that the person he had knocked from the saddle was a woman.

This woman told Dunai Ivanovich that she was Princess NASTAS`YA, the sister of Evpraksiya. She had been hunting when the two men had left with her sister and she had set out in pursuit, aiming to rescue her sister from her abductors. So taken was Dunai Ivanovich with her courage that he spared her life and asked her to become his wife. Quickly they rode to Kiev and were married at the same service as Vladimir and Evpraksiya.

The wedding feast lasted twelve days, during which a great many boasts were made. Dunai Ivanovich boasted that he was the finest archer in the land. Nastas`ya challenged him and proposed a test of their skills with the bow and arrow. A silver ring was to be placed on the head of one of them and the other would then fire an arrow down the blade of a knife and through the ring without disturbing it. Dunai Ivanovich bade his wife to have the first go and three times she succeeded. Yet when it came to Dunai Ivanovich's turn, she pleaded with him not to attempt the feat, asking him to forgive her for the foolish challenge. When Dunai Ivanovich refused, she told him of their unborn child, a child with arms to the elbow that were pure gold and legs of silver from hips to knees. Stars clustered around his temples, from every hair on his head there hung a pearl, the moon shone from his back and the sun radiated from his eyes.

Unimpressed, Dunai continued with the challenge, dipping the point of his arrow into the venom of a poisonous snake. Failing to make the target, Dunai's arrow pierced Nastas`ya's heart. As she died, they cut the baby from her womb, and it proved to be every bit as wondrous as she had said. Grief-stricken, Dunai Ivanovich sank the butt of his spear into the ground and fell on its point. Two rivers sprang up from where husband and wife lay dead. One was the River Nastas`ya and the other was the River DUNAI, which is better known today as the River DANUBE.

Ivanushka
Russian

The brother of ALENUSHKA, Ivanushka was transformed into a kid after he drank from a lake near which some goats were grazing, even though he had been warned that this was what would happen to him by his sister. When Alenushka had been trapped at the bottom of the sea by an evil sorceress who had designs on her husband, Ivanushka pined for her by the edge of the sea. After the sorceress had persuaded the tsar to kill Ivanushka, having herself taken the guise of Alenushka, Ivanushka three times went to the edge of the sea to call for his sister. On the third occasion the tsar followed him and rescued Alenushka, with whom he returned to the palace, there killing the sorceress by throwing her on to a huge bonfire.

Ivashko
Russian

The youngest son of an old peasant couple who, against his parents' better judgement, persuaded them to let him go fishing. During the day his parents came to the water's edge and brought Ivashko food and drink. However, they did not go unobserved and the witch who witnessed everything set about trapping the young boy for her supper.

Rushing to the local smith, the witch made him, under threat of being eaten himself, forge her a voice so that she would sound just like Ivashko's mother. So supplied, she hurried back to the lake and called for Ivashko to come to the shore. When he did, she grabbed the boy and made off to her home in the heart of the forest. There she ordered her daughter ALENKA to heat up the stove and roast Ivashko while she went to gather her friends, for that night they would dine on fine young human flesh.

Alenka did as her mother told her and heated up the stove, but when it was time to put Ivashko in to be cooked, the young boy tricked the girl and instead it was she who was thrust into the heart of the stove. Ivashko left the house and hid in the canopy of the forest outside.

When the witch returned with her friends, she chided her daughter for leaving the house unattended but, smelling that their meal was ready, she and her companions ate until there was nothing left apart from a few well-picked bones. After they had eaten, the witch rolled around joyfully on the grass outside her home shouting with glee about how much she had enjoyed roast Ivashko. From the top of the trees Ivashko whispered that the witch had enjoyed roast Alenka. Looking up, the witch saw Ivashko and tried to shake him from the trees, but Ivashko hung on.

Furious that she had been tricked, the witch started to gnaw at the trunk of the tree, but got only half-way before she broke her two top front teeth. Rushing to

the smith, she had him fit her with steel teeth. Back at the tree, she started to gnaw again, but now broke her two bottom front teeth. These too were replaced by the smith and the witch returned to her task. At last she gnawed through the tree, but Ivashko simply leapt to an adjoining one and the witch had to start all over again.

Just then a flock of swans and geese flew overhead and Ivashko called out to them to carry him home. Two flocks passed over but the third swooped down, picked up Ivashko and carried him back to his anxious parents.

Although the witch is not named in the story of Ivashko, most authorities agree that it is none other than BABA-YAGA, the best known of all Russian witches.

Ivo
Croatian

A hero who lived in Senj, which lies on the coast of CROATIA, opposite the island of Krk. On one occasion he was reputed to have routed 50,000 Turks with just 800 men. His death is recounted in a Croatian heroic ballad. His mother foresaw Ivo's death in a dream which she told the local priest. While in the church her son rode up to the door, his black horse covered in blood. Ivo himself was wounded in seventeen places, his severed right hand being held in his left. His mother helped him down from his horse and bathed his wounds, whereupon Ivo told her that he and his men had been returning from Italy with a vast treasure when they were ambushed three times by Turks. The first two ambushes Ivo and his men escaped from without loss. The third, however, cost Ivo all his men. As he finished the story and was blessed by the priest, Ivo died in his mother's arms.

Jafnhar

Norse and Teutonic

One of the three mysterious creatures GYLFI had a discussion with in ASGARDR, and from whom he learned the fundamentals of NORSE mythology. The other creatures are named as HAR and THRIDI.

Jarl

Norse and Teutonic

The son of HEIMDALLR, conceived during one of the god's many sojourns with mortals. He became the ancestor and progenitor of the race of warriors through his marriage to the aristocratic ERNA. Their youngest son was KONUR, the first king of DENMARK.

Jarngreipr

Norse and Teutonic

The name of the iron glove that belonged to THÓRR, some sources using the name to refer to a pair of gloves.

Jarnsaxa

Norse and Teutonic

The giant mistress of THÓRR and one of the nine WAVE MAIDENS, the daughters of ÆGIR. She was the mother of MODI and MAGNI by her lover.

Joan

British

Mythical Englishwoman who was alleged to have become Pope in 885 under the name of John VIII and was supposed to have given birth to a child during a papal procession. The myth was exposed as just that, a myth, during the seventeenth century.

John Barleycorn

British

A rustic god who was identified with the last sheaf of the harvest, and in that form was ritually burned as a sacrifice to ensure a good harvest the following year.

Jokul

Norse and Teutonic

One of the nine sons of NJÖRFE who, along with an unnamed brother, was the only one of the nine to survive a fight against the nine sons of VIKING, of whom only two remained alive: THORSTEN and THORER. Jokul killed the King of SOGN, banished Prince BELÉ and turned Princess INGEBORG into a hag. When Jokul came across Thorsten for the second time, he attempted to turn his evil magic against him, but was himself killed, his death releasing the spells under which he held the kingdom of Sogn and Princess Ingeborg.

Jól

Norse and Teutonic

The pagan midwinter festival that translates as Yule. The root meaning from which it is derived remains uncertain, though the chief suggestions connect it with the turn of the year, or an impression of a joyous festival such as Christmas. While very little is known of the original pagan festival, it appears to have been associated with cults of the dead and with fertility spirits.

Jonakur
Norse and Teutonic

The fourth husband of GUDRUNN and the father, by her, of HAMDR and SÖRLI.

Jörd
Norse and Teutonic

'Earth' and, according to Snorri STURLUSON in HEIMSKRINGLA, the daughter and wife of ODÍNN.

Jörmungandr
Norse and Teutonic

Alternative name sometimes used to refer to MIDGARDSORMR.

Jötnar
Norse and Teutonic

A generic term applied to giants, though whether this is just one race of giants, such as the FROST GIANTS, or all giants is unknown. Equally, the term might have been applied to the primeval giants such as YMIR, but as most beings in NORSE and TEUTONIC mythology seem to have been giants, it is likely that it was a term applied to every giant.

Jötun
Norse and Teutonic

The generic name given to the races of giants who were the sworn enemies of the gods and lived in JÖTUNHEIMR.

Jötunheim(r)
Norse and Teutonic

Mountainous region of south NORWAY that contains the highest mountains in Scandinavia: Glittertind at 8,000 feet and Galdhöpiggen at 8,050 feet. In mythology, Jötunheimr was the land of the giants, especially the FROST GIANTS, into which the second root of YGGDRASILL reached.

Joukahainen
Finno-Ugric

A thin LAPP who was foolish enough to challenge the power of VÄINÄMÖINEN, who chanted such powerfully magic songs that the earth trembled, huge boulders fragmented into small slivers, and copper mountains rocked. Väinämöinen changed Joukahainen's sledge into a lake, his whip into a reed on the shore of that lake, his horse into a river that fed the lake, his sword into a bolt of lightning, his bow into a rainbow, his arrows into hawks, his dog into a large boulder and his clothes into stars, clouds and water-lilies. Väinämöinen then cast the unfortunate Joukahainen up to his waist in a swamp. Leaving him there for a while, Väinämöinen returned and cast him into a meadow, and then finally threw him up to his armpits into a bog. Seeing no escape, Joukahainen promised that Väinämöinen should marry his sister AINO, but she threw herself into the sea rather than be forced to marry such an old man.

Released, Joukahainen swore he would have some form of revenge. Later, as Väinämöinen rode north for POHJOLA, Joukahainen ambushed him and shot his horse from under him, sending him tumbling headlong into the sea.

Jumala
Finno-Ugric

The supreme being, the creator to whom the oak tree was sacred. Jumala is possibly an ancient sky deity as his name is cognate with the word for dusk. Being the creator, and a sky deity, it has been suggested that Jumala was the father of ILMATER LUONNOTAR, who is known as the 'Daughter of Air' and the 'Daughter of Creation'. However, she is usually described as the daughter of ILMA. He was deposed and succeeded by UKKO as the head of the FINNO-UGRIC pantheon.

Juras Mate
Latvian
The sea goddess who was respectfully known as the MOTHER OF THE SEAS.

Juternajesta
Norse and Teutonic
The beautiful mortal maiden with whom SENJEMUNDR fell in love.

Jutes
General
Germanic people said to have originated in JUTLAND who later settled in FRANKish territory. Along with the ANGLES and the SAXONS, they invaded BRITAIN during the fifth and sixth centuries. The Jutes occupied Kent c. 450 and conquered the Isle of Wight and the opposite coast of Hampshire in the early sixth century.

Jutland
General
Peninsula of northern Europe that is separated from NORWAY by the Skagerrak and from SWEDEN by the Kattegat, with the North Sea to the west. The larger northern part today belongs to DENMARK, the southern part to GERMANY. Jutland is the assumed homeland of the JUTES, although this is by no means certain and Jutland may simply have been the region from where they embarked on their combined invasion of BRITAIN with the ANGLES and the SAXONS.

Kalevala
Finno-Ugric

The eponymous founder of the land of heroes, the exploits of whom are recounted in the KALEVALA. The land was transformed from a prosperous land into a paradise by the magical fragments of the SAMPO that VÄINÄMÖINEN managed to salvage after it had been smashed *en route* to Kalevala from POHJOLA.

Kalevala
Finno-Ugric

The chief source for the myths and legends of the FINNO-UGRIC peoples. The *Kalevala* is an epic poem that was compiled from earlier sources by Elias LÖNNROT in 1835. Being such a late compilation, it cannot be taken as a reliable source of the beliefs of the pre-Christian era, though, based on earlier material, it undoubtedly reflects them to some extent. The hero of the poem is VÄINÄMÖINEN, god of music and poetry.

Kalma
Finno-Ugric

The goddess of death and the dead whose name means 'Smell of the Corpse' and whose home was guarded by the monstrous SURMA, who at her order would seize and devour human beings with frightening speed.

Kalvaitis
Lithuanian

The divine smith who daily forges the new SUN[2]. He also makes a ring for the dawn goddess and a silver belt and golden stirrups for each of DIEVAS's sons, the DIEVO SUNELIAI.

kantele
Finno-Ugric

A kind of five-stringed lute that was made by VÄINÄMÖINEN from the jaw-bone of the huge pike that was rammed by his boat *en route*, with his brother ILMARINEN and the hero LEMMINKAINEN, for POHJOLA to steal the SAMPO from the Lady LOUHI. When Väinämöinen played the kantele all the people of Pohjola fell asleep, but the magical instrument was washed overboard while the three were making their way back to Kalevala with the sampo during a storm sent by the Lady Louhi that also smashed the sampo into tiny pieces.

Kapsirko
Russian

A poor but cunning peasant who, having been caught stealing firewood from his master, was threatened with being sent to the frozen wastelands of SIBERIA. However, his master decided that he would give Kapsirko a chance to redeem himself and set him a seemingly impossible task. Kapsirko was to steal his master's horse from a heavily guarded stable. He accomplished the task, but still his master was not satisfied, so next he told Kapsirko to steal his wife away from him.

Kapsirko achieved this by enticing the lady out of the house and bundling her into a sleigh he had waiting. He then made off with her down to a lake by which a VODYANOI, or water demon, lived. The *vodyanoi* asked Kapsirko to sell the lady to him, which Kapsirko did for a capful of money. The price was agreed and the *vodyanoi* made off into the depths of the lake with the lady, having told his servant to fill Kapsirko's cap with money. Being a cunning man, Kapsirko cut a hole in his cap and placed it on the sleigh for the water sprite to fill with money. The cap leaked everything that was placed into it into the sleigh, which was soon full with coins.

Kapsirko returned to his home and, with his new-found wealth, no longer needed to be subservient to his old master. However, after a few weeks his old master called him to his home, for he was missing his wife and wanted Kapsirko to get her back for him. He promised Kapsirko half his estate and a large amount of money if he succeeded. Kapsirko agreed and rode down to the shores of the lake, where he built himself a shelter and spent hours inside twisting a rope.

One day, while he was still working on the rope, a water sprite appeared and asked Kapsirko what he was doing. Kapsirko replied that he was making a rope from which he would make the demons of the lake swing after he had drained it of water. Quickly the sprite disappeared and repeated Kapsirko's threat to the *vodyanoi*, the water demon, and the chief of the demons and sprites who lived in the lake. He came to the surface and asked Kapsirko what he was doing. Again Kapsirko repeated his threat, to which the *vodyanoi* asked what Kapsirko wanted of him.

When Kapsirko said that he wanted his old master's wife back, the *vodyanoi* refused. Kapsirko then suggested three contests, the winner of all three to be awarded the lady. The *vodyanoi* agreed. The first test was to stand on the very

edge of the lake, where each would whistle as loudly as they could in an attempt to make the other fall into the water. The *vodyanoi* went first and Kapsirko almost fell, but when it was his turn he whistled loud and long, but also hit the *vodyanoi* with a club so that the water demon fell headlong into the water, apparently unaware that Kapsirko had hit him.

The second contest was to be a race, but Kapsirko derided the *vodyanoi*, saying that he had a grandson who could easily beat him. The demon accepted that Kapsirko's grandson was a hare and said that, as Kapsirko was so confident, maybe the hare should run rather than Kapsirko himself. Kapsirko readily agreed, for earlier he had trapped two hares. As the race started, Kapsirko let loose the first hare, which easily outran the *vodyanoi*. When the *vodyanoi* returned, severely out of breath, Kapsirko presented him with the second hare, which was as fresh as the newly formed dew.

The final contest was to be a wrestling match. Again Kapsirko tricked the *vodyanoi*, saying that his grandfather, an old bear, could easily beat the demon. The *vodyanoi* accepted this and was, of course, severely beaten as he attempted to wrestle the bear, who was not pleased to have been woken from his hibernation.

Finally the *vodyanoi* submitted and gave the lady to Kapsirko, who returned with her to his old master, who kept his promise and gave Kapsirko half his estate and a large sum of money.

Karacharovo
Russian
The village near MUROM that was the birthplace of IL `YA MUROMETS.

Kari
Norse and Teutonic
According to the ORKNEYINGA SAGA, Kari was the third son of FORNJOT, as well as

being the father of FROSTI, grandfather of SNÆR THE OLD, great-grandfather of THORRI and great-great-grandfather of Thorri's two sons, NOR and GOR, and daughter, GOI. Another version says that Kari was one of the sons of YMIR, his brothers being HLER and LOKI or LÓDURR, these three deities giving birth to the giants or monsters BELI, FENRIR, GRENDEL, GYMIR, HEL, MÍMIR, THJÁZI and THRYMR.

Karl
Norse and Teutonic
The son who was born of the union of HEIMDALLR and the mortal AMMA. He married SNOR, the pair becoming the progenitors of the peasant race.

Katya
Slavonic
A beautiful young peasant girl who had been orphaned and so inherited her parents' house. Over some time she grew conscious of the fact that she was being helped around the house by a DVOROVOI. As the years passed she was able to see him clearly – a handsome youth who had obviously fallen in love with her. Katya invited the spirit to live with her. He plaited her hair and made her promise never to undo his handiwork.

Some years later Katya realized that her lover was incapable of physical affection and, yearning for human love and affection, she met and became engaged to STEFAN. The night before her wedding, having bathed, Katya undid her hair, which had grown very long, and brushed it thoroughly before retiring. The following morning her neighbours broke into her house when their knocks went unanswered and found her still in bed. Her long hair had been twisted and knotted around her neck. She had fallen victim to the jealousy of her Dvorovoi lover and had been strangled with her own hair.

kaukai
Latvian
Subterranean spirits who are subordinate to, and ruled over by, PUSKAITIS.

Ketill
Norse
Legendary Norwegian, the hero of the *Ketils Saga Hoengs*.

Kiev
Russian
The capital of the UKRAINE and the third-largest city of RUSSIA. It lies on the confluence of the DESNA and DNEPR rivers. Founded in the fifth century, Kiev replaced NOVGOROD as the capital of Slav-dominated Russia in 882, and was the original centre of the Orthodox Christian faith after VLADIMIR I converted to Christianity *c.* 988. Kiev is the most important of the Russian cities to be mentioned in the Russian legends, as it is the seat of the court of VLADIMIR BRIGHT SUN.

Kikimora
Slavonic
A female domestic spirit who was sometimes described as the wife of the DOMOVOI. Depicted as having chicken's legs and a long beak-like nose, Kikimora could be propitiated to perform household chores for busy wives by washing the kitchen utensils in a brew made from ferns. She assisted only competent housekeepers; those who were lazy or sloppy would be punished – she would lose small items, spoil food and wake the children at night by tickling them.

Kipu-Tytto
Finno-Ugric
The goddess of sickness, best described as a hideous dwarf. She was the daughter of TUONI and TUONETAR, and the sister of KIVUTAR, LOVIATAR and VAMMATAR.

Kirbit
Russian

The tsar of an unnamed kingdom and father of the beautiful maiden Vasilisa KIRBIT`EVNA. His daughter was stolen from him by IVAN[4], whom it had been prophesied she would marry, and BULAT THE BRAVE. Giving chase, he alone survived the onslaught of Bulat. Gathering twice as many men did him no good, for Bulat killed them all again, leaving only Kirbit alive to mourn the loss of his daughter.

Kirbit`evna, Vasilisa
Russian

The beautiful daughter of Tsar KIRBIT. She lived in a tower with a gilded roof, from which she was abducted by BULAT THE BRAVE and IVAN[4], whom, it had been prophesied, she was to marry. *En route* she was kidnapped by the terrible KOSHCHEI THE DEATHLESS.

Bulat the Brave and Ivan came to the home of Koshchei to rescue her and, with her help, found out where Koshchei had hidden his soul, for without it he could not be killed. After Bulat the Brave and Ivan had successfully collected Koshchei's soul and killed him, Vasilisa returned with Ivan to his homeland, where, in fulfilment of the prophecy, she became his wife.

Kivutar
Finno-Ugric

The goddess of suffering, best described as a hideous dwarf. She was the daughter of TUONI and TUONETAR, and the sister of KIPU-TYTTO, LOVIATAR and VAMMATAR.

Kjalnesinga Saga
Norse and Teutonic

A late work that notably states that the fire in THÓRR's temple burned perpetually and was never to be allowed to go out, otherwise untold disaster would befall the people.

Knefrudr
Norse and Teutonic

A servant of ATLI who was commanded to kill the NIBELUNGEN, but did not carry out his instructions.

Kobold(s)
Norse and Teutonic

Variant name sometimes used to refer to DWARFS – somewhat ambiguously, as it can apply equally to dark and light dwarfs.

Konur
Norse and Teutonic

The first King of DENMARK, the youngest son of JARL and ERNA. He is reputed to have had the strength of eight men, could speak the language of the birds, douse fire, still the oceans, make sharp objects blunt and still troubled hearts.

Kormák
Norse

Legendary ninth-century poet and hero from ICELAND who is the subject of the *Kormáks Saga*.

Koshchei (the Deathless)
Russian

One of the most unpleasant of all the characters found in the Russian legends. Koshchei believed that he could not be killed as his soul was not kept within his body, being hidden away instead. Though the location of the hiding place can vary quite widely, the soul itself was usually hidden inside an egg. This egg was, in turn, inside a duck or another bird, which was inside a hare. The three were then hidden in some remote and inaccessible place, such as beneath a large oak tree or on an island in the middle of a huge ocean, or even under a tree on just such an island.

The egg is the symbol of life to many cultures, not just the Russian, as it is the female cell from which life will spring.

Birds' eggs, so fragile and easily broken yet containing the power to create new life, were held in awe and were usually presented to new parents upon the birth of a child. The iconography of the egg continues in many cultures, a particular example being the giving of highly decorated eggs at Easter, where they represent the resurrection of Jesus Christ.

Koshchei the Deathless finally met with his own death after he had kidnapped the beautiful Vasilisa KIRBIT'EVNA. BULAT THE BRAVE persuaded Vasilisa to find out where Koshchei kept his soul and, having uncovered it, Bulat returned to the forest home of Koshchei, broke the egg on his forehead and killed him.

kraken
Norway

An enormous round, flat, multiple-armed sea monster that is reputed to be over a mile and a half in circumference. The kraken would often be mistaken for a small island while it lay on the surface of the sea, basking, just off the coast of NORWAY, and caused a violent whirlpool when it submerged. It was first described in the 1750s by Bishop Pontoppidan, who reported that it had a huge back and long arms with which it dragged ships down to their destruction.

Kremara
Polish

The patron spirit of pigs and possibly the brother of KURWAICHIN.

Kriemhild
Teutonic

The TEUTONIC version of GUDRUNN. According to the NIBELUNGENLIED, it was Kriemhild who told HAGEN of the vulnerable spot on SIEGFRIED's back, the only place in his otherwise protected body where he could be killed. BRÜNHILDE had

Kriemhild make her husband, Siegfried, a shirt with a cross on it that would mark this one vulnerable spot, and then commissioned Hagen to stab and kill him before stealing the treasure of the DWARFS that Siegfried owned. Kriemhild herself killed Hagen after he refused to reveal the place where he had hidden the treasure, and then married ETZEL. When her new husband found out about the murder, he spurned her, so she killed him as well. Kriemhild eventually met her own death at the hands of HILDEBRAND[2].

Kronstadt
General

Known as SAARI in FINNO-UGRIC myth and legend, Kronstadt is located on Kotlin Island in the Gulf of FINLAND. Commanding the sea approaches to St Petersburg, the island has always been an important strategic site – a naval base was established there in 1703 by Peter the Great.

Krukis
Slavonic

The patron spirit of blacksmiths who also, according to some sources, watched over the welfare of domestic animals.

Kullervo
Finno-Ugric

A character from the KALEVALA who is described as a powerful but evil-minded warrior.

Kupala
Slavonic

The goddess of peace, water, magic and herbs who was, according to some sources, married to YARILO. The worship of Kupala involved ritual washing and the offering of flowers, which were thrown on to the water's surface. Curiously her rites also involved fire, for fire was considered to have the same purification qualities as water. Worshippers would run around fires and leap over the flames in order to purify themselves. Effigies of Kupala were also either burned or thrown into the water. Kupala has been equated by some with the Celtic goddess Beltane.

Kurke
Russian

The corn spirit who was conceived in the form of a cockerel. During harvest festival a young cockerel was sacrificed to Kurke and a few ears of corn were left standing in the field to feed it (cf. RUGIU BOBA).

Kurwaichin
Polish

The patron spirit of sheep and, according to some, the brother of KREMARA.

Kuu
Finno-Ugric

The MOON[3] god who was subordinate to UKKO and his consort AKKA. Kuu, the father of KUUTAR, appears to have been the brother of PAIVA, the SUN[3] god, OTAVA, the spirit of the GREAT BEAR, and ILMA, god of air and creation, though legends of the creation tend to suggest that both Kuu and Paiva were the grandchildren of Ilma.

Kuutar
Finno-Ugric

The daughter of KUU, the MOON[3] god. Her name simply means 'shining'.

Kuz`ma, Saint
Russian

Russian Orthodox saint who, according to some legends, was, along with Saint DEM`YAN, a smith who forged the first plough, although other versions of this legend name the two saintly smiths as Saint BORIS and Saint GLEB. The brothers Kuz`ma and Dem`yan, however, had nothing at all to do with smithing, for they were doctors who had been martyred. Their connection with the legends surrounding smiths stems simply from the fact that Kuz`ma sounds similar to the Russian word for a smithy, *kuznya*. As a result they became, in the Russian Orthodox calendar of saints, the patrons of smiths and craftsmen. Churches dedicated to them were often to be found in the parts of town where smiths and craftsmen carried out their business.

The plough reputedly forged by Kuz`ma and Dem`yan was of enormous proportions and was forged with implements of like size. The two smiths were reported to have used twelve golden hammers and tongs that weighed almost twelve *poods* (c. 430 lb). One particular story, of apparently Ukranian origin, tells how this plough was first used.

For some reason not told in the story, the people of southern RUSSIA angered God so greatly that he sent a fierce DRAGON[1] to wreak havoc throughout the land. Every day in a futile attempt to appease the dragon, a different family was obliged to sacrifice a son. Finally it came to the turn of the tsar to sacrifice his son, and even though many of his loyal subjects offered to send their sons in the place of the tsarevich, the dragon would not agree to this. Reluctantly the tsar led his son to the appointed place and left him to await his fate. While waiting, an angel appeared to the boy and offered him a means of escape. Teaching the tsarevich the Lord's Prayer, the angel told the youth to run as fast as he could, all the time reciting the Lord's Prayer.

For three days and nights the boy ran as fast as his legs would carry him, continually reciting the prayer, for every time he stopped his recitation, he could feel the hot breath of the dragon on his neck. Finally, on the fourth day, almost totally exhausted, he came to the smithy where Kuz`ma and Dem`yan were putting the finishing touches to the first plough mankind would have. The boy ran straight into the smithy and the two saints sought to protect him, immediately slamming the massive iron doors closed.

Outside, the dragon demanded that the two saints relinquish the boy so he could meet his allotted fate. The saints refused, so the dragon licked the iron doors, his tongue penetrating them on the fourth lick. However, as the dragon's tongue appeared through the doors the two saints caught hold of it with their red-hot pincers and, thus captive, they harnessed the dragon to the plough and made him plough a deep furrow, the great mounds of earth that this threw up becoming thereafter known as 'dragon's ramparts'.

Kuz`ma and Dem`yan were also, as the magical smiths of legend, able to forge things other than purely metal objects. In their wedding songs, Russians would ask them to forge a wedding with links so strong that they would last for ever. In this way Kuz`ma and Dem`yan also came to be regarded as the patron saints of marriage.

Kvase
Norse and Teutonic
The name used by Snorri STURLUSON to refer to KVASIR.

Kvasir
Norse and Teutonic
A mysterious being of such wisdom that he could answer any question put to him. He was created when both the ÆSIR and the VANIR spat into a cauldron. A short while later he was killed by two DWARFS named FJALR and GALR, who used his blood, which they mixed with honey, to brew the MEAD OF INSPIRATION, which ODÍNN later stole and took to ASGARDR. Whoever drank the brew was immediately inspired with wisdom and composed wondrous poetry. Thenceforth the

magical liquid was known either as KVASIR'S BLOOD or the SHIP OF THE DWARFS.

Kvasir's Blood
Norse and Teutonic
One of the names by which the MEAD OF INSPIRATION came to be known after it had been stolen from the DWARFS who had brewed it by ODÍNN and taken back to ASGARDR. It was also euphemistically known as the SHIP OF THE DWARFS. Anyone who drank the potion, which had been brewed from a mixture of the blood of KVASIR and honey, was immediately inspired to compose great poetry and was filled with immense wisdom.

Kvenland
Norse and Teutonic
According to the ORKNEYINGA SAGA, Kvenland and FINLAND were the dominion of FORNJOT.

Kylli
Finno-Ugric
A maiden who lived in SAARI (KRONSTADT) and who had a love of dancing. She was wooed by LEMMINKAINEN, the son of LEMPI, and eventually agreed to marry him on an exchange of promises. Lemminkainen promised that he would not go on any further warlike expeditions. In return Kylli promised that she would no longer go to any village dances. However, while Lemminkainen was away she broke her part of the bargain, thinking that her husband would not find out. She was seen going to the dance by Lemminkainen's sister AINIKKI, who reported her actions to her brother. Lemminkainen divorced Kylli and set out to woo the Maid of POHJA.

Kyllikki
Finno-Ugric
The mother of LEMMINKAINEN. Long after

her son had left home, having married and divorced KYLLI, Kyllikki noticed blood flowing from her son's hairbrush. Realizing that some harm had befallen him, she inquired as to his whereabouts and was told that he had travelled to POHJOLA to woo the Maid of POHJA. Having gone there herself, Kyllikki was told by LOUHI that Lemminkainen had been sent to shoot a swan of TUONELA. The SUN[3] described her son's fate to her.

Journeying to Tuonela, Kyllikki gathered together all the scraps of her son's body with a long rake. These she rejoined and healed, but the body remained lifeless. Kyllikki therefore summoned a bee and asked it to fetch her some honey from the woods, from METSOLA's meadows and then more from beyond the highest heaven. The bee did as requested and Kyllikki took the honey and anointed her dead son's corpse, which immediately came back to life.

Lada
Slavonic
The goddess of beauty.

Lædingr
Norse and Teutonic
The name of the first chain that was used by the ÆSIR in their three attempts to secure FENRIR.

Lærad
Norse and Teutonic
The name given to the topmost branch of YGGDRASILL that is sometimes erroneously used to refer to the WORLD TREE[2] itself.

Laima(-Dalia)
Lithuanian
The goddess of fate to whom lime trees were sacred. Her name is cognate with *laim*, happiness, and she was sometimes referred to as Laima-Dalia, meaning 'Happiness-Fate'. She controlled the fate of all forms of life, animal, plant and human. Some stories refer to three, or even seven, goddesses of fate, but Laima is usually conceived as a single deity.

Lame
Russian
One of the two servants of WHIRLWIND. He and his companion, ONE-EYE, are so called because that is exactly what they were. Bestowed with magical powers, they helped IVAN[1], after he had killed Whirlwind, to return to his home and once there complete the tasks set by ELENA THE FAIR that were to uncover the treachery of Ivan's brothers, PETER and VASILII[1].

Landvidi
Norse and Teutonic
The hall of the god VÍDAR within ASGARDR.

Lapland
General
Region of Europe that lies within the Arctic Circle and covers parts of NORWAY, SWEDEN, FINLAND and RUSSIA without political definition. For further information, see pages 15–16.

Lapp(s)
General
Name given to the inhabitants of LAPLAND, of whom there are about 20,000 today.

Latvia
General
One of the three BALTIC countries, along with LITHUANIA and ESTONIA. Latvian is one of the two surviving Baltic languages; the other is Lithuanian, Estonian having become extinct. For further information, see page 14.

Laufeia
Norse and Teutonic
Also NAL. The reputed mother of LOKI.

Laukpatis
Lithuanian
The patron deity of agriculture whose

name means 'Lord of the Fields'. He is sometimes wrongly called LAUKSARGIS, the name of his subordinate.

Lauksargis
Lithuanian
A patron deity of agriculture whose name means 'Guardian of the Fields'. He was subordinate to LAUKPATIS, whose responsibilities were for all aspects of agriculture. Lauksargis, on the other hand, had the specific task of protecting crops and livestock while in the fields, hence his name.

Lawkapatim
Polish
One of the three patron deities of the field, the others being DATAN and TAWALS.

Lazar
Serbian
The sole survivor of an attack by invading Turks. All the people of his village in southern MACEDONIA escaped into a tunnel in the hills – all, that is, except a single girl. She laughed at the invaders, telling them that the villagers had eluded them, but made the mistake of revealing their whereabouts. The Turks lit fires at the entrance to the tunnel and asphyxiated all those inside with the exception of Lazar, who pressed himself into the ground and crawled with such force that his tracks became the bed of a stream which flowed through the mountain and into the next valley. Lazar founded the village of Lazaropolje at the spot where he crawled from the hillside.

Leiptr
Norse and Teutonic
One of the icy rivers that flowed from HVERGELMIR, on whose banks oaths were taken.

Leire
Norse and Teutonic
The location to where GEFJUN travelled to live with SKJOLDR, ODÍNN's son and the first king of DENMARK.

Lemminkainen
Finno-Ugric
Also known as AHTI[2], Lemminkainen was the son of KYLLIKKI and LEMPI. A lively and mischievous youth, he wooed the lady KYLLI of SAARI, who eventually agreed to marry him on an exchange of promises. She promised that she would no longer attend village dances if he promised not to go on any more warlike expeditions. However, when Lemminkainen was away one day, Kylli broke her word, thinking that her husband would not find out. However, she was seen going to the dance by AINIKKI, Lemminkainen's sister, who reported what had happened to her brother. Lemminkainen divorced Kylli and set off to POHJOLA to woo the Maid of POHJA.

Arriving in Pohjola, a dark land, he drove all the men out except for a blind old cowherd called MÄRKHÄTTU, who seemed so wretched that Lemminkainen felt pity for him, much to Märkhättu's anger. Having assured himself of no competition, Lemminkainen asked LOUHI for the hand of her daughter. She set him three tasks to test his suitability. The first was to capture the ELK OF HIISI, which he did. Next he was to catch the second of Hiisi's magical beasts, a fire-breathing horse. This Lemminkainen also succeeded in doing. Finally he was to shoot a swan on TUONELA's river.

However, as Lemminkainen approached the river the cowherd Märkhättu lay in wait for him. Sending a water serpent to attack Lemminkainen, Märkhättu waited until the hero was quite dead before throwing him into the river, where TUONI's son hacked him into five pieces before hurling them into a vicious whirlpool.

At home Lemminkainen's mother, Kyllikki, realized that some harm had come to her son when she saw blood flowing from his hairbrush. Discovering that he had travelled to Pohjola, she also journeyed there, and was told that her son had been sent by Louhi to shoot a swan on Tuonela's river. The SUN[3] then told her exactly what had happened to Lemminkainen. Going to Tuonela, Kyllikki gathered together the remains of her dead son with a long rake. She rejoined and healed these pieces, but the body remained lifeless. She then asked a bee to fetch some honey from the woods, from METSOLA's meadows and from beyond the highest heaven. The bee complied, and when Kyllikki anointed her dead son's body, he was revived.

Lemminkainen later returned to Pohjola in the company of VÄINÄMÖINEN and ILMARINEN to steal the SAMPO. However, even though they managed to steal the sampo, thanks to the KANTELE of Väinämöinen sending the inhabitants of Pohjola to sleep, it was Lemminkainen who was responsible for waking them all up again when he broke into a loud and triumphant song.

Lempi
Finno-Ugric

The personification of love, the father of LEMMINKAINEN by KYLLIKKI, though whether he was also the father of AINIKKI, Lemminkainen's sister, is not recorded.

Lempo
Finno-Ugric

One of the three evil spirits which caused the axe of VÄINÄMÖINEN to slip and embed itself deep in his knee while he was carving a boat from the fragments of the spindle and shuttle of the Maid of POHJA. Lempo's companions were HIISI and PAHA.

Leontii
Russian

A priest from ROSTOV and the father of ALESHA.

Lerad
Norse and Teutonic

The name given to the very topmost branch of YGGDRASILL that hangs over ASGARDR and is the home of the eagle between whose eyes sits the falcon VEDFOLNIR. From that position the falcon can see everything that happens in each of the NINE WORLDS, his prime job being to relate what he has seen to the ÆSIR.

lesh~ii, ~y
Russian

A demon god who lived in the forest. In appearance a *leshii* was like an old man, but his skin was extremely wizened, usually blue because of his blue blood, and as rough as the bark on a tree – not that his skin could be easily seen, as he tended to be covered from head to foot with a long, shaggy coat of hair, almost always green in colour. His hair was long, unkempt and tangled, and he had strange, pale, protruding green eyes. Some representations of the *leshii* show him – for a *leshii* was almost always male – with horns and cloven hoofs. To make recognition easier for mere mortals, the *leshii* wore his shoes on the wrong feet and had no shadow.

The *leshii* had the ability to change his size and shape at will, and could appear and disappear in an instant. His flair for changing size meant that at one moment he could be small enough to hide behind a single blade of grass and the next be so tall as to tower above the tallest tree in the forest that was his home. The shape-changing ability of the *leshii* meant that he could instantly become any one of the animals in the forest, especially the wolf or the bear, who enjoyed his protection, or even a human.

As the *leshii* almost never left the forest, it was only those who entered the forest who were likely to encounter him. Since the *leshii* was the spirit that controlled the forest, people left him votive offerings in the form of eggs and pancakes. Particularly active in the spring, having hibernated through the long winter, the *leshii* enjoyed leading people astray in the thickest parts of his forest home. He could, however, be foiled by a traveller who removed all his clothes and put them on back to front, with his shoes on the wrong feet, thus imitating the *leshii*'s style of dress. Cowherds were even reported to have made pacts with *leshii* to prevent their cattle straying.

One such story tells of a peasant who built his smallholding in a remote and lonely part of the countryside. One night this peasant welcomed a passing traveller, fed him well and gave him a good bed to sleep on, and the next morning refused the man's offer of payment. The traveller then promised the peasant that from that day forth he would no longer have any trouble with his cattle. They would no longer wander off or be attacked by wild beasts, and no longer would the peasant have to tend them. Instead, all he had to do was chase them out of the yard every morning; every evening they would return well fed and give a plentiful supply of milk.

Everything went just as the traveller had said for three years, until one day the peasant could no longer quell his curiosity. Following his cattle out of the yard, he saw that they came to rest and started to graze on a lush meadow where they were watched over by an old crone who leaned heavily on her stick as she dozed, rocking gently from side to side. As the peasant spoke to her, the crone became still and then disappeared. Perplexed, the man went home, but from that day on the cattle once again needed his attention,

for the crone had been the *leshii*'s helper and the curiosity of the peasant had broken the spell that the traveller, a *leshii*, had cast.

While *leshiis* undoubtedly loved to lead people astray so that they became hopelessly lost, their favourite trick seems to have been the abduction of babies who had not been baptized, or had been left unattended. Young children who entered the forest, to fish or to gather nuts or berries, were particularly at risk from their antics.

In some regions there were whole tribes of *leshii*. Every spring they would run amok through the woods, yelling and screeching from the sheer pleasure of simply being alive. Every autumn, like the leaves on the trees among which they lived, they would die.

Líf
Norse and Teutonic
One of the two beings who will emerge from the cover of YGGDRASILL at the end of the RAGNARØKR to repeople the earth, the other being the woman LÍFDRASIR.

Lífdrasir
Norse and Teutonic
One of the two beings who will emerge from the cover of YGGDRASILL at the end of the RAGNARØKR to repeople the earth, the other being the man LÍF.

Lindormr
Norway
A land snake blown to gargantuan proportions becoming the sea serpent in the final stages of the mutation, the inveterate enemy of the HAVHEST.

Lit
Norse and Teutonic
A DWARF who got in the way of and was killed by THÓRR during the funeral of BALDR and NANNA. Thórr, angered that

he had been unable to launch HRING-HORNI, a feat that had had to be accomplished by the giantess HYRROKIN, kicked Lit on to the funeral pyre to perish alongside the bodies.

Lithuania
General
One of the three BALTIC countries, along with LATVIA and ESTONIA. Lithuanian is one of the two surviving Baltic languages, today spoken by in excess of 3 million people. The other is Latvian, Estonian having become extinct. For further information, see page 14.

Little John
British
One of the outlaw companions of ROBIN HOOD and thus one of the so-called MERRY MEN. His name comes from a joke made by Robin Hood when he was attempting to cross a fallen tree over a fast-flowing stream only to find his route blocked by a large man. When asked his name, the man replied that it was John Little, to which Robin Hood replied that it would be more appropriate if he were called Little John.

Lódurr
Norse and Teutonic
One of the three gods, the others being ODÍNN and HOENIR, who were walking along the seashore when they came across two trees that had grown from the armpits of the giant YMIR. From these they created the first man, ASKR ('Ash'), and the first woman, EMBLA (possibly 'Elm'). Odínn gave them their spirit, Hoenir gave them their intelligence and Lódurr bestowed on them their senses and their bodies. The three also created DWARFS 'like maggots in Ymir's flesh'. They then ordered the Night and the Day to drive across the sky in their chariots, as well as two blond children, the girl SUN[5] and the boy

MOON[5], who are pursued by two wolves that will eventually catch and devour them. This will bring about the end of the world and signal the start of the RAGNARØKR. It is now generally agreed that Lódurr is cognate with LOKI.

Lofn
Norse and Teutonic
A beautiful maiden who was one of the attendants of FRIGGA and whose specific role was to ease the path of true love.

Logi
Norse and Teutonic
The name assumed by Fire when he disguised himself to take part in an eating contest with LOKI, one of the tests devised by UTGARDR-LOKI for Loki, THÓRR and THJÁLFI. Even though Loki had always eaten faster than anyone else could, Logi ate even faster and consumed not just the trough full of food but also the bones of the meat and the trough as well. Some sources name Logi as Utgardr-loki's cook.

Lohengrin
Teutonic
The son of PARSIFAL, the hero of a late-thirteenth-century legend upon which Richard WAGNER based his opera *Lohengrin* (1845–8). Lohengrin came to the aid of ELSA OF BRABANT, summoned from the GRAIL temple and transported to her realm in a swan-boat drawn by an angel. There he defeated her suitor, Frederick de TELRAMUND, and married Elsa, though he warned her that she must never ask his name. Having borne Lohengrin two children, Elsa finally asked the taboo question and Lohengrin was immediately borne away again in the swan-boat. Lohengrin subsequently married the Princess BELAYE, but was murdered by her parents who thought that their daughter was held under an enchantment. Belaye died of grief and the

name of her country was changed to Lothringen (Lorraine) in his honour.

Lokasenna
Norse and Teutonic

A relatively late work that is alone in supporting the view that LOKI was the murderer of BALDR. A point worthy of note from this version of the story is the inclusion of the mistletoe, a plant that is not native to ICELAND, the home of Snorri STURLUSON. This may be the result of a misunderstanding by Sturluson of his sources, for NORSE tradition says that there was once a wonderful sword called MISTILLTEINN ('Mistletoe'), and SAXO GRAMMATICUS alludes to Baldr being killed with just such a magical weapon. However, further confusion may arise from the shaping of the mistletoe into a dart, for this could derive from a version of the story of Baldr which says that he was killed by a charmed stick being pointed at him, a common and well-known feature of the art of the SHAMAN, which is referred to several times in association with ODÍNN, Baldr's father.

Lok~i, ~e
Norse and Teutonic

A minor fire god, one of the ÆSIR, but one of the most brilliant, devious and ambiguous of all the immortals, as well as the father, by ANGRBODA, of the wolf FENRIR, the serpent MIDGARDSORMR, who is sometimes called JÖRMUNGANDR, and HEL, the goddess of the UNDERWORLD[4]. A blood brother of ODÍNN, Loki was a handsome and loquacious seducer and an inveterate schemer. He had an endless talent to amuse, a sly sense of humour and never stopped talking, though his main attributes can be described only as demonic. While he outwardly supported his kith and kin, he never stopped seeking new ways to discomfort them and in this he was frequently successful. His charm

seems to have been irresistible and his double-dealing knew no bounds – he once betrayed even the mighty THÓRR, though he also accompanied the god to recover his mighty hammer, MJOLLNIR, which had been stolen by THRYMR.

Loki also accompanied Thórr and THJÁLFI to UTGARDR, a giant realm. Having reached the great hall of the king, UTGARDR-LOKI, the three of them were invited to display their skills to the king, who commented disparagingly on their puny appearance. Loki was pitted against a character named LOGI in an eating contest, and while Loki ate quickly, Logi ate even faster and consumed not only the food but also all the bones as well, and even the trough. Utgardr-loki later revealed that Loki had been pitted against the incarnation of fire.

His malicious nature could not be controlled and eventually overflowed at a banquet held by ÆGIR to which all the gods had been invited, except Loki, since by that time he had succeeded in infuriating all the Æsir. However, just as the banquet was really getting going, the doors of the hall flew open and there stood Loki, demanding a place. Ægir asked the gods to vote whether or not Loki should be admitted, the vote of Odínn swinging the result in Loki's favour. Yet no sooner had he taken his seat at the table than he started a tirade that ridiculed each and every god present. Having successfully destroyed the reputation of all of them, Loki then turned his attention to the goddesses.

Thórr's wife, the faithful, innocent SÍF, whose golden hair Loki had once stolen, came to the garrulous god with a cup of mead and pleaded with him to hold his tongue. Loki simply retorted by announcing in a loud voice that he had held Síf, naked and acquiescent. However, as he mentioned Thórr's name the hall was filled with the sound of Thórr's approaching chariot. The god strode into the hall and raised Mjollnir above Loki, who immediately backed off. As he was sidling out of the great hall, he turned back to the assembled company and prophesied the RAGNARØKR, the time when the rule of the gods would come to an end and the world would be destroyed by the forces of evil.

Loki is perhaps best remembered for his involvement in the death of BALDR, the best loved of all the gods, who had been rendered invulnerable to all things except mistletoe. Loki sharpened a dart of mistletoe, which he gave to the blind HÖDR and then guided that god's arm so that the dart struck home, Baldr immediately falling dead. Later, after the gods had sought to bring Baldr back from the Underworld but failed, because the giantess THOKK refused to weep at his death, the gods chased after Loki as they felt certain that he had disguised himself as Thokk, thus assuring that Baldr would have to remain in NIFLHEIMR. Loki fled and changed himself into a salmon in an attempt to escape. Eventually, however, he was netted and made to pay for his complicity in the death of the god by being tied over three stones with the entrails of one of his sons, a serpent being placed above him so that venom from its open mouth dripped into his face. SIGYN, Loki's devoted wife, attempted to keep the poison out of her husband's face by catching it in a bowl, but every time she went to empty the contents the venom fell back into Loki's face. The agonizing pain caused him to writhe, and it is that writhing that makes the earth tremble. Loki will have to remain in this terrible position until the Ragnarøkr. When that disastrous time comes, Loki will be at the helm of the ship NAGLFARIB, which is made of dead men's nails. This ship he will sail across the waters that flood the surface of the earth, bringing with him the first of

the FROST GIANTS to attack Asgardr. Finally Loki will be pitted against HEIMDALLR and they will kill each other.

Lönnrot, Elias
General
A Finnish philologist and folklorist (1802–84) who was born in Sammatti in Nyland. He studied medicine and was a district medical officer for twenty years in Kajana. During this time he carried out extensive folklore studies, and this led to his being appointed professor of Finnish at Helsinfors (today Helsinki) in 1853; he held the position until 1862. His major achievement was the collection of popular oral lays, which he organized into a long, connected poem of ancient life in the far north. This poem, the KALEVALA, appeared in a shorter version in 1835 and a longer one in 1849. While the poem remains the greatest single source of pre-Christian FINNO-URGRIC beliefs, it cannot be regarded as wholly reliable, as Lönnrot undoubtedly applied a fair degree of artistic licence to his research to complete the poem in a literary style.

Lonzaric, Petar
Croatian
A notorious gambler from the thirteenth century who was playing cards outside the church of Saint Vid in Rijeka (Vid being the Slav form of Vitus) and losing badly. Enraged by his bad luck, he began to blaspheme, blaming the saint for his misfortune. Throwing yet another losing hand of cards on to the ground, he raced into the church and began hurling accusations at God. Not content with that, he snatched up a large stone and hurled it at the crucifix hanging above the altar. The figure on the cross began to bleed and Petar Lonzaric suffered divine retribution for his actions. As he left the church, the ground opened up and swallowed him – except for one hand, which remained

thrust from the ground in a spasm of death. The governor of the city ordered the hand to be sliced off and cremated.

This legendary event is commemorated in the church, where a bronze hand dangles from the cross above the altar, and a stone is attached to the figure of Christ with an inscription to the effect that the attack of Petar Lonzaric took place some time in 1296.

Lorelei
Teutonic

A large rock or cliff on the River RHINE near Sankt Goarshausen in Germany about which a famous legend exists concerning the remarkable echo. A beautiful maiden called Lorelei was said to have drowned herself in despair at that spot, only to rise as a nymph who would sit on the rock combing her hair as she sang to lure sailors to their deaths. She features in several notable poems, including '*Die Lorelei*' by the Romantic poet Heine. The Lurlei Rock to the south of Koblenz is some 430 feet high.

Lorride
Norse and Teutonic

One of the daughters of THÓRR.

Louhi
Finno-Ugric

The ruler of POHJOLA and mother of the Maid of POHJA. She promised the hand of her daughter to LEMMINKAINEN if he could complete three tasks. The first and second, being the capture of HIISI's two magical beasts, Lemminkainen successfully completed. The third, to shoot a swan on TUONELA's river, he did not complete as MÄRKHÄTTU ambushed and killed him.

Later Louhi promised VÄINÄMÖINEN the hand of the Maid of Pohja if he would forge for her a SAMPO, giving him a horse and sledge to take him back to his own

land, KALEVALA. There, Väinämöinen had his brother, the divine smith ILMARINEN, forge the required item. Ilmarinen took the sampo to Louhi in Pohjola, and there married the Maid of Pohja, even though Louhi advised her daughter to marry the much older Väinämöinen. Following the death of the Maid of Pohja, Ilmarinen returned to Pohjola to ask Louhi for the hand of her other, unnamed, daughter. Louhi refused, so Ilmarinen abducted the girl, who was unfaithful to him, so he turned her into a seagull.

Later, Väinämöinen, Ilmarinen and Lemminkainen came to Pohjola to steal the sampo for their own land, as its magical properties had transformed Pohjola into a land of plenty. Louhi raised a terrible storm to pursue the three thieves, during which the sampo was smashed, but Louhi eventually had to give way to the powers of Väinämöinen and the remains of the sampo.

Loviatar
Finno-Ugric

A hideous dwarf, swarthy-faced and crinkle-skinned and the source of all evil, she was the most terrible of all of the daughters of TUONI and TUONETAR, her sisters being KIPU-TYTTO, LOVIATAR and VAMMATAR. She became, by the WIND[2], the mother of nine monsters: PLEURISY, COLIC, GOUT, TUBERCULOSIS, ULCER, SCABIES, PLAGUE, CANCER and ENVY.

Lygni
Norse and Teutonic

The king who wanted to marry HIORDIS but was rejected by her in favour of SIGMUNDR, a choice that was to prove fatal, for Lygni then marched his army against that of Sigmundr, who was killed in the battle.

Lytir
Sweden

A Swedish god who is referred to in the FLATEYJARBÓK. It is now thought that Lytir may have been a title of FREYR as, like that god, Lytir was also taken around in a cart or covered wagon. The *Flateyjarbók* tells how King EIRÍKR INN SIGRSAELI drove the wagon to a certain place and then waited until the cart grew heavy, a sign that Lytir had arrived. The king then drove the cart back at speed to his royal hall, where he welcomed the god and consulted him.

Lytuvonis
Lithuanian

In LITHUANIA, god of rain.

Maan-Eno
Estonian

In ESTONIA, the name for AKKA, the consort of the supreme being UKKO and joint creator of man.

Macedonia
General

Ancient Macedonia occupied parts of Greece, Bulgaria and the former Yugoslavia. Today there are, in effect, two Macedonias. One is a mountainous region of northern Greece and the other is now an independent country formed from the former federal republic of Macedonia that was part of former Yugoslavia.

Mader Akka
Finno-Ugric – Lapp

The wife of MADER ATCHA, she was responsible for the creation of the body of man, while her husband created the soul. Mader Akka is the LAPP equivalent of the deity otherwise known in FINNO-UGRIC mythology simply as AKKA.

Mader Atcha
Finno-Ugric – Lapp

The divine creator, husband of MADER AKKA. He created the soul, the life force of man, while his wife created the body. Mader Atcha is the LAPP version of the supreme being otherwise known in FINNO-UGRIC mythology as UKKO.

Madoc, Prince
British – Wales

Legendary prince of Gwynedd, Wales, who was alleged to have discovered the Americas and to have been a direct ancestor of light-skinned, Welsh-speaking Indians in the American West.

Mælare
Norse and Teutonic

Lake at OLD SIGTUN, modern Sigtuna on the Uppsalfjord, where, according to Snorri STURLUSON, ODÍNN moved his palace after having made peace with King GYLVE through the offices of GEFJUN. There Odínn built a great temple and performed sacrifices according to the customs of the ASALAND people, before giving dominions to each of the DIAR.

Mælstrom
Norse and Teutonic

The primeval whirlpool whose name has passed into modern usage.

Magni
Norse and Teutonic

Son of THÓRR by the giantess JARNSAXA, Magni is said to own a part of MJOLLNIR, his father's mighty hammer, and will be one of those to survive the RAGNARØKR, along with his brother MODI, when they will take possession of Mjollnir.

Maid Marian
British

The legendary companion of ROBIN HOOD. She was said to have been of noble birth, some versions of the story going so far as to say that she was a relative of the absent but true king of England. Having suffered at the hands of the SHERIFF OF NOTTINGHAM, Maid Marian joined Robin Hood and his MERRY MEN in SHERWOOD FOREST as an outlaw, and there remained until the throne was restored to the rightful king. Popular versions of the story say that she then married Robin Hood.

Majas Kungs
Latvian
In LATVIA, god of the home, a version of ZEMEPATIS.

Major Oak
British
The name given to a large oak tree in the middle of SHERWOOD FOREST that legend makes the headquarters of the band of outlaws under the leadership of ROBIN HOOD, his so-called MERRY MEN, who stole from the rich and gave to the poor to save them from the oppression of the SHERIFF OF NOTTINGHAM.

Malaran
Sweden
Lake that was supposedly formed when GEFJUN ploughed the island of SJÆLLAND out of SWEDEN, the resulting hole quickly filling with water. Since the shapes of the lake and the island bear no resemblance to each other, this cannot be true.

Mana
Finno-Ugric
An alternative name for TUONI, lord of the dead, which gives rise to the variant MANALA for TUONELA, the land of the dead.

Manala
Finno-Ugric
The land of MANA, an alternative name for the dark land of the dead, TUONELA.

Managarmr
Norse and Teutonic
A wolf, the offspring of JARNSAXA and FENRIR.

Manaheimr
Norse and Teutonic
A term sometimes used to refer to MIDGARDR, the domain of mankind that is also known as SWITHIOD THE LESS. The term appears to be fairly late, possibly post-Christian, and was probably brought into use at about the time that GODHEIMR began to be used to refer to ASGARDR.

Mani
Norse and Teutonic
A minor MOON goddess who drove her horse ALSVIDUR ('All Swift') across the sky every night. Tradition says that she saw the way HIUKI and BIL were being treated by their father and brought them up to her domain to save them, making them her water-bearers.

Mannigfual
Norse and Teutonic
A massive ship that, according to a FRISIAN tradition, was owned by the giants. Its scale can be assessed from the fact that youths told to climb the masts were old men by the time they got back down again.

Mannu
Finno-Ugric
The spirit of the earth, though not necessarily MOTHER EARTH. Some have suggested that as the dead are usually buried, Mannu led to the variant name for the lord of the dead, TUONI, and thence led to the variant of MANALA for TUONELA. This theory has never been substantiated.

Mara
Norse and Teutonic

The personification of the nightmare and the form in which the NORSE witch or succubus often chose to haunt male victims.

Marfida
Siberia – Tungus

The wife of IVAN THE MARE'S SON. One of three sisters who used to fly, wearing heron skins, to decorate the arrows of Ivan and his two 'adopted' brothers, IVAN THE MOON'S SON and IVAN THE SUN'S SON. When Ivan the Mare's Son hid the heron skins, she swore to marry him. Her sisters married the other two Ivans.

All was well until a serpent started to visit their home during the day and suck their blood. All three Ivans were killed during a battle with the serpent, who carried Marfida and her sisters off to its UNDERWORLD[1] lair. Ivan the Mare's Son was restored to life by his mother, along with his two brothers. Lowered into the Underworld, he killed the serpent and rescued the three maidens. However, Ivan the Moon's Son and Ivan the Sun's Son left him in the Underworld and made off with all three women. Ivan the Mare's Son, restored to life once more by his mother and rescued from the Underworld, killed his false brothers. Making himself wings from feathers plucked from the heron skins he had hidden, he flew away with Marfida and her sisters to their homeland.

Marfusha
Russian

The oldest daughter of an ageing peasant, stepdaughter to his second wife and stepsister to two younger daughters of the couple. Although the favourite of the man, Marfusha was hated by her stepmother, who made her do all the household chores, calling her lazy and idle, even though her own two daughters did nothing from morning to night. Finally the stepmother decided that Marfusha should marry. One winter's morning she made the girl carry all her belongings to the sleigh and told her browbeaten husband to take the girl out into the forest, where she was to be left for her husband to come and greet her, the husband she had chosen for the girl being none other than MOROZKO, the FROST[1] demon.

Saddened by the almost certain death of his daughter, the man obeyed his wife and left Marfusha in the middle of the forest. Growing colder by the minute, Marfusha heard Morozko approaching. As he arrived, he asked her three times if she was warm enough and each time, although frozen half to death, she replied that she was quite warm. Finally Morozko had pity on the girl, wrapped her in warm furs and gave her wondrous gifts.

The following morning the father reappeared, sure that he would be taking a frozen corpse back to the house. To his delight, he instead conveyed home the wondrously clothed Marfusha. The stepmother was horrified that her plan had backfired, but, seeing the finery that Morozko had bestowed on Marfusha, insisted that her own daughters must now be left in exactly the same place.

This they were, but when Morozko came to them, they both complained bitterly about the cold and he simply froze them to death. The name of only the oldest of these two girls is known: PARAKHA. When the father collected the bodies and took them home, his wife at first berated him for killing her daughters, but she was finally made to realize by her husband, who could no longer stand her scolding, that it was all her fault, and from that day his wife loved Marfusha and did all the work the unfortunate girl had been made to do before.

Marfusha finally married the son of a

neighbour and lived happily for many years, the gifts given to her by Morozko acting as her dowry.

Märkhättu
Finno-Ugric

A blind, ageing cowherd who lived in the land of POHJOLA. When LEMMINKAINEN drove all the men out of Pohjola, he took pity on Märkhättu, much to the old man's chagrin, and allowed him to remain. To have his revenge, Märkhättu lay in wait for Lemminkainen beside the river of TUONELA when LOUHI sent Lemminkainen there to shoot a swan. As the hero came to the river, Märkhättu released a water serpent, which killed Lemminkainen. Märkhättu then threw the body into the river, where it was cut into five pieces and thrown into a fierce whirlpool by TUONI's son.

Marko, Prince
Serbian

A historical figure in SERBIA who became a legendary hero. He was a man of enormous strength – his mace alone weighed more than 180 lb – and considerable cunning, with an inexhaustible capacity for alcohol. He was chivalrous, fearless and passionate, though he was also capable of the most ruthless brutality, even to women. Marko was in league with the supernatural mountain nymphs (see VILA) and owned a horse named SARAC, which was the fastest in the world and had the power of speech. Sarac, like his master, also had a considerable liking for alcohol, often sharing his wine with him.

Marko is described as a very large man, though whether he was a giant is open to speculation. He has very dark, almost black, eyes and a black moustache as large as a six-month-old lamb. He wears a *kalpak*, a fur hat, and a cloak made of wolf skins. Across his back is slung a spear and from his belt hangs a damascened sword.

From Sarac's saddle hang his huge mace and a large wineskin.

In poetry and popular tradition Marko was identified with resistance against the invading Turks, the exemplar of heroic valour and the embodiment of the spirit of true independence. In historical fact he became, like a good many other Serbs, a vassal of the Turkish invaders, fighting for the Sultan against the Christians at the Battle of Rovine in ROMANIA in 1394. Popular legend says that before that battle he prayed to God to give the Christians the victory, even if it meant that he lost his life.

Legend tells of his death in the following manner. One morning he was riding Sarac along a road when the normally sure-footed horse stumbled and wept, omens Marko immediately recognized as evil. Instantly a *vila* appeared and told him that as none could kill him and none should own Sarac but Marko, his time had come to die.

Marko knew this was a message from God and accepted that, having attained the age of 300, Sarac being 160 years old, their time of deliverance had come. Marko killed Sarac and gave his trusted friend an elaborate burial. He then broke his sword and spear, and threw his mace over the mountains and far out to sea before laying down to die.

A continuation of this legend says that a priest found his body and took it to Mount ATHOS, burying it there. A more popular belief says that Marko never died but instead, like King ARTHUR, sleeps in a cave in the mountains, to rise again in a time of great need. One BULGAR variant embroiders this, saying that Marko sleeps in the cave with his beard wound several times around him.

Marzanna
Polish

The goddess of fruit and fruit trees.

Mashen`ka
Russian

An eight-year-old girl who was abducted by a lonely bear. Though her parents feared she had been eaten, the bear simply wanted someone to live with him and keep him company. The bear felt sorry for Mashen`ka, because she pined for her parents, and told her to bake some pies for them which the bear would deliver. Mashen`ka baked the pies, then warned the bear not to eat any of them, saying that she would see him if he did, and quietly hid herself in the bottom of the basket.

On his way to the village where Mashen`ka's parents lived, the bear sat down to eat one of the pies. Inside the basket Mashen`ka warned him that she could still see him, so the bear hurried on his way. Three times this happened, until the bear reached the village and left the basket outside Mashen`ka's house before running back into the forest. As Mashen`ka's parents opened the basket, their daughter leapt out.

For some time Mashen`ka would not leave the house for fear of the bear returning. When it did, however, it came only to say goodbye and to forgive Mashen`ka for tricking him. As he left he threw a leather bag into the house. For several days neither Mashen`ka nor her parents would touch the bag, but in the end curiosity overcame them and, when they opened it, a large quantity of gold and silver coins poured out. From that day on Mashen`ka and her parents lived a life of ease.

Mati-Syra-Zemlya
Russian

The earth goddess, whose name is a title which means 'Moist-Mother-Earth'. She is not often referred to by name in the myths of ancient RUSSIA. She was often called upon to witness oaths and con-tracts, a common method being the placing of a handful of soil on the head before taking a vow. This made the vow sacred, for MOTHER EARTH could not be cheated. Her cult dated from very early times, as is inevitable in any agrarian society. However, unlike elsewhere, her cult did not develop.

Matushka
Russian

Matushka is the Russian for 'little mother' and was almost always used to refer to the River VOLGA.

Mauthe Dog
British – Manx (Isle of Man)

Variant name for the MODDEY DHOO.

Mead of Inspiration
Norse and Teutonic

A drink that was brewed from the blood of KVASIR by FJALR and GALR, the DWARFS who had murdered him. The dwarfs drained the blood into three containers, a cauldron called ODHROERIR and two bowls called BODEN and SONR. They then mixed the blood with honey and fermented the mixture. Anyone who drank the resulting potion was inspired with great wisdom and the ability to compose wondrous poetry. Eventually, to save their own lives, the dwarfs were obliged to give the brew to SUTTUNGR, the son of the giant GILLINGR, whom the dwarfs had mur-dered. It was subsequently stolen from Suttungr's daughter GUNNLOD by ODÍNN, who took it to ASGARDR in the form of an eagle, and thenceforth the concoction was known either as KVASIR'S BLOOD or SHIP OF THE DWARFS.

Medeine
Lithuanian

Goddess of the forest, whose name is known only from thirteenth-century texts.

Megingjörd
Norse and Teutonic

The BELT OF STRENGTH that doubled THÓRR's strength whenever he buckled it up.

Meness
Latvian

The MOON[4] god who is known as MENUO in LITHUANIA. Meness was said to have married the WEAVER OF THE STARS, though whether he had earlier marriages, as Menuo did in Lithuanian myth, remains unknown.

Menglod
Norse and Teutonic

A divine maiden, though perhaps not a goddess, who was wooed by the hero SVIPDAGR.

Menia
Norse and Teutonic

According to Snorri STURLUSON in HEIMSKRINGLA, Menia and FENIA were enormously strong giantesses who were brought to SWEDEN by FRODE to grind gold and bring good luck to both him and his domain. Other sources say that the giantesses were taken to DENMARK by King FRODI for the same purpose, the variation apparently being a confusion.

Menuo
Lithuanian

The MOON[2] god who is known as MENESS in LATVIA. Wearing a starry robe, he travelled across the night sky in a chariot drawn by grey horses. He married SAULE but later fell in love with AUSRINE, for which he was punished by PERKUNAS, who broke him into pieces.

Mephistopheles
Teutonic

The name given to the DEVIL, or the devil's advocate, in the legends of FAUST, and to whom Faust was alleged to have sold his soul in return for one moment of complete contentment.

Mermaid
General

Mythical female sea creature, the male version being the merman, having a human upper half and the tail of a fish rather than legs. Both the dugong and seals have been mooted as possible origins for the mermaid legends.

Merseburg Charm(s)
Teutonic

The name given to two pagan spells that name various TEUTONIC deities.

Merry Men
British

The name given to the band of outlaws who lived in SHERWOOD FOREST under the leadership of ROBIN HOOD.

Metsola
Finno-Ugric

The frost spirit who may also have been the goddess of the woodlands or of pastures. She appears in the myth of LEMMINKAINEN when KYLLIKKI summoned a bee to collect honey from Metsola's meadows with which she would anoint and so rejuvenate her son.

Middle Earth
Norse and Teutonic

The literal meaning of MIDGARDR, the domain of mankind that lies midway between ASGARDR and NIFLHEIMR.

Midgardr
Norse and Teutonic

Also MANAHEIMR. The region, surrounded by an unnavigable ocean, in which men live, it is also known as MIDDLE EARTH, the literal translation of Midgardr. The region was said to have been created from the carcass of YMIR, or AURGELMIR, the giant who had been killed by the ÆSIR deities ODÍNN, VILLI and VÉ. They placed the body of the giant in the centre of the universe to form the land itself. They then formed the lakes and the seas from his blood, the earth from his flesh, mountains from his bones, rocks and pebbles from his teeth, jaws and smaller broken bones, and the grass from his hair. From Ymir's eyebrows they built a wall around Midgardr to protect the region from the FROST GIANTS. They then took his skull and, supported at the four cardinal points by DWARFS whom they had also formed like 'maggots in Ymir's flesh', they formed the vault of the heavens.

Midgardsormr
Norse and Teutonic

A monstrous serpent, one of the offspring of LOKI and ANGRBODA. It was thrown into the sea by ODÍNN, its tail in its mouth, where it completely encircled the earth. This was not, however, the last contact any of the ÆSIR had with the serpent, though it was THÓRR who was always pitted against it.

On the occasion when Thórr, Loki and THJÁLFI travelled to UTGARDR, Thórr was matched against Midgardsormr by UTGARDR-LOKI, who disguised the serpent as a huge grey cat. Try as he might, Thórr could lift only a single paw of the monstrous animal, but while Thórr admitted defeat, Utgardr-loki seemed satisfied with his achievement.

Thórr had one other notable encounter with the serpent, though this time he knew exactly who he was up against. Taking the guise of a youth, Thórr invited the giant HYMIR to join him on a fishing expedition. Hymir readily agreed and went to fetch some bait. While he was gone, Thórr cut the head off Hymir's largest oxen, apparently concealing it on the boat before Hymir returned. Thórr then rowed out to sea at such a rate that Hymir began to fear for his safety, his consternation growing even greater as they rowed straight past the usual fishing ground until at last Thórr stopped and cast his line, which had been baited with the ox head. It wasn't long before Midgardsormr took the bait. Exerting all his strength, Thórr attempted to haul the serpent from the depths, something he was able to do only after he had stamped holes in the bottom of the boat and braced himself against the sea-bed. As the monster came to the surface Thórr lifted MJOLLNIR, but as the blow descended the frightened Hymir cut the line and Midgardsormr slipped back beneath the waves. Furious, Thórr swept Hymir over the side of the boat and then strode back to the shore, while Hymir floundered out at sea.

Thórr's contests with the serpent appear to be a NORSE version of a widespread myth of the storm or fertility god's struggle with a monster, the story of Utgardr-loki being told in the EDDA poem *HYMISKVIDA*. The underlying theme of the myths is, of course, the battle of good against evil, though Midgardsormr cannot always be regarded as evil, for if it did not encircle the earth the world would crumble and disintegrate. This is well illustrated by the fact that in neither of the above stories does Thórr actually manage to defeat the serpent, rather simply exerting his authority over it.

Only at the RAGNARØKR will the serpent break free and then the world will be destroyed. The great serpent will rise from the depths of the ocean, spouting venom. At the sound of HEIMDALLR's horn the gods will ride out of ASGARDR to do battle, Thórr against Midgardsormr, each one killing the other.

Mielkki
Finno-Ugric

The wife of the minor god of the woods

TAPIO and mother, by him, of NYYRIKKI and TUULIKKI. All four were invoked by huntsmen to aid them in making a good kill.

Mikula (Selyaninovich)
Russian

A legendary ploughman whose story appears to be fairly late, possibly fifteenth-century, though in foundation it appears to be much older and may have some historical background. This story illustrates quite clearly the way in which the peasants regarded their rulers, for the prince in this story, VOL`GA SVYATOSLAVOVICH, is much less of a hero than the humble Mikula, though Mikula is by no means an ordinary peasant.

Vol`ga Svyatoslavovich was the nephew and godson of Prince VLADIMIR BRIGHT SUN, Grand Prince of KIEV. His uncle had given him dominion over three towns, along with the peasants who lived in the surrounding lands. As was his right, Vol`ga could raise taxes from his subjects, and it was on one such trip around his domain that he came into contact with Mikula.

Riding out of the palace and into the countryside, Vol`ga and his entourage heard the sound of a ploughman whistling and calling to his horse, the sound of the plough cutting its furrow and the grating of the ploughshare as it struck a stone. However, no matter how fast they rode they were unable to catch the ploughman up. For two and a half days they rode hard, chasing the elusive sound, until finally they came upon him.

Whistling as he ploughed, the plough-man, Mikula, tore up tree stumps that lay in his path, roots and all, and cast aside huge boulders. The plough was pulled by a light bay mare and the plough itself was of maple with a coulter of damask steel, the share of silver, the handles of red gold and the tugs that coupled the plough to the mare were made of silk. Mikula himself is described as a man of tremendous masculine beauty, with eyes as keen as a falcon's, his hair worn in tight ringlets and his brows as black as sable. He wore a black velvet tunic, a soft felt cap and boots of green Morocco leather with extremely pointed toes and very high heels.

Mikula and Vol`ga exchanged good wishes, but when Vol`ga told Mikula the purpose of his journey the ploughman warned the prince of a band of robbers on his chosen route. These robbers lay in wait by a bridge over the River SMORODINA, where they cut through the planks of the bridge so that travellers fell into the water and were drowned. Mikula told the prince that he had been that way just three days previously and these robbers had attempted to waylay him as he travelled home carrying two skins filled with salt that weighed 100 *poods* (c. 3,600 lb) each. When the robbers had demanded money from Mikula to let him pass, he had laid 1,000 of them out.

Hearing this, Prince Vol`ga invited Mikula to join his party, which he was pleased to do, and unharnessed his horse. However, after a short while Mikula began to worry about his plough, for he had left it in the open and it might easily be stolen. Vol`ga sent five of his men back to hide the plough, but they could not even begin to move it. Ten men then went back, but they had no more success. Finally Vol`ga's entire company attempted to move the plough, but it still would not budge. Seeing this, Mikula walked into the field, lifted the plough from the ground with one hand and hid it himself behind a willow bush, after he had carefully cleaned it off.

With the plough safe, Mikula urged his little mare on. When it trotted, Vol`ga had to urge his steed into a gallop. When

Mikula gave his mare her head, Vol`ga was left far behind. Calling out for Mikula to stop, Vol`ga caught up with him and, having been suitably impressed with Mikula's strength and prowess, made him lord of his three towns and bade him collect the taxes in his place.

Milky Way

1 *Russian*

Russian peasants believed that the souls of their departed loved ones crossed the celestial bridge of the Milky Way to reach the MOON[1], which was to be their eternal abode.

2 *Lithuanian*

As in RUSSIA, the Milky Way, or BIRD'S WAY, was believed to be a bridge across which the souls or spirits of the dead travelled to reach their eternal abode, the realm of DAUSOS, which lay beyond the slippery high hill of the sky, though some equate Dausos with the MOON[2]. It was just one of the routes by which the departed could make the journey, other options open to them being to make the long climb up the slippery high hill of the sky, to ride on horseback, to travel in the smoke of the cremation fire or to travel in a boat such as that used every day by the SUN[2] as it made its way home at night.

Mime

Norse and Teutonic

The literal translation of REGINN, the divine smith.

Mimingus

Norse and Teutonic

According to the story of BALDR's death as related by SAXO GRAMMATICUS, Mimingus was a SATYR who lived in an OTHERWORLD kingdom and owned a magical sword which HÖDR required if he were to kill Baldr. Hödr travelled to the

kingdom, stole the sword and wounded Baldr, who died three days later.

Mim(m)ingr

Norse and Teutonic

A sword made by VÖLUNDR for his son HEIME. Other sources say that this sword was made by MÍMIR or MIMINGUS.

Mím(i)(r)

Norse and Teutonic

The origins of Mímir are a little confused. He may have originally been the giant who made the marvellous sword MIMMING, and in this case is perhaps cognate with MIMINGUS. However, he also has associations with the WELL OF URDR and YGGDRASILL, although his association with the Well of Urdr is differentiated from his own spring in Snorri STURLUSON's account, which is briefly as follows.

The spring of Mímir rose from beneath the second root of Yggdrasill in JÖTUNHEIMR, the land of the FROST GIANTS. Anyone who drank from this spring was immediately empowered with great wisdom. Though Mimir originated from the homeland of the great enemies of ASGARDR, he actually lived with the ÆSIR. Following the war between the Æsir and the VANIR, he was sent, along with the silent HOENIR, as the hostages called for by the truce between the two factions. However, as Hoenir never spoke, the Vanir felt that they had been cheated and so beheaded Mímir and sent his head back to Asgardr. ODÍNN, who had sacrificed one of his eyes for the right to drink from the spring of Mímir and was thus called the 'One-Eyed', sang a spell over the head which brought it back to life and gave it the power of speech, and from that day forth he consulted it in any crisis.

Mistillteinn

Norse and Teutonic

'Mistletoe', a wondrous sword that was

owned by various heroes, such as HROMUNDR GREIPSON. As the story of the death of BALDR includes the use of mistletoe, especially in the version where LOKI fashions the dart, it may well be, as SAXO GRAMMATICUS implies, that it was this sword that HÖDR stole from MIMINGUS in order to kill Baldr.

Mjollnir
Norse and Teutonic

THÓRR's war hammer that had been made for him by the DWARFS BROKK and SINDRI, and with which he protected ASGARDR from its enemies. While the hammer makes an appearance in almost all the stories surrounding Thórr, there are only two in which it is the central player.

In the first it is stolen by THRYMR, a FROST GIANT, who held it to ransom, saying that he would return it only if FREYJA married him. HEIMDALLR, usually silent but here either finding his voice or writing down his message, suggested that Thórr should disguise himself in a wedding veil and take the place of Freyja. Reluctant at first to wear female clothing, Thórr finally consented to play his part in the subterfuge and set off for JÖTUNHEIMR with LOKI.

The two were greeted rapturously by the giants. However, Thórr almost gave himself away at the wedding feast when he ate not only eight salmon but also an entire ox, and washed the lot down with three barrels of mead. Loki quickly explained that 'Freyja' had been unable to eat for eight days with excitement at the prospect of becoming Thrymr's wife. Again Loki explained away the staring eyes that the giant glimpsed through the veil when he stooped down to embrace his 'wife', this time saying that 'Freyja' had also been unable to sleep. Finally, as was the custom, Thrymr laid his wedding gift, in this case Mjollnir, in 'Freyja's' lap. Immediately, Thórr took hold of his

weapon, threw off his disguise and quickly disposed of Thrymr and all the wedding guests.

On another occasion the drunken HRUNGNIR boasted that he would not only sink Asgardr beneath the waves but also make off with Freyja and SÍF, challenging the furious Thórr to a duel in the process. To support Hrungnir, the Frost Giants made MOKKURKALFI ('Mist-calf'), a man of clay. So prepared, Hrungnir strode on to the field of combat brandishing a huge whetstone and carrying a stone shield. Thórr then advanced, wearing his iron gloves and his BELT OF STRENGTH, and brandishing Mjollnir. His attendant was THJÁLFI.

Hrungnir hurled his whetstone at Thórr, who simply replied by releasing Mjollnir, which smashed the whetstone into thousands of tiny pieces. One piece lodged itself in Thórr's forehead (see GRÓA) before continuing on its destructive path and smashing Hrungnir's skull.

Moddey Dhoo
British – Manx (Isle of Man)

Also called the MAUTHE DOG, this famous spectral hound was reputedly most often sighted at Peel Castle, Douglas, where it used to stand guard, terrifying both those who kept the castle and those who attacked it.

Modeina
Polish

One of the two patron deities of the forest, the other being SILINIETS.

Modgudr
Norse and Teutonic

The guardian of GJALLARBRÚ, the golden bridge that spanned the River GJALL and led to HELGRIND, the gates of the UNDERWORLD[4]. Described by some sources as a girl, though an exact description does not exist except that she was skeletal, she is said to have told HERMÓDR[1] of the crossing of BALDR in the company of five troops of dead horsemen. Her exact role remains uncertain. In some senses she served to admit the dead to NIFLHEIMR, while in others she appears almost like the Greek Cerberus, preventing the dead from leaving again.

Modi
Norse and Teutonic
One of the two sons of THÓRR and the giantess JARNSAXA, his brother being MAGNI. They will both survive the RAGNARØKR, after which they will possess their father's hammer, MJOLLNIR.

Modir
Norse and Teutonic
The wife of FADIR and mother, by HEIMDALLR, of JARL, which made her the progenitor of the race of warriors.

Mokerkjálfi
Norse and Teutonic
Alternative spelling of MOKKURKALFI.

Mokkurkalfi
Norse and Teutonic
Also MOKERKJÁLFI. 'Mist-calf', a giant man made of clay by the FROST GIANTS to support HRUNGNIR after he had, in a drunken stupor, threatened to sink ASGARDR and abduct FREYJA and SÍF, a threat he capped by challenging THÓRR to a duel.

Montenegro
General
A part of the former Yugoslavia, Montenegro was part of SERBIA from the late twelfth century until it became independent, under Venetian protection, when Serbia was defeated by the Turks in 1389. It was forced to accept Turkish suzerainty in the late fifteenth century, but was never completely subdued. A monarchy was founded in 1851 and Montenegro became a sovereign principality under the Treaty of Berlin in 1878.

Moon
1 *Russian*
Like the SUN[1] and certain elemental characters such as FROST[1] and WIND[1], the Moon is not usually given a name in the later Russian folk-tales. Earlier stories call him (or her, for the Moon is sometimes feminine) MYESYATS. Some say that the Sun and the Moon were brother and sister, and that every spring they would come together to talk about what they had been doing and what they had seen. Sometimes, however, the Moon would be angry with her brother and would block out his light. Such occurrences were usually short-lived, as the Moon could not remain angry for long, but the early peoples thought that the Moon first ate the Sun and then spat him out again. The Sun and the Moon both feature in the story of Raven RAVENSON, though this story has more to do with man's stupidity than with either celestial object.

The Moon is also widely regarded as an eternal abode for the souls of the dead, each soul crossing the celestial bridge of the MILKY WAY[1] to reach their final resting place.

2 *Lithuanian*
Like the Russians, the ancient Lithuanians believed that the souls of the departed crossed the BIRD'S WAY (the MILKY WAY[2]) to reach their eternal abode, the Moon. As the realm of DAUSOS was also considered the land of the dead, positioned as it was beyond the slippery high hill of the sky, this has led to conjecture that in LITHUANIA Dausos was the name for the Moon, though not a deification of

it. That honour was reserved for MENUO, who is described as having travelled across the night sky in a chariot drawn by grey horses while wearing a starry robe. He is known as MENESS in neighbouring LATVIA. He married SAULE, the SUN[2] goddess, but later fell in love with AUSRINE, the MORNING STAR[2], for which he was punished by PERKUNAS, who broke him into pieces, thus explaining the phases of the Moon.

3 *Finno-Ugric*

Deified as KUU, the Moon was subordinate to both UKKO and his consort, AKKA. The father of KUUTAR, Kuu appears to have been the brother of PAIVA, the SUN[3] god, OTAVA, the spirit of the GREAT BEAR, and possibly also ILMA, the god of air and creation, though legends of Ilma suggest that both Kuu and Paiva were his grandchildren.

4 *Latvian*

Meness, the equivalent of MENUO. He was said to have married the WEAVER OF THE STARS.

5 *Norse and Teutonic*

The blonde girl whom the ÆSIR set in the sky after they had formed MIDGARDR from the corpse of YMIR. At the same time they placed a blond boy in the sky who became the SUN[5]. They are chased across the skies by wolves. At the start of the RAGNARØKR the great wolf FENRIR will catch both the Sun and the Moon, and for three years, prior to the destruction of the gods and of the world itself, the bitter FIMBULVETR will shroud the earth.

Morning Star

1 *Latvian*

AUSRINE, the personification of the planet VENUS in the dawn sky.

2 *Lithuanian*

AUSEKLIS, the equivalent of AUSRINE.

3 *Slavonic*

One of the two AURORAS, ZVEZDA DENNITSA, who is, along with her sister, ZVEZDA VECHERNYAYA, the EVENING STAR, the daughter of, and attendant on, the SUN[1] god DAZHBOG[1]. She and her sister had the specific task of grooming their father's horses. They were the sisters of the two, or three, ZORYA.

Morozko

Russian

The FROST[1] demon who features most notably in the story of MARFUSHA, on whom he took pity when she was left to be his bride, freezing her two stepsisters to death when they complained of the cold.

Another story concerning the frost does not name Morozko directly. In this a peasant pays homage to the WIND[1], who appears as a man with tousled hair, dishevelled clothing and a swollen face and lips. This offends both the SUN[1], who appears as a chubby man with rosy cheeks, and Frost, who appears as a thin man with grey hair and bushy white eyebrows. The Wind, however, promises that neither shall ever harm the peasant. That winter, afraid that the frost might harm him, the peasant swore not to venture from his home, but was finally forced to do so when he ran out of firewood. As he walked through the forest he felt the frost attacking him, so he broke into a run. Soon he was warm and thanked Frost for making him move more quickly, so keeping himself warm. Angered by this, Frost swore that he would make the man suffer horribly, so, when the man had removed his hat and gloves so that he could chop wood, Frost froze them solid. Returning to his garments, the man saw that they were frozen, so set about them with the blunt edge of his axe. Frost only just managed to escape the onslaught and crept away badly beaten and bleeding. The Wind stayed quiet throughout this episode, for it knew that Frost was not really dangerous without his intervention.

The Wind also helped the peasant the following summer when the Sun tried to scorch him, blowing gentle, cooling breezes and making small clouds scurry across the sky, blotting out the Sun and dropping a soothing rain on the man. Neither Frost nor Sun ever bothered the peasant again.

Moscow
General

Capital of RUSSIA, lying some 400 miles southeast of St Petersburg. Founded as the city-state of Muscovy in 1127, it was destroyed by the Mongols during the thirteenth century, but rebuilt in 1294 by Prince Daniel (d. 1303) as the capital of his principality. During the fourteenth century the city was under the rule of Alexander Nevski, Ivan I and Dmitri Donskai, and became the foremost political and religious power in Russia. The city was burned in 1571 by the khan of the Crimea, and ravaged by fire in 1739, 1748, 1753 and 1812, the last instance being either accidental or to stop Napoleon's troops from taking possession. In 1918 Moscow became the capital of the RSFSR (Russian Soviet Federal Socialist Republic) and of the USSR (Union of Soviet Socialist Republics) in 1922.

Mother Earth
Russian

Though the personification of Mother Earth is not usually given a name in the Russian legends, her true name, or rather title, is MATI-SYRA-ZEMLYA. She is essential to many of the stories. In the story of Dobrynya NIKITICH, he calls upon her to open up and swallow the vast lake of blood he finds himself stranded in

after slaying a hideous twelve-headed DRAGON[1].

Mother Earth came into existence, so the legends tell us, when a little duck laid an egg on a small island that rose out the primeval ocean. The egg rolled off the island and broke into two, the lower half forming the earth and the upper half forming the sky. This is remarkably similar to the FINNO-UGRIC story of ILMATER LUONNOTAR and the duck which laid its eggs on the goddess's knees in the primeval ocean.

Mother of the Seas
Latvian

Respectful name by which JURAS MATE, the sea goddess, was known.

Mothers, The
Norse and Teutonic

Name given to a triad of goddesses of plenty who were worshipped during the Roman period and who represented triple aspects of the Earth Mother.

Motovun
Croatian

Town on the Istra peninsula of northern CROATIA that was the home of VELI JOZE, a giant who, in a fit of temper, shook the town tower with such force that it began to lean and was badly cracked, in which condition it still remains.

Mundilfari
Norse and Teutonic

The giant father of MANI and SOL, the MOON[5] and the SUN[5].

Muninn
Norse and Teutonic

'Memory', one of the two ravens that brought news from all over the world to ODÍNN, the other bird being HUGINN, 'Thought'.

Murkwood
Norse and Teutonic
The home of the SWAN MAIDENS, from where they flew to the shores of a lake in WOLFDALES and to which they suddenly returned after having spent seven years there with their respective husbands.

Murom
Russian
City to the east of MOSCOW and southwest of Gorky that was the home of IL`YA MUROMETS, giving him his epithet, which simply means 'of Murom'.

Múspell
Norse and Teutonic
The sons of the Hordes of SURTR which will survive the RAGNARØKR and rise against the sons of the good gods, who will fight under the leadership of the resurrected BALDR.

Múspellheimr
Norse and Teutonic
One of the two primeval lands, Múspellheimr was the southern region of fire and light. To the north lay NIFLHEIMR, the land of ice and snow. In between was the space GINNUNGAGAP, in which sparks from Múspellheimr met the icy discharges of Niflheimr and thawed them, slowly revealing through the melting ice the giant YMIR.

Múspellheimr was also the home of SURTR, the fire fiend, who will, at the start of the RAGNARØKR, lead his hordes to shatter the rainbow bridge BÍFROST before joining the giants and monsters on the plain of VÍGRÍDR before VALHALLA, on to which the gods of ASGARDR will ride to do battle.

Muxdi
Siberia – Tungus
Alternative sometimes used instead of DZULI.

Myesyats
Slavonic
Myesyats, the MOON[1] god, appears widely throughout Slavonic mythology and legend, though later stories always tend to leave him nameless. In fact, in the UKRAINE Myesyats marries the SUN goddess, though the Sun is almost always thought of as masculine, and it would seem that it is this confusion that led later story-tellers to leave the name out.

Subsequent Russian belief only adds to this confusion. Early tales say that Myesyats was the old, balding adviser to DAZHBOG[1], the Sun. Later the gender of Myesyats changed, making her a young Moon goddess who married Dazhbog in the summer, left him in winter and was reunited with him the following spring. She and Dazhbog were the parents of all the stars and, when they had marital differences, caused violent earthquakes.

Mysingr
Norse and Teutonic
The leader of the VIKINGS who is named as having murdered FRODI.

Naaki
Finno-Ugric
The spirit of lakes and rivers. A shape-shifter and extremely dangerous, Naaki would emerge from the waters twice daily, at dawn and dusk, to walk on the earth. He was reported to have caused the death by drowning of many men foolish enough not to throw a placatory coin into the water. Naaki was subordinate to AHTI[1], though was not adverse to drowning men for his own perverse pleasure.

Nabbi
Norse and Teutonic
A DWARF who is named as a master smith.

Naglfar(i)
Norse and Teutonic
1 The first husband of NIGHT[2] and father by her of AUD.
2 A ship made from dead men's nails that will sail across the floods that cover the earth with LOKI at the helm, bringing the FROST GIANTS to fight the gods during the RAGNARØKR.

Nágrind
Norse and Teutonic
Alternative name for HELGRIND.

Naharvali
Norse and Teutonic
Tribe whom TACITUS reported wor-shipped the twin deities known as ALCIS in forest sanctuaries, their priests wearing ornate, effeminate costumes. Other than this reference, no other evidence has

been found of this cult among the NORSE and TEUTONIC peoples.

Nainas
Russian
The personification of the Northern Lights, the AURORA BOREALIS[2], who was betrothed to NIEKIA, the daughter of the MOON[1], but never married to her after the intervention of PEIVALKÉ and his father, the SUN[1].

Nal
Norse and Teutonic
Alternative name for LAUFEIA, the reputed mother of LOKI.

Nanna
Norse and Teutonic
Beautiful divine maiden who in one version of the story of BALDR was that god's wife, dying of grief after LOKI had tricked HÖDR into throwing the mistletoe dart. However, in the version recorded by SAXO GRAMMATICUS, Nanna was loved by both Baldr and Hödr, who fought to gain her hand, Hödr eventually marrying her. The version given by Saxo Grammaticus is now thought to be the earlier of the two.

Narvi
Norse and Teutonic
Variant of NORVI.

Nastas`ya, Princess
Russian
Daughter of the King of LITHUANIA and

sister to Princess EVPRAKSIYA. When Dunai IVANOVICH and Dobrynya NIKITICH travelled from KIEV to Lithuania to request the hand of Evpraksiya for VLADIMIR BRIGHT SUN, Nastas`ya was away hunting. When she returned to find her sister had been taken away, she followed, vowing to return with her sister or die in the attempt.

She caught up with Dunai Ivanovich, Dobrynya Nikitich and her sister but, for reasons that remain unknown, she did not attack. Instead she rode away, but was followed and unseated from her horse by Dunai Ivanovich. However, her courage so impressed him that he asked her to become his wife and, riding to Kiev, the pair were married at the same ceremony as Vladimir Bright Sun and Evpraksiya.

During the wedding feast her new husband boasted that there was no finer archer than he. Nastas`ya rose to the bait and challenged her husband, proposing that a silver ring should be set up on the head of one and the other should fire an arrow along the blade of a knife and then through the ring. Dunai Ivanovich invited his wife to go first and three times she successfully did so. Then, as it came to Dunai Ivanovich's turn, she implored him not to try and to forgive her for her foolishness. Dunai Ivanovich refused to listen to her, so she implored him, not for her sake, but instead for the sake of their unborn child, whom she said would be the most wondrous child ever born. He would have arms of pure gold from the shoulders to the elbows, legs of pure silver from the hips to the knees, stars would cluster around his temple, the moon would shine from his back and the sun would radiate from his eyes.

Dunai Ivanovich still refused to listen and, dipping the tip of his arrow in snake venom, promptly shot Nastas`ya through the heart. As she lay dying, they cut the child from her womb, and he proved to be everything that she had foretold. Grief-stricken, Dunai Ivanovich planted his spear in the ground and threw himself on its point. From the place where the two died there sprang up two rivers, the Nastas`ya and the DUNAI, the latter better known today as the River DANUBE.

Nastas`ya of the Golden Braid
Russian
Wife of Bel BELYANIN and mother of PETER, VASILII[1] and IVAN[1]. When WHIRL-WIND abducted her, she was rescued, many years later, by her youngest son, Ivan, although Peter and Vasilii tried to claim her rescue for themselves.

Nastrondr
Norse and Teutonic
Region of NIFLHEIMR to which HEL sent the spirits of evil people after their death and where NIDHOGGR the DRAGON[2] chewed up their earthly remains.

Nehalennia
Norse and Teutonic
The goddess of plenty who was worshipped on Walcheren Island in Roman times.

Nerthus
Norse and Teutonic
Also HLODIN. According to TACITUS, Nerthus was a fertility goddess particularly venerated in DENMARK who was carried around the country in a cart and worshipped on island sanctuaries. Human sacrifice seems to have played an important part in her cult, some authorities seeking to claim that this explains many of the Iron Age corpses found in Danish peat bogs, as these sacrifices were mainly carried out by throwing the victims into the bogs.

This goddess has many associations with NJÖRDR, whose name is, in fact, the Old

NORSE equivalent of Nerthus. It now seems increasingly likely that Nerthus and Njördr were brother and sister, though once they were thought to have possibly embodied male and female principles of the same deity, as their cults share many features.

Nibelung~en, ~s
Teutonic

A race of DWARFS said to live in NORWAY, among whom were such famous figures as GUDRUNN, and in whose land SIGURDR sought out and married BRYNHILDR the VALKYRJA. The Nibelungen owned a great treasure which was guarded by the ELF[3] king ALBERICH, from whom it was stolen by Sigurdr (SIEGFRIED). The story is told in the NIBELUNGENLIED, which recounts the legend of Siegfried and the lives of many other well-known TEUTONIC figures.

Nibelungenlied
Teutonic

'Lay of the Nibelungen', an anonymous twelfth-century German epic poem that is derived from earlier sources and embodies a story to be found in the EDDA. The poem tells the story of SIEGFRIED (the equivalent of SIGURDR) and the revenge of KRIEMHILD (GUDRUNN). It also relates the stories of many other famous TEUTONIC characters such as BRÜNHILDE, GUNTHER, HAGEN and ATLI.

Nidavellr
Norse and Teutonic

One of the NINE WORLDS, the land of the DWARFS that was located on the same level as MIDGARDR, JÖTUNHEIMR and SVARTALFHEIMR.

Nidhad
Norse, Teutonic and Anglo-Saxon

The Old English equivalent of NIDUDR.

Nidhoggr
Norse and Teutonic

'Corpse-tearer', a flying DRAGON[2] that visited NASTRONDR to eat the corpses of those HEL had sent to that region of NIFLHEIMR as punishment for leading evil lives. Nidhoggr also appears as the serpent that lies coiled around and gnawing at the roots of YGGDRASILL in the company of numerous other, smaller serpents.

Nidudr
Norse and Teutonic

The king of SWEDEN who attacked VÖLUNDR while he slept, took him captive, confiscated all his property and then marooned him, hamstrung, on an island. There Völundr was visited by Nidudr's sons, whom he murdered, ornamenting their remains as jewels which he sent back to Nidudr. Fascinated by the breast ornament she had received, BODVILDR, Nidudr's daughter, visited Völundr, who got her drunk and raped her before flying away on wings he had made himself, proclaiming that he had had his vengeance.

Niekia
Russian

The daughter of the MOON[1] who was betrothed to NAINAS. However, as the SUN[1] wanted to betroth her to his son PEIVALKÉ, the Moon sent her daughter to be raised on the earth by an elderly couple. Eventually the Sun discovered her whereabouts and took her up to meet his son, a journey that left her badly burned. She refused to marry Peivalké, so, in his fury, the Sun threw the unfortunate Niekia back into her mother's arms. She pressed her into her heart, her image still visible to this day on the surface of the Moon.

Niflheimr
Norse and Teutonic

One of the two primeval regions, the

northern land of snow and ice. To the south lay MÚSPELLHEIMR, the southern land of fire and light. Between them lay the GINNUNGAGAP, in which sparks from Múspellheimr met the icy floes from Niflheimr and slowly melted them, revealing beneath the ice the giant YMIR, from whose body the gods formed the earth.

Niflheimr later came to be associated with the goddess HEL, whereupon it became the UNDERWORLD[4], the land of the dead, into which the third root of YGGDRASILL reaches. From beneath this root the spring HVERGELMIR, the source of all rivers, bursts forth.

Night

1 *Russian*

Though Night does not have any specific legends surrounding him as a character, the legends of BABA-YAGA the witch say that he, along with the SUN[1] and DAY[1], is under the command of the witch. In these tales he is described as a horseman with a black face, dressed from head to foot in black, and riding the deepest black horse imaginable, complete with a black saddle and harness. He is the brother of Day, who is his complete opposite, though his relationship to the Sun is never revealed. Some say that the Sun may be the father of both Day and Night, but this is never disclosed in any of the stories in which Night appears.

2 *Norse and Teutonic*

Also NOTT. The daughter of giant NORVI, she had three husbands: NAGL-FARI[1], ANNAR and DELLINGR.

Nightingale

Russian

A brigand, half-bird and half-man, who lived in a nest in a tree beside a stream called SMORODINKA. For thirty years he had controlled the road between CHERNIGOV and KIEV, killing any who tried to pass with his whistle. When IL`YA MUROMETS travelled down the road, he tried to dismount the great knight, but only succeeded in making his horse stumble. Quickly regaining his balance, Il`ya Muromets shot an arrow at the brigand which hit him in the temple, knocked him senseless and made him fall off of his perch. Il`ya Muromets tied him up and took him into Kiev, where he displayed him to prince VLADIMIR BRIGHT SUN before taking him out on to the steppe and beheading him.

Nikitich, Dobrynya

Russian

Friend of Dunai IVANOVICH and his companion when Dunai Ivanovich travelled from the court of VLADIMIR BRIGHT SUN in KIEV to LITHUANIA to bring back Princess EVPRAKSIYA to be Vladimir's bride. In Lithuania he ran amok at the royal court, thus persuading the king to allow his daughter to marry Vladimir Bright Sun, whom he held in very low esteem. Dobrynya Nikitich brought the princess back to Kiev by himself after Dunai Ivanovich had set off after a mysterious marauder who had circled their camp at night.

Dobrynya, however, is probably best known as a DRAGON[1] slayer. Having killed the young of a she-dragon, Dobrynya was warned by his mother never to return to the SOROCHINSK Mountains, where the dragon lived, and to stay away from the River PUCHAI. Dobrynya ignored what he thought were the ramblings of an old woman and was soon back in dragon-hunting country.

Tired and dusty from his long journey, Dobrynya stripped off his clothes and, leaving them and his horse on the bank, dived into the River Puchai. No sooner had he stepped into the fast-flowing waters than he saw fire and sparks leaping into the air, accompanied by thick black smoke. Out of this smoke emerged a twelve-headed she-dragon, the dragon whose offspring Dobrynya had previously killed. As the dragon asked Dobrynya what she should do with him, the knight saw his chance and dived beneath the waters, coming ashore on the opposite bank to where his clothes and weapons lay, his horse having been frightened away when the dragon appeared.

Just as he thought his time was finally up, Dobrynya caught sight of a priest's hat lying in the grass. As a BOGATYR, a knight of Holy RUSSIA, he knew that this would make a formidable weapon, but when Dobrynya lifted it up he found it to be extremely heavy. As the dragon flew towards him Dobrynya brandished the hat and severed the dragon's heads. As the dragon dropped to the ground, Dobrynya leapt on to her and readied himself to finish her off.

The dragon begged for mercy and promised never to raid the lands of Holy Russia again and never to carry off any more Russian people. Dobrynya likewise promised never to return to the Sorochinsk Mountains and, having made their pact, Dobrynya released the dragon.

Since he had lost his horse and his weapons, Dobrynya had to make his way back to Kiev, his home, on foot. When he arrived there, he found that in his long absence a disaster had befallen the court of Prince Vladimir Bright Sun. The very dragon whom Dobrynya had spared had broken her word and, flying over the city, had carried away the Princess ZABAVA, Vladimir's favourite niece, holding her between her jaws. Vladimir Bright Sun called together his knights and challenged them to rescue the unfortunate maiden.

ALESHA, the son of the priest LEONTII, told Vladimir that Dobrynya appeared to know the dragon responsible quite well, adding that he believed the dragon regarded Dobrynya as her brother. When Vladimir Bright Sun heard this, he commanded Dobrynya to bring back the girl or be beheaded.

Returning home, Dobrynya explained what had transpired to his mother and complained that he would have to walk to the Sorochinsk Mountains as he had no horse. His mother told him of his father's old chestnut horse which stood, stuck in its own dung, within the stables. Telling her son to clean up the horse and feed it, she also advised him to get a good night's sleep. Dobrynya followed his mother's advice to the letter, and the following morning mounted the chestnut and made ready to leave. Just as he was about to spur the horse on, his mother gave him a silken whip, telling him to whip the horse should its strength ever be failing.

Placing the whip in his pocket, Dobrynya spurred the horse, which cleared the walls of the city in a huge leap and sped off faster than the eye could follow. In no time at all they had reached the foothills of the Sorochinsk Mountains. There the ground teemed with the young of the she-dragon. Dobrynya set about them, riding over their dead bodies, but gradually, having been bitten badly, the horse began to falter. Remembering the words of his mother, Dobrynya took the whip from his pocket and gently whipped his mount between the ears and hind legs. Instantly the vigour of the horse returned, and they finally came to the cave of the she-dragon.

Needless to say, she was not happy to see Dobrynya and complained bitterly about the death of her offspring, but more so about the fact that Dobrynya, a knight of Holy Russia, had broken his word. Dobrynya retorted that it was she who had first broken their pact and demanded the return of Zabava. When the dragon refused, Dobrynya attacked her. For three days the pair fought, until finally Dobrynya was victorious. However, Dobrynya now found himself stranded in the middle of a vast lake that had formed from the dragon's blood, a lake that the earth would not soak up.

Calling on MOTHER EARTH, he commanded her to open and swallow the dragon's blood. Instantly a huge chasm appeared and the lake drained. Dobrynya climbed down from his horse and entered the network of caves in which the dragon had lived. Inside he found, and released, many hundreds of Russians before coming upon Princess Zabava in the very last chamber. Leading her outside, he perched her in front of him on his horse and returned to Kiev, travelling at the same incredible speed.

Nikolai of Mozhaisk, Saint
Russian

The patron saint of sailors. He features in the story of SADKO, the richest merchant in NOVGOROD, who was imprisoned beneath the sea by the SEA TSAR. As a reward for having helped Sadko escape from his watery fate, a magnificent cathedral to his honour was built by Sadko in his home city.

Nine Worlds
Norse and Teutonic

Term used to cover the various regions that constituted the creation, all of which ODÍNN could see while sitting on HLIDSKJÁLF. It is perhaps impossible to produce a definitive list, because of the confusion between the different sagas and legends. However, as best as can be determined, they were:

The bottom level:
HEL and NIFLHEIMR, though later the two merged.

The middle level:
JÖTUNHEIMR, the land of the giants; MIDGARDR, the land of mankind; NIDAVELLR, the land of the DWARFS; SVARTALFHEIMR, the land of the dark elves.

The top level:
ALFHEIMR, the land of the light elves; VANAHEIMR, the home of the VANIR; ASGARDR, the home of the ÆSIR.

Nip
Norse and Teutonic
The father of NANNA.

Njál
Norse
The tragic hero of NJÁLS SAGA, or BRENNU-NJÁALS SAGA ('The Saga of Njall's Burning') from ICELAND.

Njáls Saga
Norse
Popularized and shortened version of the BRENNU-NJÁALS SAGA.

Njörd(r)
Norse and Teutonic
The chief of the VANIR who lived at NÖATÛN, 'the boat enclosure'. He ruled over the sea and its waves, helped fishermen and gave sailors who honoured him smooth passages, but could wreck those who did not pay him the proper respect. He slowly gained ascendancy over the old god of the sea, ÆGIR. His name is the Old NORSE equivalent of NERTHUS, whom TACITUS described as a fertility goddess who was carried around in a cart and particularly revered in DENMARK. Both deities, Njördr and Nerthus, share many attributes of cult, leading to speculation that they may be brother and sister, or that Njördr started out as Nerthus and later underwent a change of gender when the society passed from being matriarchal

to patriarchal. Other theories suggest that Njördr and Nerthus were male and female principles of the same, androgynous deity.

Following the war between the ÆSIR and the Vanir, Njördr and his son FREYR went to live in ASGARDR. There, at least according to Snorri STURLUSON, SKADI, the daughter of the giant THJÁZI sought to avenge her father by attacking Asgardr. In preference to fighting a woman, the Æsir suggested that Skadi should marry one of their number. She readily agreed, hoping to be able to choose BALDR, but the gods hid themselves so that all that was visible were their feet, and when Skadi picked she found that she had chosen Njördr. Their marriage was not a happy one, for Skadi hated living by the sea and he found the inland regions totally alien. Thus they separated each winter, he returning to the sea and she to her hunting in the mountains.

Another version by Snorri Sturluson, the YNGLINGA SAGA from HEIMSKRINGLA, says that Njördr started out life as a mortal who succeeded the incarnate ODÍNN as the sole King of SWEDEN. His people believed that he ruled over not only the people but also the seasons, and thus ensured the prosperity of his subjects. During his reign all the DIAR, or gods, died and so after his own death the people elevated him to the heavens.

Njörfe
Norse and Teutonic
Originally the enemy of VIKING and HÁLF-DAN, Njörfe eventually came to regard them both as his close friends, though his sons were not so keen.

No Bigger than a Finger
Russian
A tiny boy who was born when his mother cut off her little finger while baking an apple pie. Having gone out to the fields to help his father plough, he told him that, if anyone offered to buy him, he should be sold for as high a price as his father could get. Then he told his father to rest and climbed up to the horse's ear, where he gave it instructions and quickly finished the ploughing.

Just then a rich landowner came by and was amazed to see the horse ploughing the field by itself. When the father explained that his diminutive son was giving it instructions, the landowner paid a very high price for him and put the tiny boy in his pocket. No Bigger than a Finger gnawed a hole in the pocket, jumped to the ground and started for home.

That night, resting behind a blade of grass, he overheard three thieves who were planning to steal a bull. Persuading them that he could be of help, the tiny boy was taken along and led out the finest bull, which the thieves shared among themselves, leaving only the offal for No Bigger than a Finger, who laid down to sleep beside it. During the night a hungry wolf came along and swallowed the offal and the tiny youth.

Alive in the wolf's stomach, No Bigger than a Finger made life very hard for it, as each time it stalked a flock of sheep, a tiny voice rang out to warn the shepherd. Finally the wolf pleaded with No Bigger than a Finger to crawl out of his stomach. The boy agreed, provided that the wolf agreed to take him home. Back at the village, No Bigger than a Finger crawled out of the wolf's insides and took hold of it by the tail. Too weak to run away, the wolf was easily killed by No Bigger than a Finger's old parents, with whom the minuscule young boy was reunited.

Nöatûn
Norse and Teutonic
'The boat enclosure', the home of NJÖRDR, the chief VANIR god. Some sources say that Nöatûn was in ASGARDR,

while others say that it was situated by the sea.

Nor
Norse and Teutonic

The eponym of NORWAY, the ORKNEYINGA SAGA says that Nor was the son of THORRI and brother of GOR and GOI. Three years after the disappearance of his sister Goi, he and his brother Gor vowed that they would seek her out, Nor being assigned the mainland to search and Gor all the islands. They were both unsuccessful in their quest until they came to the region known as HEIDEMARK, which was ruled over by King HROLF of BJARG, and there they found their sister, whom the king had abducted and made his wife.

Nordri
Norse and Teutonic

The DWARF who was placed at the northern cardinal point to support the skull of YMIR by ODÍNN, VILLI and VÉ, who used that skull to form the dome of the sky. The south was supported by SUDRI, the east by AUSTRI and the west by WESTRI.

Nornagesta
Norse and Teutonic

A bard who possessed the gift of eternal youth, which was unwittingly bestowed on him by SKULDR, who, having taken offence at some slight made against her, ordered that Nornagesta should die when a candle next to him burned down. However, one of the other NORNS simply snuffed the candle out, and thenceforth Nornagesta carried it with him wherever he went. At the age of 300 he became a Christian on the order of OLÁFR TRYGGVASON, who commanded Nornagesta to set fire to the candle to prove that his conversion to a new faith was more than simple lip service. Nornagesta complied, and when the candle burned right down he died.

Norn(s)
Norse and Teutonic

The equivalent of the Fates of classical Greek mythology, the Norns were the personification of fate or destiny. They were usually depicted in the form of virgin goddesses situated beneath YGGDRASILL, the WORLD TREE[2], an ash whose roots connect heaven (ASGARDR), earth (MIDGARDR) and hell (NIFLHEIMR). Their similarity to Greek mythology is very marked. There were three goddesses in both cultures, and in each these represented the past, the present and the future. The Norn of the past was URDR ('Fate'), of the present VERDANDI ('Being') and of the future SKULDR ('Necessity'). The Norns were guardians of the WELL OF URDR, and every day they tended and watered Yggdrasill, plastering it with clay from the well to preserve it. The three goddesses also wove webs of great complexity, though haphazard design, these webs invariably being destroyed by Skuldr shortly after they had been completed. Urdr and Verdandi were benevolent towards mortals, but Skuldr was quick to take offence for the most trivial of reasons.

Norse
General

Generic term that denotes origin from NORWAY, though later use of the term also encompassed Scandinavia in its entirety, ICELAND and GREENLAND. Upon the advent of Christianity the Norse religion was banned (in 1000), but it was re-recognized by the Icelandic government in 1973.

Norvi
Norse and Teutonic

Also NARVI. The giantess mother of NIGHT[2].

Norway
General

Country of northwest Europe, on the Scandinavian peninsula, bounded to the east by SWEDEN and to the northeast by FINLAND and RUSSIA. Originally inhabited by LAPPS and other nomadic peoples, Norway was gradually invaded by GOTHS and remained under the control of local chieftains until unified by Harald Fairhair (r. 872–933) as a feudal country. From the eighth to eleventh centuries, VIKINGS from Norway raided and settled in many parts of Europe, as well as ICELAND and GREENLAND.

Christianity was introduced in the eleventh century by Olaf II, who was overthrown in 1030 by rebel chiefs backed by Canute. His son Magnus I regained the throne in 1035. Haakon IV (1217–63) made the monarchy hereditary and established the authority of the crown over the Church and the nobles. DENMARK and Norway were united by marriage in 1380, and from 1397 Sweden, Denmark and Norway were united under a single sovereign until 1523, when Sweden broke away. Norway remained under Danish rule until 1814, when it was ceded to Sweden. Norway rebelled and Sweden invaded. Finally a compromise was reached whereby Norway kept its own parliament but remained united with Sweden under a single monarch – a situation that obtained until 1905, when conflict between the Norwegian parliament and the Swedish crown forced Norway to declare its independence. This independence was confirmed by plebiscite and Prince Carl of Denmark was elected king as Haakon VII. He ruled for fifty-two years, until his death in 1957, and was succeeded by his son Olaf V.

Nothung Sword
Norse and Teutonic

The sword that was forged by SIGURDR (SIEGFRIED) and later used by him to slay FÁFNIR, the DRAGON[2] that guarded the hoard of gold owned by the DWARFS.

Nott
Norse and Teutonic

The goddess of the night, the daughter of the giant NORVI. She had three husbands, though some sources simply refer to the three as her lovers. They were NAGLFARI, to whom she bore AUD; ANNAR, to whom she bore a daughter named ERDA; and DELLINGR, whose son by her was called DAG[1] Her horse was called HRIMFAXI.

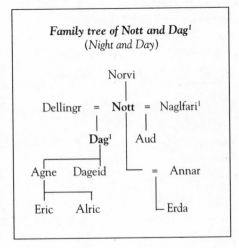

Family tree of Nott and Dag[1]
(Night and Day)

Norvi

Dellingr = **Nott** = Naglfari[1]

Dag[1]   Aud

Agne   Dageid   = Annar

Eric   Alric   Erda

Novaya Zemlya
Russian

Island group within the Arctic Circle off the northeast of RUSSIA which is rich in seals and walruses, and is virtually uninhabited except for a few Samoyed.

Novgorod
Russian

City on the Volkhov River in northwest RUSSIA that was a major trading city in medieval times. The original capital of Russia, Novgorod was founded at the invitation of the people by RURIK, the chief of the VIKINGS, in 862. The Viking merchants who went there quickly became fully assimilated into the native Slav population. The capital was moved to KIEV in 912, but this did little to harm the prosperity of Novgorod. It developed a strong municipal government which was run by the leaders of the various craft guilds and, until the thirteenth century, flourished as a major commercial centre – a fact well illustrated in the legend of SADKO.

Novgorod became one of the principal members of the HANSEATIC LEAGUE, but by then its economy had already started to decline. This was hastened under the rule of the BOYARS, nobles who had wrested power from the guilds in 1416. In 1476 Novgorod came under the control of IVAN THE GREAT and was sacked in 1570 by IVAN THE TERRIBLE.

Nyyrikki
Finno-Ugric

One of the offspring of the minor wood god TAPIO and his wife, MIELKKI. His sibling was TUULIKKI. All four were invoked by huntsmen seeking a good kill.

Oberon

French

The King of the Fairies, the husband of
TITANIA. Oberon first appears in English
literature in a prose translation by Lord
Berners (c. 1534) of the French romance
Huon de Bordeaux, in which he is made
the illegitimate son of Julius Caesar.
Other sources say that Oberon was the
father of ROBIN GOODFELLOW (one of the
names used for PUCK) by a human girl.
Possibly his most famous appearance
comes in *A Midsummer Night's Dream* by
William SHAKESPEARE. Here much is
believed to be owed to the earlier French
work and in the play Oberon is shown as
a magical figure served by the impish
Puck.

Octa

Anglo-Saxon

Son of HENGIST and brother to EBISSA,
AESC, HARTWAKER, SARDOINE and
RENWEIN.

Odd

Norse and Teutonic

Legendary hero and traveller whose story
appears in the *Orvar-Odds Saga*.

Odhroerir

Norse and Teutonic

The name of one of the vessels into
which FJALR and GALR drained the blood
of KVASIR, whom they had killed, and
then mixed with honey to brew the MEAD
OF INSPIRATION.

Odín(n)

Norse and Teutonic

The chief god of NORSE mythology,
known as TÎWAZ, WODAN or WOTAN by
the TEUTONIC peoples, and WODEN or
GRIM by the ANGLES and SAXONS. A sky
god, the eloquent god of the human spirit
and patron of heroes, god of wisdom, culture, the dead and death itself. The poet
who made all human laws, his name
means 'Master of Fury'. The head of the
ÆSIR, Odínn was a fearsome god of justice
as well as being the Lord of Battle, and
thus also the god of war and victory,
warriors dedicating themselves to Odínn
being known as BERSERKIRS. He was the
brother of VILLI and VÉ, their parents
being named as BÖRR, son of BÚRI, and
BESTLA, daughter of YMIR the giant, whom
the three gods killed, the blood from the
massacre causing a great flood that killed
all but one of the original race of FROST
GIANTS. This survivor, BERGELMIR, sailed
away over the flood to found the new race
of giants, the sworn enemies of the Æsir.

From the carcass of Ymir the three gods
formed the land of mankind, MIDGARDR.
They created the surface of the earth from
Ymir's flesh, in which they also put, like
maggots, the DWARFS. They made the seas
and lakes from Ymir's blood, the mountains from his bones, rocks and pebbles
from his teeth, jaws and smaller broken
bones, and the grass from his hair. They
then built a wall around Midgardr, to protect it from the Frost Giants, using Ymir's
eyebrows. Finally they took the dead
giant's skull and formed the dome of the

sky, which they supported by placing four dwarfs at the cardinal points.

A short while later, while walking on the seashore, Odinn, HOENIR and LÓDURR came across two trees which had grown from Ymir's armpits. From these they created the first man, ASKR ('Ash'), and the first woman, EMBLA (possibly 'ELM'). Odínn gave them their spirit, Hoenir gave them their intelligence and Lódurr gave them their bodies and their senses. They then created DAY[2] and NIGHT[2], whom they commanded to drive across the sky in their chariots, and then contrived two blond children, the girl SUN[5] and the boy MOON[5]. These children, whom the gods also commanded to perpetually traverse the skies, were chased by wolves, who will eventually catch and devour the Sun and Moon, this event heralding the end of the world, the RAGNARØKR, during which time Odínn will be pitted against FENRIR, each killing the other.

Odínn resides in ASGARDR in the silver-roofed hall, VALASKJÁLF, in which stands the HLIDSKJÁLF, the seat from which he was able to survey all the corners of the world and where he was brought information and news by the ravens HUGINN and MUNINN. He also travelled extensively astride his wondrous eight-legged horse, SLEIPNIR. Odínn, in his role as the war god, stirred up conflict and strife with his spear GUNGNIR. He then welcomed the souls of heroic slain warriors, who were brought to him by the VALKYRJA, to the palace of VALHALLA, there to feast all night on pork and mead, milked from the goat HEIDRUN, and to sally forth to do battle all day, every day. The husband of FRIGGA, though he was also married at some stage to FJORGYNN, Odínn was the father of THÓRR, BALDR, HÖDR, HEIMDALLR, ULLR, VÍDAR, HERMÓDR[1] and VALI. He was known as the 'All Father' as well as 'the One-Eyed', this latter name

coming from the story that he had sacrificed an eye in exchange for the right to drink from the spring of MÍMIR. His other names were 'Father of Battle', 'God of the Hanged' and 'God of Cargoes'.

In both the Norse and Teutonic cultures, Odínn was regarded with mixed feelings as, like his Teutonic counterpart Woden, Odínn, so it seems, could not be wholly trusted. On one notable occasion he promised HARALDR HILDITONN, King of DENMARK, that he would provide him with divine protection in return for the souls of all those the king killed. Having made the promise, the god then stirred up trouble between Haraldr Hilditonn and his friend King RINGR, even going so far as to teach Ringr how to draw up his troops in the invincible wedge formation, before taking the place of Haraldr Hilditonn's charioteer for the ensuing battle. Odínn then threw the luckless king from the chariot and stabbed him to death.

Just as Odínn could be treacherous, he could also be overtly generous to his favourites. For example, he bestowed a magnificent sword on SIGMUNDR, the VOLSUNG, and gave his son SIGURDR (the Teutonic SIEGFRIED) a splendid horse.

Odínn's titles are of great interest as they demonstrate the complexity of the god. As the 'Father of Battle' he stirs up strife and revels in the resulting wars. This also surfaces with his title 'God of the Hanged', though this has a dual meaning. First, it reflects the custom of hanging people, especially defeated enemies, and animals on trees in his honour, as often as not having run them through or stabbed them while they were hanging there. However, it also tells of the time when Odínn sacrificed himself on YGGDRASILL for nine days, during which time he neither ate nor drank, before peering down to take hold of the runes of knowledge, after which he was freed to be reborn as a youth. This story,

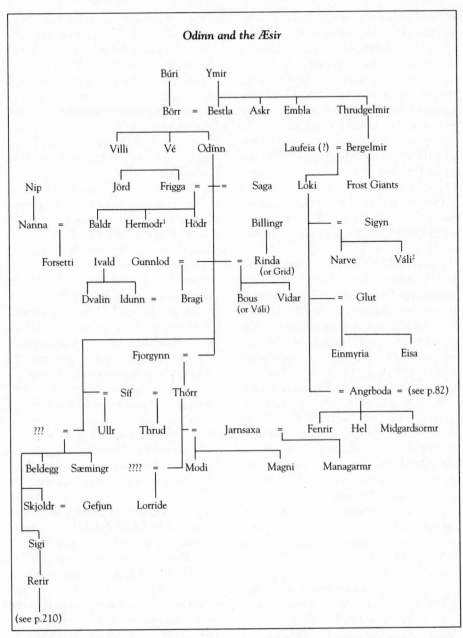

Odinn and the Æsir

(see p.210)

which appears in the HÁVAMÁL, was originally believed to have been a post-Christian development, but is now thought to refer to the symbolic death of the SHAMAN by means of which he perceived hidden wisdom.

Yggdrasill was also sometimes referred to as 'Odínn's steed', a reference that has been taken to symbolize the characteristic ascent of a ladder or a tree by a shaman to commune with the heavens. Further references to the shamanistic traits of Odínn

179

are to be found in the YNGLINGA SAGA, which talks of his faculty to send out his spirit in the form of an animal or bird, a skill that possibly alludes to the ravens Huginn and Muninn, while his horse Sleipnir is also characteristic of the shaman's mystical steed. On Sleipnir the god travels to NIFLHEIMR to consult with the dead, and on another famous occasion he lends the stallion to Hérmódr to travel to ask the goddess HEL to release the spirit of Báldr, while in the late EGILS SAGA OK ASUMNDAR the god leads a giantess down to the UNDERWORLD[4]. All these stories suggest that Odínn was, in fact, a shaman deity.

Much like his Greek counterpart Zeus, Odínn fathered many heroes on mortal women. Following the death of Baldr at the hands of Hödr, Odínn visited the Princess RINDA and fathered on her the son BOUS, his sole intent being that the resulting son should grow into manhood and then avenge the death of Baldr by killing Hödr – as eventually came to pass.

In the YNGLINGA SAGA from HEIM-SKRINGLA, Snorri STURLUSON adds a great deal to the mythology of Odínn, but most of this is simply from the mind of the author and has no true place in Norse tradition. In this version, which is briefly given below, Sturluson makes Odínn a divine mortal. (Note that the spellings are those used by Sturluson; where necessary extra cross-references are given in square brackets.)

Odín was a chief who lived in the main city of ASGAARD, which lay within the land immediately to the east of TANAKVISL, that land being identified with ASIA, which Sturluson calls ASALAND or ASAHEIM and from which he says the name Æsir is also derived. The city was a great centre for sacrifice, custom decreeing that twelve temple priests both directed the people in their daily lives and oversaw the sacrifices. These priests were called DIAR – a rare name for the old gods that is believed to have been imported in the ninth or tenth centuries from Ireland, or DROTNER – a word that means 'lord', but does not appear to have any direct relevance to the ancient gods; it was later widely used to refer to both God and Christ. All the people of Asgaard served and obeyed these Diar.

Odín had two brothers, Vé and VILJE, who on one occasion divided the realm between themselves when Odín was away for an extended period, and both took turns in being married to Frigg, Odín's wife. However, as soon as Odín returned the land was reunited and his brothers apparently pardoned.

Shortly afterwards Odín and his army went to war against the people of VANA-LAND. The battle raged for a long time, until a truce was called, when it was decided to exchange hostages so that another war would not erupt. The Vanaland sent NJÖRD and his son FREY, while the people of Asaland reciprocated by sending HÖNE and the wisest of all their number, Mime [MÍMIR]. The people of Vanaland then sent a third hostage, their wisest, who was called KVASE.

However, as Höne never spoke, the people of Vanaland felt they had been cheated, so they beheaded Míme and sent the head back. Odín smeared it with herbs and sang spells over it to return to it the power of speech, and by thus doing learned many things from the head that became the fount of all wisdom in Asaland. Odín then made Njörd and Frey priests of the sacrifice – Diar – and Njörd's daughter FREYA a priestess of the sacrifice. It was she who first taught the people of Asaland their magic arts. Both Frey and Freya were the children of Njörd by his sister, whom he had married according to Vanaland custom – a custom that was forbidden in Asaland.

Having established the hierarchy within Asaland, Odín left Vé and Vilje as regents in his absence and set out with all the Diar and many other people. First they travelled west to GARDARIKE (Russia) and then south to SAXLAND (northern Germany), the latter falling under his jurisdiction after their conquest, thereafter being governed by some of Odín's many (unnamed) sons. Finally Odín travelled north and took up residence on an island called ODINSÖ.

From there he sent Gefion [GEFJUN] across the straits to discover new lands and to bring him news of them. She came to King GYLVE, who gave her a ploughgate of land. In order to ensure that the land she was given was as large as possible, Gefion travelled to JÖTUN-HEIMR, which according to Sturluson lay to the northeast of SWEDEN, and there bore four sons to a giant whom she then transformed into oxen. These she yoked to a plough, and with them ploughed the land so hard that the area broke away from the land. This was SJÆLLAND (Zealand – the largest of the Danish islands). There she married SKJOLDR, the progenitor of the Danish Skjoldungs dynasty and a son of Odín, the pair establishing their home at LEIRE, near Roskilde in Sjælland.

Having, through the interaction of Gefion, made peace with King Gylve, Odín moved his residence to Lake MÆLARE at OLD SIGTUN (modern Sigtuna on the Uppsalfjord). There he built a great temple and performed sacrifices according to the customs of the people of Asaland. He then gave dominions to each of the Diar. Njörd lived in NÖATÛN, Frey in Upsal [UPPSAL], HEIMDAL in the HIMINBERGS, THÓR in THRUDVANG and Baldr in BREIDABLIK,

though each of these names is actually the name of the residence of each of the Diar, so they are not real place-names.

Odín had the ability to change his shape in any way he liked and spoke in rhyme so convincingly that everyone who heard him believed him implicitly. He and his temple priests were songsmiths and were responsible for teaching the general population that art form. In battle Odín could strike his enemies blind or deaf or simply fill them with such dread that they turned and fled. Their weapons would become blunt and their arrows would fall to the earth but a few inches in front of them. His men, on the other hand, would rush forward, clothed only in animal skins, their minds whipped into a frenzy, and were able to kill with a single blow while remaining invulnerable to both iron and fire. In this fighting frenzy, which has led to the modern use of the word 'berserk', the men were often considered to have magical powers, but it is not thought that the frenzy was induced by use of hallucinogens.

With words alone Odín could quench fire, still the stormy seas and turn the wind to whichever direction he desired. He also owned a ship called SKÍDBLADNIR (Sturluson mistakes the ownership of this magical vessel, which actually belonged to Freyr), which he could roll up like cloth, and he always carried with him on his journeys the head of Mime. Sometimes Odín would call up the dead from the ground, or even hang himself beside hanged or sacrificed men, an act that earned him the title 'Lord of the Hanged', or 'Sovereign of Ghosts'. His two ravens, Huginn and Muninn, to whom he had given the powers of speech, brought him news and information from every corner of the world.

Odín could bring on death, ill-luck or bad health, and take the strength, cunning and intelligence from one person and give it to another. He knew where all the treasures of the earth were kept and understood the sounds made by the earth, hills, stones, trees and grass, and thus bound those who dwelt in them to him, and when the fancy took him, he simply went in and took what he wanted. Gradually people began to sacrifice to Odín and the Diar, and started to revere them as gods (this is the first indication of the godly status of Odín and his entourage made by Sturluson).

As a god, Odín established laws and customs. He decreed that dead men should be burned with their possessions, the ashes to be either cast into the sea or buried in the ground. Thus, so he said, everyone worthy of doing so would be admitted to Valhalla, bringing with them their earthly riches.

Odín then married SKADE, who had previously married Njörd, and had many sons by her, among them SÆMINGR, to whom Earl HAKON the Great said he could trace back his divine descent. Finally Odín died in his bed at SWITHIOD THE LESS, having shortly before death been sacrificed to himself with his spear, saying that he was going to ascend to GODHEIMR (a name that is clearly post-Christian in derivation). The Swedish believed that he had returned to ancient Asgaard, would live there for all time and make himself known to them before each and every battle. To some he gave victory and those who died he welcomed as his eternal guests, and in this way all could feel that they had been the fortunate ones.

In this complex rendition of the chronology of Odínn, Sturluson makes many assumptions and embroiders many of the stories to make them fit into his own personal idea of the god and his ascendancy. To Sturluson the god was a man, though no mere mortal, and through his prowess became so revered by the populace that he became a god. When all is said and done, and ignoring the inconsistencies in Sturluson's account, there may have been some historical foundation to this theory, for in many countries a man could be elevated to the ranks of the gods purely through the deeds of his life, and who is to say that the ancient Norse tradition did not also follow this path. Obviously several aspects of the Sturluson account are post-Christian in conception, but it remains a fascinating elucidation that is well worth close scrutiny.

Odinsö
Norse and Teutonic
Island where, according to Snorri STURLUSON, ODÍNN once had a residence.

Od(r)
Norse and Teutonic
The first husband of FREYJA, whom he soon deserted. As a result Freyja spent the rest of her existence in a strange mixture of mourning and promiscuous behaviour.

Oesc
Anglo-Saxon
Variant of AESC, though some sources cite Oesc as a grandson of HENGIST rather than his son.

Offa
British
Historical king of Mercia (757–96), said to have built Offa's Dyke, – an earthwork on the English-Welsh border.

ogre(s)
General
The name given specifically to a man-eating giant.

Okoln~ir, ~ur
Norse and Teutonic
Variant for BRIM~IR, ~UR.

Oku-Thórr
Norse and Teutonic
'Thórr the Charioteer', a title of THÓRR in his role as the god of thunder who drives a chariot drawn by goats.

Oláfr
Norse and Teutonic
Brother of HÁLFDAN SVARTI, with whom he shared the kingdom.

Oláfr Geirstadaálfr
Norse
Olaf, ELF[3] of Geirstad, an early historical king of NORWAY at whose tomb sacrifices were made and votive offerings left.

Oláf(r) the Holy
Norse
The local name given to Saint Olaf, a historical king of NORWAY who ruled between 1016 and 1030.

Oláfr Tryggvason
Norse and Teutonic
The FLATEYJARBÓK tells the story of the Norwegian GUNNARR HELMINGR, who, having offended King Oláfr Tryggvason, fled to SWEDEN. There, in the temple of FREYR, he was attracted to the god's wife, the beautiful young priestess. Later that year, when it came round to the time for Freyr's autumn progress from his temple to bless the land, Gunnarr Helmingr was invited to accompany it even though the priestess felt that Freyr might not be pleased. Soon after their departure from the temple, the party found themselves in the midst of a severe blizzard and everyone except Gunnarr Helmingr and the priestess abandoned the god. Gunnarr Helmingr led the wagon on for a while and then stopped to rest, even though the priestess

said that Freyr would attack them.

In desperation Gunnarr Helmingr called on the god of Oláfr Tryggvason – that is, the Christian God – and with his help overcame Freyr, who then departed and left the couple alone. Gunnarr Helmingr destroyed the image of Freyr, dressed himself in the god's finery and took his place. The couple then continued on their journey and were greeted with delight at the feast to be held in Freyr's honour when the people saw that their god had assumed human form and could thus join them. They were delighted when the god demanded rich clothes and gifts in the place of the normal human sacrifice, and were overjoyed when they learned that the priestess was pregnant. Shortly afterwards, having heard that Oláfr Tryggvason demanded his return, Gunnarr Helmingr stole away secretly, taking with him all his godly gifts and the priestess.

Old Sigtun
Norse and Teutonic
The name given to modern Sigtuna on the Uppsalfjord by Snorri STURLUSON, who says that ODÍNN had his residence at Lake MÆLARE at Old Sigtun.

Oleg
Russian
A historical prince of KIEV who died in 912. According to the Russian chronicles, he asked his wizards how he was to die and they told him that he would be killed by his favourite horse. Reluctantly Oleg banished the animal from the court and had it released far out on the steppe. Many years later, Oleg heard that the horse had died and rode out to a spot where he was shown the animal's skeleton. Dismounting, he placed a foot on the skull of the animal, upon which a poisonous viper shot out of an eye socket and bit him on the ankle. Several days later Oleg died, thus fulfilling the prophecy.

Ollr

Norse and Teutonic
Variant of ULLR.

Olrun

Norse and Teutonic
One of the VALKYRJA and sister of ALVIT and SVANHVIT. These three were allegedly raped by EGIL, VÖLUNDR and SLAGFIDR, which would seem to identify them as the SWAN MAIDENS.

Onar

Norse and Teutonic
According to Snorri STURLUSON in *HEIM-SKRINGLA*, Onar, whom Sturluson also calls ANAR, was a DWARF who was the husband of NIGHT[2], their daughter being EARTH.

One-Eye

Russian
One of the two servants of WHIRLWIND. He and his companion, LAME, are so called because that is exactly what they were. Bestowed with magical powers, they helped IVAN[1] after he had killed Whirlwind to return to his home, and once there completed the tasks set by ELENA THE FAIR that were to uncover the treachery of Ivan's brothers PETER and VASILII[1].

Orgelmir

Norse and Teutonic
Little-used variant for YMIR.

Orkney(s)

General
Group of about ninety islands off the northeast coast of Scotland. They were conquered by Harald I (Fairhair) in 876, becoming Norwegian territory. They were pledged to James III of Scotland in 1468 for the dowry of Margaret of DEN-MARK and were annexed in 1472 as the dowry remained unpaid.

Orkneyinga Saga

Norse and Teutonic
Pseudo-mythical history of the kings of ORKNEY that is attributable to Snorri STURLUSON and includes the story of NOR, GOR and GOI.

Orsel

Slavonic
Variant name for URSULA.

ort

Finno-Ugric – Cheremiss
The Cheremiss name for HALTIJA, the concept of a spirit or soul with which all things, animate and inanimate, are imbued.

Orvandil(l)

Norse and Teutonic
Variant of AURVANDILL.

Ossetes

Russian
Descendants of the SARMATIANS living in the CAUCASUS region of Ossetia, hence their name. Speaking the Persian language Ossetic, the Ossetes were conquered by the Russians in 1802. These people tell a story very similar to that of the passing of King ARTHUR which might have been carried to the area by the Romans, though this has never been established.

Ostrogoths

General
A branch of the GOTHS who settled near the BLACK SEA some time around the second century AD. They were conquered by the HUNS in 372 and regained their independence in 454. Under Theodoric the Great the Ostrogoths conquered Italy between 488 and 493, but disappeared as a recognizable nation after Justinian I, the Byzantine emperor, retook Italy between 535 and 555.

Otava
Finno-Ugric
The spirit of the GREAT BEAR, the constellation Ursa Major in the northern celestial hemisphere, whom VÄINÄMÖINEN asked to teach him how to escape from his gloomy home during his thirty years of gestation.

Otherworld
General
Common to many cultures is the concept of the Otherworld. To some it is the land of the dead, but to most it is a spiritual land where strange beings and creatures abide. It can usually be reached by the living after a long and torturous journey, but only those of extreme cunning – or luck – ever return. In that way it is almost seen as a sort of limbo, a land between life and death through which all must pass and from which only those with the knowledge, ability or help of the gods can ever hope to return.

Otr
Norse and Teutonic
'Otter', the son of HREIDMAR, so called as he liked to spend his days in the form of an otter swimming in the rivers. Following his accidental death at the hands of LOKI, who thought he was simply killing an animal, his father and brothers, REGINN and FÁFNIR, compelled the ÆSIR to steal the hoard of gold that was owned by ANDVARI the DWARF and pay it to them as compensation.

Otso
Finno-Ugric
A woodland spirit who appears, without reference to his name, in the story of ILMARINEN, when he is invoked by the unnamed daughter of LOUHI to help her escape from Ilmarinen, who has abducted her. The result of this action was for Ilmarinen to turn the unfaithful girl into a seagull.

Ottar Heimski
Norse and Teutonic
'Ottar the Simple', a devotee of FREYJA, by whom he was helped to discover the secret of his ancestry from HYNDLA while in a disagreement with ANGANTYR over a piece of property. As Ottar Heimski was able to recite his ancestry, he won the dispute.

Overturn Mountain
Russian
A giant who appears in the story of IVAN[2]. During his flight from home to escape from his yet-to-be-born sister, whom he had been told would be a terrible witch, Ivan sought to live with Overturn Mountain, but was told that, even though the giant would have taken him in, he did not have long to live, as he would die as soon as he had overturned the mountain range he was working on.

Later, as Ivan was returning to his home from the safety of the home given to him by SUN'S SISTER, he found that Overturn Mountain had only two mountains left to topple. As he did not want to see his friend die he threw down a brush that Sun's Sister had given him, which caused a huge mountain range to spring up from the earth. These mountains Overturn Mountain later toppled into the path of the witch as she chased Ivan back to the home of Sun's Sister, thus delaying her for long enough to allow Ivan to reach safety.

Ovinnik
Slavonic
The spirit of the barn that looked like a large black cat with fiery eyes but had a fierce bark. If fed, the Ovinnik would protect the barn and its occupants. If forgotten, then the spirit would become malevolent and help itself to the livestock in the barn.

Paha
Finno-Ugric

One of the three evil spirits, the others being LEMPO and HIISI, who directed the axe of VÄINÄMÖINEN while he was building a boat from the fragments of the spindle and shuttle of the Maid of POHJA. The three caused the axe to deflect so that Väinämöinen drove it hard into his knee.

Paiva
Finno-Ugric

The god of the SUN[3], who is possibly the brother of KUU, the MOON[3] god.

Parakha
Russian

The oldest of the two stepsisters of MAR-FUSHA, the only one of the two to be named. Unlike Marfusha, she and her unnamed sister died from the cold when left to be married to the FROST[1] demon MOROZKO.

Parsifal
Teutonic

The father of LOHENGRIN whose name is actually the German version of Perceval.

parstukai
Lithuanian

Alternative name for BARSTUKAI, though it is possibly a simple misspelling.

Patrimpas
Slavonic

The god of rivers, streams and springs, but not of lakes.

Peivalké
Russian

The son of the SUN[1]. When he announced to his father that he wanted to find a bride, his father replied that the MOON[1] had just had a daughter and he would approach the Moon about a betrothal. The Moon was horrified at the prospect and protested that the Sun would scorch her delicate daughter, but the Sun simply waived her objections aside. She then told the Sun that her daughter was already betrothed to NAINAS. At this the Sun became so angry that everyone on the earth had to take cover.

To protect her daughter, the Moon sent her to be raised on earth by an elderly couple, who called her NIEKIA. Finally the Sun became aware of Niekia's existence and carried her up to meet his son, but she was severely scorched and was adamant that she would not marry Peivalké. Furiously the Sun flung Niekia back into the arms of the Moon and her mother pressed her to her heart, the image of her face remaining visible to this day on the surface of the Moon.

Pellervoinen
Finno-Ugric

A minor deity, the god of vegetation and guardian of fields and crops.

Perkonis
Prussian

The thunder god, the equivalent in PRUSSIA of PERKUNAS. His sanctuaries contained a fire that was never allowed to go out.

Perkons
Latvian
The thunder god, the equivalent in LATVIA of PERKUNAS and PERKONIS.

Perkunas
Lithuanian
The thunder god, the equivalent in LITHUANIA of PERKONS, PERKONIS, PERUN and PYERUN. Perkunas was perceived as a vigorous red-bearded man brandishing an axe who was drawn, rattling, across the sky in a chariot pulled by a billy goat. These attributes make him remarkably similar to the Norse god of thunder, THÓRR, which leads to the conjecture that Perkunas is a variant of that deity.

Perkunas lives in a castle on the top of the slippery hill of the sky (see DAUSOS) where, as the agent of good and justice, he attacks the DEVIL with his thunderbolt. He also dispenses justice to mankind, either striking down wrong-doers with his thunderbolt or striking their homes with lightning. The thunderbolt of Perkunas is, as in many other mythologies, conceived as a symbol of fertility and in spring the thunder of Perkunas is held to purify the earth of the evil spirits of winter and bring it back to life.

Perun
Czech
The god of thunder, elsewhere known as PYERUN, PERKONIS, PERKONS and PERKUNAS. He is attended by the god of the storm wind, VARPULIS.

Peter
Russian
Son of Bel BELYANIN and NASTAS`YA OF THE GOLDEN BRAID, and brother to VASILII[1] and IVAN[1]. After Ivan had rescued their mother from WHIRLWIND, he and Vasilii stranded their young brother and tried to claim the rescue for themselves. The truth finally came out and their father wanted to have them executed. Ivan interceded, and Peter married the tsarita of the SILVER KINGDOM and Vasilii the tsarita of the COPPER KINGDOM, while Ivan married ELENA THE FAIR, the tsarita of the GOLDEN KINGDOM, each maiden having been rescued by Ivan when he freed his mother.

Phol
Norse and Teutonic
With a name that should possibly be VOL, Phol was the companion of VOLLA. Perhaps a fertility deity, Phol and his associate are mentioned in the second MERSEBERG CHARM.

Picts
British
The name given to the people who inhabited northern Britain in Roman times, their first appearance being recorded near to the close of the third century AD. About the time of the Roman withdrawal they were raiding Britain and the Saxons are thought to have been invited to the country to oppose them. Geoffrey of Monmouth says that they were almost wiped out by King ARTHUR, and would have been had not their priests interceded.

The racial identity of the Picts is almost certainly Celtic, calling themselves *Priteni* in their own language. It is this name that has, so some say, given rise to Britain. The Irish called them Cruthin, a name which they also applied to a Pictish race, the Picti, who lived in Ireland. The name means 'Painted Folk', which is how the Romans described them. Although the Picts probably preceded the ancient Britons, the Venerable Bede says that they arrived after, coming from SCYTHIA, an area that today lies within the UKRAINE in southern RUSSIA. Geoffrey of Monmouth stresses that the Picts were defeated by Marius, the British king who is said to have given the Pictish people Caithness. The medieval Irish poet Mael Mura of Othain claims that the Picts came from Thrace. There were two main Pictish kingdoms, the northern and the southern, the latter being divided into four states: Atholl, Circinn, Fife and Fortrenn.

Wherever or whatever their origins, the principal kings of the Pictish kingdom during the late fifth and early sixth centuries were said to have been Galem I (495), Drust III and Drust IV (510–25), Drust III alone (525–30), Gartnait III (530) and Cailtram (537). This list should, however, be treated with extreme caution, as Pictish history is, to say the least, scant.

Pied Piper
Teutonic
According to the famous legend, in 1284 a piper rid the town of HAMELIN of a plague of rats by playing a magical tune on his pipe. The rats followed the music which the piper played all the way to the banks of the River WESER, where they fell in and drowned. However, although the town council had agreed to pay the piper a certain amount if he rid the town of rats, they changed their minds once he had completed the task. In retaliation the piper played a new tune as he walked through the town, and this time it mesmerized the children, who followed him out of the town and into the foothills of the mountains, where a door opened through which the piper and the children vanished.

The source of this legend may have been the emigration of young Germans during the thirteenth century to colonize the east, or possibly the ill-fated departure of the German children on the Children's Crusade of 1212. Whatever the source, the story of the Pied Piper remains one of the best known of all German legends.

Plague
Finno-Ugric
One of the nine monstrous offspring of LOVIATAR and WIND[2]. The other monsters are named as PLEURISY, COLIC, GOUT, TUBERCULOSIS, ULCER, SCABIES, CANCER and ENVY.

Pleurisy
Finno-Ugric
One of the nine monstrous offspring of LOVIATAR and WIND[2]. The other monsters are named as being COLIC, GOUT, TUBERCULOSIS, ULCER, SCABIES, PLAGUE, CANCER and ENVY.

Pohja
Finno-Ugric
The family name of the ruling family of the realm of POHJOLA. It is most widely used in the story of VÄINÄMÖINEN and ILMARINEN, in which the daughter of LOUHI, the ruler of Pohjola, is simply referred to as the Maid of Pohja. It is quite conceivable that Pohja is just a misspelling of Pohjola.

The Maid of Pohja was the youngest daughter of Louhi. At first wooed by the hero LEMMINKAINEN, she was later promised to Väinämöinen provided he made a SAMPO for Louhi and performed several tasks that the Maid herself set him. The tests set Väinämöinen by the Maid were to split a horsehair with a blunt knife, to tie an egg in knots though no knot was to be apparent in it, to peel a stone, to cut a pile of ice without causing any splinters and finally to carve a boat from fragments of her spindle and shuttle. Väinämöinen completed all but the last, for while he was building, or carving, the boat, the three evil spirits LEMPO, HIISI and PAHA caused his axe to slip and imbed itself deep in his knee. Unable to think of any binding spell, incorporating the words of the origin of iron, which could heal the deep wound, Väinämöinen went to a nearby village to seek help. Eventually, after having been turned away by a great number of people, Väinämöinen found an old man who healed him.

Having failed in his tasks, Väinämöinen returned to his homeland of KALEVALA, where he had his brother Ilmarinen, the divine smith, forge the sampo and take it to Louhi. There Ilmarinen married the Maid of Pohja. She was killed some years later by some bears.

Pohjola
Finno-Ugric

The northernmost country, sometimes equated with LAPLAND but usually considered to be much further north than that. A snowy wasteland ruled over by LOUHI, it was transformed into a beautiful land of prosperity and plenty by the magical SAMPO forged by the divine smith ILMARINEN, who married Louhi's daughter, the beautiful Maid of POHJA.

Polevik
Slavonic

A spirit of the fields whose appearance varied according to geographical location. Sometimes he was dressed all in white and sometimes he had grass for hair, or he was a dwarf whose skin was the colour of the earth and had eyes of different colours. Drunkards or travellers who slept in his fields were likely to be attacked, or even murdered, for Polevik was very jealous of the sanctity of his home.

Polovoi
Russian

The spirit of the fields whose hair was as green as the grass.

Poludnitsa
Russian

The goddess of the fields in northern RUS-SIA. Represented as a tall, beautiful woman dressed in white, she was attended by POLOVOI. While a patron deity of agriculture, Poludnitsa would also punish those who worked in the fields at midday, for she had decreed that this was a time of rest. She would also sometimes lure young children into cornfields and lose them there.

Porevik
Baltic Coast

'Power', an alternative name for SVANTOVIT in which the iconography of the god shows five rather than the usual four faces.

Potyk, Mikhail
Russian

A knight who made a pact with his wife, AVDOT`YA, that when one of them died the other would follow them into the tomb. Avdot`ya died first and Mikhail, good to his word, was lowered in beside her, although he did take with him a rope that was attached to the church bell so that, if he changed his mind, he could ring and summon assistance.

Lighting a candle, Mikhail sat down beside the body of his wife. Around midnight he saw many snakes entering the tomb, one of which turned into a dragon spouting fire and smoke. Unafraid, Mikhail drew his sabre and cut off the beast's head, which he rubbed on to his dead wife's body. Magically she was brought back to life and, ringing the bell, both Mikhail and Avdot`ya were released from the tomb to spend many more happy years alive.

Prester John
General

First mentioned by the chronicler Otto of

Freising, this legendary monarch was thought to have ruled in either ASIA or Africa. It was said that he attacked Ecbatana and defeated the Medes and the Persians, whose capital it was. A letter said to have been written by Prester John appeared in Europe during the twelfth century (perhaps c. 1185). It described the various wonders of his kingdom and became vastly popular. Marco Polo identified him with an Asiatic ruler, but the fourteenth-century Jordanus de Sévérac placed his kingdom in Ethiopia.

Prussia
General
A state in northern GERMANY from 1618 until 1945, though the duchy of Prussia had been founded in 1525. An independent kingdom until 1867, Prussia then became a dominant part of the North German Confederation, and in 1871 became part of the German Empire under the Prussian Kaiser Wilhelm I. For further information, see page 14.

Puchai, River
Russian
An extremely fast-flowing river that rose in the SOROCHINSK Mountains and above which a terrible twelve-headed she-DRAGON[1], who lived in the mountains, liked to fly so that she could pick off unsuspecting people bathing in the river. On one such occasion the dragon attacked Dobrynya NIKITICH, but he almost killed the dragon. Later, after the dragon had abducted Princess ZABAVA, contrary to the pact Dobrynya Nikitich had made with the dragon, the knight came to her lair and killed her, so releasing the princess and all the dragon's other captives.

Puck
British
Also called ROBIN GOODFELLOW or

HOBGOBLIN. A peculiarly British earth spirit, a decided but very distant relative of the classical Greek deity Pan. He is much less amorous and confined his mischief to doing the housework in return for some titbit such as cream or a cake. According to a biography written about Puck in 1588, he was the result of a union between a young girl and a 'hee-fayrie', one of his attributes being the ability to change his shape at will. He was especially fond of turning himself into a horse. It was not uncommon for travellers to stumble across him in this guise and mount him, only to find themselves in the middle of a stream with nothing between their legs save their saddle.

Unlike his colleagues the fairies, Puck is a coarse being, a trait that is reflected in his other, earthy names: GRUAGACH, URISK, BOGGART, DOBIE and HOB. He is perhaps most famous as the impish messenger of OBERON in William SHAKESPEARE's A Midsummer Night's Dream.

Puskaitis
Latvian
A subterranean deity who lived beneath an elder bush and ruled over the BARSTUKAI and KAUKAI. He rewarded those who worshipped him and left him votive offerings by sending his subjects to them with gifts of corn.

Pyerun
Russian
The god of thunder, known elsewhere as PERKONIS, PERKONS, PERKUNAS and PERUN. His name is possibly cognate with Parjanya, an epithet of the Hindu god Indra. Pyerun was represented with a head made of silver and a gold moustache. In the tenth century there was an idol of Pyerun in NOVGOROD near Lake IL`MEN`, around which six eternal fires burned.

Regarded as the lord of the universe, Pyerun lived in the sky and had absolute control over the weather. When angry, he caused thunderstorms and sent lightning to strike down people who had offended him. Belemnite fossils, the arrow-like internal bone of a creature similar to a cuttlefish, used to be regarded by those who found them as missiles flung down by Pyerun and were thus called 'thunder arrows'.

God of war also, Pyerun carried a bow and arrows as well as a heavy cudgel, a spear and a battleaxe. The protector of soldiers, he could bestow victory on those he favoured, and it was for this reason, when military or commercial treaties were concluded, that Russians swore to keep to their word by their naked swords and by Pyerun. Very much an exclusive deity, Pyerun had no priests, his rites being performed by princes and military leaders.

Cockerels and other animals were offered to Pyerun, though human sacrifices in his honour were also not uncommon. One such recorded victim was a Viking living in KIEV who was chosen by VLADIMIR I to be the sacrificial victim following a successful raid. The Viking, a Christian, refused to be the votive for a pagan god, but was nonetheless sacrificed as Vladimir I had ordered.

In c. 988, when Vladimir I made the political decision to accept Christianity as part of a pact with the Byzantine emperor BASIL II – a pact that also included his marriage to ANNA, the sister of Basil – Vladimir I ordered that all the pagan idols be destroyed. That of Pyerun, which stood outside his palace in Kiev, was tied to a horse, beaten with metal rods and finally cast into the waters of the River DNEPR. With Christianity as the official faith in RUSSIA, Pyerun was simply replaced with the prophet Elijah, or IL`YA as he was known in Russia, for according to the Old Testament Elijah shared many of Pyerun's powers, such as being able to call down rain or fire from heaven.

R

Radigast
Baltic Coast
A deity with similar attributes and characteristics to SVANTOVIT, known only through the writings of SAXO GRAMMATICUS, the Danish chronicler.

Rafnagaud
Norse and Teutonic
'God with the ravens', a name used to refer to ODÍNN that associates him with the ravens HUGINN and MUNINN that brought him news from all four corners of the earth.

Ragnar Lodbrog
Norse and Teutonic
Variant of RAGNAR LODBRÓKR.

Ragnar Lodbrókr
Norse and Teutonic
A heroic DRAGON[2]-slayer whose story appears in the *Ragnars Saga Lodbrókr*, and whose sons are said to have conquered England. Ragnar Lodbrókr was the husband of ASLAUG, and thus the son-in-law of SIGURDR and BRYNHILDR.

Ragnarøk(k)r
Norse and Teutonic
'The Twilight of the Gods', a story that was greatly popularized by Richard WAGNER in his *GÖTTERDÄMMERUNG* (GÖTTERDÄMMERUNG being the TEUTONIC equivalent). It will be heralded by a time on earth during which mankind will perform all manner of vile and inhuman crimes, though the downfall of mankind

is simply their response to the example set them by the gods, who had commissioned a giant to build them a wonderful palace, but, as the time came to pay, asked LOKI to find a way out of their obligation. Loki was, naturally, delighted to do so, but seeing that the gods could not be trusted, mankind turned their back on them and began to dishonour their own oaths and contracts. All the confusion was brought to a head by the death of BALDR and the imprisonment of Loki under the dripping venom of a serpent. War will break out throughout the world, during which the great wolf FENRIR will catch the SUN[5] and the MOON[5], and for three years the bitter FIMBULVETR, a time of extreme darkness and cold, will cover the earth. Giants from the UNDERWORLD[4] and the VALKYRJA will all take part in the war and the earth will be rent asunder by violent earthquakes that will free all the monsters of the Underworld.

Spouting venom, the vast serpent MIDGARDSORMR will rise from the depths of the ocean and flood the earth. Across these turbulent waters will come the ship NAGLFARI[3], steered by HRYMR, or Loki, carrying the FROST GIANTS to join the other giants and monsters congregating on the plain of VÍGÍRDR that lies before VALHALLA. SURTR, the fire fiend, will lead his forces to join the massing horde from MÚSPELLHEIMR and in the process shatter the rainbow bridge BÏFROST.

Summoned by a blast on GJALLARHORN from HEIMDALLR, the gods will ride forth from ASGARDR behind ODÍNN to do battle.

Each of the ÆSIR will find himself pitted against his mortal foe: Odínn against the wolf Fenrir; THÓRR against Midgardsormr; FREYR against Surtr; TYR against GARMR; and Heimdallr against Loki. All but Surtr will die in the conflict. Without the gods, the universe will be thrown out of equilibrium. The stars will fall from the sky and the world will begin to distort. Surtr will then shroud the earth in a purifying fire that will destroy all the corpses, as well as mankind, the flames reaching down into NIFLHEIMR and up into Asgardr, causing everything to sink beneath the waves.

However, the earth will rise once more as the waters recede, the seas returning to their basins and the rivers to their courses, the earth emerging refreshed and green from beneath the waters, and the daughter of the sun goddess will take her mother's place, driving her chariot across the skies. Baldr will rise again from the dead to rule, along with HÖDR, in a palace built from the ruins of Odínn's Valhalla. The new pantheon of gods will be completed by two sons of Odínn, two of BÖRR and two of Thórr. Finally, from the shelter of YGGDRASILL will emerge LÍF and LÍFDRASIR, who will marry and repeople the world.

Some sources speak of the Ragnarøkr as having occurred already, while others speak of it as still to come. Since many of the images have definite post-Christian influences, it is hard to determine whether the sources that speak of the Ragnarøkr as having already happened are actually referring to the introduction of Christianity as the reason for the destruction of the gods, rather than to the actual cataclysmic end of the world, as the original myth surely must have intended.

Rakgnhildr
Norse and Teutonic
A daughter of HARALDR GOLDBEARD who

married HÁLFDAN SVARTI. They had a son named HARALDR[2], who was raised in SOGN by Haraldr Goldbeard. When Haraldr Goldbeard died the kingdom passed to the young Haraldr, but he died when he was just ten years old. Hálfdan Svarti immediately rode north to Sogn when he learned of his son's death and there claimed the heritage and dominion of his son without opposition.

Ran
Norse and Teutonic
A sea goddess, the sister and wife of ÆGIR. She was much feared as she not only captured drowned sailors in her nets, entertaining them in her hall at the deepest point of the ocean, but also drowned sailors as the whim took her. Even though Ran was feared by those still alive, it seems that to die at her hands was not so bad. The mead flowed as freely in her realm as it did in VALHALLA, and all welcomed to her domain would be entertained in style in her glittering palace. It was even said that sailors might appear at their own funerals if Ran had received them with particular enthusiasm. One way of ensuring that this was the case would be to carry gold while at sea, for Ran loved gold.

Randwer
Norse and Teutonic
The son of ERMENRICH, he was falsely accused by SIBICH of sleeping with his father's wife, SWANHILDR. Ermenrich had the pair of them put to death.

Ratatoskr
Norse and Teutonic
The name of the squirrel that ran between the serpent NIDHOGGR at the base of YGGDRASILL and the eagle, Nidhoggr's inveterate foe, that perched on its topmost branches, carrying insulting messages between them.

Rati
Norse and Teutonic
An augur owned by ODÍNN.

Raumarike
Norse and Teutonic
Kingdom of EYSTEIN which was subdued by HÁLFDAN SVARTI. However, no sooner had Hálfdan returned to WESTFOLD than King Eystein resubjugated Raumarike. Hálfdan immediately set off and retook Raumarike, and then pursued the defeated Eystein to HEIDEMARK, where he once again defeated him. However, the pair were eventually at peace, after which Hálfdan gave Eystein half of the domain of Heidemark.

Rauni
Finno-Ugric
An alternative name for AKKA that means 'Mountain Ash', the name arising from the fact that the rowan, or mountain ash, was sacred to Akka.

Ravenson, Raven
Russian
A raven who, along with the SUN[1] and the MOON[1], helped an old peasant pick up a measure of rye grain after he had carelessly spilt it, each of them receiving one of the man's three daughters as his wife. Raven Ravenson chose the youngest girl, the Moon chose the middle daughter and the Sun chose the oldest one. When the girls had been taken away to live with their new husbands, the father set out to see each in turn.

First he travelled to his oldest daughter, who was now living happily with the Sun. There she cooked him pancakes, using the heat from her husband's head to cook them. When the old man tried the same thing at home nothing happened. Next he visited his middle daughter and the Moon. There he took a bath, the light he needed to see by being provided by one of the Moon's fingers. Again he tried the same thing at home using his own finger and got the expected result – nothing. Finally he went to visit his youngest daughter and Raven Ravenson. There he spent the night securely tucked under the wing of the raven. When he tried the same thing at home, choosing to sleep in the chicken coop, he was all right while he stayed awake, but immediately crashed to the ground when he fell asleep.

This story serves but a single purpose – to illustrate the stupidity of man.

Regin(n)
Norse and Teutonic
'Mime', a smith, the son of HREIDMAR and the brother of FÁFNIR and OTR. The foster father of SIGURDR, he asked that hero to kill Fáfnir after he had stolen the treasure of ANDVARI, fully intending later to double-cross his foster son and keep the booty for himself. However, having killed Fáfnir, Sigurdr ate his heart and so learned the language of the birds, who told him that his foster father was planning to kill him. Some sources say that this Reginn was not the foster father of Sigurdr, but a mortal who was appointed by ELF[2] to become the tutor of Sigurdr.

Renwein
Anglo-Saxon
Also RONWEN and HROTHWINA. Daughter of HENGIST and sister to EBISSA, OCTA, AESC, HARTWAKER and SARDOINE. Her original ANGLO-SAXON name appears to have been Hrothwina, both Ronwen and Renwein being Latinizations.

Rerir
Norse and Teutonic
The son and heir to SIGI. He and his wife remained childless until FRIGGA took pity on them and sent the goddess GNA to them with a magic apple. The couple shared the fruit and nine months later

VOLSUNGR was born. They both died while their son was still an infant.

Rhine
Norse and Teutonic
River of central Europe in the depths of which the gold of the DWARFS was hidden by GUNNARR and GUTTORMR after they had stolen it from SIGURDR. It was also the home of the LORELEI, the siren-like maiden who lured sailors to their deaths on the rocks on which she sat combing her hair and singing a beautiful song.

Ríg
Norse and Teutonic
The hero of the *Rígspula*, a poem to be found in the EDDA. Ríg journeyed over the earth to visit the three classes of man – earl, farmer and thrall – spending a night in the home of each and each time sleeping between the man and his wife. The three children who were born as a result of these visits were to become the ancestors of each social class.

The preface to the poem identifies Ríg with HEIMDALLR, while the poem itself suggests that it may have been influenced by Celtic, especially Irish, literature.

Riger
Norse and Teutonic
Alias employed by HEIMDALLR to enable him to pass undetected among mankind.

Rind(a)
Norse and Teutonic
A princess, though of what kingdom remains unknown, on whom ODÍNN fathered BOUS or VÁLI[1] with the idea that he should grow up and kill HÖDR and thus avenge the death of BALDR, plans which came to fruition. Rinda became deified as the goddess of the frozen earth, as she was by all accounts frigid after her encounter with Odínn. She is often confused with the daughter of King BILLINGR whom

Odínn tried but failed to seduce. It seems likely that the two were once one and the same.

Ringr
Norse and Teutonic
A king, the son of VIKING and the close friend of King HARALDR HILDITONN. For some unknown reason, ODÍNN stirred up trouble between the two and taught Ringr how he should draw up his troops in the all but invincible wedge formation.

Ringric
Norse and Teutonic
The kingdom of SIGURDR RINGR.

Robin Goodfellow
British
Variant sometimes used to refer to PUCK.

Robin Hood
British
Legendary outlaw and the champion of the poor against the rich. He is traditionally named as Robin of Loxley, a dispossessed nobleman who took to living in SHERWOOD FOREST, Nottinghamshire, during the reign of King Richard I (1189–99). His constant enemy was the SHERIFF OF NOTTINGHAM, against whom he fought with a band of outlaws who were euphemistically referred to as his MERRY MEN, though their circumstance would seem to have suggested that they had little or nothing to be merry about. Among this band of robbers were characters with such evocative names as WILL SCARLET, LITTLE JOHN, Alan A'DALE and FRIAR TUCK. His love was MAID MARIAN, a lady of noble, some say royal, birth. She had also suffered at the hands of the Sheriff of Nottingham and went to live with Robin Hood in Sherwood Forest, the base for their robbing expeditions being a famous tree known as the MAJOR OAK.

The legends surrounding Robin Hood probably owe their origins to the general peasant discontent of the fourteenth century, and as such have been linked with earlier Celtic legends of a green man of the woods. Robin Hood appears in many ballads that date from the thirteenth century, but his first datable appearance is in William Langland's *Piers Plowman* (c. 1377).

Rod
Russian

A male deity who, along with his female counterparts the ROZHANITSY and the spirits of dead ancestors, protected the home. Rod was originally the god of husbandmen, though his attributes went far beyond this. He was a universal deity, the god of heaven, rain and the thunderbolt, who had created both the world and all life on it. He created man, established the importance of the family and united his devotees into one nation. His wife was called ROZANICA, though as this word is always plural, it implies that Rod had many wives, polygamy being a common trait among pagan Slavonic peoples. Later Rod was toppled from his position at the head of the pantheon by PYERUN (or any of that deity's variants, according to nation) and was thus reduced to his role as protector of the home and guardian of ancestors.

Rognvaldra
Norse and Teutonic

An historic earl and poet of ORKNEY who lived between 1135 and 1158.

Romania
General

Country of southeastern Europe, on the BLACK SEA, that is bounded to the north and east by RUSSIA, to the south by Bulgaria, to the southwest by the former Yugoslavia and to the northwest by Hungary. The earliest-known inhabitants of Romania merged with invaders from Thrace to form an indigenous people who became subject to Rome, which made the country the province of Dacia. Following the withdrawal of the Romans in 275, Romania was occupied by GOTHS, and from the sixth to the twelfth centuries it was overrun by HUNS, BULGARS and Slavs, among others. The present country came into existence in 1859.

Ronwen
Anglo-Saxon

Variant of RENWEIN, which is the Latinization of HROTHWINA.

Roskva
Norse and Teutonic

The female servant of THÓRR, her brother THJÁLFI being the male servant. They were the children of a farmer whose goats had been slaughtered and were brought back to life by the god. They were taken into the service of the god after one had been restored lame, as Thjálfi had broken a leg bone to get at the bone marrow, an act that greatly annoyed the god.

Rossthiof
Norse

A magician from FINLAND who used his powers to draw travellers into his kingdom, where he killed them and stole all their belongings. He also had the power to predict the future and was once made to use this by HERMÓDR[1] when he predicted that a son of ODÍNN would be killed but avenged by another, then unborn, son. The two he was talking about were BALDR and BOUS or VALI[1].

Rosterus
Norse and Teutonic

The name of a smith who was none other than ODÍNN in disguise – one of the many disguises the god adopted in his attempts to mate with RINDA.

Rostov
General

Port on the River DON in southwest RUSSIA some fourteen miles east of the Sea of Azov. Modern Rostov dates from 1761 and is linked by both river and canal to Volgograd on the River VOLGA.

Rozanica
Slavonic

The wife of ROD. Since her name is plural, this suggests that Rod had more than one wife – polygamy was common among Slavonic peoples. After Rod had been toppled as the head of the pantheon by PYERUN, Rozanica herself (or themselves) appears to have been replaced, especially in RUSSIA, by the ROZHANITSY.

Rozhanitsy
Russian

A collective name for a group of female deities who, along with ROD and the spirits of dead ancestors, protected the home. They also presided over the birth of children and animals, and ensured that the land was always fertile. At their festival in September, offerings of bread or porridge, honey mead and cheese were made to them in a ceremony that would today resemble a harvest festival.

Rugavit
Baltic Coast

A deity with similar attributes and characteristics to SVANTOVIT, known only through the writings of SAXO GRAMMATICUS, the Danish chronicler. cf. RADIGAST, who is similarly described.

Rugiu Boba
Lithuanian

A female votive made from the last sheaf of the harvest, her name meaning 'Old One of the Rye'. She was honoured at the harvest festival ceremony, when a feast would be held at which she was the guest of honour. She would then be kept for a year, until a new figure was made to replace her. What became of the old figure is unknown, but one suggestion is that it was buried in the last field to be harvested.

Rurik
Norse and Russian

The chieftain of the VIKINGS who founded the city of NOVGOROD, the original capital of RUSSIA, at the invitation of the people.

rus~alka, ~ulka
Russian

A water nymph (plural *rusalki*), sometimes malevolent, sometimes benevolent, who, like the LESHII, lived in the forest. Although they principally lived in the waters that flowed through the forest, they would quite often climb out and lie on the banks of the river or lake, or climb a tree that hung over the still waters below, their favourite occupation being to comb their flowing golden or green hair while admiring their beauty in the water. On clear, moonlit nights they would assemble to dance and sing, weaving garlands out of the forest flowers. A *rusalka* could not live for long out of the water, but as long as she carried her comb she was not in danger, for that gave her the magical ability to conjure up water when she needed it, no matter where she was.

Rusalki were thought to be the spirits of drowned girls, so in appearance they were almost human, though their characteristics depended on their surroundings. *Rusalki* of soft and sunny southern rivers were nubile and attractive, while those from the cold north were stern, cruel and ugly. Their skin was exceptionally translucent and pale, and they sometimes had tails, so may have originated as land-bound mermaids. Like *leshii*, they possessed the power to transform their appearance, though they were severely limited in this ability, for they could only change into animals that lived in the water, such as fish or toads and frogs. Some accounts say that during the winter the *rusalki* lived in the water, coming ashore during the summer to live in the forest.

Sad and lonely figures, *rusalki* would often attempt to find themselves a companion who could be lured to their death and thus join them in their underwater crystal palaces. Young children were fair game, and they tried to tempt them with baskets of fruit and nuts, or biscuits. However, what every *rusalka* really desired was for a young man to join them, and in an attempt to lure young men into their power they would leave the water and call out young men's names at random. If a young man in the forest was foolish enough to reply, then the *rusalka* had him in her power. The *rusalka* would then make him join her in her games, only to finally drown him in the water. If this did not work, for some men appeared to have a resistance to the charms of a *rusalka*, she would tease and tickle him until he fell down from exhaustion. Then the *rusalka* would drag him into the water. Peasants who believed in the existence of *rusalki* always remembered to wear a cross, or to cross themselves when swimming or crossing a stretch of water, for this would render the *rusalka* powerless to harm them.

Some stories tell of how men, captivated by the unearthly beauty of a *rusalka*, tried to live an ordinary life with them. One such story concerns a young seal hunter by the name of Ivan SAVEL`EVICH who came from ARCHANGEL. Passing the winter on the bleak island of NOVAYA ZEMLYA, well within the Arctic Circle, to hunt seals, he spent many a lonely night alone in his hut playing his balalaika. One night the oil in his lamp ran out and

he continued to play in the dark. As he did, he heard the sound of someone dancing inside his hut. Knowing he was alone, he was frightened and quickly refilled and relit his lamp. There was no one there. The following night the same thing happened. Finally he hid the lit lamp behind a thick curtain and, as soon as the sound of dancing started, he drew back the curtain to reveal a young girl.

She explained to Ivan that she was a *rusalka* but, as she had a human father, she was able to remain out of the water for as long as she liked if she was in the presence of only one person. Ivan fell hopelessly in love with the *rusalka* and they spent the winter together. However, when spring came Ivan had to return to his home to sell his catch. On parting, the *rusalka* gave him instructions as to how he might find her again.

Some time later Ivan found he could not live without the *rusalka*. Remembering what she had told him, he sought out her home, climbed a tree that hung above the water and, directly on the stroke of midday, dived into the water. As he reached the bottom of the river, his love rushed out from the weeds and embraced him. Ivan stayed for quite some time beneath the waters of that river, but finally he longed for home. Remembering that anyone could be protected from the charms of the *rusalka* by the holy cross, he made the sign and was immediately transported back home, and, having crossed himself, would never be able to return to his love.

Russia

General

Massive country that has both European and Asian components. The name was originally used to refer to the pre-Revolutionary Russian Empire, and then incorrectly to refer to the Union of Soviet Socialist Republics (USSR), but since the collapse of Communism the name has once again come back into common usage to refer to the whole country.

The southern steppes of this huge country were originally inhabited by nomadic peoples, and the northern forests by Slavonic peoples who gradually spread southwards and slowly assimilated with the indigenous population. During the ninth and the tenth centuries VIKINGS established cities such as NOVGOROD and KIEV at the invitation of the Russian people. In c. 988, under the influence of Kiev, the Russian peoples were temporar- ily united into an empire and Christianity was introduced from Constantinople. For further information, see pages 12–13.

Ruthene(s)

General

The inhabitants of Ruthenia or Carpathian Ukraine, a region of central Europe on the southern slopes of the Carpathian Mountains. Dominated by Hungary from the tenth century, the Ruthenes remained under the influence of Austria and Hungary until the First World War.

Saari
Finno-Ugric

The ancient name for KRONSTADT, the home of the maiden KYLLI, who married LEMMINKAINEN but was later divorced by him for breaking her marital promise.

Sadko
Russian

A poor musician from NOVGOROD who played the *gusli*, a stringed instrument similar to a psaltery and shaped like a flat wooden box which was laid across the knees and plucked with the fingers. Sadko earned his living by playing at banquets, but one day fell from favour, for a reason which is not given, and so, saddened and worried by this, he went to the shores of Lake IL`MEN`, where he began to play. He had played all day long and far into the dusk, when he saw a huge wave forming out on the lake. Tremendously scared, he ran all the way back to Novgorod.

Three days later, still out of favour, he returned to the shores of Lake Il`men`, where he sat down to play. Again a huge wave formed on the lake and he ran away. A further three days passed before Sadko plucked up enough courage to return to the lake. Once more he played until the huge wave appeared, but this time he did not turn and run but sat and waited.

Out of the wave appeared the SEA TSAR, though this may have been the personification of Lake Il`men`, and thanked Sadko for so regally entertaining his guests. As a reward he told Sadko that the very next day he would be invited to play at a banquet at which some of the richest men of Novgorod would be present. At this banquet the rich men would start to boast about their wealth and their possessions. The Sea Tsar told Sadko that he too should make a boast, stating that he could tell them where to find a fish with golden fins swimming within the waters of Lake Il`men`.

The following day, just as he had been told, Sadko was invited to play at a magnificent banquet and, sure enough, as the rich men began to get drunk, they started to boast. In a loud voice Sadko made the boast he had been told to. When the rich men poured scorn on Sadko, he challenged them as he had been instructed, wagering his head against the shops and merchandise of the men. Six men took Sadko up on his wager and, collecting a silken net, Sadko led the men to the shores of Lake Il`men`, where he cast the net three times into the waters, each time hauling it in with a fish with golden fins struggling within its mesh.

The men were obliged to keep their word and soon Sadko became one of the richest merchants in all Novgorod, but, having become accustomed to his wealth, he forgot to thank the Sea Tsar, who had made it all possible for him.

Returning from a long sea voyage during which Sadko had sold all of his merchandise and reloaded his fleet of ships with gold, silver, jewels and pearls, the fleet became strangely becalmed on the open sea, for though the sails flapped in the wind and the waves lapped against the hulls, the ships did not move forwards. Sadko immediately guessed what was wrong and ordered that a barrel filled with red gold be thrown into the sea as a tribute to the Sea Tsar, whom they had forgotten to honour on their countless previous voyages.

Still the ships did not move, even after they had tossed numerous other barrels filled with valuables over the side. Finally Sadko suggested that they draw lots and make a human sacrifice, but Sadko tried to trick his men by writing his name on a twig while the men wrote theirs on gold coins. The human sacrifice would be the name that was on the first lot to reach the bottom of the sea. Sadko fully expected his lot to float, but to his dismay it sank while the gold coins floated. Realizing that the Sea Tsar wanted him alone, he called for writing materials to make his will. Then, having lowered an oak raft into the sea and taking only his *gusli* with him, he bade farewell to his men and was cast adrift. Immediately the ships were released and sailed off towards Novgorod, leaving Sadko alone.

Having nothing else to do, Sadko lay back on the raft and quickly fell asleep. When he awoke he found himself on the sea-bed close to a white palace that was the home of the Sea Tsar. As soon as the Sea Tsar had chided him for never making tribute, he ordered Sadko to play his *gusli*. As Sadko played, the Sea Tsar began to dance until the sea was whipped into a frenzy, many people dying as a result. Soon people began to pray to Saint NIKOLAI OF MOZHAISK, the patron saint of sailors, to save them.

Beneath the sea Sadko continued to play and the Sea Tsar continued his frenzied dance. As he played, Sadko was confonted by an old man who bade him stop, but Sadko could not as he was under the spell of the Sea Tsar. The old man then instructed Sadko to break the strings and

the pegs of his *gusli* so that it would be impossible for him to continue playing. This Sadko did and the storms abated.

Seeing that Sadko could no longer play, for his *gusli* had been ruined, the Sea Tsar tried another way of keeping Sadko beneath the sea for ever. He offered him his choice of wife from hundreds of beautiful maidens. As instructed by the old man, he chose the very last maiden, a beautiful girl by the name of CHERNAVA, and, exactly as instructed, did not consummate the marriage but instead fell into a deep sleep.

When he awoke Sadko found himself on the banks of the River Chernava, his fleet sailing towards him down the River Volkhov into Novgorod. Released from the grip of the Sea Tsar, Sadko kept a promise to the old man who had appeared to him on the sea-bed and built a cathedral in honour of Saint Nikolai of Mozhaisk in Novgorod, for it had been none other than the saint himself who had appeared to help him. This was the last time Sadko ever sailed the seas, staying safely at home in Novgorod instead.

Sæhrimnir
Norse and Teutonic
The boar that was slain every day by ANDHRIMNIR and cooked in the cauldron ELDHRIMNIR to feed the warriors in VALHALLA. No matter how much the warriors ate, there was always sufficient to go around and every night the boar was restored to life in time to be butchered again the next day.

Sæmingr
Norse and Teutonic
A son of ODÍNN who went to live in MIDGARDR, where he became a king.

Sævarstod
Norse and Teutonic
The island on which VÖLUNDR was ham-

strung and marooned by NIDUDR, and where he was visited by Nidudr's sons, whom he killed, and the Princess BODVILDR, whom he raped, thus avenging himself on Nidudr.

Saga
Norse and Teutonic
A mistress of ODÍNN who lived in the hall of SOKKVABEKK, where she was visited every day by the god, who used the excuse of going there for a drink.

Saltyk
Russian
The king of INDIA in the legend of Volkh VSESLAV`EVICH, by whom he is killed.

sampo
Finno-Ugric
An undefined talisman that was forged for LOUHI, the Lady of POHJOLA, by the divine smith ILMARINEN as part of the agreement between Louhi and VÄINÄ-MÖINEN after the latter had asked for the hand of the Maid of POHJA, Louhi's daughter. Väinämöinen returned to his homeland of KALEVALA, where he told his brother Ilmarinen to forge the required item.

Ilmarinen took the feathers from a swan, the milk from a barren heifer, a small amount of barley grain and the finest sheep's wool he could find and cast them into his furnace, upon which he summoned a huge number of slaves to stoke the fire. Every day Ilmarinen checked the forge to see what had been created in the flames. Many marvellous objects came from within the furnace: a golden bowl, a red-copper ship, a golden-horned heifer and a plough with silver-tipped handles, golden share and copper frame. Recognizing them as evil, Ilmarinen broke each of these into pieces and threw them back into the inferno. At last, among the flames, the wonderful

sampo, with a beautifully decorated cover, appeared. One side of the sampo was a flour mill, one side a slate mill and the third a coin mill.

Ilmarinen took the sampo to Pohjola and presented it to Louhi. Her daughter, preferring the young Ilmarinen to Väinämöinen, married the divine smith. The sampo had such wondrous powers that it transformed the snowy wastelands of Pohjola into a glorious land of plenty. When Ilmarinen later returned to Pohjola to ask for the hand of Louhi's other daughter, the Maid of Pohja having died, he reported the prosperity back to Väinämöinen. Together Väinämöinen, Ilmarinen and LEMMINKAINEN travelled to Pohjola to steal the sampo for their own land. Having successfully stolen the magical item, it was smashed to pieces during the storm Louhi sent after the three thieves. However, enough survived to transform Kalevala into a land of prosperity and plenty. What happened to Pohjola after the loss of the sampo remains untold.

Sarac
Serbian
The horse of Prince MARKO whose name simply means 'Piebald'. Described as the fastest horse in the world, Sarac had the gift of speech and the same capacity for alcohol as his master, whose wine he always shared. Sarac was killed by Marko at the age of 160, Marko himself being 300. He was given an elaborate burial before Marko lay down and died.

Sardoine
Anglo-Saxon
Daughter of HENGIST and sister to EBISSA, OCTA, AESC, HARTWAKER and RENWEIN.

Sarmatian(s)
Russian
An ancient barbarian people who lived in

RUSSIA during the Roman period. Their descendants, the OSSETES, still inhabit the CAUCASUS. The Ossetes have a story about their hero BATRADZ that bears great similarity to the story of the passing of King ARTHUR. It was possibly brought to them by Roman soldiers.

Satære
Teutonic
God of agriculture who became increasingly associated with LOKI.

Satyr
Norse and Teutonic
A woodland creature with pointed ears, two horns on the forehead and an animal's tail. The satyr is, in reality, a creature from Graeco-Roman mythology. It possibly owes its place in the NORSE and TEUTONIC traditions either from contact with the Greeks and the Romans or from a confusion by later writers with SATÆRE.

Saule
Lithuanian
The SUN² goddess who lives, with her daughters, in a castle that was located either at the far ends of the seas or beyond the tops of the slippery high hill of the sky (see DAUSOS). Every day she would drive her chariot, drawn by tireless fiery steeds, across the sky. As the evening approached, she would rest her horses and wash them in the sea before retiring to her castle home. Sometimes she would ride down the slopes of the slippery high hill of the sky to her apple orchard in nine chariots drawn by 100 horses. The red setting sun was said to be one of her precious apples slipping from her hand, the goddess weeping fiery red tears that would shine from the mountainside.

Sometimes Saule was regarded as sailing the seas in a golden boat, or was simply a jug from which light was poured, her daughters washing it every evening in the sea. Saule was closely associated with the MOON² god MENUO, or MENESS, and the unnamed sons of DIEVAS, who were known as the DIEVO SUNELIAI.

Savel`evich, Ivan
Russian
A young seal hunter who lived in ARCHANGEL in northern RUSSIA who, according to one story, became captivated by the unearthly beauty of a RUSALKA. Passing the winter on the bleak island of NOVAYA ZEMLYA, well within the Arctic Circle, to hunt seals, Ivan spent many lonely nights alone in his hut playing his balalaika. One night the oil in his lamp ran out and he continued to play in the dark. As he did so he heard the sound of someone dancing inside his hut. Knowing that he was alone, he was frightened and quickly refilled and relit his lamp. The hut was empty. The following night the same thing happened. Finally he hid the lit lamp behind a thick curtain and, as soon as the sound of dancing started, he drew back the curtain to reveal a young girl.

She explained to Ivan that she was a rusalka but, as she had a human father, she was able to remain out of the water for as long as she liked if she was in the presence of only one person. Ivan fell hopelessly in love with the rusalka and they spent the winter together, during which time everything they ever wanted or needed magically appeared. However, when spring came Ivan had to return home to sell his catch. On parting, the rusalka gave him instructions as to how he might find her again.

Some time later Ivan found he could not live without the rusalka. Remembering what she had told him, he sought out her home, climbed a tree that hung above the water and, directly on the stroke of midday, dived into the water. As he reached the bottom of the river, his love rushed out from the weeds and embraced him. Ivan stayed for quite some time beneath the waters of that river, but finally he longed for home. Remembering that anyone could be protected from the charms of the rusalka by the holy cross, he made the sign and was immediately transported back home, and, having crossed himself he would never be able to return to his love.

Saxland
Norse and Teutonic
According to Snorri STURLUSON, ODÍNN travelled to Saxland from RUSSIA, and from there to ODINSÖ. Saxland is Sturluson's name for the 'land of the SAXONS' – that is, Saxony.

Saxnot
Teutonic and Anglo-Saxon
Called SEAXNEAT by the ANGLO-SAXONS, Saxnot was an old SAXON war god whose name may mean 'Sword companion'. Following his introduction to England, he was cited as the ancestor of the kings of Essex.

Saxo Grammaticus
General
A Danish chronicler (*c.* 1150– *c.* 1220) who was born on SJÆLLAND and became either clerk or secretary to Bishop Absalon of Roskilde. Saxo Grammaticus is best remembered for his monumental GESTA DANORUM, a Latin history of the legendary and historical kings of Denmark down to 1186. Probably written between 1185 and 1216, it is the only source of some of the legendary figures of the BALTIC coast, such as RADIGAST.

Saxon(s)
General
General term used for TEUTONIC invaders who came to BRITAIN in the fifth century AD, although the Saxons were only one of the peoples who invaded the country. They were accompanied by the ANGLES (hence the term ANGLO-SAXON) and the JUTES. The invasions by these barbarian peoples, who had neither armour nor cavalry, started some time between 440 and 460. The languages spoken by the various invading peoples gradually converted into a single tongue referred to as Anglo-Saxon by Cambridge scholars and Old English by Oxford scholars. These invaders, whom BEDE[2] divided into three groupings, formed the ancestors of the modern English people.

Scabies
Finno-Ugric
One of the nine monstrous offspring of LOVIATAR and WIND[2]. The other monsters are named as PLEURISY, COLIC, GOUT, TUBERCULOSIS, ULCER, PLAGUE, CANCER and ENVY.

Sceaf
Norse, Teutonic and Anglo-Saxon
Child who drifted on to the coast of DENMARK in an open boat with his head resting on a sheaf of corn. He later became the king of the Danes and founder of the Danish people. Sceaf's story is told by William of Malmesbury, and he is thought to be identifiable with SCYLD SCEFING through the similarity of parts of their stories.

Scotland
General
Country of northern Europe that forms the northern part of the British Isles. Once a sovereign country in its own right, Scotland was first settled by CELTS from Ireland (called Scotti, hence Scotland) some time around the fourth century BC, the Highland regions of the country remaining impregnable to the Romans thanks to the tenacity of the PICTS and the Scots. Scotland became a part of the

United Kingdom when James VI of Scotland became James I of England and Scotland in 1603.

Scyld Scefing
Norse, Teutonic and Anglo-Saxon
The first king of the Danes, referred to in BEOWULF, which says that he drifted ashore in an open boat and after his death was put out to sea on the tide. It is this aspect that has led to his being identified with SCEAF. In NORSE tradition he was known as SKJOLDR, a son of ODÍNN, who lived with GEFJUN at LEIRE.

Scythia
General
Region to the north of the BLACK SEA between the Carpathian Mountains and the River DON, the original inhabitants of which were, from the middle of the fourth century AD, slowly superseded by the SARMATIANS.

Sea Tsar
Russian
The god of the oceans who, in one account, is also the spirit of Lake IL`MEN`. He also features in a second story concerning the poor musician SADKO, who became the richest merchant in NOVGOROD with his help. But no matter how often Sadko sailed the open seas, he forgot to pay tribute to the Sea Tsar, until one day his ships became strangely becalmed, even though the wind still filled the sails and the waves still lapped at the hulls.

Set adrift on an oak raft by the sailors as an offering, Sadko fell asleep, only to find himself under the sea in the presence of the Sea Tsar when he awoke. The Sea Tsar ordered Sadko to play his *gusli*, a musical instrument, which he did. The Sea Tsar began a frenzied dance which whipped the seas into a fury. Many people drowned in the storm, but those who survived prayed for salvation to Saint NIKOLAI OF MOZHAISK, the patron saint of sailors. Saint Nikolai helped Sadko to escape from the Sea Tsar by telling him to break his instrument. The Sea Tsar then attempted to hold on to Sadko by having him marry one of his daughters. As instructed by Saint Nikolai, Sadko chose the very last maiden to be offered to him, a girl by the name of CHERNAVA. As directed, Sadko did not consummate the marriage, and when he awoke the morning after his wedding he found himself on the banks of the River Chernava, near his home city of Novgorod.

Seaxneat
Anglo-Saxon
The ANGLO-SAXON name for SAXNOT.

seidr
Norse and Teutonic
A form of magical trance divination that was allegedly invented by FREYJA.

Senjem~undr, ~andr
Norse and Teutonic
Giant who fell in love with JUTERNAJESTA, a mortal. She rejected him, saying that he was far too old and ugly. Senjemundr, more than a little piqued by this response, decided that he would kill the maiden and so, from a distance of some eighty miles, fired an arrow straight at her. The arrow would have killed the girl had it not been for the intervention of TORGE, another of Juternajesta's giant suitors. He threw his huge hat into the air and it caught the arrow. Senjemundr saw this and took off on his horse, fearing that Torge would now exact his revenge. That, however, was unnecessary, as just then the SUN rose and turned the hat, the arrow and the fleeing giant to stone.

Serbia
General
Republic within the former Yugoslavia that was settled by pagan Serbs in the

seventh century AD, Christianity being adopted almost 200 years later. In c. 1169 the Serbs were united as a single kingdom, and under Stephen Dushan (1331–55) they founded an empire that covered most of the BALKANS. However, following their defeat at Kosovo in 1389, the Serbs came under the domination of Turkey, which annexed Serbia in 1459. Following uprisings between 1804 and 1816, and a war from 1876 to 1878, Serbia became an independent kingdom. After the First World War, it was one of the principalities that became Yugoslavia.

Sessrymnir
Norse and Teutonic
The hall of FREYJA within ASGARDR, though she is also associated with FOLKVANG. Sources that specifically name Sessrymnir as Freyja's hall say that it was located in her realm of Folkvang. It was also said to have been so well built that it was impregnable, the only chance of admittance being if Freyja herself opened its doors.

Shakespeare, William
General
English dramatist and poet (1564–1616). Born in Stratford-upon-Avon, Warwickshire, the son of a wool dealer, he was educated at the grammar school and in 1582 married Anne Hathaway. In 1583 they had a daughter, Susanna, and in 1595 twins, Judith and Hamnet (d. 1596). Established in London by 1589 as an actor and playwright, Shakespeare was England's unrivalled dramatist until his death. He is still considered as the country's greatest playwright. His dramas, written in blank verse, can be broadly divided into lyric plays, comedies, historical plays and tragedies. He also wrote numerous sonnets. He retired to Stratford-upon-Avon in 1610 and died there on 23 April 1616.

Shaman
General
The term shaman originates with the Tungus people of the Siberian Arctic. They gave the name to their priestly magicians and seers, who practised a form of what is now popularly known as 'charismatic religion'. The female counterpart of the shaman is the SHAMANKA. The word itself means 'one who is excited' or 'one who is raised up', the priest or priestess in question being said to have the power of entering the spirit world at will, where its denizens can be brought under his or her command. In some instances the journey of the shaman is symbolized by climbing a tree or a ladder, thus connecting the rites of the shaman to the WORLD TREE[1&2]. In others he or she is spoken of as flying, usually in bird form, or riding a magical horse. The shaman is also believed to have the ability, like the gods he or she could communicate with, to send his or her spirit out at will to summon other spirits, and to exorcize those who cause illness or any other harm.

Though in certain cases the role of shaman might pass down from generation to generation, he or she was usually 'chosen' by a spirit who would inhabit the body of the unwilling individual until it could be driven out. While the spirit was within its host, that person would take to living in the woods until at length he or she underwent an ecstatic enlightenment during which the secrets of the universe were revealed. The individual then accepted his or her role in life, and acknowledged the particular spirit aids. The spirit then returns to the spirit world, where it waits to be contacted by the new shaman.

Shamanka
General
The name given to a female SHAMAN.

shazka
Russian

One of the three major categories of Russian legend, along with the BYLINA and the BYLICHKA. Unlike the *byliny*, the *shazkas* are pure fantasy. The commonest name for the hero in these stories is IVAN, one of the commonest of Russian proper male names. No matter whether the hero comes from a royal or a noble family, or whether he is a peasant or even the off-spring of an animal, he is always brave and kind, and is usually beset by some personal misfortune which he ultimately overcomes.

Sheriff of Nottingham
British

The cursed enemy of ROBIN HOOD and his band of followers. The high taxation imposed by the sheriff, with taxes forcibly collected by his henchmen, led to great unrest among the peasantry, who were increasingly forced into exile as a result. These outlaws existed by stealing the king's meat (deer) within the confines of SHERWOOD FOREST, where they hid from the soldiers. It was not until they came under the leadership of Robin Hood, a dispossessed nobleman, that they took on any form, and from that date until Richard the Lion Heart returned from the Crusades, they fought an unending guerrilla war against the sheriff, notably stealing from the rich and giving to the poor, so that as often as not the taxes that had just been collected were quickly redistributed by Robin Hood and his MERRY MEN.

Sherwood Forest
British

Hilly stretch of woodland in north Nottinghamshire that was, before extensive deforestation, one of the royal forests. It is best known as the hideout of ROBIN HOOD and his MERRY MEN, whose head-quarters are alleged to have been the MAJOR OAK, a site that is now a popular tourist attraction.

Ship of the Dwarfs
Norse and Teutonic

One of the names given to the MEAD OF INSPIRATION after it had been taken to ASGARDR by ODÍNN, where it was also known as KVASIR'S BLOOD.

Siberia
General

Asiatic region of RUSSIA that extends from the Urals to the Pacific Ocean. Having a harsh and inhospitable climate, Siberia is perhaps best known for its labour camps, where the Communist regime of the old USSR would exile political dissidents and criminal prisoners.

Sibich
Norse and Teutonic

A liar who told ERMENRICH that his son RANDWER had been sleeping with SWANHILDR. Even though the accusation was groundless, Ermenrich had the unlucky pair put to death.

Siegfried
Teutonic

The TEUTONIC form of SIGURDR, one version of his story being told in the NIBELUNGENLIED, though it is thought that the story may have a historical background. It was certainly current by c. 700. While a great deal of both the NORSE and Teutonic versions of the story are the same, the latter, which is given here, has a slightly different ending.

Siegfried came to a hill where he found BRÜNHILDE asleep in a circle of fire within which WODEN had condemned her to lie until she was wakened by one who could penetrate the fiery curtain. Siegfried woke her and gave her a cursed ring as a token of his love. Having married

Brünhilde, Siegfried travelled to the homeland of KRIEMHILD, where he drank a draught that made him forget all about the VALKYRJA. He married Kriemhild and then persuaded her brother GUNTHER to seek the hand of Brünhilde. However, Gunther was unable to penetrate the fiery circle, so Siegfried assumed his identity and pledged Gunther's troth in his place.

Brünhilde was aware of the trickery involved and yet resolved to see her part through to its conclusion. During the wedding feast Kriemhild mocked her for the ease with which she had been tricked into marriage with Gunther, so Brünhilde began to plan her revenge. So far the Norse and Teutonic versions tally, but hereafter the story differs.

Siegfried, having bathed in the blood of FÁFNIR, the DRAGON[2] he had slain with the NOTHUNG SWORD, was invulnerable except for one spot between his shoulder blades that had been masked from the protective bath by a leaf. Brünhilde persuaded Kriemhild to make her husband a shirt that had a cross on it that marked Siegfried's weak spot, and then incited HAGEN, who had been told just what the cross meant, to stab Siegfried while he slept and then steal the treasure of the DWARFS. This was done, but when Kriemhild demanded that Hagen turn the treasure over to her he refused, so she killed him.

Far from showing any remorse at the death of Siegfried, Kriemhild immediately married again, this time to ETZEL, the Teutonic mythological name for ATTILA THE HUN. However, when he found out about her murderous habits Etzel refused to have anything more to do with her. She eventually met her death at the hands of HILDEBRAND[1].

siela
Baltic
The living spirit, or power of life, that does not depart with the dead spirit or *VELE*, instead being reincarnated in animals or plants, especially trees.

Síf
Norse and Teutonic
The golden-haired wife of THÓRR, the most innocent of all the divine wives, whom LOKI said he had once held naked in his arms (he did once cut off her beautiful hair) and whom the drunken HRUNGNIR said he would abduct. She may have appeared innocent on the surface, but she in fact bore ULLR to ODÍNN, the child being raised by Síf and Thórr.

Sigar
Norse and Teutonic
King of NORWAY and father of SIGNY. He executed HARBARDR, the lover of Signy, for the murder of his sons, after which Signy took her own life.

Sigemund
Anglo-Saxon
The ANGLO-SAXON name for SIGMUNDR.

Siggeir
Norse and Teutonic
King of the GOTHS and VOLSUNGS and the husband of the churlish SIGNY. When he made the mistake of angering SIGMUNDR and SINFIOLTI, he paid with his life.

Sigi
Norse and Teutonic
A son of ODÍNN, emperor of the HUNS and the father of RERIR. A particularly nasty individual, Sigi once murdered a hunting companion simply for having killed more game than he had. In his old age he himself was murdered by a member of his wife's family.

Sigmundr
Norse and Teutonic
Known to the ANGLO-SAXONS as SIGE-

MUND, Sigmundr was the father of SIGURDR, the VOLSUNG, who was born to him posthumously.

Signy
Norse and Teutonic
The daughter of King SIGAR of NORWAY, she took her own life when her lover, HARBARDR, was executed by her father for the murder of her brothers.

Some sources make Signy the twin sister of SIGMUNDR and the churlish wife of SIGGEIR, by whom she bore two sons. To test the merit of these children she set them a challenge. Both failed, one boy being killed by Sigmundr, the other being much luckier and escaping with only a caution that he must do better.

However, Signy had never been overly fond of her husband, whom she thought ineffectual and weak – feelings that were not improved when he killed her father and nine of her ten brothers. She decided that if the first two children she had had with her husband were not up to the high standards she demanded, no children by him would be. She thus changed her appearance and spent three nights of incest with her brother, the result of the illicit union being SINFIOLTI.

Sigrdrifa
Norse and Teutonic
One of the VALKYRJA.

Sigrún
Norse and Teutonic
One of the VALKYRJA, said to have been the mistress of HELFGI HUNDINGSBANI.

Sigtyr
Norse and Teutonic
'God of Victory', a title given to ODÍNN.

Sigurdr
Norse and Teutonic
Hero who appears in the EDDA as well as

in the NIBELUNGENLIED, though in the latter he is known by his TEUTONIC name, SIEGFRIED. The Teutonic version of his story, told under that heading shows marked similarities with the Norse version, but also distinct differences, particularly in the ending.

Sigurdr was a VOLSUNG, the posthumously born son of SIGMUNDR. He was raised by his foster father, REGINN, the smith, who persuaded him, when he had come of age, to kill FÁFNIR, the DRAGON[2] that guarded the gold of the NIBELUNGEN, even though Fáfnir was in fact Reginn's brother. The gold that he protected had originally belonged to ANDVARI the DWARF, but the ÆSIR had been compelled to steal it from him by Reginn, Fáfnir and their father, HREIDMAR, in recompense for the accidental death of OTR, Hreidmar's third son. Reginn and Fáfnir then killed Hreidmar, Reginn's intention being that they should share the booty, but Fáfnir made off with it and changed himself into a fearsome serpent.

Sigurdr sought out Fáfnir, possibly riding the wondrous horse given to him by ODÍNN, and killed him. He then ate Fáfnir's heart and was thus empowered to understand the language of the birds. They told him that Reginn was planning to double-cross him and keep the gold all for himself, so Sigurdr killed Reginn as well. However, this destined him for a life of sorrow, since among the treasure was the ring of Andvari, which brought a curse to whosoever owned it.

Some time later Sigurdr came to a hill on the crest of which, within a fiery circle, lay BRYNHILDR, the beautiful VALKYRJA who had been condemned to sleep there until one brave enough could breach the flames to wake her. Sigurdr managed the feat and gave her Andvari's ring as a token of his love. He then travelled to the land of the Nibelungen, the original owners of the golden treasure, and there drank

Family Tree of Sigurdr

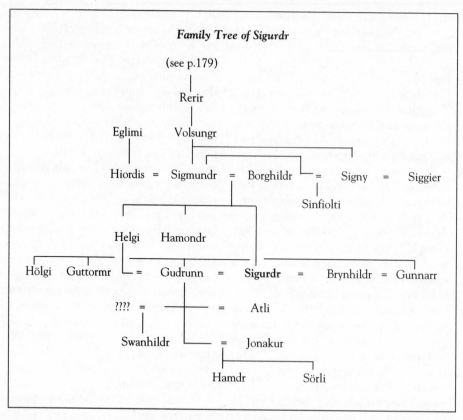

(see p.179)

Rerir

Volsungr

Eglimi

Hiordis = Sigmundr = Borghildr = Signy = Siggier

Sinfiolti

Helgi   Hamondr

Hölgi   Guttormr   = Gudrunn = **Sigurdr** = Brynhildr = Gunnarr

???? =   = Atli

Swanhildr   = Jonakur

Hamdr   Sörli

a potion that made him forget his love for Brynhildr. This led him into marriage with the cunning GUDRUNN. Later, obviously still having knowledge of his former love, Sigurdr persuaded his new brother-in-law GUNNARR to seek Brynhildr's hand.

Gunnarr was not of the same metal as Sigurdr as he could not penetrate the fiery curtain that surrounded the Valkyrja, so Sigurdr assumed his likeness and plighted his troth to Brynhildr in place of Gunnarr. The pair exchanged rings, so that Sigurdr once again held Andvari's cursed jewel, which he later passed on to Gunnarr. It appears that Brynhildr was fully aware of the trick being played on her, but she determined to see her role through to the end.

At the wedding feast of Brynhildr and Gunnarr, Gudrunn began to mock the Valkyrja about how easy it had been to trick her into marriage. At the same time the potion given to Sigurdr wore off and he was once again filled with love for Brynhildr, a situation that Gudrunn was also quick to pick up on. Furious at the deception, Brynhildr swore to have her revenge on Sigurdr. She persuaded her brother-in-law GUTTORMR to kill Sigurdr while he slept and then, filled with remorse, killed herself. The luckless pair shared the same funeral pyre. Gudrunn quickly remarried, her new husband being ATLI, King of the HUNS.

Sigurdr Ringr
Norse and Teutonic
The king of RINGRIC who wished to marry INGEBORG, a goal he achieved along with a yearly tribute from HELGÉ and HÁLFDAN.

Sigyn
Norse and Teutonic
The devoted third wife of LOKI who bore his mortal sons VÁLI[2] and NARVE. After her husband had been bound over three rocks with the entrails of one of his own sons by the ÆSIR, she attempted to prevent the venom from the open mouth of the serpent placed above him falling into his face by catching it in a bowl. However, every time she had to empty the container the poison would once again reach Loki's face and he would writhe in agony, making the earth tremble and thus causing earthquakes. Loki is destined to remain in this painful situation until the advent of the RAGNARØKR.

Siliniets
Polish
One of the two forest spirits, the other being MODEINA.

Silver Kingdom
Russian
One of the three kingdoms of WHIRLWIND that were located on a plateau at the top of some tremendously high mountains. The tsarita of this kingdom, a prisoner of Whirlwind, lived in a silver palace that was guarded by DRAGONS[1]. She was set free by IVAN[1], along with her sisters, the tsaritas of the COPPER KINGDOM and the GOLDEN KINGDOM, when he killed Whirlwind and released his mother, NASTA`YA OF THE GOLDEN BRAID. She married PETER, one of the two brothers of Ivan. Her sister the tsarita of the Copper Kingdom married VASILII[1], while ELENA THE FAIR, the tsarita of the Golden Kingdom, married Ivan.

Simul
Norse and Teutonic
The name of the pole that was carried by HIUKI and BIL, along with a pail named SOEG.

Sindr
Norse and Teutonic
One of the nine WAVE MAIDENS, the giantess daughters of ÆGIR.

Sindri
Norse and Teutonic
Also EITRI. The brother of BROKK.

Sinfiolti
Norse and Teutonic
The oldest son of SIGMUNDR who was incestuously born to his sister SIGNY. A brave child right from the start, unlike the sons Signy had born to her husband SIGGEIR, Sinfiolti had his metal tested when Signy sewed his clothes to his skin and then tore them off. Sinfiolti responded with laughter. Sinfiolti and his father had many adventures together. On one occasion they transformed themselves into wolves and savaged everything in sight, revelling in the carnage so much that they turned on each other, an act that led to Sigmundr killing his son. However, luckily for them a passing raven gave Sigmundr a magic leaf with which he restored his son to life.

At the instigation of Signy, Sinfiolti killed Signy's sons by Siggeir, though some sources say that the oldest of these had been killed prior to Sinfiolti's birth by Sigmundr. For this crime Siggeir decreed that both Sigmundr and Sinfiolti should be buried alive, which they were, but before they had been put into the ground Signy had given her son Sigmundr's magic sword, and with this he was able to hack his way out of their tomb. The pair then went to the hall of Siggeir and set it alight, trapping all the men inside but letting the women escape. Signy, however, feeling that she had had enough of life, decided to stay, breaking the news to Sigmundr that Sinfiolti was his son moments before her death. Sigmundr later married BORGHILDR, who poisoned Sinfiolti.

Sjælland
Norse and Teutonic
The ancient name for ZEALAND, the largest of the Danish islands, which is said to have been separated from the mainland when GEFJUN ploughed the area in order to be given it by King GYLFI.

Skad~i, ~e
Norse and Teutonic
The daughter of the giant THJÁZI who was, according to Snorri STURLUSON in HEIMSKRINGLA, the wife of NJÖRDR. Seeking to avenge the death of her father, Skadi attacked ASGARDR, but the gods preferred not to fight a woman. Instead they proposed that she should marry one of their number. She readily agreed, hoping that she would be allowed to marry BALDR, but when the time came for her to choose her husband all the gods hid so that only their feet remained visible. Skadi chose the most perfectly formed pair of feet, sure that these would belong to Baldr, but instead it was Njördr whom she had chosen. Though disappointed, Skadi went through with the marriage. However, theirs was not to be a happy life together, for she disliked living by the ocean and he could not abide the mountains. So in the winter they separated, he returning to his home by the sea and she to her hunting in the mountains. Some sources name Skadi as the mother of FREYR, though this is not the accepted picture of his parentage, as it would have been impossible for him to come to Asgardr as one of the two VANIR hostages along with his father if Njördr did not marry Skadi until some time later. Sturluson adds that SIGURDR allegedly claimed his descent from Skadi, but again this is not the accepted situation.

Skíalf
Norse and Teutonic
The wife of AGNE, King of SWEDEN, whom she killed by strangling him with her necklace in what was possibly a ritual execution in her role as a priestess of FREYJA.

Skídbladnir
Norse and Teutonic
A magical boat that was said to have belonged to FREYR, and which had been made by DVALIN[1] the DWARF. Large enough to carry all the ÆSIR, the boat could be folded down, or rolled up, so that it fitted in a pocket when not in use It could sail in any direction, as it always had a following wind. It is this aspect that has led some sources to attribute its ownership to ODÍNN.

Skinfaxi
Norse and Teutonic
The horse that pulls the chariot of DAG[1].

Skírnir
Norse and Teutonic
The servant of FREYR who acted as go-between for the god, who had fallen in love with GERDR. Skírnir travelled to the UNDERWORLD[4] kingdom of Gerdr's father and pledged Freyr's undying love for her, offering gifts that included golden apples and the great ring DRAUPNIR. Gerdr refused Freyr's suit, at which point Skírnir turned nasty and threatened to cast a spell that would exile her to a cave at the very edge of the world, and there she would be left to wither and die. Gerdr consented and nine days later, in a grove sacred to Freyr, the couple were married.

Skjoldr
Norse and Teutonic
The son of ODÍNN, husband of GEFJUN, King of DENMARK and ancestor of the Danish royal house. He is cognate with SCYLD SCEFING.

Skögul

Norse and Teutonic

According to Snorri STURLUSON in *HEIM-SKRINGLA*, Skögul was one of the VALKYRJA.

Sköll

Norse and Teutonic

The wolf that pursues the SUN[5] across the sky, the chase ending at the start of the RAGNARØKR, when he will catch and devour it.

Skrymir

Norse and Teutonic

'Big Fellow', a giant whom THÓRR and his companions, *en route* to UTGARDR, came across as he slept. When he awoke he appeared amiable and offered to carry the luggage of the god and his party, and duly packed it all away into his sack. However, soon the giant, who took massive strides, left the party far behind, so that by the time they came across him again he was fast asleep.

Tired and hungry, Thórr tried to loosen the sack so that they might get at their provisions, but even his strength was no match for the knots Skrymir had tied. In anger, Thórr struck Skrymir with MJOLLNIR, but the giant simply opened a single eye, remarked that he had been hit by a leaf and promptly went back to sleep. A second blow produced little better, as Skrymir simply remarked that an acorn must have fallen from a tree. Thórr and his companions spent a hungry, restless night.

By morning Thórr was so incensed that he took a third, furious swipe at the giant, this time sinking his hammer up to its shaft in the skull of Skrymir. The giant sat up, rubbed his head and announced that a bird must have dropped something on to him. Rising, he took his leave of Thórr and his companions, adding that they would meet giants larger than he in Utgardr and should therefore remember their manners at all times. Some sources say that Skrymir was none other than UTGARDR-LOKI in disguise.

Skrymsli

Norse and Teutonic

A giant who beat a peasant at a game of chess and thus won the servitude of that peasant's son. The peasant called upon the gods ODÍNN, LOKI and HOENIR for assistance, Loki eventually saving the boy's life.

Skuldr

Norse and Teutonic

'Necessity', one of the three NORNS, the virgin goddesses of fate or destiny who guard the WELL OF URDR at the foot of YGGDRASILL. They have been likened by many to the three Fates of classical Greek tradition. The other two were URDR and VERDANDI.

Slagfi~dr, ~nn

Norse and Teutonic

One of the three sons of WADA, King of the Finns, his brothers being VÖLUNDR and EGIL. The three brothers took the three SWAN MAIDENS to be their wives. When their wives flew back to their original homeland, Egil and Slagfidr went in search of them, while Völundr remained in WOLFDALES, where he worked as a smith.

Sleipnir

Norse and Teutonic

The wonderful eight-legged horse of ODÍNN on which the god journeyed over the face of the earth. On one notable occasion Odínn lent his fabulous steed to his son HERMÓDR[1], at the request of FRIGGA, so that he might travel down to NIFLHEIMR to request the return of BALDR's spirit from the goddess HEL. On its back Hermódr easily leapt over the HELGRIND, the gates of the UNDERWORLD[4].

Slovenia
General

Constituent republic of the former Yugoslavia that was settled by Slovenes (a Slavonic people) some time during the sixth century AD and was, until 1918, the Austrian province of Carniola. Following the First World War, Slovenia was one of the republics of Yugoslavia, becoming autonomous in 1946 and voting to secede from Yugoslavia in September 1989.

Smorodina
Russian

River that VOL`GA SVYATOSLAVOVICH was intending to cross in order to collect the taxes due to him. However, MIKULA SELYANINOVICH warned him of a band of robbers that lay in wait under the bridge over the river, watching those who crossed through the cracks between the planks. Vol`ga Svyatoslavovich never crossed the river, but sent Mikula Selyaninovich in his place.

Smorodinka
Russian

A stream that ran across a road that led from CHERNIGOV to KIEV. Beside this stream lived the brigand NIGHTINGALE, who killed all who attempted to pass with his whistle. He was finally defeated, having let no one pass for thirty years, by IL`YA MUROMETS.

Snær the Old
Norse and Teutonic

According to the ORKNEYINGA SAGA, Snær the Old was the son of FROSTI, and thus the grandson of KARI. This work also says that he was the father of THORRI and the grandfather of NOR, GOR and GOI.

Snor(r)
Norse and Teutonic

The wife of KARL.

Snotra
Norse and Teutonic

The omniscient goddess of virtue who was one of FRIGGA's numerous attendants.

Soeg
Norse and Teutonic

The name of a pail carried by BIL and HIUKI, along with a pole named SIMUL.

Sogn
Norse and Teutonic

Kingdom of HARALDR GOLDBEARD, the kingdom passing to HARALDR[2], the son of HÁLFDAN SVARTI and RAGNHILDR. However, Haraldr died when he was just ten years old and the kingdom passed, unopposed, to his father. Hálfdan Svarti left HYSING and HELSING as his regents in Sogn, but they usurped the kingdom and Hálfdan Svarti was forced to fight them at VINGULMARK, and thus assumed sole power over the kingdom.

Sokkvabekk
Norse and Teutonic

The hall within ASGARDR of the goddess SAGA.

Sökmime
Norse and Teutonic

A giant whose hall, according to the YNGLINGA SAGA, SWEGDE entered from beneath (or through) a huge boulder, at the beckoning of DURNIR, and was never seen again, the entrance immediately closing after him.

Sol
Norse and Teutonic

As within many cultures and mythologies, Sol was the name given to the personification of the SUN[5], perhaps owing its name to contact with Roman culture.

Son(r)
Norse and Teutonic
One of the bowls used by the DWARFS FJALR and GALR to catch the blood of KVASIR.

Sörli
Norse and Teutonic
The son of GUDRUNN by JONAKUR.

Sorochinsk Mountains
Russian
Mountain range that was the home of a twelve-headed she-DRAGON[1] that was killed by Dobrynya NIKITICH after she had abducted Princess ZABAVA from the court of Prince VLADIMIR BRIGHT SUN in KIEV. The mountain range was the source of the River PUCHAI, an extremely fast-flowing river above which the dragon liked to fly and pick off unsuspecting people who foolishly bathed in its waters.

Soté
Norse and Teutonic
A notorious pirate who once stole an armband that had been forged by VÖLUNDR.

Sprite(s)
General
A generic term for any small and elusive being such as a GOBLIN, ELF[3] or GNOME. Sprites appear in the mythologies of many cultures and are usually portrayed, if not in definite goblin, elf or gnome form, as small, mischievous beings who are usually associated with specific locations such as woodlands, marshes or lakes.

Starkadr
Norse and Teutonic
A legendary hero who is referred to in sagas and the EDDA. The relatively late GAUTREKS SAGA relates how King VIKARR prayed to ODÍNN for a good wind, the king and his men drawing lots to see who should be sacrificed as payment. The lot fell to Vikarr, who quickly decreed that they should hold a symbolic sacrifice. Thus the king stood with the intestines of an animal around his neck like a noose, while Strakadr uttered the ritual dedication. However, as Starkadr struck the king with a stick – part of the dedication – the stick turned into a sword and the intestines into a noose Starkadr found that he had performed a true sacrifice to the god which left Vikarr dangling from the tree dead.

Stefan
Slavonic
Peasant who became engaged to KATYA, who, on the night before the wedding, was strangled in bed with her own hair by her jealous DVOROVOI lover.

Stein
Norse and Teutonic
A mansion to the east of SWITHIOD THE GREAT that SWEGDE came to while seeking GODHEIMR. Near to the entrance, under a huge boulder, sat DURNIR, who beckoned Swegde to enter the portal within the stone (or beneath it), for there he would meet ODÍNN. Without a moment's hesitation, Swegde entered the stone, which instantly closed behind him. The YNGLINGA SAGA says that he entered the hall of a giant named SÖKMIME and was never seen again.

Stribog
Russian
The god of air, but more specifically the god of wind.

Sturluson, Snorri
Norse – Iceland
Early thirteenth-century Icelandic scholar (1178–1241) who compiled an anthology of pagan stories that became known as the *Prose EDDA*. Born to a gifted family

that had newly risen to a position of influence in the west of ICELAND, he was raised in Oddi, the great cultural centre in the south. He went there at the age of three and did not leave until he was twenty-three. His foster father for this period was Jon Loftsson, the grandson of Sæmund Sigfusson (1056–1133), the first northerner to have studied in France and the author of a now lost Latin work on the kings of NORWAY. Jon Loftsson's wife was the illegitimate daughter of King Magnus Bareleg of Norway.

Sturluson's education in Oddi, and his subsequent career as a lawyer (he was the law-speaker of the general assembly, 1215–18), landowner, politician and poet gave him a deep understanding of the past. He spent two periods away from Iceland in Norway, the first between 1218 and 1220, and the second from 1237 to 1239. His history of the kings of Norway, the HEIMSKRINGLA, was written between c. 1223 and 1235, the culmination of a century of historical research and composition in his home country. Sturluson was accused of treason by the King of Norway and was murdered by his brother in 1241.

Styrbjörn
Norse and Teutonic
An opponent of EIRÍKR INN SIGRSAELI.

Suaixtis
Prussian
The god of light, but not the sun god. His name probably means 'Star'.

Sudri
Norse and Teutonic
The DWARF placed in the south to support the skull of YMIR, from which the gods ODÍNN, VILLI and VÉ had formed the vault of the sky. The north was likewise supported by NORDRI, the east by AUSTRI and the west by WESTRI.

Sukhman
Russian
Knight at the court of VLADIMIR BRIGHT SUN who, during a feast, boasted that he would catch for his prince a snowy white swan without harming it. Riding away, he was disappointed to find that where the wild fowl usually gathered, on that day there was not even the smallest duck to be seen. Riding on further to the River DNEPR, he was surprised to find that the waters, usually a racing torrent, were moving at a snail's pace, silted up with sand. When Sukhman asked the river the meaning of this, the river replied that a TARTAR army some 40,000 strong was camped upstream, continually trying to build bridges across her, and that she had used up almost all her strength washing these bridges away.

Sukhman realized that if the Tartar army managed to cross the river then KIEV would be lost. Goading his horse into an enormous leap, he cleared the river in a single bound. There he uprooted a huge tree, said in some accounts to have weighed ninety *poods* (c. 3,240 lb), which he wielded as a giant club to ravage the Tartar army, killing all but three of them. These three hid and ambushed Sukhman as he rode back towards Kiev, their arrows striking him in his side. Pulling the shafts out, Sukhman killed the three Tartars and then plugged his wounds with leaves and herbs before riding back to Kiev.

There he was greeted by Vladimir Bright Sun, who asked for his swan. Sukhman related what had happened, but Vladimir thought that Sukhman was simply making excuses and so had him thrown into a deep dungeon. Nevertheless, he dispatched Dobrynya NIKITICH to investigate Sukhman's claims, and when Dobrynya Nikitich returned with conclusive proof, Vladimir Bright Sun released Sukhman and apologized to him. Sukhman refused the apology, however, and, riding away from Kiev, unplugged his wounds, from which his blood gushed forth to form the fast-flowing river that carries his name.

Summer
Norse and Teutonic
The personification of the season, one of the very earliest of all NORSE and TEUTONIC deities. He was the beloved of everyone and everything except WINTER.

Sun
1 Russian
Though many folk-tales are told about the Sun, none of them refer to DAZH-BOG[1], the earlier solar god. By the time paganism had been forgotten, the Sun had become connected with death, just as the MOON had. Russians would always try to bury their dead just before sunset, so that the Sun might carry away the departing soul on its downwards journey.

One folk-tale refers to the Sun as a beautiful maiden with wings like an angel. A peasant once came to a cottage at the end of the world, where the earth and the sky meet. Welcomed into the house, he had retired before sunset but awoke to hear the old woman talking to her daughter. Peering through a crack in the curtain, he saw the maiden sitting at the table eating her supper, her dress radiating a brilliant light that warmed the room. After her meal the girl hung her dress up and her mother covered it with a thick cloth, darkness falling immediately. The following morning the maiden put on her dress and left the house, and as she did so the night became day.

In some folk-tales the Sun marries human girls; in others he either warms men who have honoured him or tries to scorch men who have offended him.

In one such story (see MOROZKO) he appears as a chubby man with rosy cheeks. However, stories of the witch BABA-YAGA say that the Sun is under her command, along with DAY[1] and NIGHT[1], and in these stories the Sun is described as a horseman, dressed from head to foot in scarlet, riding a scarlet stallion. He starts his journey from Baba-Yaga's cottage and returns there when his day's work is done.

2 Lithuanian
In some Lithuanian legends it is said that, at the end of the Sun's daily journey across the sky, he would travel from west to east in a boat across the night sky to be ready for the next day. Others change the gender of the Sun and name her as SAULE. Still others say that the new Sun was forged every morning by the divine smith KALVAITIS.

3 Finno-Ugric
In Finno-Ugric mythology the god of the Sun is named as PAIVA, who is possibly the brother of KUU, the MOON[3] god. Some also suggest a relationship between both OTAVA, the spirit of the GREAT BEAR, and ILMA, the god of air and creation.

4 Baltic Coast
On the Baltic Coast the god of the Sun remains unnamed but is said to be the offspring of SVANTOVIT. This bears comparison with the Lithuanian Sun goddess SAULE, who in this context might be seen as the daughter of Svantovit.

5 Norse and Teutonic
The blonde girl who was ordered by the ÆSIR to drive her chariot across the sky during the DAY[2], while her companion, the blond boy MOON[5], was ordered to do the same at NIGHT[2]. They are chased across the sky by wolves who will one day catch and devour them, an event that will herald the RAGNARØKR.

Sun's Sister
Russian
Given no specific name, the Sun's Sister appears in the story of IVAN[2], which tells how she helped the young tsarevich escape from the cannibalistic clutches of his sister, a fearsome witch. This story says that she lives on the earth, but also tells of a palace she has in the heavens, the sun itself.

Surma
Finno-Ugric
The guardian monster of TUONELA, the land of the dead, which was ruled over by TUONI and TUONETAR, aided by their daughters KIPU-TYTTO, KIVUTAR, VAMMATAR and LOVIATAR. Surma was perceived as a monstrous animal with an ever-open jaw ready to catch the unwary, and so became the personification of sudden death. Surma was also seen, like the Greek Cerberus, as a guard who prevented the dead from leaving, rather than stopping the living from entering, Tuonela.

Surtr
Norse and Teutonic
The fire giant who resides in MÚSPELL-HEIMR, the southern land of fire and light. At the start of the RAGNARØKR he will lead his host to join the other giants and monsters on the plain of VÍGRÍDR, shattering the rainbow bridge BÍFROST as they come. During the ensuing battle Surtr will be pitted against FREYR, whom he will kill. He alone will survive the carnage, and will then burn the earth, destroying all the corpses, along with mankind, and as the flames reach up to the heavens, the earth will sink beneath the waters.

Suttungr
Norse and Teutonic
The son of GILLINGR and brother of BAUGI. After his father had been killed by

FJALR and GALR, evil DWARFS, Suttungr threatened to drown them unless they gave him the MEAD OF INSPIRATION by way of compensation. This the dwarfs did, and Suttungr, very proud of the fact that the divine liquid was now his, told the world about it. News of the brew reached the gods and it was subsequently stolen from Suttungr's daughter GUNNLOD by ODÍNN, who seduced her in the form of the mortal BOLWERK and took it to ASGARDR.

Svadi
Norse and Teutonic
According to the ORKNEYINGA SAGA, Svadi was a giant from DOVRE mountain and the father of HROLF of BJARG, King of HEIDEMARK. Hrolf abducted GOI, the sister of NOR and GOR, who later came to seek her out. Nor and Hrolf fought for a long time without any result, so it was finally decided that Nor should marry Hrolf's sister, while Hrolf himself kept Goi.

Svadilfar~i, ~e
Norse and Teutonic
The sire of SLEIPNIR who appears in the myth of the building of the wall around ASGARDR, where he is described as the stallion of the FROST GIANT commissioned by the ÆSIR to complete the mammoth task in a year.

Svafa
Norse and Teutonic
One of the VALKYRJA.

Svalin
Norse and Teutonic
A magical shield that protected the NINE WORLDS from the heat of the SUN[5] and reduced it to a bearable level.

Svanhvit
Norse and Teutonic
One of the VALKYRJA and sister of OLRUN

and ALVIT. All three were allegedly raped by EGIL, VÖLUNDR and SLAGFIDR, which would seem to identify them as the SWAN MAIDENS.

Svantovit
Baltic Coast
Also SVENTOVIT, IAROVIT, POREVIT and TRIGLAV. The principal deity of the Slavonic people inhabiting the BALTIC coastal districts, god of gods, and father of the SUN and fire. His chief temple was at ARCONA, where Svantovit was depicted in four aspects on a carved wooden pillar. The god held a bull's-horn cup in his right hand which was annually filled with wine, which would then seep away or evaporate. The amount left in the cup at the end of the year signified the coming year's prosperity. No wine left in the cup would spell disaster.

A white stallion, sacred to Svantovit, was kept in his temple and beside his statue hung its saddle and bridle, along with Svantovit's sword and war banner. The stallion was also, like the wine, a means of divination. It would be driven by the god's priests through a twisting course made up of spears stuck into the ground and the forecast for the coming year would be good if it did not disturb any of the spears, but bad if they were dislodged, the degree of bad luck depending on the number of spears uprooted. Early chroniclers, such as SAXO GRAMMATICUS, are the only sources to mention Svantovit, and they are very patchy. Similar deities known as RADIGAST, RUGAVIT and YAROVIT are described in these early texts. While each has similar attributes to Svantovit, they are all plainly different and may simply be aspects of Svantovit.

Svar~og, ~izic
Russian
God of the sky, his name is cognate with the Sanskrit *svar*, bright, clear or shining. The father of the two most important elemental deities, DAZHBOG[1], the god of the SUN[1], and SVAROZHICH, the god of fire, Svarog was considered as the father of the gods.

Svaro~zhich, ~gich
Russian
The god of fire, the son of SVAROG and brother of DAZHBOG[1], the god of the SUN[1]. He and his brother were considered the two most important elemental deities, for in a land where it is cold for many months of the year the Sun and fire provided the people with warmth and light. As Dazhbog retired for the night, so Svarozhich would take his place, warming the people and lighting their homes.

Svarozhich lived in an oast house where a fire burned in a deep pit over which sheaves of corn had been laid to dry prior to threshing. Corn was the usual votive offering to Svarozhich, a custom which survived into the last century. Another custom that survived well after paganism had died out was the taboo on anyone cursing while the domestic fire was being lit, for it was believed that as Svarog had given fire so he could take it away again.

Svartalfheimr
Norse and Teutonic
The domain of the dark elves, as opposed to ALFHEIMR, the realm of the light elves.

Sva~sud(r), ~rud(r)
Norse and Teutonic
The father of SUMMER and thus one of the earliest of all deities. He is described as being both gentle and beautiful.

Sveinsson, Brynjólfr
Norse
The discoverer (*c.* 1643) of the collection of poems written by a group of anonymous

Norwegian poets between the ninth and twelfth centuries that forms the *Poetic* EDDA.

Sventovit
Baltic Coast
Simple variant of SVANTOVIT.

Svetozar
Russian
The father of VASILISA OF THE GOLDEN BRAID, her two unnamed brothers, and of IVAN THE PEA, though the latter was conceived when his wife, the tsarita, inadvertently swallowed a small pea. He was succeeded, after his death, by Ivan the Pea.

Sviagríss
Norse and Teutonic
'Piglet of the Swedes', a torque owned by ATHLIS, King of SWEDEN.

Svipdagr
Norse and Teutonic
Hero who wooed the divine maiden MENGLOD.

Svyatogor
Russian
The last of the giants. There are two accounts of how Svyatogor met with his end. In the first his strength was put to the test by IL`YA MUROMETS, who rode to the Holy Mountains to find the giant, for he had heard that Svyatogor was one of the mightiest of men.

Coming to the Holy Mountains, Il`ya Muromets saw an enormous man, larger than any he had ever seen before, riding towards him. Knowing at once that this was the giant Svyatogor, he spurred on his horse and struck the giant a mighty blow with his huge mace. Svyatogor did not even wince and rode lazily on. Again Il`ya struck him and again the giant did not even flinch. The third time Il`ya struck

out, however, the giant jerked upright in his saddle. Seeing who had hit him, he deftly picked Il`ya up by the hair and dropped him into his pocket.

Some time later Svyatogor's horse stumbled and complained that carrying two knights was too much, even for him. Svyatogor took Il`ya out of his pocket and, seeing that he was a knight of Holy RUSSIA, suggested that the two of them should ride together, as brothers. This they did for many days, until they came to a huge stone coffin lying beside a tree.

Il`ya leapt off his horse and lay down in the coffin. It was far too large for him, but fitted Svyatogor perfectly. Even though Il`ya pleaded with him not to put the lid on, Svyatogor did just that. However, when he asked Il`ya to remove the lid, Il`ya found it far too heavy. Three times he hit it with his mace, but each time he hit it a steel band closed around the coffin, securing the lid.

Svyatogor blew some of his strength into Il`ya so that he could use the giant's own sword, but this just made matters worse, for two steel bands closed around the coffin every time it was hit with the sword. Resigning himself to his fate, Svyatogor had Il`ya tie his horse to the tree to die there beside its master. Il`ya did as asked and sadly rode away from the coffin, knowing that Svyatogor, the last of the giants, would shortly be no more.

The second account of the giant's demise is possibly the older of the two. Svyatogor often boasted of his great strength, going so far as to say that he could even lift MOTHER EARTH. One day, while out riding, he came across a small bag lying in his path. Unable to move it with the end of his staff, he dismounted and, with tremendous effort, managed to raise the bag as high as his knees. In doing so he sweated so heavily that his sweat became blood and, sinking deep into the earth under the weight of the bag, he could not save himself from his end.

Swan Maidens
Norse and Teutonic
Three maidens who lived in MURKWOOD, from where they flew in costumes made from swans' feathers to the shores of a lake in WOLFDALES, where they were discovered by VÖLUNDR, EGIL and SLAGFIDR, the three sons of WADA. They married the brothers and spent seven years with them before flying home to Murkwood. Some sources identify the three Swan Maidens with the VALKYRJA sisters ALVIT, OLRUN and SVANHVIT.

Swanhildr
Norse and Teutonic
The VALKYRJA daughter of GUDRUNN.

swastika
Norse, Teutonic and Anglo-Saxon
A well-known symbol that appears to have been a fire emblem and which, according to some authorities, signified THÓRR's lightning. It was especially popular with TEUTONIC peoples.

Sweden
General
Country of northern Europe on the BALTIC Sea. It is bounded to the west by NORWAY and to the northeast by FINLAND. Southern Sweden has been inhabited since at least the sixth millennium BC. From their bases in Sweden, VIKINGS sailed mainly east between 800 and 1060, and founded the principality of NOVGOROD. During the middle of the twelfth century the Swedes in the north were united with the GOTHS in the south and accepted Christianity.

Swegde
Norse and Teutonic
According to the YNGLINGA SAGA,

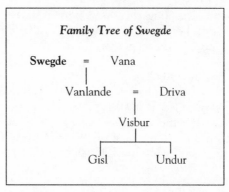

Family Tree of Swegde

Swegde = Vana
|
Vanlande = Driva
|
Visbur
|
Gisl   Undur

Swegde married VANA and had a son named VANLANDE. He then set out to seek GODHEIM. After a while he came to a mansion called STEIN to the east of SWITHIOD THE GREAT. Near to the entrance, under a huge boulder, sat DURNIR, who beckoned Swegde to enter the portal within the stone (or beneath it), for within he would meet ODÍNN. Without a moment's hesitation, Swegde entered the stone, which instantly closed behind him. The *Ynglinga Saga* says that Swegde entered the hall of a giant named SÖKMIME and was never seen again.

Swithiod the Great
Norse and Teutonic
The ancient, legendary name for RUSSIA, which Snorri STURLUSON calls GODHEIM, which he makes the home of ODÍNN and the other deities. Within Swithiod the Great there are a great many kingdoms, races of men and languages. There are giants, DWARFS, blue men (a possible reference to Celts), and many kinds of strange and terrible creatures, including the obligatory DRAGONS[2]. At the southern edge of Swithiod the Great, on the south side of the mountains that lie beyond the inhabited regions, there runs a river that is properly called TANAIS (the modern River DON), but was formerly called TANAKVISL or VANAKVISL. This river flows into the BLACK SEA, its route forming the land known as VANALAND or VANAHEIM

221

and separating the world into its three parts: Vanaland, ASIA to the east and Europe to the west.

Swithiod the Less
Norse and Teutonic
Also called MANAHEIMR, Swithiod the Less was the legendary name for SWEDEN and was the home of the descendants of the gods who lived in SWITHIOD THE GREAT.

Syn
Norse and Teutonic
The goddess of all trials and tribunals who guarded the entrance to FRIGGA's hall against all unwelcomed visitors. Once she had decided to refuse admittance, she was unmovable, and even appeals to higher deities within the pantheon would not make her change her mind.

Tacitus, Publius or Galius Cornelius
General
Roman historian (*c*. 55–120). Having studied rhetoric in Rome, he rose to eminence as a pleader at the Roman bar, and in 77 married the daughter of Agricola. By 88 he was praetor and a member of one of the priestly colleges. In 89 he left Rome for GERMANY and did not return until 93. This journey led to the writing of his *Germania*, a monograph of immense value on the ethnography of the region. Tacitus copied much from earlier historians and was biased in his republican ideals and hatreds, his work today often being obscured by condensation.

Tanais
Norse and Teutonic
According to Snorri STURLUSON, the River Tanais (the modern River DON) ran along the southern edge of the mountains in the south of SWITHIOD THE GREAT and was formerly called TANAKVISL or VANAKVISL. This river flows into the BLACK SEA, its route forming the land known as VANALAND or VANAHEIM and separating the world into three parts: Vanaland, ASIA to the east and Europe to the west.

Tanakvisl
Norse and Teutonic
According to Snorri STURLUSON, one of the former names of the River TANAIS, along with VANAKVISL. The river is better known today as the DON.

Tanngnjostr
Norse and Teutonic
'Tooth-cracker', one of the goats owned by THÓRR.

Tanngrisnr
Norse and Teutonic
'Tooth-gnasher', one of the goats owned by THÓRR.

Tannhäuser
Teutonic
Legendary thirteenth-century *Minnesinger* (lyric poet and song writer), according to whom the classical Roman goddess Venus held her court on the mountain VENUS-BERG. The legends say that Tannhäuser worshipped HOLDA, or FRIGGA, though he eventually went to ask absolution of the Pope. However, that absolution was not forthcoming, the Pope's reply being that those who worshipped pagan gods must expect eternal damnation. Tannhäuser's only chance of salvation, he said, was if the papal staff began to bloom. As this was impossible, Tannhäuser went back to his old ways and sacrificed himself to Holda. Three days later, the Pope's staff began to show green buds and a messenger was dispatched to take the news of his absolution to Tannhäuser. However, Tannhäuser was never absolved, as he had died before his request was answered, and as a result he has to spend eternity in the passionate embraces of the lascivious Holda.

Tapio
Finno-Ugric
A minor deity, god or spirit of the woods. Along with his wife, MIELKKI, and their children, NYYRIKKI and TUULIKKI, he was invoked by huntsmen to help them make a good kill.

Tartar(s)
General
A Turkic, mainly Muslim people who are the descendants of the followers of Genghis Khan. They today live mainly in Tartar and Uzbekistan, to where they were deported from the Crimea in 1944, and southwestern SIBERIA. Their language belongs to the Altaic grouping.

Tawals
Polish
One of the three gods of the field, the other two being DATAN and LAWKAPATIM.

Teiwa
Teutonic
A name that linguists consider may be an archaic form of TÎWAZ.

Tell, Wilhelm (William)
Teutonic
Legendary fourteenth-century Swiss archer who was reputed to have refused to do homage to the Habsburg badge at Altdork on Lake Lucerne, though other versions say that he refused to salute the hat of GESSLER, the tyrannical Austrian bailiff, that had been placed on a pole. Whatever it was that Tell refused to pay his respects to, he was made to shoot an apple from the head of his son, which he did before turning his crossbow on to Gessler and shooting him with a second bolt. This symbolized the refusal of the Swiss people to submit to the external authority of Albert I of Austria.

The first written account of the legend dates from 1474, the period during which the Swiss were at war with Charles the Bold of Burgundy, but the actual basis of the story, the man showing his prowess with the crossbow, is far older.

Telramund, Frederick de
Teutonic
The suitor who besieged ELSA OF BRABANT, claiming that she was betrothed to him. He was defeated by LOHENGRIN, who came from the GRAIL temple in a swan-boat.

Teutonic
General
Of or pertaining to the Germanic peoples commonly referred to as Teutons. The term is used extensively throughout this book to refer to the Germanic peoples of Europe, since to use the term Germanic would encompass too many people (see GERMANY).

Thing(r)
Norse and Teutonic
The Thing was, and still remains, a Scandinavian public assembly or court of law.

Thjálfi
Norse and Teutonic
One of the servants of THÓRR, the other being his sister ROSKVA. They were the children of a farmer whose goats had been slaughtered and then restored to life by Thórr. However, one was restored lame, as Thjálfi had broken a leg to get at the bone marrow, an act that greatly annoyed the god and led to the children being offered as servants in order to placate him. Thjálfi became Thórr's trusted friend and even accompanied him when he travelled to UTGARDR. There Thjálfi ran a race against HUGI and lost, though it was later revealed that he did not stand a chance as Hugi was none other than thought in disguise.

Thjázi
Norse and Teutonic
The giant father of SKADI who black-mailed LOKI into helping him steal the APPLES OF YOUTH and abduct the goddess IDUNN. Immediately the ÆSIR began to age, and when they discovered the part played by Loki they threatened that god with death if he did not recover both Idunn and the apples. Loki used his extreme deviousness to disguise himself as a falcon and flew into Thjázi's home while the giant was away fishing. There he turned Idunn into a nut and, holding her in his beak and clutching the apples in his talons, flew back to ASGARDR. When Thjázi returned and found both the goddess and the apples had gone, he chased after Loki in the form of an eagle. However, the Æsir saw him coming and, by setting fire to a heap of woodshavings, singed his wings so that he fell to the ground, where he was easily overcome and killed. Skadi later travelled to Asgardr to have her revenge, but rather than fight, the Æsir had her choose one of their number to be her husband. She chose NJÖRDR, though she had hoped to pick BALDR.

Thokk
Norse and Teutonic
The giantess who refused to weep for the loss of BALDR, stating as the reason for her decision that, as he had been of no use to her alive, he might as well stay where he was. The decision of Thokk was to prove the undoing of LOKI, for the ÆSIR believed that she was none other than that devious god in disguise. They chased after the god, who changed himself into a salmon in his attempt to escape, but he was eventually netted. The Æsir then tied Loki across three stones with the entrails of one of his own sons, the open mouth of a serpent directly above him so that it dripped venom into his face. There Loki is destined to remain, his writhing causing earthquakes, until the RAGNARØKR.

Thora
Norse and Teutonic
The daughter of HAKON and wife of ELF[2].

Thord Freysgodi
Norse and Teutonic
A priest of FREYR.

Thor~er, ~ir
Norse and Teutonic
A son of VIKING and brother of THORSTEN.

Thorgerdr Holgarbrudr
Norse and Teutonic
'Bride of Helgi', a fertility goddess who was associated with FREYR and particularly worshipped in HALOGALAND, northern NORWAY. Her devotee, who referred to the goddess as his wife, was one Jarl HARKON, while SAXO GRAMMATICUS says that she was married to one of Freyr's relatives and along with all her companions became a prostitute, a reference that undoubtedly suggests that the cult of Freyr involved temple prostitution. Later sagas associated the goddess with TROLLS and other unnatural fiends.

Thorgrímr Thorsteinsson
Norse and Teutonic
A priest of FREYR who was killed by the outlaw GISL, his brother-in-law.

Thorhallr Veldimadr
Norse and Teutonic
'The Hunter', a devotee of THÓRR who travelled to VINLAND.

Thorólfr Mostrarksegg
Norse and Teutonic
'Beard of Most', a legendary Norwegian from the island of Most who was said to have been one of the first colonists of ICELAND.

Thór(r)

Norse and Teutonic

Also known as DONAR. One of the ÆSIR, the giant son of ODÍNN and FJORGYNN, though his parents are usually given as Odínn and FREYA, he was god of thunder and lightning, war and agriculture, and the champion of the gods, though he was also somewhat simple, or just gullible. He wore iron gloves and his BELT OF STRENGTH and wielded his hammer, MJOLLNIR. He drove a chariot whose wheels could be heard rumbling through the universe, occasionally hurling his thunderbolt at the world below him either in rage or simply due to his irritable nature. His ill-temper was famous and those who offended him ran the very real risk of having his thunderbolt hurled in their direction or their ship blown on to the rocks as the god blew out his cheeks, cheeks that were covered by his great red beard, in frustration. Thórr was, so it appears, the god of the soldier rather than of the hero, the latter falling under the protection of his father, Odínn. NORSE poets seem to have almost always depicted Thórr as at one with the common infantryman. In battle he would behave with a rash bravado, screaming at the top of his voice, hurling his body towards the foe while swinging his hammer around his head. Such a sight must surely have filled his enemies with dread, and therein lies the truth behind Thórr. He was a god who could terrorize with ease and yet who could be commensurately favourable to those who were devoted to him, these devotees being the common man.

Thórr married SÍF, celebrated for her beautiful fair hair, remaining faithful to her – a trait not common in ASGARDR. His children were said to be as strong as he was, among them MAGNI and MODI. Thursday is named after him.

Through his association with the ferocity of the storm, Thórr has also become associated with fertility, for his thunderbolt is both a terrible weapon and a phallic symbol. His hammer, which represented the power of lightning, was held to afford devotees some degree of protection, for many examples of hammer-shaped charms exist, while the hammer and the associated SWASTIKA symbol also appear on inscriptions that invoke the god or bless the dead. The swastika has also been found on ANGLO-SAXON funerary jars, and from this it has been inferred that it is a fire emblem as well as possibly signifying Mjollnir. The dual nature of the hammer, as symbol and weapon, is to be found in the stories of Thórr's journey to UTGARDR, and in the events following the theft of Mjollnir by Thrymr.

Although Thórr is usually considered invincible, in the *Prose* EDDA Snorri STURLUSON tells the story of his journey to Utgardr in the company of Loki. *En route* the gods rested at a farm, where Thórr slaughtered a number of goats, his sacred animal, for a meal. After they had eaten, the god laid out all the bones and chanted a spell over them which immediately restored them to life. However, one of the goats was restored lame as, during the meal, THJÁLFI, the farmer's son, had broken a leg bone to extract the marrow. This act so annoyed the god that the farmer offered his son and his daughter, ROSKVA, as servants to the god.

The following day the party journeyed through a great forest until, at nightfall, they came to a strange building with a gaping hole in one side. They entered the curious structure and lay down to sleep. However, they were soon disturbed by an earthquake, which caused them to retreat further into the building, where they found a passage. They hid in the passage, with Thórr guarding its entrance, and there spent a restless night through which they were constantly disturbed by a terrible roaring noise.

In the morning they crept out of the building to find a sleeping giant whose snores had been the roaring noise that had kept them awake, the earthquake having been caused when he lay down, while their shelter for the night had been none other than one of the giant's gloves. Hastily Thórr began to buckle up his Belt of Strength, but the giant awoke and introduced himself as SKRYMIR. He then offered to carry all their belongings, packing them into his own sack. He then set off, with Thórr and his companions struggling to keep up, but so huge were Skrymir's strides that the giant was soon out of sight. They finally caught up with him as night fell once more, only to find him asleep.

Tired and hungry, they tried to untie Skrymir's sack, but even Thórr's strength was not enough to undo the knots. Angered by this Thórr, crashed Mjollnir down on to the sleeping giant's head. He awoke, rubbed his head, commented that a leaf must have hit him and promptly went back to sleep. Thórr hit him again, harder, with much the same result, though this time Skrymir complained that an acorn must have fallen on him.

Thórr and his companions spent a cold and hungry night and at dawn, summoning up all his strength, the god hit the giant once more, this time with such force that Mjollnir sank into Skrymir's skull up to its shaft. Sleepily the giant awoke, complained that a bird must have dropped something on him and then rose. Before he took his leave of Thórr and his companions, Skrymir warned them that in Utgardr they would meet giants much larger than he was and that they should therefore always remember their manners. With that he left and Thórr, Loki, Thjálfi and Roskva travelled on until, at last, they came to Utgardr, where they were greeted by the giant king UTGARDR-LOKI, who commented disparagingly on

their diminutive size and invited them to demonstrate their various skills.

Loki, the first to take up the challenge, was to face a character by the name of LOGI in an eating contest. However, even though Loki ate quickly, Logi consumed not only the meat but also all of the bones as well as the eating trough. Thjálfi then ran a race against HUGI, who beat him hands down. Thórr then took on three challenges, the first of which was to empty at a single draught the horn of wine he was offered. However, after three huge gulps he had only slightly lowered its level. Then, upon the suggestion of Utgardr-loki, he attempted to lift the king's cat, a huge grey monster. Try as he might, using all his enormous strength, Thórr just managed to lift a paw. Utgardr-loki then suggested that the god might like to wrestle his ageing foster mother. Thórr mustered up all his strength and approached the wizened old crone, but try as he might he could not throw her, while she had no difficulty forcing him down on to one knee and might have succeeded in throwing him had Utgardr-loki not intervened and stopped the contest.

The following morning the travellers were taken to the gates of the kingdom by Utgardr-loki himself. There, before bidding them farewell, he explained that Loki had been pitted against the incarnation of fire (logi) and that Thjálfi had run against the personification of thought (hugi). Thórr, he explained, had tried to drink the sea, whose level he had managed to lower appreciably, had tried to lift the serpent MIDGARDSORMR, which had been disguised as the cat, and had tried to wrestle old age (elli). Furious at the deception, Thórr swung Mjollnir, at which Utgardr-loki and his domain instantly vanished, leaving the party quite alone in the forest.

The appearance of goats in this story as Thórr's sacred animal is worthy of attention. His chariot was said to have been drawn by two he-goats rather than by horses, which perhaps indicates that he originated as an agricultural deity, only later gaining his warlike personality. The goats that drew his chariot never let him down, on one occasion drawing him to the gates of NIFLHEIMR. At the end of the day, if the god felt hungry, he would kill and eat them, making sure that he always carefully set aside their hides and their bones. The following morning, as in the story of Thjálfi, he would restore them to life by touching them with Mjollnir.

The giant Thrymr, one of the FROST GIANTS, stole Mjollnir and held it to ransom, demanding the goddess FREYJA as payment for its return. HEIMDALLR, who here appears to have found his voice, unless of course he wrote down the idea, suggested that Thórr should assume the guise of the goddess and travel to JÖTUNHEIMR to recover his beloved weapon. At first Thórr was reluctant to put on woman's attire, but he eventually consented, his companion on the trip being the ever-resourceful LOKI.

The two gods, both of whom were in disguise, though the disguise assumed by Loki is unrecorded, were welcomed joyously at Jötunheimr. However, Thórr almost gave the game away during the wedding feast by eating not only eight salmon but also a complete ox, and washing the meal down with three barrels of mead. Loki was quick to explain that for eight days 'Freyja' had been unable to eat due to the excitement she felt at her forthcoming marriage. Thrymr then bent down to embrace his bride, but was somewhat startled by the glaring eyes he caught sight of through the veil. Once more Loki saved the day by explaining that 'Freyja' had also been unable to sleep. Finally, as custom dictated, Thrymr laid his wedding gift, Mjollnir, in the lap of 'Freyja' to cement their marriage.

Immediately Thórr took hold of his hammer, threw off the veil and killed Thrymr and all the guests.

Thrymr and his guests were not the only giants to be killed by Thórr. Among the others were GEIRRØDR, as well as the unnamed giant who built, though did not complete, the wall that surrounded ASGARDR. One duel with a giant is of particular interest as in its later stages it introduces the concept of woman as doctor, for in NORSE culture only women were permitted to practise this art. The duel was against HRUNGNIR, whose head and heart were said to be made of stone. The tale is especially interesting as it is now thought that it alludes to a temple cult in which the image of the god had a flint in his forehead from which devotees would strike a spark to light their torches.

In a drunken stupor Hrungnir had boasted that he would not only abduct Sif, Thórr's wife, and FREYJA, but also sink Asgardr. He then challenged Thórr, already angered by these insults, to a duel. The Frost Giants created MOKKURKALFI, a man of clay, to support Hrungnir, who, carrying a huge whetstone and holding a massive stone shield, advanced on to the field of combat. Thórr then came out wearing his gloves of iron and his Belt of Strength, brandishing Mjollnir and attended by THJÁLFI, his servant.

Hrungnir let his whetstone fly at the god, who responded by loosing Mjollnir, which shattered the whetstone before shattering Hrungnir's head. Fragments of the whetstone flew in all directions, one of them embedding itself in Thórr's forehead. To have this fragment removed, Thórr went to GRÓA, a VOLVA, who tried to charm it out. However, while she was going through her rituals, Thórr began to speak of the occasion when he had brought her husband, AURVANDILL, out of Jötunheimr in a basket, and how he had, when the man had suffered a frost-bitten toe, amputated the offending digit, which he then hurled into the heavens to form the star AURVANDILL'S TOE. Gróa became so engrossed in the story that she forgot to complete her incantations and the fragment remained in Thórr's forehead.

Thórr's battles with the serpent Midgardsormr – one such has already been described – are the Norse equivalent of the widespread myths of the storm-god doing battle with a vile monster. While Thórr appears to have been defeated in his contest with the serpent in the guise of Utgardr-loki's cat, the comments of the king suggest that if he had been successful, that would have heralded a great disaster, for the combatants cannot live without each other, the purpose of the contest being the struggle itself. This is the case in the story that follows as well.

Assuming the guise of a youth, Thórr went to the giant HYMIR and asked for his company on a fishing trip. Hymir agreed and went to fetch some bait, and while he was absent Thórr beheaded the giant's largest oxen and hid this in the boat. Shoving off, Thórr rowed so swiftly that the giant began to fear for his life – fear that was compounded when the god rowed straight past the traditional fishing ground and out to sea. Eventually Thórr stopped and immediately cast his line, which he had baited with the ox head.

After a short time Midgardsormr took the bait and Thórr attempted to reel him in. Eventually, having stamped holes in the bottom of the boat and bracing himself on the sea-bed, he succeeded in bringing the serpent to the surface, where god and monster stared at each other. However, as Thórr raised Mjollnir to strike Midgardsormr dead, Hymir cut the line and the serpent slid back to the ocean depths. Furious, Thórr swept Hymir into the sea and then waded back to the shore. In this case, it would appear that Thórr had gained the upper hand,

though if he had actually killed the serpent the world would have fallen, for Midgardsormr coils his body around the world and holds it together.

It is only at the RAGNARØKR that the serpent will break free and rise from the depths, spouting venom. God and monster will then meet in one final battle and will kill each other.

Thorri
Norse and Teutonic

According to the ORKNEYINGA SAGA, the son of SNÆR THE OLD, his own sons being named as NOR and GOR, and his daughter as GOI. Thorri was a great believer in the value of worship and every year held a sacrificial feast at midwinter that locally became known as 'Thorri's Sacrifice'. One winter at this time his daughter Goi disappeared and, even though a thorough search was made for her, she could not be found. A month later Thorri prepared to make another sacrifice in an attempt to find out what had happened to his daughter, this sacrifice becoming known as 'Goi's Sacrifice'. However, no matter what they did, they just could not discover what had occurred. It was not until Nor and Gor set out to find their sister

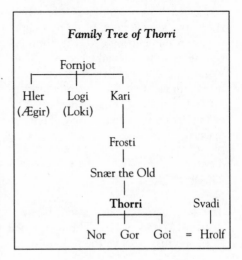

Family Tree of Thorri

Fornjot

Hler (Ægir) — Logi (Loki) — Kari

Frosti

Snær the Old

Thorri — Svadi

Nor — Gor — Goi = Hrolf

that she was discovered.

The Icelandic calendar names Thorri as the month that starts in the third week of January, and Goa (derived from Goi) as the following month. During pre-Christian times, sacrifices were held at the beginning of both months, sacrifices that echo the myth, though the myth is undoubtedly the later.

Thorsten
Norse and Teutonic
One of the nine sons of VIKING and brother of THORER. Following a war between his father and NJÖRFE, started when one of Njörfe's sons struck out in anger during a ball game and killed one of Thorsten's brothers, Thorsten became a pirate. In this role he encountered JOKUL, another of Njörfe's sons, who had killed the King of SOGN, banished Prince BELÉ and turned Princess INGEBORG into a hag. Jokul now turned his evil magic against Thorsten, but was himself killed, his death releasing the spells under which he held the kingdom of Sogn and Princess Ingeborg.

Thorsten and Belé became firm friends and joined up with ANGANTYR, with whom he recovered the ship ELLIDA that had been given to Viking by ÆGIR. They conquered the ORKNEYS, of which Angantyr became king, pledging himself to pay an annual tribute to Belé, thus suggesting that he actually became Belé's vassal. Thorsten and Belé then regained a magic torque that had been forged by VÖLUNDR from a pirate named SOTÉ before returning home, where Thorsten married Ingeborg, their son being FRITHIOF.

Thrall
Norse and Teutonic
The son born of the union between HEIMDALLR and EDDA. Thrall married THYR and they became the progenitors of

the race of serfs, or thralls. Legend records that neither Thrall nor his wife were the most beautiful of people.

Thridi
Norse and Teutonic
One of the three curious creatures that discoursed with GYLFI while he was in ASGARDR in the guise of GANGLERI, the other two being HAR and JAFNHAR.

Thrud
Norse and Teutonic
The daughter of THÓRR and SÍF. Her hand in marriage was sought by ALVIS, a DWARF, and while Thrud was willing, and the whole of the ÆSIR gave their blessing, Thórr was not so keen. The god denigrated the dwarf for his diminutive size, and then bombarded him with tricky questions for hours until the SUN rose in the sky and the unfortunate Alvis was turned to stone.

Thrudgelmir
Norse and Teutonic
The father of BERGELMIR, this six-headed giant was one of the original FROST GIANTS who had been born from between the toes of YMIR.

Thrud~heimr, ~vang
Norse and Teutonic
The home of THÓRR within the realm of ASGARDR, though some sources talk of Asgardr lying within the domain of Thórr, which is in this case called Thrudvang. This would seem to suggest that some sources consider Thrudvang or Thrudheimr the name of the entire upper level of the NINE WORLDS.

Thrymheimr
Norse and Teutonic
The home of THJÁZI and SKADI, it seems that Thrymheimr was a kingdom within the boundaries of JÖTUNHEIMR.

Thrymr
Norse and Teutonic
One of the FROST GIANTS, the son of KARI, he stole MJOLLNIR and refused to return it unless FREYJA was delivered to him to become his wife. The gods of ASGARDR debated what to do. HEIMDALLR suggested that THÓRR should assume the guise of Freyja and travel to JÖTUNHEIMR to recover his property. At first reluctant, as this meant dressing in female garb, Thórr finally agreed, setting off in the company of LOKI.

The pair were joyously greeted by the Frost Giants, but twice Thórr was almost discovered during the wedding feast. The first occasion was when he ate eight salmon and a whole ox, and then washed the meal down with three barrels of mead. Loki was quick to explain that 'Freyja' had been so excited by the prospect of her forthcoming marriage that she had been unable to eat for eight days. Thrymr then bent down to embrace his veiled bride and was surprised by the staring eyes he glimpsed. Again Loki saved the day by adding that 'Freyja' had also been unable to sleep.

Finally, as custom dictated, Thrymr laid his wedding present, Mjollnir, in the lap of his bride. Immediately Thórr took hold of his weapon, threw off his veil and killed Thrymr and all the wedding guests returning triumphant to Asgardr.

Thunor
Norse, Teutonic and Anglo-Saxon
A name for TÎWAZ, whom the ANGLO-SAXONS also called TIG.

Thyr
Norse and Teutonic
The wife of THRALL.

Tig
Anglo-Saxon
One of the ANGLO-SAXON names for TÎWAZ.

Titania
French and British
The queen of the FAIRIES, wife of OBERON. She is perhaps best known from A Midsummer Night's Dream by William SHAKESPEARE, in which she quarrels with her husband over a changeling boy.

Tîw(az)
Teutonic and Anglo-Saxon
The name by which the TEUTONIC and ANGLO-SAXON people referred to the sky father, though by the first century AD the position of Tîwaz was, it seems, under challenge by the war god WODAN. A sternly just god, he was later replaced in the pantheon by ODÍNN, who shares his sacrificial practices and appears to combine attributes and characteristics of both Tîwaz and Wodan. The NORSE peoples referred to Tîwaz and TYR. The day Tuesday is derived from 'Tîw's Day'.

tjetajat
Finno-Ugric
Name given to a village SHAMAN, considered as a wizard who was in contact with the gods and the spirits of the dead.

Torge
Norse and Teutonic
One of the giant suitors of the mortal JUTERNAJESTA who saved his love from the arrow fired at her by SENJEMUNDR, whom she had rejected. Torge threw his immense hat into the path of the arrow; arrow, hat and Senjemundr being turned to stone moments later as the SUN[5] rose. Whether or not Torge was rewarded by marrying the maiden is not recorded.

Tree of Life
1 *Russian*
    An alternative name for the WORLD TREE[1].
2 *Siberia – Yakut*
    The world pillar of YRYN-AL-TOJON,

the 'white creator Lord'. Though the Tree of Life is not given a particular name, it does appear in one YAKUT myth in which a youth is nourished by AJYSYT from her milk-laden breasts after she has arisen from the roots of the tree. This myth combines the cosmic Tree of Life and the mother goddess in one sustaining and nourishing entity.

Triglav
Slovene
Name by which SVANTOVIT was worshipped in SLOVENIA, depicted with just three faces instead of the usual four.

Triglav, Mount
Slovene
The highest mountain of the Julijske Alps in northeastern SLOVENIA and the highest peak in the former Yugoslavia. Mount Triglav lies about eight miles south of the Austrian border, to the east of Bled, and was considered by the Slovenes as the home of the gods, a sort of Slovene Mount Olympus. It was on this mountain that the chamois with golden horns, ZLATOROG, was hunted.

Troll(s)
Norse and Teutonic
An evil spirit who is often likened to a kind of DWARF. Usually malicious and extremely ugly, with fir trees growing from their heads, Trolls live in caves and other dark areas, such as below bridges, where they trap unsuspecting travellers and demand a tribute from them under threat of an extremely unpleasant death. A Troll might thus be seen as a minuscule OGRE, though tradition does not necessarily make Trolls small, like dwarfs.

Tuberculosis
Finno-Ugric
One of the monstrous offspring of LOVIATAR and WIND^2. The other monsters are named as PLEURISY, COLIC, GOUT, ULCER, SCABIES, PLAGUE, CANCER and ENVY.

Tugarin
Russian
A vile, heathen monster who is described as being a giant with a girth the size of two fully grown oak trees. His eyes were set wide apart – some accounts say a full arrow's-length apart – and his ears were almost eight inches long. Inflicting his presence on the court of Prince VLADIMIR BRIGHT SUN at KIEV, he was insulted by ALESHA, whom he attempted to kill at a banquet in the royal palace by throwing his knife at him. EKIM, Alesha's squire, caught the knife, so Tugarin challenged Alesha to meet him out on the steppe.

Alesha did so in the guise of a pilgrim, but Tugarin thought he would have the upper hand, for he made himself a pair of wings out of paper on which he flew while sitting astride his powerful horse. Alesha, however, prayed for rain, which spoilt the wings. Crashing to the ground, Tugarin rushed at Alesha on his horse, fully intending to trample him into the ground, but Alesha hid in the horse's flowing mane and struck Tugarin's head from his shoulders with the heavy staff he was carrying. Alesha then stuck Tugarin's head on to the end of the staff and rode back into Kiev on Tugarin's horse.

Tugarin is a prime example of the way the traditional DRAGON^1 developed in the later epic stories, the BYLINY, for he was human in form but had the power to fly like a dragon, albeit on paper wings.

Tungus
Siberia
Ancient, indigenous people who endured the rigours of life in the wastelands of SIBERIA.

Tuonela
Finno-Ugric

The UNDERWORLD, the land of the dead that was ruled over by the TUONI and TUONETAR and their hideous, dwarf-like daughters LOVIATAR, KIVUTAR, VAMMATAR and KIPU-TYTTO. The entrance to the realm was guarded by the monstrous SURMA, the personification of sudden death.

VÄINÄMÖINEN travelled to Tuonela, where Tuoni's son tried to trap him. The hero, however, turned himself into a serpent and escaped. LEMMINKAINEN was not quite so lucky when he came to Tuonela on the third of the tests set him by LOUHI. He was ambushed by MÄRKHÄTTU, who threw his body into the river, where Tuoni's son cut it into five pieces which he threw into a whirlpool. Lemminkainen's mother, KYLLIKKI, later gathered the pieces together and revived her son.

Tuonetar
Finno-Ugric

The consort of TUONI, queen of the land of dead, TUONELA, and mother of four hideous, dwarf-like daughters, LOVIATAR, KIVUTAR, VAMMATAR and KIPU-TYTTO, as well as other unnamed children, such as the son who cut up the corpse of LEMMINKAINEN.

Tuoni
Finno-Ugric

Ruler of TUONELA, the land of the dead, husband of TUONETAR and father, by her, of LOVIATAR, KIVUTAR, VAMMATAR and KIPU-TYTTO, four hideous, dwarf-like daughters, as well as at least one unnamed son, who was responsible for cutting up LEMMINKAINEN's corpse.

Turkic
General

Of or pertaining to Turkey, its peoples and its languages.

Tursas
Finno-Ugric

A hideous water fiend who was an attendant upon AHTI[1]. In one fragment of a myth, Tursas was reported to have risen from the depths of the oceans and fired the hay cut by the VIRGINS OF THE WAVES.

Tuulikki
Finno-Ugric

The offspring of TAPIO and MIELIKKI whose sibling was NYYRIKKI. All four were invoked by hunters to help them make a good kill, for they are minor woodland deities.

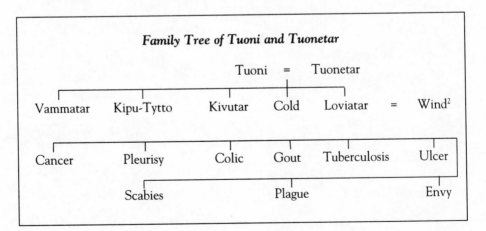

Family Tree of Tuoni and Tuonetar

Twilight of the Gods
Norse and Teutonic
The literal meaning of both the RAGNAR-
ØKR and GÖTTERDÄMMERUNG.

Tyr
Norse and Teutonic
Also known as TÎWAZ. The north
European equivalent of the classical
Greek Zeus or the Roman Jupiter. Born
from the sweat of the giant YMIR, Tyr was
the father of the giants and shared the
same hierarchy as DONAR and WODAN.
Some sources name Tyr as the son of
FRIGGA by either ODÍNN or the giant
HYMIR, the latter apparently being a confusion between Ymir and Hymir.
Associated with the light of heaven itself,
he also had some connection with the
idea of legal government, but later
became far less associated with peaceful
purpose and was altered into a war god
who was reputed to be able to determine
the outcome of battles.

Tyr once succeeded in catching the
wolf FENRIR with the chain GLEIPNIR, the
wolf refusing to submit unless one of the
ÆSIR placed his arm in his mouth. Tyr
volunteered and Fenrir promptly bit off
his right hand. During the RAGNARØKR he
will be pitted against GARMR, the hound
of Hel, and each will slay the other.

Tyrfing(r)
Norse and Teutonic
A magical sword that was made by the
DWARFS and subsequently owned by
ANGANTYR.

Ukko
Finno-Ugric
The 'Ancient Father Who Rules the Heavens', the god of the air and sky who succeeded JUMALA as the supreme deity, the head of the FINNO-UGRIC pantheon. Married to AKKO, the goddess of the mountain ash, Ukko supported the world and was, in turn, supported by PAIVA, the SUN³, KUU, the MOON³, OTAVA, the spirit of the GREAT BEAR, and ILMA, the air. Controlling all the elements, Ukko was invoked by man only when all other gods had failed to help.

Ukko is depicted as wielding a jagged stick, symbolic of the thunder he alone controls. The oak tree was sacred to him. Holding it aloft, Ukko caused the clouds to gather and made the rain descend.

Ukraine
General
A constituent republic of the southeast of RUSSIA since 1923, the capital of which is KIEV. A state by the ninth century, it was under Polish rule from the fourteenth century. East Ukraine was absorbed by Russia in 1667 and the rest in 1793 from Austrian rule. The Ukrainian language belongs to the Slavonic branch of the Indo-European family. It is closely related to Russian, sometimes being referred to as 'Little Russian', though this term is unliked by the Ukrainian people.

Ulcer
Finno-Ugric
One of the monstrous offspring of LOVIATAR and WIND². The other monsters are named as PLEURISY, COLIC, GOUT, TUBERCULOSIS, SCABIES, PLAGUE, CANCER and ENVY.

Ulfheônar
Norse and Teutonic
'Wolf-skin-clad Ones', a term that was sometimes used to refer to the BERSERKIRS.

Ulfrun
Norse and Teutonic
One of the nine WAVE MAIDENS, the giantess daughters of ÆGIR.

Ullr
Norse and Teutonic
Also HOLLR, OLLR and VULDR. An inhabitant of ASGARDR, the god of winter, hunting, archery, death and skiing, the son of SÍF and ODÍNN, who was raised as the stepson of THÓRR. He is possibly to be considered as the husband of the giantess SKADI. Ullr, who was possibly the lover of FRIGGA, was the next deity in importance after Odínn, but never achieved great popularity or cult because of the severity of the season with which he is associated. Sources say that for two months of each year, summer, Ullr was forced to live in NIFLHEIMR. The AURORA BOREALIS¹ was believed to be Ullr putting on a display of his powers for both gods and humans alike.

Underworld
1 *Russian*
Though the Underworld is not a rec-

ognized domain of the dead in Russian legend, it does appear in the TUNGUS story from SIBERIA of IVAN THE MARE'S SON as the realm of a huge serpent who feeds on the blood of MARFIDA and her sisters. When the serpent is wounded by Ivan the Mare's Son, it returns after three days, riding in a cloud of fire, surrounded by its army of demons.

Some Russian legends connect the witch BABA-YAGA with the realm of the dead, though this is never specifically called the Underworld. Some authorities go so far as to say that her cottage, with its chicken's legs, stands where the land of the living meets the land of the dead. In this context Baba-Yaga may be seen to be protecting the entrance to the Underworld, her role being similar to the Greek Cerberus: rather than stopping anyone entering the Underworld, she is there to keep the dead from escaping. In the story of Ivan the Mare's Son, her role seems to have been replaced by the heroic Ivan, for his house is also in a clearing in the middle of a forest.

2 *Finno-Ugric*

The land of the dead, TUONELA, the realm of TUONI and TUONETAR, their hideous daughters LOVIATAR, KIVUTAR, VAMMATAR and KIPU-TYTTO, and the guardian monster SURMA, who, like BABA-YAGA, may be seen as protecting the entrance to the Underworld.

3 *Lithuanian*

The realm of PUSKAITIS and the subterranean *BARSTUKAI* and *KAUKAI*. Though it is not necessarily the land of the dead, it was certainly considered as a realm whose occupants affected the fertility of the ground, for the *barstukai* were believed to influence the harvest.

4 *Norse and Teutonic*

The domain of the goddess HEL that is called NIFLHEIMR. The Underworld was one of the two primeval regions that existed before man had been created, a northern land of snow and ice, characteristics that appear to have carried through to the land of the dead, which had to be entered through the HELGRIND gates.

Undines
Norse and Teutonic

Friendly female water spirits that are to be considered as the NORSE version of mermaids, though they were said to inhabit both fresh and salt water.

Undur
Norse and Teutonic

Son of VISBUR and brother of GISL. The witch HULDR arranged for them to kill their father without being either detected or suspected of the crime.

Unicorn
General

A fabulous beast that is common to the mythology and folklore of a great many different cultures and is represented as a beautiful white horse with a single horn, usually conical or helical in form, projecting from the centre of its forehead. Very occasionally it is depicted as a young goat. Tradition says that it is a proud, wild and shy creature that can be caught only by a virgin if she sits very still, for then it will lay its head in her lap and immediately become tame. It is also believed that should all the unicorns be killed, then a terrible fate will befall mankind.

Upinis
Lithuanian

The god of rivers to whom white suckling pigs were sacrificed to ensure the purity of the waters.

Uppsal(la)
Sweden

City located in a fertile plain some forty-five miles northwest of Stockholm. Until the end of the thirteenth century Uppsala was the residence of the Swedish kings and is still an archbishopric. The city boasts the oldest university in northern Europe (1477) and SWEDEN's largest library. Three miles to the north of the city lies Old Uppsala, which is famous for its royal burial mounds dating from the sixth century.

Uproot Oak
Russian
A giant who appears in the story of the young tsarevich IVAN[2]. While the boy is fleeing from his home to escape his soon-to-be-born sister, who will be a cannibal witch, Ivan asks Uproot Oak to take him in. Uproot Oak would have done so, but he was due to die when he had cleared the forest he was working on. Later, after Ivan had found sanctuary with SUN'S SISTER, the young man was returning to his home to find out what had happened to his family. *En route* he met up again with Uproot Oak and, seeing that he had only two trees left to topple, threw down a comb that had been given to him by Sun's Sister, from which a huge forest of sturdy oak trees sprang up.

These trees were later to delay the witch as she pursued Ivan, for Uproot Oak blocked the road with a huge pile of tree trunks and the witch had to gnaw her way through them before she could continue the chase.

Urdr
Norse and Teutonic
Also WURDR. 'Fate', one of the three virgin NORNS who guarded her well, appropriately named the WELL OF URDR, that lay at the foot of YGGDRASILL. Her associates, sometimes said to be her sisters, were VERDANDI and SKULDR. Every day they watered Yggdrasill and plastered it with clay, thus ensuring its survival.

Urisk
British
One of the variant names given to PUCK.

Ursula
Slavonic
Also HORSEL and ORSEL. Goddess of the MOON[1] who was feasted on 21 October. Following the advent of Christianity, her importance was recognized and she became Saint Ursula.

urt
Finno-Ugric – Votyak
The VOTYAK name for HALTIJA, the concept or belief that all things, animate and inanimate, possess a soul or spirit.

Utgardr
Norse and Teutonic
Mysterious kingdom of giants like JÖTUNHEIMR that was ruled by UTGARDR-LOKI and was once memorably visited by THÓRR, LOKI, THJÁLFI and ROSKVA.

Utgardr-loki
Norse and Teutonic
The ruler of UTGARDR, the kingdom of giants from which he took his name. On one famous occasion he was visited by THÓRR, LOKI, THJÁLFI and ROSKVA, and challenged the three men to complete a series of impossible tasks after having made disparaging remarks about their diminutive size.

Loki, the first to take up the challenge, was to face a character by the name of LOGI in an eating contest. However, even though Loki ate quickly, Logi consumed not only the meat but also all of the bones, as well as the eating trough. Thjálfi then ran a race against HUGI, who beat him hands down. Thórr next took on three challenges, the first of which was to empty at a single draught the horn of wine he was offered. However, after three huge gulps he had only slightly lowered its level. He then, upon the suggestion of Utgardr-loki, attempted to lift the king's cat, a huge grey monster. Try as he might, and using all his enormous strength, Thórr just managed to lift a paw. Utgardr-loki then suggested that the god might like to wrestle his ageing foster mother. Thórr mustered up all his strength and approached the wizened old crone, but try as he might he could not throw her, while she had no difficulty forcing him down on to one knee and might have succeeded in throwing him had Utgardr-loki not intervened and stopped the contest.

The following morning the travellers were taken to the gates of the kingdom by Utgardr-loki himself. There, before bidding them farewell, he explained that Loki had been pitted against the incarnation of fire (*logi*) and that Thjálfi had run against the personification of thought (*hugi*). Thórr, he explained, had tried to drink the sea, whose level he had managed to lower appreciably, had tried to lift the serpent MIDGARDSORMR, which had been disguised as the cat, and had tried to wrestle old age (*elli*).

Furious at the deception, Thórr swung MJOLLNIR, at which Utgardr-loki and his domain instantly vanished, leaving the party quite alone in the forest.

Vafthrudnir

Norse and Teutonic

A clever giant who was once challenged to a contest by GANGRAD (ODÍNN in mortal disguise), the loser forfeiting his head. Gangrad answered all the giant's questions and then fired his quota at Vafthrudnir, who managed to answer them all until the last, which was to repeat the words Odínn had whispered into the ear of his dead son BALDR. Immediately Vafthrudnir realized that his competitor was none other than the god in disguise, for who else could possibly answer such a question. No matter that he had been tricked, Vafthrudnir admitted that he had been honourably defeated and willingly offered his head.

Väinämöinen

Finno-Ugric

God of music and poetry, the greatest hero of all the FINNO-UGRIC myths, and the hero of the KALEVALA, the epic poem that is the main, if somewhat unreliable, source of Finno-Ugric pre-Christian beliefs.

Väinämöinen was the son of ILMATER LUONNOTAR. Gestating for thirty years, he mused on how he might escape from his gloomy prison. At length he called on the SUN[3], PAIVA, and the MOON[3], KUU, to release him, and on the spirit of the GREAT BEAR, OTAVA, to teach him how to escape, but none replied. Growing bored, he hammered on the castle gates with the nameless finger (the ring finger). With his left big toe he breached one wall and,

on hands and knees, he drew himself across the threshold and fell from his mother into the sea, already an old man.

Väinämöinen was the first man to clear and till the soil, much to the envy of others. One such man, the LAPP JOUKAHAINEN challenged his power, making Väinämöinen chant such powerful and magical songs that the earth trembled, copper mountains rocked and huge boulders cracked into minute slivers. Väinämöinen changed Joukahainen's sledge into a lake, his whip into a reed that grew on the shore of that lake and his horse into a river that fed the lake. His sword he turned into a bolt of lightning, his bow into a rainbow and his arrows into hawks. Joukahainen's dog became a huge boulder, and his clothes clouds, stars and water-lillies. Väinämöinen now turned his attention to the peasant. First he cast him into a swamp up to his waist, then into a meadow and finally into a bog up to his armpits. Realizing that there was no other escape, Joukahainen promised that Väinämöinen could marry his sister AINO if he was released, but Aino threw herself into the sea rather than be married to such an old man.

Väinämöinen now sought the advice of his mother, who, stirring on the sea-bed, told him to seek a wife in the northern land of POHJOLA. As Väinämöinen rode north, *en route* to the snowy wastelands of Pohjola, Joukahainen ambushed him and shot his horse out from under him. Väinämöinen tumbled into the sea, where a storm blew him out of sight of land. For eight days he was swimming until an eagle spotted him and carried him to the borders of Pohjola. There, abandoned in a strange land where he could find no path, Väinämöinen wept.

His sobs attracted the attention of the Maid of POHJA, the young and beautiful daughter of LOUHI, the ruler of Pohjola. Louhi promised Väinämöinen the hand of her daughter if he would forge for her a SAMPO, and added that she would also guide him out of the snowy wastes of Pohjola and return him to his own fertile land of KALEVALA, where yellow cornfields waved in the breeze and birdsong filled the skies.

Väinämöinen admitted that he could not forge the required item, but promised instead to send his brother ILMARINEN, the divine smith. Louhi warned him that only the maker of the sampo would be able to marry her daughter, and then gave Väinämöinen a horse and sledge to take him home, adding that he must not stop or even look up from the sledge during the journey.

As Väinämoinen rode home he heard the sound of a loom being worked hard and, forgetting the prohibition placed on him by Louhi, looked up and saw the Maid of Pohja sitting on a rainbow weaving a golden cloth. Inviting her to become his wife, she agreed, provided that he complete several tasks for her. Eagerly he agreed and set about them. The tasks set Väinämöinen by the Maid of Pohja were to split a horsehair with a blunt knife; to tie an egg in knots though no knot was to be apparent in it; to peel a stone; to cut a pile of ice without causing any splinters; and finally, to carve a boat from fragments of her spindle and shuttle. Väinämöinen completed all but the last, for while he was carving the boat, the three evil spirits LEMPO, HIISI and

PAHA caused his axe to slip and become deeply embedded in his knee. Unable to think of any binding spell incorporating the words of the origin of iron that would heal the wound, Väinämöinen went to a nearby village, where he finally gained the help of an old man who healed him. Having failed in his last task, Väinämöinen returned to Kalevala and there set about building a ship to carry him back to Pohjola. This episode in the life of Väinämöinen is one of the most interesting sections of the *Kalevala*, for its references both to Väinämöinen's adventures in the UNDERWORLD[2] and to binding spells.

At each stage of his ship-building, Väinämöinen sang the appropriate charm or spell to bind the work together. However, when he came to join the planks, he found that he had forgotten three vital words. Search as he might, he could not find them anywhere, so he set out for TUONELA, the Underworld, land of the dead.

The journey took three weeks, the first of which he marched through shrubland, the second through woods and the third through thick forests. Finally he came to the black river which guarded the entrance to Tuonela. There he saw LOVI-ATAR and KIPU-TYTTO, two of the hideous daughters of TUONI and TUONETAR, rulers of Tuonela, washing their clothes in the dark waters. Väinämöinen persuaded them to carry him across the river to the land of MANALA, where he was welcomed by Tuonetar, who offered him a mug of beer crawling with worms and frogs, adding that he would never be allowed to leave.

As Väinämöinen rested from the long journey he had undertaken, Tuoni's unnamed son threw a net of steel over him and dragged him down to the very deepest part of the river to prevent him from escaping. Väinämöinen changed himself into a steel serpent, slid between the mesh and made his way back to the far bank of the river.

Leaving Tuonela, Väinämöinen sought the advice of a shepherd, who told him to go to the giant ANTERO VIPUNEN, who lay beneath the earth. Väinämöinen did so and, once there, felled the various trees that grew from the giant: the poplar that grew from his shoulders, the birch from his temples, the fir from his forehead, the alder from his cheeks, the willow from his beard and the wild pine from between his teeth.

Next Väinämöinen thrust his iron staff into Antero Vipunen's throat. The giant gagged and swallowed Väinämöinen, staff and all. Once inside the giant, Väinämöinen, ever resourceful, turned his shirt into a forge and his shirt sleeves and coat into a pair of bellows. He created an anvil from one of his own knees and a hammer from one of his elbows. Väinämöinen then set to work, hammering so violently that the anvil sank into Antero Vipunen's heart until, unable to endure any more, the giant spat up Väinämöinen and gave him the missing words that enabled him to complete building his ship.

During all this time Ilmarinen, his brother, had forged the sampo and had delivered it to Louhi, becoming betrothed to the Maid of Pohja in the process. Väinämöinen did not know of this and so set sail in his newly completed ship for Pohjola, intending to woo the Maid of Pohja himself. Although he arrived in Pohjola before his brother, who chased after him learning of his intent, and even though Louhi advised the Maid of Pohja to marry Väinämöinen, the Maid chose Ilmarinen.

Much later, after the Maid of Pohja had died, Ilmarinen returned to Pohjola to seek the hand of Louhi's other, unnamed daughter. Louhi refused, so Ilmarinen simply abducted the girl, but she played him false and Ilmarinen turned her into a seagull. Returning to Kalevala, Ilmarinen told his brother how the sampo had transformed Pohjola from a barren, snowy wasteland into a land of prosperity and plenty. Väinämöinen, accompanied by Ilmarinen and LEMMINKAINEN, then set sail for Pohjola, intending to steal the sampo. *En route* their ship rammed a huge pike, from whose jaw-bone Väinämöinen made a KANTELE, whose music was so sweet that it sent the entire population of Pohjola to sleep.

Having stolen the sampo, the three thieves turned their ship around and headed back towards Kalevala. However, Lemminkainen started to sing a loud and triumphant song which woke Louhi and all her people. Seeing that the sampo had been stolen, Louhi raised a huge storm which pursued the fleeing thieves and caught them up. During the storm the kantele was washed overboard and the sampo smashed, but Väinämöinen managed to salvage sufficient of this magical item to cause Louhi to give up and to transform Kalevala into a land of wondrous prosperity.

Väinämöinen is also reputed to have brought the benefit of fire to mankind. UKKO first struck fire from his fingernail with his sword, but in a moment's carelessness dropped it. It fell to earth, where it was swallowed by a trout, which was swallowed by a salmon, which was in turn swallowed by a pike. Väinämöinen caught the fish and cut it, together with the two fish inside it, open. The fire escaped and, after having burned down an entire forest, Väinämöinen caught it and imprisoned it in a metal jug.

At the end of his life Väinämöinen sailed away in a copper boat to a land reserved for the likes of him that was simply described as being half-way between heaven and earth.

Vak
Norse and Teutonic
One of the aliases assumed by ODÍNN so that he might travel incognito among mortals.

Valaskjálf
Norse and Teutonic
The silver-roofed home of ODÍNN in ASGARDR in which stood the HLIDSKJÁLF, the seat from which the god could survey the entire world. Sitting there, he was brought news by the ravens HUGINN and MUNINN. Valaskjálf should not be confused with VALHALLA.

Valfadir
Norse and Teutonic
'Father of the Dead', a title given to ODÍNN in his role as host to slain warriors in VALHALLA.

Valgrind
Norse and Teutonic
Alternative name for HELGRIND, the gates to NIFLHEIMR.

Val~halla, ~holl
Norse and Teutonic
The hall that stands by the plain of VÍGRÍDR to which the heroes who have fallen in battle are welcomed, to join ODÍNN's personal band of warriors. Those who gain entry to Valhalla are selected by one of the twelve VALKYRJA. From this glittering palace with golden walls and ceilings of burnished shields the valiant set out each morning to do battle, and return each night to feast on boar's meat and drink mead.

Váll
Norse and Teutonic
1 The son of ODÍNN and RINDA and brother to VÍDAR. Deliberately conceived to avenge the death of BALDR, in which case he is usually referred to as BOUS, he will be one of those to survive the RAGNARØKR.
2 The son of LOKI and SIGYN who killed his brother NARVE.

Valkyr~ja, ~ie
Norse and Teutonic
'Choosers of the Slaughtered', the name given to the twelve warlike handmaidens of ODÍNN who were supposed to hover over battlefields and select those who were to die before conducting them to VALHALLA, where they would spend eternity in the company of Odínn, and to be entertained by him. The Valkyrja (Valkyrie is a Latinization) were armed and mounted, and in some accounts rode to the battlefield, where they sometimes not only selected those who were to die that day but also guarded their favourites from death. The Valkyrja were always depicted as young, blonde, long-haired, blue-eyed maidens who wore elaborate breastplates, were armed with long lances and shields, and wore golden helmets on their heads.

From comparatively early times the Valkyrja were conceived as riding wolves rather than horses. One Irish poem from the time of the VIKINGS speaks of them weaving the fate of men in entrails. They bathed the battlefield in blood, and on one occasion are spoken of as rowing through a sea of blood as more blood rains down from the skies above. It is quite possible that the Valkyrja were deifications of the priestesses who chose the human victims for sacrifices to Odínn and then performed the ritual slaughter.

Many different names are given for the Valkyrja. Though said to number only twelve, there appear to be many more than there should be. Some, such as BAUDIHILLIE, are erroneous, but among the true Valkyrja are BRYNHILDR, GÖLL, GÖNDUL, GUDR, GUNN, HERFJOTURR, HILDR, HLADGUNNR, HLOKK, HRIST, SIGRDRIFA, SIGRÚN and SVAFA.

Valtam
Norse and Teutonic
One of the aliases assumed by ODÍNN so that he might travel incognito among mortals.

Vammatar
Finno-Ugric
The goddess of illness, one of the hideous daughters of TUONI and TUONETAR, her sisters being the equally ugly LOVIATAR, KIVUTAR and KIPU-TYTTO.

Vampire
Slavonic
In Slavonic demonology the vampire was a corpse that returned to 'life' at night to suck the blood of the living, the victim of the vampire's bite in turn also becoming one of the 'living dead'. This is, of course, the source of the now famous Dracula story. The vampire seems to have originated as a DRAGON[1] who ate the moon, such occurrences being believed to bring the dead back to life. The name itself is borrowed from the Serbian *vampir*. In certain cases the vampire had the ability to shape-shift at will, the most common target animal being the wolf, though bats were also common. These vampires were known as *vukodlak*, which literally translates as 'wolf's hair'. Common superstition still holds that when a WEREWOLF dies it becomes a vampire.

Vana
Norse and Teutonic
According to the YNGLINGA SAGA, a VANAHEIMR maiden who married SWEGDE and bore him a son, VANLANDE.

Vana~dis, ~brudh
Norse and Teutonic
'Betrothed of the VANIR', sometimes used to refer to FREYJA.

Vanaheimr
Norse and Teutonic
The realm of the VANIR.

Vanakvisl
Norse and Teutonic
According to Snorri STURLUSON, one of the former names, along with TANAKVISL, of the river TANAIS (the modern River DON).

Vanaland
Norse and Teutonic
Variant for VANAHEIMR that is used by Snorri STURLUSON, who says that it lay along the route of the TANAIS and formed one of the three regions of the world that were delineated by the river: Vanaland, ASIA to the east and Europe to the west.

Vandal(s)
General
A Germanic people related to the GOTHS. In the fifth century AD the Vandals moved from north GERMANY to invade Roman GAUL and Spain, many settling in Andalusia, the region at that time being known as Vandalitia. Others reached North Africa in 429. The Vandals sacked Rome in 455 but accepted Roman suzerainty during the sixth century.

Vanir
Norse and Teutonic
One of the two principal groupings of deities, the other being the ÆSIR. The Vanir, whose number included NJÖRDR, FREYR and FREYJA, were fertility deities, peaceable and benevolent and at their best during the summer months, the gods of farming and commerce. They fought a long battle against the Æsir which neither side won. As a result, a truce was organized and each side decided to exchange hostages. As a result Njördr and Freyr went to live in ASGARDR, while the Æsir reciprocated by sending HOENIR and

the wise MÍMIR. However, since Hoenir never spoke, the Vanir felt that they had been cheated, so they beheaded Mímir and sent his head back to the Æsir. ODÍNN sang a charm over the head and smeared it with herbs, thus restoring it to life, and gave it the power of speech. Thenceforth the god consulted the head in any crisis as it had become the fount of all wisdom.

This story possibly reflects the decline of the Vanir and the ascendancy of the Æsir as the main pantheon within the NORSE and TEUTONIC traditions, and seems to illustrate that rather than the Æsir becoming the sole pantheon the two were assimilated, each group retaining a particular function but, as the swapping of hostages shows, also sharing some attributes.

Another story says that at the end of the inconclusive war the two sides met to discuss the terms of peace. All the assembly spat into a cauldron, from which they created KVASIR, a being of such great wisdom that he could answer any question posed of him. Kvasir, however, was killed by two DWARFS, who mixed his blood with honey to brew the MEAD OF INSPIRATION. Later Odínn managed to steal this brew and take it to Asgardr, where it became known either as KVASIR'S BLOOD or the SHIP OF THE DWARFS.

Vanlande
Norse and Teutonic

The son of SWEGDE and VANA. According to Snorri STURLUSON in HEIMSKRINGLA Vanlande married DRIVA, who beseeched the witch HULD to either cast a spell over her husband so that he would return to FINLAND or kill him. Vanlande immediately felt the desire to return to Finland, but his friends and counsellors advised him not to, so he simply lay down to sleep. After a short while Vanlande awoke and called out to his advisers that the MARA (the nightmare was the way the

NORSE witch or succubus often chose to haunt male victims) was trampling him. His men hastened to his side, but they were too late and he died. In this story the Mara is said to have been the power of GRIMHILDR's daughter.

Vara
Norse and Teutonic

One of the numerous attendants of FRIGGA, Vara was responsible for the keeping of oaths and promises, for punishing perjurers and for justly rewarding those who kept their word no matter what.

Varpulis
Czech

The god of the storm wind and an attendant of the thunder god PERUN.

Vasilii
Russian

1 Son of Bel BELYANIN and NASTAS`YA OF THE GOLDEN BRAID, and brother to PETER and IVAN[1]. After Ivan had rescued their mother from WHIRLWIND, Vasilii and Peter stranded their young brother and tried to claim the rescue for themselves. The truth finally came out and their father wanted to have them executed. Ivan interceded, and Peter married the tsarita of the SILVER KINGDOM, Vasilii married the tsarita of the COPPER KINGDOM, and Ivan married ELENA THE FAIR, the tsarita of the GOLDEN KINGDOM, each maiden having been rescued by Ivan when he freed his mother.

2 Son of Tsar Vyslav ANDRONOVICH and brother of DMITRII and IVAN[6]. Vasilii and Dmitrii waylaid their brother Ivan when he was returning home with the FIREBIRD, the HORSE WITH THE GOLDEN MANE and ELENA THE BEAUTIFUL, and killed him. Vasilii won Elena the Beautiful when he and Dmitrii cast

lots, while his brother received the Horse with the Golden Mane. The Firebird they presented to their father as proof that they had completed the quest for the fabulous bird. After Ivan had been restored to life with the WATER OF LIFE AND DEATH and had returned to the royal palace, Vasilii and Dmitrii were thrown into the deepest dungeon by their father for their treachery.

Vasilisa of the Golden Braid
Russian

The beautiful daughter of Tsar SVETOZAR. For the first twenty years of her life she lived alone, save for her maids and ladies-in-waiting, in her room at the top of a tall tower. She earned her epithet because her hair reached her ankles and was worn in a single plait. News of her wondrous beauty spread far and wide, and soon offers of marriage were being received. Her father was in no hurry and waited until the appropriate time to announce that she would choose a husband.

As Vasilisa had never been outside her room, she longed to see the fields and the flowers that lay beyond the palace. Finally her father agreed to let her out just once. As she strolled around, picking the pretty flowers, she wandered away from her ladies-in-waiting. As she did so a strong wind sprang up which lifted the unfortunate girl clean off the ground and carried her far away to the land of a fierce DRAGON[1], who imprisoned her in a golden palace that stood on a single silver pillar.

Heartbroken by her disappearance, her parents dispatched her two brothers to find her. After two years they came to the land of the dragon and saw Vasilisa behind a barred window within the strange palace. As they entered the palace, the dragon returned and, being challenged by the two young men, deftly

picked one up and dashed him against his brother, so killing both of them.

Vasilisa at first starved herself, but then vowed that rather than die she would escape from the palace. Pretending to be nice to the dragon, she learned that there was only one who could beat him and he was named IVAN THE PEA, but the dragon laughed as he told her this, for he did not believe that such a person existed. Indeed, at that time, Ivan the Pea had yet to be born.

Back at her home, Vasilisa's mother was heartbroken at the lack of news of her children. Walking in her garden one hot day, she became thirsty and drank from a small stream that ran through the garden, failing to see that she had also swallowed a small pea that was in the water. The pea started to swell within the tsarina, and after the appropriate time she gave birth to a son whom she called Ivan the Pea.

Ivan the Pea grew at a tremendous rate until, at the age of ten, he was the strongest and fattest knight in all the kingdom. Learning of the fate of his brothers and sister, Ivan the Pea set out to find them. After travelling for three days, he came to a house on chicken's legs that revolved in the wind. The old crone who lived in the house gave Ivan the Pea directions to the land of the dragon on the understanding that he would bring her some of the magic water owned by the dragon that would once again make her young.

Finally Ivan the Pea arrived at the palace of the dragon, but when Vasilisa found out who he was she begged him to leave and save his life. Ivan the Pea would not hear anything of the sort, and instead went to the palace smithy and asked the old smith to make him a mace weighing 500 *poods* (18,000 lb). The mace took forty hours to make and took fifty men to lift it, but Ivan the Pea picked it up in a single hand and tossed it into the air, where it disappeared from sight. He returned to the palace and asked to be told when the mace was sighted. Three hours later a frightened messenger told Ivan the Pea that the mace had been spotted and the boy deftly caught it in one hand, the impact having no effect on him, although it did make the mace bend slightly. At that Ivan the Pea simply laid it across his knee and bent it straight again.

Shortly afterwards the dragon returned to the palace, which would normally have begun to revolve on its single silver pillar as he approached. This time it did not even move an inch, warning the dragon that there must be something, or someone, extremely heavy inside.

The dragon, who had the body of a man but the head of a serpent, flew in through one of the windows riding a winged black horse. Spying Ivan the Pea, the dragon leapt at him, but Ivan the Pea jumped nimbly to one side. As the dragon crashed to the floor, Ivan the Pea launched his enormous mace at it. As it made contact, it smashed the dragon into thousands of tiny pieces. However, the mace did not stop and crashed through the walls of the palace, only coming to rest many hundreds of miles away.

Refusing the request of the beleaguered kingdom that the dragon had ruled over to become their tsar, Ivan the Pea appointed the smith who had made his mighty mace. Next, remembering the promise he had made to the old crone in the forest, he located the magic water owned by the dragon, the WATER OF LIFE AND DEATH. He carefully filled a flask with the water and then sprinkled some more over the bodies of his dead brothers, who came back to life, rubbing their eyes as if they had just woken from a deep sleep.

All four then returned to their homeland, stopping en route to deliver the flask of the magic water to the crone in the forest. Once home, Vasilisa took a husband, and, following the death of their father, Ivan the Pea became tsar.

Even though the crone in the forest is not named, most authorities agree that she is none other than the witch BABA-YAGA.

Vasilisa the Beautiful
Russian

Vasilisa the Beautiful was the only daughter of a merchant whose wife died when the girl was just eight years old. As she lay dying, her mother gave Vasilisa her blessings and a doll, saying that if ever Vasilisa needed guidance all she had to do was feed the doll and it would tell her what to do. A short time later the merchant married for the second time. His new wife was a widow who had two daughters of her own.

Vasilisa's stepmother and stepsisters were jealous of her beauty and did everything they could to make her life a misery. They gave her all the hardest jobs to do and were always complaining. However, Vasilisa completed each task with ease, for all she had to do was feed the doll her mother had given her and, while she passed the time picking flowers or walking in the meadows, the doll did all the work that had been set for her.

The years passed and the merchant spent much of his time away from home. On one such occasion the stepmother moved the entire family to the edge of a very dark forest in the middle of which BABA-YAGA had her home. Every day some excuse would be found to send Vasilisa into the forest, but every time the doll guided her and kept her clear of Baba-Yaga's house. One night in autumn the stepmother and her daughters let all the fires in the house go out and, telling Vasilisa to fetch a light from Baba-Yaga, they pushed her out of the house.

After talking with her doll, who assured her that no harm would befall her as long as they were together, Vasilisa left the house and started into the forest. Deeper and deeper she went, and just as dawn was breaking, she was passed by a galloping horseman whose face and clothes were white, as were his horse and its harness. Just as the sun was rising she was passed by a second racing horseman. This time the rider's face and clothes were scarlet, as was his horse. Vasilisa walked deeper and deeper into the forest until, well into the evening, she came to the clearing in which Baba-Yaga's house stood.

The sight she saw froze her to the spot. A high fence of human bones circled the cottage, which stood slowly turning in the slight breeze. Human skulls adorned the fenceposts. The gate consisted of a pair of human legs, the bolts were a pair of human hands and the lock a mouth with razor-sharp teeth. As Vasilisa stood there, a third horseman passed her, riding swiftly through the gates, which magically opened to admit him. This rider was entirely black and rode on the blackest horse Vasilisa had ever seen. As horse and rider passed through the gate, they disappeared from view and night instantly fell. Light soon returned to the scene, though, for the eyes of the skulls that sat atop the fence started to glow until the clearing was lit as brightly as it would have been in the middle of the day.

As Vasilisa stood in the strangely lit clearing she heard an awful noise coming from the forest. Suddenly Baba-Yaga herself came into view, riding in a mortar which she rowed with a pestle before brushing away all trace of her passage with a broom. Stopping at the gates, she saw Vasilisa and asked her the reason she was there. When Vasilisa told her that she had come for a light, Baba-Yaga said that she would give her one provided that she worked for her for a time, warning that failure to complete any task set would result in her being eaten by the witch.

For two days Baba-Yaga set Vasilisa seemingly impossible tasks, such as separating earth from poppy-seeds, but each task was carried out with ease by the doll. All Vasilisa had to do was cook for the witch, a task she enjoyed and which the doll did not, for fear of falling into the fire thanks to her small size. On the third evening Baba-Yaga told Vasilisa that, as her mother had blessed her, she was free to leave, first answering a single question which she allowed Vasilisa to ask. Vasilisa wanted to know who the three horsemen were whom she had seen. Baba-Yaga explained that they were her servants, DAY[1], SUN[1] and NIGHT[1]. Leading the girl to the gate, she took one of the skulls down from the fence and placed it on a pole before handing it to Vasilisa, who then made her way back to the cottage where her stepmother and stepsisters eagerly awaited her return.

Outside the cottage Vasilisa made to throw away the skull, but it told her not to. Entering the cottage Vasilisa was warmly welcomed as, since she had left, they had been unable to light anything in the cottage and had spent five miserable days in the dark and the cold. However, when they took the skull from Vasilisa it stared straight into their eyes. No matter where they hid, the skull managed to fix its gaze on them, and by morning all three had been burned to a cinder.

Leaving the cottage the next morning, Vasilisa buried the skull and went to the town to await the return of her father. While waiting, the doll wove some spectacular thread which a seamstress took to the tsar. When he saw it he asked for the spinner of such a thread to be brought to him. As Vasilisa entered, the tsar fell instantly in love with her and made her his wife.

Vasilisa the Wise

Russian

A princess from a remote and unnamed kingdom who had the ability to change her shape at will, though she usually chose to assume that of a frog. It was in this guise that IVAN[5] found her.

Ivan was the youngest son of an unnamed tsar and one of his three concubines, each of whom had presented him with a son. Unsure which of them should rule after him, he told each to go into a field and to fire a single arrow with his name written on it in a different direction. Wherever the arrows landed they would rule, and each would marry the daughter of the house his arrow had landed in. The princes did as instructed and set off to find their arrows.

Ivan was at first unable to locate his arrow. However, after three days' searching he came across a small hut, made of reeds, in the middle of a swamp. Inside there sat a large green frog with his arrow in its mouth. The frog saw Ivan and bade him enter, changing the hut into a pretty summerhouse so that it was large enough to accommodate him.

The frog then magically made a table laden with food appear and then, when Ivan had eaten, told him that, unless he consented to marry her, he would never leave the swamp. Realizing that the frog was some kind of enchantress, Ivan agreed, whereupon the frog discarded its skin and stood before him in her real guise as a beautiful maiden. She told him that she would wear her frog skin during the day, but would appear as he now saw her every night.

Returning home, Ivan was at first ridiculed for wanting to marry the frog, but finally his father consented and the two were married, the frog keeping her word and appearing as the beautiful woman every night. For a long time Ivan and his wife lived happily. Then the tsar devised three tests for each of his son's wives. The first was to sew a fine shirt. The frog easily won, for she had had the garment magically made. The second test was to embroider, in one night, a tapestry. Again the frog easily won, for she commanded the winds to bring her the finest tapestry from her father's kingdom. Finally the tsar commanded each to bake him a loaf of bread. This time the two other wives tried to cheat by spying on the frog, but each produced disastrous results, while the frog produced the finest loaf ever seen.

To congratulate each of his daughters-in-law, the tsar organized a huge banquet in their honour. Distraught, Ivan knew he would be the laughing stock of the kingdom if he brought a frog to the banquet. Telling him to go on ahead, the frog changed into the beautiful maiden and arrived at the banquet in the finest horse and carriage anyone in the kingdom had ever seen. As the feast drew to a close Ivan made an excuse and left early, so he could arrive home ahead of his wife. There, in an attempt to keep his wife in her womanly form, he found and burned her frog skin. When his wife returned, she told him that had he waited just a while longer she would have been his for ever. Instead she told him that her name was Vasilisa the Wise and then disappeared, having instructed him to travel to the land of eternal sunlight to seek her.

Ivan set out to find his wife. After a long journey he found himself in front of a small wooden hut on chicken's legs that revolved slowly in the wind, the home of the witch BABA-YAGA. Entering the hut, he was confronted by the angry witch, but when he explained the purpose of his visit she agreed to help him. She told him that his wife flew in every day to see her. After she had made herself comfortable, Ivan was to take a firm hold of her and not to let go, even when she changed her shape.

Finally she would turn into an arrow, which, Baba-Yaga told him, he must break over his knee. Then, and only then, would Vasilisa be his for ever.

Shortly afterwards Vasilisa flew in on her magic carpet. Making herself comfortable, she did not see Ivan as he leapt out of his hiding place and caught hold of her. Instantly she began to change her shape, and in his surprise Ivan let her wriggle free and fly away. Baba-Yaga advised Ivan to visit Vasilisa's middle sister, for the witch knew that Vasilisa also visited her. Ivan thanked the witch and made his way to the home of Vasilisa's middle sister. There the very same thing happened, so the middle sister sent Ivan on to visit their youngest sister.

There he was told that this time he must not fail, for if he did he would never see Vasilisa again. After Vasilisa had arrived, Ivan pounced on her and hung on for all he was worth. Finally, realizing that she could not escape him, Vasilisa changed herself into an arrow, which Ivan broke across his knee. Instantly Vasilisa assumed her human form and told him that she was his for ever. Together they rode back on Vasilisa's flying carpet and lived happily together, Ivan becoming his father's heir.

Vasud
Norse and Teutonic
A very unlikeable and unfriendly god who was the father of VINDSAL and thus the grandfather of WINTER, which would make him an extremely early deity.

Vavaquisl
Norse and Teutonic
One version of Snorri STURLUSON's work calls the land on the River DON, the home of the VANIR, Vavaquisl. However, this appears to be a transcription error for VANAKVISL.

Vé
Norse and Teutonic
One of the sons of BÖRR and BESTLA, his brothers being ODÍNN and VILLI. The three killed YMIR, the blood of the giant flooding the earth and drowning all the FROST GIANTS with the exception of BERGELMIR, who sailed away across the flood to found a new race of Frost Giants who were to become the mortal enemies of the ÆSIR.

From the corpse of Ymir the three gods formed MIDGARDR. They made the seas and lakes from his blood, the earth from his flesh, in which they created the race of DWARFS like 'maggots', the mountains from his bones, rocks and pebbles from his teeth, jaws and smaller broken bones, and the grass from his hair. From the eyebrows of the giant they formed a wall around Midgardr to protect it from the Frost Giants. They then completed the creation process by setting four dwarfs at the four cardinal points to hold up Ymir's skull, which formed the dome of the sky.

Some sources say that once Odínn spent so long away from ASGARDR that Vé and Villi split the kingdom between themselves, along with FRIGGA, who apparently had no objection to sleeping with both of them.

Vecha
Norse and Teutonic
One of the aliases assumed by ODÍNN so that he might travel incognito among mortals.

Vedfolnir
Norse and Teutonic
The name of the falcon that sat between the eyes of the eagle in the topmost branches of YGGDRASILL. His eyes were so keen that he saw everything that happened in each of the NINE WORLDS, events that he duly related to the gods.

Vegtam
Norse and Teutonic
Alias used by ODÍNN when he travelled down to NIFLHEIMR to consult a seeress about the prophesied death of BALDR, only to be told what he already knew.

vele(s)
Baltic
Generic term applied to the spirits of the dead. They are believed to live in families, similar to their families when alive, in villages in sandy hills.

Veles
Russian
A nature deity who was regarded as the patron of cattle and of merchants. Following the adoption of Christianity by VLADIMIR I, Veles became Saint VLASII, who is depicted in Russian iconography surrounded by sheep, cows and goats.

Veli Joze
Croatian
Literally translated as 'Big Joe', Veli Joze was a giant who lived at MOTOVUN on the Istra peninsula of northern CROATIA. A valiant warrior, he once, in a fit of fury against a tyrannical feudal lord, wrapped his arms around Motovun tower and shook it with all his might. The tower cracked and began to lean to one side, a state it remains in to this day. Veli Joze did not escape unpunished. Two iron rings were fixed to the side of a nearby canyon from which he was suspended, though whether he died there is not recorded.

Vellamo
Finno-Ugric
The consort of AHTI[1].

velnias
Baltic
The name given to a malevolent spirit of the dead.

Venus
General
The nearest planet in the solar system to the earth, it lies nearer to the sun than the earth and thus shows phases. It is most famous as the MORNING STAR[1,2&3] or the EVENING STAR – the first 'star' visible in the dusk sky or the last star to disappear at dawn. Many cultures around the world have connected the planet Venus with deities personifying the daily death of the sun, and its wondrous rebirth the following morning.

Venusberg
Teutonic
Mountain, identified with Hörselberg in Thuringia, in the caverns of which, according to the TANNHÄUSER legend, the classical goddess Venus held her court.

Veraldargód
Norse and Teutonic
A name that is sometimes used to refer to FREYR, the most usual source of this variant being the works of Snorri STURLUSON.

Verdandi
Norse and Teutonic
One of the three virgin goddesses, the NORNS, who guard the WELL OF URDR at the foot of YGGDRASILL, the WORLD TREE[2], that they daily tend, water and plaster with clay. The other two were URDR and SKULDR.

Vetehinen
Finno-Ugric
An evil water spirit, the companion of TURSAS, and, with Tursas, an attendant of AHTI[1].

Vídar
Norse and Teutonic
A son of ODÍNN and the giantess GRID, and the brother of VÁLI[1]. His death was avenged by his father, who killed FENRIR,

though some sources say that he will kill Fenrir, survive the RAGNARØKR and avenge the death of his father.

Vígrídr
Norse and Teutonic
The name of the plain that is situated before VALHALLA. During the RAGNAR-ØKR all the monsters, fiends and giants will congregate here prior to the gods riding out of ASGARDR to meet them in their final battle.

Vikarr
Norse
The relatively late GAUTREKS SAGA tells the story of Vikarr, King of the VIKINGS, who prayed to ODÍNN for a favourable wind. He and his men then drew lots to find out who should be sacrificed to the god in payment. The lot fell to Vikarr, who quickly suggested that they should hold a symbolic hanging. However, as the king stood with entrails wound around his neck like a noose and the man STARKADR uttered the ritual dedication and struck the king with a stick, that stick turned into a sword and impaled the king, while the entrails turned into a rope and the king was hanged.

Vikhor`
Russian
A wicked enchanter who had stolen the mother or sister of a prince and was per-sonified as a WHIRLWIND. Popular belief held that if a knife could be thrust into the heart of a Whirlwind then it would injure or kill the wizard or devil riding in its midst. It is not clear whether Vikhor` is the name of the character simply referred to as Whirlwind in the story of IVAN[1], but it seems likely.

Viking
Norse and Teutonic
The eponymous hero who was greatly revered by the VIKINGS. The son of HALOGE, a king of NORWAY, though some sources say that Haloge was none other than LOKI in disguise, Viking was born on the island of BORNHOLM in the BALTIC Sea. At the age of fifteen his prowess came to the attention of HUNVOR, a princess who lived in SWEDEN, where she was being troubled by a giant. Viking set sail, armed only with ANGURVADEL, the magic sword of his father, and promptly killed the giant. He would have married Hunvor on the spot but was considered too young, so spent some years sailing around the North Sea, where he befriended a man named HÁLFDAN. He finally returned to Sweden and married Hunvor, Hálfdan accompanying him and marrying her servant INGEBORG.

Over the following few years Viking and Hálfdan took great pleasure in raid-ing other countries, their particular delight being the rape of women before putting them to the sword. However, the pair remained faithful to their wives, which suggests that for NORSE people rape did not interfere with relationships, being an acceptable form of lust that glorified their cause. Hálfdan and Viking also made friends with a king named NJÖRFE.

After Hunvor had died, Viking placed their son RINGR with foster parents and remarried, having nine further sons, the same number as Njörfe. However, even though the parents were on the friendliest of terms, their sons hated each other. Most of the time their fury was contained in a game of ball, but during a match one of Njörfe's sons was killed by one of Viking's children. As a result, Viking banished the offending child and his brothers willingly followed him into exile. Before they left Viking gave his eldest son, THORSTEN, the sword Angurvandel.

Njörfe's sons were far from satisfied with simple banishment. They followed

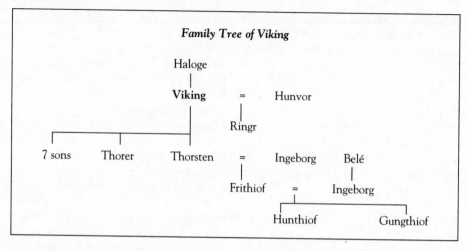

Family Tree of Viking

the exiled sons of Viking and engaged them in battle, at the end of which only two of Viking's sons – Thorsten and THORER – and only two of Njörfe's – JOKUL and another – were still alive. The two pairs swore their undying hatred for each other, the sons of Viking being sent to the court of Hálfdan, from where Thorsten set out on his own adventures, during the course of which he killed Jokul.

Vikings
Norse and Teutonic
Also called Norsemen, though known as 'Danes' in England and Ireland, the Vikings were Scandinavian sea warriors who raided Europe between the eighth and eleventh centuries, and often settled in the countries they attacked. For example, in France they were given Normandy. The Vikings conquered England in 1013 under Sweyn I, his son Canute being the king of England, DENMARK and NORWAY. In the east they created the first state in RUSSIA, as well as founding the city of NOVGOROD. Excellent mariners, the Vikings reached the Byzantine Empire in the south, and Ireland, ICELAND, GREENLAND and North America in the west.

Noted for the barbarity of their raids, the Vikings were able to penetrate far inland in their shallow-draught, highly manoeuvrable longships. They plundered for gold and other riches, killing men and children with abandon before raping the women and putting them to the sword as well. It was the need for an organized resistance against the Vikings that accelerated the development of the feudal system. The Vikings actually successfully invaded BRITAIN twice, first in their guise as Vikings and second in 1066 under the leadership of William the Conqueror as Normans.

vila
Serbian
A woodland nymph (plural *vile*) who is possibly similar in characteristics to the Baltic VELE.

Vilcinus
Norse and Teutonic
King who met the goddess WACHILT in a forest, the goddess subsequently rising from the depths of the ocean to arrest the progress of his ship to tell him that she was to bear their son. Vilcinus took her home and she gave birth to the great WADA before disappearing. Later Wachilt once more rose from the sea, to save her

grandson WIDIA from those who sought to kill him, and took him down to her sea-bed palace.

Vilje
Norse and Teutonic
Version of VILLI used by Snorri STURLU-SON.

Villi
Norse and Teutonic
One of the three sons of BÖRR, son of BÚRI, and BESTLA, the daughter of YMIR. His brothers were ODÍNN and the VÉ. The three killed their grandfather Ymir, the blood of the giant flooding the earth and drowning all the FROST GIANTS with the exception of BERGELMIR, who sailed away across the flood to found a new race of Frost Giants who were to become the mortal enemies of the ÆSIR.

From the corpse of Ymir the three gods formed MIDGARDR. They made the seas and lakes from his blood, the earth from his flesh, in which they created the race of DWARFS like 'maggots', the mountains from his bones, rocks and pebbles from his teeth, jaws and smaller broken bones, and the grass from his hair. From the eyebrows of the giant they formed a wall around Midgardr to protect it from the Frost Giants. They then completed the cre-ation process by setting four dwarfs at the four cardinal points to hold up Ymir's skull, which formed the dome of the sky.

Vimir
Norse and Teutonic
The river in which THÓRR almost drowned after GEIRRØDR's daughter had stood astride the river and made it flood. Thórr hurled a huge rock at the giantess and then, pulling on a rowan tree that hung over the water, managed to haul himself to safety.

Vindsal(ir)
Norse and Teutonic
The son of VASUD and the father of WINTER.

Vingnir
Norse and Teutonic
The husband of HLORA and one of the foster parents of THÓRR who used the alternative name of VINGTHÓRR in his honour.

Vingolf(r)
Norse and Teutonic
The name of a hall within ASGARDR where the gods and goddesses came together, not only to discuss matters of concern but also to enjoy each other's company.

Vingthórr
Norse and Teutonic
Honorific assumed by THÓRR as a mark of respect to VINGNIR, his foster father, his foster mother being HLORA, for whom he chose the name HLORRIDI as tribute. Together these foster parents constitute sheet lightning, an attribute of their ward.

Vingulmark
Norse and Teutonic
Realm of King GANDALF, half of the king-dom falling to HÁLFDAN SVARTI after the two had fought without result.

Vinland
Norse
A settlement on the northeastern seaboard of America that was founded by settlers from GREENLAND who were origin-ally from ICELAND.

Virgins of the Waves
Finno-Ugric
Unknown sea deities, possibly a form of sea nymph or even MERMAID, who appear in a fragment of a myth concerning

TURSAS in which this hideous water demon is said to have fired the hay cut by these Virgins of the Waves.

Visbur
Norse and Teutonic
Son of VANLANDE who was killed by his sons GISL and UNDUR, the witch HULDR arranging it so that the sons were neither detected nor suspected of the crime.

Visigoths
General
One division of the GOTHS, a Germanic people who settled near the BLACK SEA some time around the second century AD. Their eastern neighbours were the OSTROGOTHS. The Visigoths migrated to Thrace, from where, under Alaric, they raided Greece and Italy between 395 and 410, sacked Rome and established a kingdom in southern France. Expelled from France by the FRANKS, the Visigoths settled in Spain, their kingdom there lasting until the Moorish conquest of 711.

Vizi-ember
Finno-Ugric – Magyar
An extremely unlikeable and unattractive water god who lived in rivers and lakes and regularly demanded human sacrifices.

Vjofn
Norse and Teutonic
One of the multitude of FRIGGA's attendants whose role was that of conciliation. She aimed to keep the peace in all situations, whether it was reuniting quarrelling lovers or finding a peaceful solution to wars. Her position is therefore something of a paradox in a culture that glorified warfare at every opportunity.

Vladimir I
Russian
Also known as Saint Vladimir, or Vladimir the Great, the first Christian sovereign of RUSSIA. Born *c.* 956, the son of SVYATOSLAV, Grand Prince of KIEV, he became Prince of NOVGOROD in 970 and, following the death of his father in 972, he seized Kiev from his brother in 980. Consolidating the Russian realm from the BALTIC to the UKRAINE, he extended its dominions into Galicia, LITHUANIA and Livonia, making Kiev his capital city. Until 987 he, like his people, worshipped the pagan gods such as PYERUN, but in 987 or 988 he formed a pact with the Byzantine emperor BASIL II, married Basil's sister ANNA and accepted Christianity. He was, with his great-grandson VLADIMIR II, amalgamated into the legendary hero VLADIMIR BRIGHT SUN.

Vladimir II
Russian
Correctly known as VLADIMIR MONOMAKH or VLADIMIR MONOMACHUS, Vladimir II was born in 1053, the great-grandson of VLADIMIR I. He became the Grand Prince of KIEV in 1113 by popular demand, and therefore became ruler of RUSSIA instead of the prior claimants of the Svyatoslav and Iziaslav families, thus founding the Monomakhovichi dynasty. A popular, powerful and peaceful ruler, he ruled until his death in 1125 and was, with his forebear Vladimir I, amalgamated into the legendary hero VLADIMIR BRIGHT SUN.

Vladimir Bright Sun
Russian
A legendary figure who was created from two historical princes of KIEV, VLADIMIR I (*c.* 956–1015) and VLADIMIR MONOMAKH (1053–1125). According to the legends, the BOGATYRI, or Holy Russian knights, gathered at his court before setting off on their adventures in the defence of their country.

Vladimir Monomachus
Russian
Latinized form of VLADIMIR MONOMAKH.

Vladimir Monomakh
Russian
The correct name by which VLADIMIR II, the founder of the Monomakhovichi dynasty and ruler of RUSSIA from 1113 to 1125, was known.

Vlasii, Saint
Russian
Saint created from the older pagan patron of cattle and merchants, VELES. In Russian religious iconography he was depicted surrounded by cows, sheep and goats.

vodyanoi
Russian
The chief of the water demons that inhabit any particular stretch of water, whether river or lake. He is usually portrayed as a fat, jolly man with a long beard and tangled green hair, though he could assume any shape, from a log to a beautiful maiden. He lives in an underwater home with his wife and children and has total control over the other water sprites and demons, such as the sad RUSALKA, who also live in the same tract of water. Sometimes his babies would stray from home and be caught in the nets of fishermen. If the fishermen gently replaced them in the water, he would reward them with a good catch, but if they did not he would vent his anger on them, tearing their nets and capsizing their boats.

Some legends said that the *vodyanoi* tended a herd of his own cattle on dry land and would creep out at night to pasture them on the peasants' land. On these occasions he would be dressed as an ordinary peasant, but was instantly recognizable for his clothes were always damp and he left a trail of wet footprints wherever he went.

Usually a benevolent being, his favourite sport being to ride on the backs of large fish, the *vodyanoi* could also become angry – for example, when humans tampered with his possessions or forgot to return his offspring to the water. Early legends said that a *vodyanoi* would claim a life in compensation every time a new water mill was built, for the *vodyanoi* tended to favour the still waters of the millpond. To safeguard the mill the peasants would slaughter a chicken or a horse and throw it into the water. They would also cross themselves before swimming or stepping into the water to bathe, just in case the *vodyanoi* was angry and tried to drown them.

However, despite all this the *vodyanoi* were not always regarded as demons, and, as the story of KAPSIRKO demonstrates, they were easily tricked. Even though the *vodyanoi* were immortal, they aged like humans, and were rejuvenated according to the phases of the MOON[1].

Vol
Norse and Teutonic
The companion of VOLLA who is usually named as PHOL, though this form, it is thought, might actually be correct.

Volga, River
Russian
The longest river in Europe, some 2,290 miles in total. It rises in the Valdai plateau and flows into the Caspian Sea fifty-five miles below Astrakhan, having drained most of the central and eastern parts of RUSSIA. In the Russian legends the river is affectionately referred to as *matushka*, which translates as 'little mother'.

Vol`ga Svyatoslavovich
Russian
Nephew and godson of VLADIMIR BRIGHT SUN, who had given him a princedom

that consisted of three towns and their surrounding lands, and lordship over all the peoples living within that domain. He is best known from a legend, possibly as late as the fifteenth century, in which he sets out to collect taxes from his subjects but is warned of robbers in the vicinity by the ploughman MIKULA SELYANINOVICH, who so impresses him with his strength and prowess that Vol`ga makes the ploughman lord of his domain, empowering Mikula to collect the taxes in his place.

Volla
Norse and Teutonic
The companion of PHOL or VOL.

Volos
Slavonic
A god of war who may simply have been an aspect of PERUN/PYERUN. The Russians specifically made him the god of animals as well as of war, making him an attendant of Pyerun. With the advent of Christianity, Volos became absorbed into the cult of Saint Vlas (Saint Blaise). When disease attacked farm animals, a sheep, a cow and a horse would be tied together by their tails and driven over a ravine and finished off with boulders. This sacrificial offering to Volos continued well into the Christian era and perpetuated memory of the pagan god.

volshebnye shazka
Russian
The largest subdivision of SHAZKA. Literally translated as 'wonder tales', these take place in fantasy lands which are inhabited by fabulous beings such as BABA-YAGA, KOSHCHEI THE DEATHLESS and MOROZKO the FROST[1] demon. The stories all follow the same basic format. The hero must find some way to enter the fantasy world, which may lie beyond the horizon, under the sea or in the sky, and

there overcome any number of obstacles until he wins the prize he came to seek, such as the release of a beautiful maiden, the return of his mother or wife, or a fabulous and magical object, such as the WATER OF LIFE AND DEATH. Like the simple *shazka*, they have no historical grounding and are pure make-believe, unlike the BYLINY, which have at least some historical background. Stories that deal with the UNDERWORLD[1] may appear to be *volshebnye shazka*, or even *shazka*, but they are in fact BYLICHKA, a specific grouping of stories that deal with the supernatural.

Volsung(s)
Norse and Teutonic
Legendary family, founded by VOLSUNGR, whose most famous members were SIGMUNDR and his son SIGURDR.

Völsunga Saga
Norse
The NORSE version of the story of SIGURDR (the TEUTONIC equivalent, the NIBELUNGENLIED, concerns SIEGFRIED). It is now thought that the *Völsunga Saga* was possibly written *c.* 1270–80.

Volsungr
Norse and Teutonic
Eponymous founder of the legendary VOLSUNG family. Volsungr was the father of SIGMUNDR and SIGNY (as well as nine other sons), and thus the grandfather of SIGURDR. Volsungr became the king of the HUNS following the death of his father, RERIR.

Völundr
Norse and Teutonic
One of the sons of WADA, King of the Finns, his brothers being EGIL and SLAGFIDR. Their story is told in the epic *Volundr*. Völundr was known as WELAND by the ANGLO-SAXONS, a name that was

later to be corrupted into WAYLAND.

Völundr, Egil and Slagfidr lived in WOLFDALES, where they came across the three SWAN MAIDENS, whom they married. However, seven years later the Swan Maidens returned to their native home in MURKWOOD, so Egil and Slagfidr set out to try and find them, Völundr remaining at home in Wolfdales, where he worked as a smith. One night he was taken captive by the men of King NIDUDR as he slept. The king requisitioned his sword and gave the smith's ring to his daughter, Princess BODVILDR. Völundr was then hamstrung and marooned on the island of SÆVARSTOD, where he was secretly visited by Nidudr's two sons, who were curious to see the treasure attributed to Völundr. However, Völundr tricked and murdered them, burying their bodies in a dunghill. He kept their heads, which he mounted in silver, made jewels from their eyes and breast ornaments from their teeth. The two skulls he sent to Nidudr, the jewels to their mother and the breast ornaments to their sister, Bodvildr. Having had her curiosity aroused, Bodvildr visited Völundr, who raped her and, then having proclaimed that he was avenged, flew off on a pair of wings he had made for himself.

Voluspá
Norse and Teutonic
Anonymous poem that combines elements from at least three accounts of the creation of the world, if not more. It also supports the account of SAXO GRAMMATICUS in attributing the death of BALDR to HÖDR alone.

Volva
Norse and Teutonic
A seeress, such as GRÓA. These seeresses were associated with FREYJA, who was alleged to have taught them the technique of trance divination known as SEIDR.

Von
Norse and Teutonic
The name of the river that was said to flow from the mouth of FENRIR.

Vör
Norse and Teutonic
'Faith', one of FRIGGA's attendants who had knowledge of the future.

Vseslav`evich, Volkh
Russian
One of the most ancient Russian heroes, a mighty wizard and hunter, the son of Tsarevna Marfa VSESLAV`EVNA and a snake who impregnated her when she stepped on him. His birth was hailed as that of a great man, for the sky was lit up by the brighest moon ever seen, and a huge earthquake rocked the land and made all the animals of both land and sea run to find a safe hiding place.

At the age of just one and a half hours he first talked to his mother and told her not to swaddle him, but rather to equip him with a suit of shining armour, including a helmet of solid gold. He also told her that she was to give him a heavy lead mace. By the age of ten Volkh was fully educated and had learned other skills, such as the ability to change his shape at will. At twelve he began to gather an army of youths, a task which took him three years, but by the age of fifteen he had assembled some 7,000, all of them the same age as he was.

A short time after this a rumour reached KIEV that the king of INDIA was threatening to invade RUSSIA. Immediately Volkh and his army set forth for that far-off land. Each night, as his troops slept, Volkh would change himself into a vicious wolf and hunt down the animals that were needed to feed his army. Some nights, wanting to give his men a change from red meat, Volkh would change himself into a falcon and harry swans, geese and ducks.

Nearing the borders of India, Volkh changed himself into a wild ox and bounded away from his army to spy out the land ahead. Reaching India, he changed himself into a falcon and flew straight to the palace of King SALTYK, whom he overheard talking to his wife, who was warning him of Volkh's approach. Knowing that his advance had been reported, Volkh changed himself into a stoat and ran all over the palace, seeking out the king's armaments. He gnawed through bow strings, removed the flints from firearms and buried them, and ruined as much as he could find. Then he changed himself into a falcon once again and flew back to where his men were waiting.

Marching them relentlessly on towards India, they finally arrived at the walls of the capital city. There appeared to be no entry, but Volkh changed himself and his entire army into ants, and they crawled through tiny gaps until they were inside. Changing his men back into their human form, he commanded them to slaughter everyone, save for 7,000 beautiful maid-ens, one for each of them. He himself went straight to the royal palace. There he forced his way into King Saltyk's chamber, swung him about his head and smashed him on to the floor, which shattered him.

Volkh then divided the spoils of the land among his men, who married the 7,000 maidens who had been spared, and Volkh and his men settled in that land, Volkh ruling wisely over them and taking the captive queen to be his wife.

Vseslav`evna, Marfa
Russian
The mother of Volkh VESLAV`EVICH, whom she conceived when she stepped on a serpent which wound itself around her and impregnated her, her son, a great wizard, being born in KIEV.

Vuldr
Norse and Teutonic
Variant of ULLR.

Vyeles
Russian
The specific Russian name for the god of war who was, elsewhere, known as VOLOS.

Wachilt
Norse and Teutonic
Goddess who met King VILCINUS in the forest and subsequently rose from the depths of the ocean to arrest the progress of his ship to tell him that she was to bear their son. Vilcinus took her home, where she gave birth to the great WADA before disappearing. Later she once more rose from the sea, to save her grandson WITTICH from those who sought to kill him, and took him down to her sea-bed palace.

Wad~a, ~e
Norse and Teutonic
The giant son of WACHILT and VILCINUS, and the father of VÖLUNDR. Wada was especially connected with great stones and the sea, and was particularly revered in DENMARK and by the ANGLO-SAXONS, the latter of whom referred to him by his variant Wade.

Wælcyrge
Norse, Teutonic and Anglo-Saxon
An eighth- and ninth-century term meaning 'Chooser of the Slain' that appears to be a corruption of VALKYRJA.

Wagner, Richard
General
German composer (1813–83) who revolutionized the nineteenth-century conception of opera, seeing it as a wholly new art form in which musical, poetic and scenic elements should be unified. His operas include *Tannhäuser* (1845),

Lohengrin (1850) and *Tristan and Isolde* (1865). In 1876 the first performance of his masterpiece *Der Ring des Nibelungen*, a sequence of four operas, was performed at the Festival Theatre in Bayreuth that Wagner had founded in 1872. His last work, *Parsifal*, was produced in 1882.

Walgino
Polish
The patron god of cattle.

Walpurgisnacht
Teutonic
The eve of May Day on which, according to TEUTONIC belief, the witches would congregate on the Brocken, the highest peak of the Harz Mountains in Germany, to dance.

Water of Life and Death
Russian
A magical water that was owned by the DRAGON[1] which abducted VASILISA OF THE GOLDEN BRAID. It was used by IVAN THE PEA to restore his two brothers to life when he rescued his sister Vasilisa from the dragon. Ivan the Pea, keeping a promise, also gave some of the life-restoring water to an old crone who lived in a small wooden house on chicken's legs in a forest and which revolved in the wind, for she had given him directions to the land of the dragon.

The Water of Life and Death also makes an appearance in the story of IVAN[6]. Here it was used by a shape-changing wolf to restore Ivan to life after he had been ambushed and killed by his brothers, DMITRII and VASILII[2], who were jealous that Ivan had obtained the FIREBIRD and also managed to secure the HORSE WITH THE GOLDEN MANE and the maiden ELENA THE BEAUTIFUL.

Wave Maidens
Norse and Teutonic
Generic name given to the nine giantess daughters of ÆGIR, though this connection is by no means certain. They are named as ATLA, AUGEIA, AURGIAFA, EGIA, GJALP, GREIP, JARNSAXA, SINDR and ULFRUN. All nine are said to have simultaneously given birth to the god HEIMDALLR, the son of ODÍNN, who had come across the giantesses playing in the sea while he wandered through MIDGARDR.

Wayland
Anglo-Saxon
ANGLO-SAXON variant of WELAND which was, in turn, a variant of VÖLUNDR. His name is thought to have been brought to BRITAIN, together with his father's WADE and his son's WIDIA, by the SAXONS. The name Wayland survives in several English names, such as Wayland Wood near Watton in Norfolk, a place traditionally associated with the story *The Babes in the Wood*. The most famous occurrence of the name is undoubtedly Wayland's Smithy, a prehistoric long barrow near Uffington, Oxfordshire.

Wealtheow
Norse, Teutonic and Anglo-Saxon
Queen of the Danes, the wife of HRODGAR.

Weaver of the Stars
Latvian
The wife of MENESS, the MOON[4] god.

Wecta
Anglo-Saxon
According to the line of descent claimed by HENGIST, Wecta was the son of WODEN and great-grandfather of Hengist.

Weland
Norse, Teutonic and Anglo-Saxon
A late variant of VÖLUNDR that was, in turn, to lead to the variant WAYLAND.

Well of Urdr
Norse and Teutonic
Also called the 'Spring of Fate', the Well of Urdr lay at the foot of YGGDRASILL and was tended by the three NORNS, URDR (from whom the well takes its name), VERDANDI and SKULDR. Daily the three virgin goddesses watered the WORLD TREE[2] and plastered it with clay taken from the well to preserve it.

Weohstan
Norse, Teutonic and Anglo-Saxon
The father of WIGLAF.

Werewolf
General
The legends that surround a person who metamorphoses into a wolf at night, but reverts to human form by day, may have come from the BERSERKIRS, the warriors dedicated to ODÍNN who wore bear- or wolf-skin shirts into battle and drove themselves into a martial frenzy. Some werewolves are thought to have had the ability to change their form at will, but others changed involuntarily under the influence of the full moon. It is this latter that has become the most popular concept of the man-wolf. Common superstition still holds that when a werewolf dies it becomes a VAMPIRE.

Weser
Teutonic
The river that runs near to HAMELIN and

in which legend says the PIED PIPER drowned the rats that had been plaguing the city.

Westfold
Norse and Teutonic
According to Snorri STURLUSON in *HEIMSKRINGLA*, Westfold was the seat HÁLFDAN SVARTI established at the age of eighteen, sharing half the kingdom with his brother OLÁFR.

Westri
Norse and Teutonic
The DWARF placed at the western cardinal point to support the dome of the sky that had been formed by the gods ODÍNN, VILLI and VÉ from the skull of YMIR. The east was supported by AUSTRI, the north by NORDRI and the south by SUDRI.

Whirlwind
Russian
The personification of a whirlwind who is sometimes referred to as VIKHOR`. In one story he abducts NASTAS`YA OF THE GOLDEN BRAID, the wife of Bel BELYANIN and mother of PETER, VASILII[1] and IVAN[1], and keeps her in a wondrous palace encrusted with diamonds and other precious stones on a plateau on the top of some very high mountains. There he also holds three maidens captive as the tsaritas of three kingdoms, the COPPER KINGDOM, the SILVER KINGDOM and the GOLDEN KINGDOM, the tsarita of the latter being ELENA THE FAIR. Each of the four palaces in his realm was guarded by multi-headed DRAGONS[1] which could be placated with water drawn from a well nearby.

Whirlwind renewed his strength periodically from a barrel containing a magic water that bestowed great strength on anyone who drank from it. He also kept a second barrel containing a water which sapped strength. It was these two barrels that were ultimately to be his downfall.

Ivan and his two brothers set off to search for their lost mother, Ivan finally discovering her after climbing the tall mountains and passing through the three kingdoms to reach her. There Nastas`ya of the Golden Braid told him of Whirlwind's secret, and by drinking from the strength-increasing barrel, and then swapping it with the strength-sapping one, Ivan was able to defeat Whirlwind, cutting off his head with a single blow and then burning his body before scattering the ashes in the wind.

Whirlwind had two servants, LAME and ONE-EYE, who could work wondrous magic and, after the death of Whirlwind, served Ivan.

White God
Slavonic
Known as BYELOBOG, or BYELUN in RUSSIA, the White God is the personification of good, light and life. He is opposed by CHERNOBOG, the BLACK GOD, the personification of evil and the cause of all misfortune. White God is the literal translation of the root words of the name Byelobog: *byeli*, white, and *bog*, god.

White Horse
Anglo-Saxon
The symbol of the ANGLO-SAXON people which is still a common sight around BRITAIN, particularly in Wiltshire and Oxfordshire, where huge horses have been carved on to the faces of hills and can be seen for many miles. The most famous is perhaps at Uffington, Oxfordshire, quite close to WAYLAND's Smithy. It has been discovered that some are not SAXON in origin, but are much later, sometimes even nineteenth century. However, no matter whether they date from the Dark Ages or are Victorian copies, they remain one of the

most enigmatic reminders of days when England was overrun by barbarians who were to become the direct descendants of the modern English people.

White Russia
General
Translation of Belorussia, a constituent republic of western RUSSIA.

White Youth
Finno-Ugric – Yakut
The father of mankind, simply known as the WHITE YOUTH, who was fed by the spirit of the WORLD TREE². He is possibly cognate with both HEIMDALLR and BYELOBOG.

Widia
Anglo-Saxon
The ANGLO-SAXON name for WITTICH.

Wiglaf
Norse, Teutonic and Anglo-Saxon
The son of WEOHSTAN and kinsman to BEOWULF. He alone stood beside his age-ing king to fight a DRAGON² that had been attacking Beowulf's kingdom. Together they killed the monster, but not before Beowulf received a mortal wound.

Wihtgils
Anglo-Saxon
The father of HENGIST and, according to Hengist's claimed line of descent, the great-great-grandson of WODEN.

Wild Hunt
General
Common throughout Europe is the con-cept of the Wild Hunt, a spectral hunt that survives in folklore to this day during which the ghostly figures of riders may be seen. In England the Wild Hunt was said to have been witnessed in both Devon and Somerset. Most famously it was said to have been led by King ARTHUR, who rode in procession to Glastonbury, Somerset, either at noon or on clear nights that were lit by a full moon.

Will Scarlet
British
One of the companions of ROBIN HOOD and thus one of his MERRY MEN.

Wind
1 *Russian*
In many of the Russian folk-tales the Wind is referred to simply as that, with no name. Earlier stories call the god of the wind STRIBOG. In one (see MOROZKO) the nameless wind appears as a man with tousled hair, a swollen face and lips, and wearing dishevelled clothing. He can be either benevolent or malevolent, and is said to give rise to demons whenever he blows hard.

Later legends talk of not one but three gods of the wind: the gods of the North, East and West Winds, who lived on the oceanic island of BUYAN. Of these, only the West Wind is given a name: DOGODA.

2 *Finno-Ugric*
Though the Wind remains unnamed in FINNO-UGRIC mythology, he is said to have been the father, by LOVIATAR, of nine terrible children: PLEURISY, COLIC, GOUT, TUBERCULOSIS, ULCER, SCABIES, PLAGUE, CANCER and ENVY. He is also said to have stirred life in ILMATER LUONNOTAR as she lay in the primeval ocean and by him conceived the hero VÄINÄMÖINEN.

3 *Czech*
Though the Czech people do not have a single god of the wind, their god of the storm wind, potentially the most dangerous and an attendant on the god of thunder, PERUN, is named as VARPULIS.

Winter
Norse and Teutonic
An early deity, the son of VINDSVAL and grandson of VASUD. The inveterate enemy of SUMMER.

Witta
Anglo-Saxon
According to the line of descent claimed by HENGIST, Witta was the grandson of WODEN and grandfather of Hengist.

Wittich
Norse and Teutonic
The son of VÖLUNDR, thus the grandson of WADA. The ANGLO-SAXONS called him WIDIA. When his life was being threatened, his grandmother WACHILT rose from the depths of the ocean and took him to her sea-bed palace.

Wlencing
Anglo-Saxon
Son of AELLE and brother to CISSA and CYMEN. He and his brothers accompanied their father when he defeated the Britons.

Wod~an, ~en
Teutonic and Anglo-Saxon
The TEUTONIC name for ODÍNN, the NORSE god who seems to have been an amalgamation of the Teutonic deities Wodan and TÎWAZ. The variant Woden was used by the ANGLO-SAXONS. He was the god of war, who by the first century AD appears to have been challenging Tîwaz for the position as the head of the Teutonic pantheon – a position he eventually adopted. As head of the pantheon, Wodan was regarded as the ancestor of all earthly kings and was invoked before every battle. His name is still commemorated in Wednesday or Wodan's Day.

He was at first thought of as the god of the night, the magical ruler of the land of the dead who thundered across the skies at the head of a vast army, his host comprising the souls of dead warriors, while he was dressed in a great flowing cloak and a broad-brimmed hat. As he rose to supremacy, he was no longer to be found at the head of the army, but rather remained at home in his great hall, from where he invoked the spirits of self-sacrifice and heroism, deciding the outcome of all wars and dispensing either reward or punishment. He became an increasingly cruel god and demanded both animal and human sacrifices, human victims usually being crucified in trees, where their bodies were cut to shreds.

His name means 'Master of Fury' and comes from *wode*. The Anglo-Saxons took his worship to England, where he was also known as GRIM, a term that denotes someone wearing a hood that covers their face, and is cognate with the Old Norse GRIMR, a title applied to Odínn and which today survives in such English place-names as Grim's Dyke. His function as the leader of the WILD HUNT survives in the story of HERNE THE HUNTER, among others. The semi-legendary Anglo-Saxon leader claimed his descent from Woden, stating that he was that god's great-great-grandson. Wodan was clearly the master of the powers of darkness and death, and thus has a SHAMANistic element to his character that become even more apparent in his Norse counterpart Odínn.

The second MERSEBURG CHARM mixes Norse and Teutonic tradition, as in this Wodan is associated with BALDR, though Baldr is of Norse origin – a confusion suggesting that Wodan was a name used throughout the Teutonic lands, or that Baldr was imported as the Teutonic tradition had no counterpart.

Wode
Norse and Teutonic
Variant for FRIGGA.

Wolfdales
Norse and Teutonic
The home of VÖLUNDR, EGIL and SLAG-FIDR. It was to a lake in Wolfdales that the three SWAN MAIDENS flew, where they were discovered by the three brothers who made them their wives.

World Tree
1 *Slavonic*
Also known as the TREE OF LIFE[1]. Common to many mythologies and religions is the concept of a World Tree whose roots reach down to the UNDERWORLD[1] and whose branches reach up to heaven. Usually such a tree was considered to grow in the exact centre of the world. Later traditions tended to treat the World Tree with some contempt, though in SIBERIA it retained its importance for much longer, as the SHAMAN climbed a tree in order to gain magic powers.

One late story illustrates the manner in which the World Tree was treated long after the disappearance of paganism. This tells of a peasant couple who were so poor that they were reduced to living off acorns from the forest. One acorn rolled into their cellar, where it began to grow. When it reached the floor of their home they simply cut a hole for it to grow through. They did the same when it reached their roof. Now they had a tree growing straight through their home.

Finally the time came when they could find no more acorns in the forest, so the man climbed the tree to gather acorns from it instead. Among its uppermost branches he found a magnificent cockerel and a handmill. Quickly he seized both and climbed back down to his wife below. Wondering what they would have to eat that day, the old woman turned the handle on the mill. To their delight pies and pancakes began to tumble from the mill. From that day forth, they no longer felt the pangs of hunger.

Some time later a wealthy merchant was passing through the forest. He stopped at their house and was hospitably welcomed and fed from the mill. Seeing the mill, the merchant offered a high price for it, but the couple would not sell it. Instead the merchant simply stole it and returned home. Knowing that the couple could not go after him, for no one would believe their word against his, the cockerel said that he would return their mill to them, and flew off to the home of the merchant.

Perching on the man's gate, the cockerel crowed that the merchant should return the mill. Hearing this, the man ordered his servants to throw the cockerel into the well. There the cockerel simply drained the water and flew on to the man's balcony, where it repeated its demands. This time the man had his cook throw the cockerel into the stove. In the midst of the flames the cockerel spat out all the water from the well and flew right into the heart of the man's house. As the man ran away, the cockerel seized the mill and flew back to the old couple in the wood.

2 *Norse and Teutonic*
The common way of referring to YGGDRASILL.

Wotan
Teutonic
Variant of WODAN.

Wurdr
Norse and Teutonic
Variant of URDR.

Wyrd
Norse, Teutonic and Anglo-Saxon

The mother of the three virgin NORNS, though the ANGLO-SAXONS actually regarded her as one of the Norns, the name being seen as their variant of URDR. It is thought that the memory of the three goddesses who determined man's life persisted until at least SHAKESPEARE's day, the 'three weird sisters' of *Macbeth* possibly being a representation of them. This is supported by an illustration in the first edition of Holinshed's *Chronicles* (1577) which shows the three sisters standing beneath a tree which would appear to be a direct derivation of YGGDRASILL.

Y

Yakut(s)
General

A Turkic-speaking people living near the Lena River in northeast SIBERIA, one of the coldest regions on earth. Today there is an institute in Yakutsk, the coldest point in the Arctic, for studying the permafrost there. Very few of the beliefs of the ancient Yakut people have survived. Turkic is an Ural-Altaic language and thus closely related to FINNO-UGRIC.

Yarilo
Slavonic

A goddess of peace who, in later times, changed gender and became the god of spring, fertility and erotic or sexual love. Depicted as a barefoot youth dressed in a white cloak and adorned with a crown of wild flowers, Yarilo rode on a white horse, his left hand holding a bucket of wheat. Ceremonies honouring Yarilo were commonplace as recently as the eighteenth century, these consisting of a planting rite in spring and the ritual burning of his/her effigy in summer.

Yarovit
Baltic Coast

A deity, having some of the attributes of SVANTOVIT and possibly simply an aspect of that deity. His existence is only known through the writings of the Danish chronicler SAXO GRAMMATICUS.

Ydalir
Norse and Teutonic

The hall within ASGARDR that was the home of ULLR.

Yggdrasil(l)
Norse and Teutonic

The WORLD TREE[2], a sacred ash that spans heaven, earth and hell. An evergreen, it is tended by the three virgin NORNS, who live at its foot, where they guard the WELL OF URDR, from which they daily take water to nourish the tree and clay which they plaster on its bark to preserve it.

Yggdrasill has three roots, with a spring that rises beneath each one. The first root reaches into NIFLHEIMR, the UNDERWORLD[4], the land of the dead, and beneath it rises the spring HVERGELMIR, the source of all earthly rivers. The second root runs into JÖTUNHEIMR, the land of the FROST GIANTS, and under it rises the spring of MÍMIR, which gives great wisdom to all who drink from it. The third root reaches into ASGARDR, the home of the gods. It is under this root that the Well of Urdr rises, a site where the gods regularly gathered to confer.

At the base of the tree, curled around the trunk, lies the huge serpent NIDHOGGR, along with many smaller snakes, all of whom constantly gnaw at the tree's roots. On the topmost branch an eagle perches with a hawk named VEDFOLNIR on its head, or between its eyes. This eagle was the inveterate enemy of Nidhoggr. Between them the squirrel RATATOSKR scurried, carrying insulting messages from one to the other. Within the branches of the tree lived the goat HEIDRUN and the four stags DAIN[2], DUNEYR, DURATHOR and DVALIN[2].

Following the RAGNARØKR both LÍF and

LÍFDRASIR will emerge from the shelter of Yggdrasill's branches to repopulate the world, thus perpetuating the necessity of Yggdrasill to the very existence of the world and all life upon it.

Ymir
Norse and Teutonic

Also FORNJOTNR and ORGELMIR. The first of the immortals, the primeval father of the giants. Created when sparks from MÚSPELLHEIMR met the icy floes of NIFLHEIMR in the GINNUNGAGAP, the resulting thaw revealing the giant in the ice. Two trees grew from Ymir's armpits and these were to later become the first man, ASKR, and the first woman, EMBLA. From between his toes the race of FROST GIANTS grew. Ymir was fed by the primordial cow AUDHUMLA, whose licking of the salt-encrusted rocks freed the man BÚRI, whose son BÖRR married BESTLA, Ymir's daughter. Their children were the gods ODÍNN, VILLI and VÉ.

Ymir was killed by his three grandsons, the blood from the carnage covering everything and drowning all the giants with the exception of BERGELMIR, who sailed away across the flood to found a new race of giants who were to become the mortal enemies of the ÆSIR.

From the corpse of Ymir the three gods formed MIDGARDR, the world of men. The flesh of the giant became the earth, in which the gods also created DWARFS like 'maggots'. From the blood they formed the seas and the lakes, the mountains were formed from the bones, rocks and pebbles from the teeth, jaws and smaller broken bones of the giant, while the grass was formed from the hair. To protect the newly created earth the three gods placed Ymir's eyebrows around its perimeter as a wall to keep out the Frost Giants. Finally the gods placed four dwarfs at the four cardinal points and had them support Ymir's skull, which became the dome of the sky.

Yngling
Norse and Teutonic

According to Snorri STURLUSON in the YNGLINGA SAGA from HEIMSKRINGLA, FREYR was also known as YNGVE. For a long time after the death of Freyr, this was considered a name of honour, so much so that his descendants have ever since been called Yngling.

Ynglinga Saga
Norse and Teutonic

Saga which refers to the SHAMANistic characteristics of ODÍNN, and talks of the ability of that god to send out his spirit in the form of an animal or bird to far-off lands to return with news and other information.

Yngve
Norse and Teutonic

According to Snorri STURLUSON in the YNGLINGA SAGA from HEIMSKRINGLA, FREYR was also known as Yngve. For a long time after the death of Freyr, this was considered a name of honour, so much so that his descendants have ever since been called YNGLING.

Yryn-al-tojon
Siberia – Yakut

The 'White Creator Lord', the supreme being of the YAKUT people. He lives in, or above, the TREE OF LIFE[2], the cosmic pillar, in whose roots the mother goddess AJYSYT lives and from where she rises to suckle those in need of nourishment and sustenance.

Zabava, Princess
Russian

The favourite niece of Prince VLADIMIR BRIGHT SUN. She was abducted from the gardens of the royal court at KIEV by a twelve-headed she-DRAGON[1] and carried away, between the dragon's jaws, to the dragon's lair in the SOROCHINSK Mountains. She was later rescued by Dobrynya NIKITICH, who killed the dragon after an epic three-day battle.

Zaltys
Lithuanian

The grass snake who was believed to be lucky and with whose head AITVARAS was sometimes perceived.

Zealand
General

Variant name for SJÆLLAND, the main island of DENMARK.

Zemepatis
Lithuanian

Also known as ZEMININKAS. The brother of ZEMYNA, Zemepatis is the god of the homestead, sometimes being called DIMSTIPATIS, this latter name being cognate with *dimstis*, home, and *patis*, father. In LATVIA, the equivalent is MAJAS KUNGS.

Zemes Mate
Latvian – Lett

The name given to MOTHER EARTH by the Lett people who inhabited LATVIA but were more closely related to people from LITHUANIA. The Lithuanian equivalent to Zemes Mate is ZEMYNA.

Zemininkas
Lithuanian

Alternative name for ZEMEPATIS.

Zemyna
Lithuanian

In LITHUANIA, the name for MOTHER EARTH. Sometimes referred to as the sister of ZEMEPATIS, god of the home, Zemyna is also known as 'Mother of the Fields', 'Mother of Springs', 'Mother of Forests', 'Blossomer' and the 'Bud-raiser'.

Zlatorog
Slovene

A white chamois with golden horns that lived on the slopes of Mount TRIGLAV in northeastern SLOVENIA. Once Zlatorog was pursued by hunters, who were, naturally, after the animal's golden horns. Zlatorog outwitted the hunters by leading them to the edge of a precipice, over which all but one of the hunters fell. This survivor managed to wound Zlatorog and out of this wound sprang a red flower, which Zlatorog ate and was immediately cured. Some accounts say that this flower was a red carnation, the emblem of Slovenia.

Z~orya, ~arya
Slavonic

A collective term applied to the two daughters of DAZHBOG[1], their names being ZORYA UTRENNYAYA and ZORYA

VECHERNYAYA. Sometimes there are three daughters included under this title, but the third, the goddess of midnight, remains nameless. Although each of the named Zorya has a specific task to carry out at her father's palace, all three are appointed guardians of the unnamed deity who has been chained to the constellation Ursa Major (the GREAT BEAR), for if he breaks loose then the world will come to an end. Some accounts say that they watch over the constellation in case the bear, or hound, imprisoned within breaks free. The Zorya are sisters to the ZVEZDA.

Zorya Utrennyaya
Slavonic

One of the two, sometimes three, daughters of DAZHBOG[1]. The goddess of dawn, and sister to ZORYA VECHERNYAYA, Zorya Utrennyaya opens the gates to her father's palace so that he might ride forth at the start of the SUN[11]'s journey. Her sister, the goddess of dusk, closes them again after Dazhbog has returned home. There is sometimes a third sister, the goddess of midnight, but she remains nameless. The two, or three, sisters are collectively known simply as the ZORYA, and are sisters to Dazhbog's other daughters, ZVEZDA DENNITSA and ZVEZDA VECHERNYAYA, who are, in turn, simply known collectively as the ZVEZDA.

Zorya Vechernyaya
Slavonic

One of the two, sometimes three, daughters of DAZHBOG[1]. The goddess of dusk, and sister to ZORYA UTRENNYAYA, Zorya Vechernyaya closes the gates to her father's palace at night after he has returned home at the end of the day. There is sometimes a third sister, the goddess of midnight, but she remains nameless. The two, or three, sisters are collectively known simply as the ZORYA,

and are sisters to Dazhbog's other daughters, ZVEZDA DENNITSA and ZVEZDA VECHERNYAYA, who are, in turn, known collectively as the ZVEZDA.

Zroya
Slavonic

The virgin goddess of war who is closely associated with PYERUN or his various incarnations.

Zvezda
Slavonic

A collective name given to ZVEZDA DENNITSA and ZVEZDA VECHERNYAYA. The two Zvezda are the daughters of DAZHBOG[1] and the sisters of the two, sometimes three, ZORYA. They are also sometimes described as the two AURORAS.

Zvezda Dennitsa
Slavonic

The MORNING STAR[3], one of the two ZVEZDA, sister to ZVEZDA VECHERNYAYA and the two, or three, ZORYA, all four, or five, being the daughters of DAZHBOG[1]. Both she and her sister, ZVEZDA VECHERNYAYA, the EVENING STAR, are described as having married MYESYATS, the MOON[1], and became the mother of the stars by him. The specific task of Zvezda Dennitsa and her sister was to groom the horses that daily pulled their father's chariot across the sky.

Zvezda Vechernyaya
Slavonic

The EVENING STAR, daughter of DAZHBOG[1] and sister to ZVEZDA DENNITSA, as well as the two, sometimes three, ZORYA. She is said to have married MYESYATS, the MOON[1], and to have been the mother of the stars by him, but her sister Zvezda Dennitsa is also said to have done this. Zvezda Vechernyaya and Zvezda Dennitsa had the specific job of grooming their father's white horses.

BIBLIOGRAPHY

The main sources that have been consulted during the compilation of this work follow. While some of the books listed in the original language may be available in a translated form, those given below, particularly for Russia, are the core texts from which translations have been made. I am indebted to my contacts in Russia, who have supplied me with rough translations of the stories they were told as children by their parents and which, I have no doubt, they are telling their own children. Many of these have, to the best of my knowledge, never been written down before.

Afanas`ev, A. N., *Narodnye russkie legendy*, Moscow, 1916

– *Narodnye russkie shazki*, Vol. 1, Academia, 1936

– *Poeticheskie vozzreniya slayan no prirodu*, Vols. 1–3, Moscow, 1865–9

Azadovskii, M. (ed.), *Russkaya shazka*, Vols. 1 and 2, Moscow–Leningrad, 1931

Baktin, V., *Shazki Leningradskoi oblasti*, Leningrad, 1976

Branston, Brian, *Gods of the North*, Thames & Hudson, London, 1955

Crossley-Holland, Kevin, *The Norse Myths*, André Deutsch, London, 1980

Davidson, H. R. Ellis, *Gods and Myths of Northern Europe*, Penguin Books, Harmondsworth, 1964

– *The Viking Road to Byzantium*, Allen & Unwin, London, 1976

– *Scandinavian Mythology*, rev. edn, Hamlyn, London, 1982

– *Pagan Scandinavia*, Hamlyn, London, 1984

– *Lost Beliefs of Northern Europe*, Routledge, London, 1993

Downing, C., *Russian Tales and Legends*, Oxford University Press, Oxford, 1956

Esping, Mikael, *The Vikings*, Piccolo, London, 1982

Gimbutas, Marija, *The Balts*, Thames & Hudson, London, 1963

– *The Goddesses and Gods of Old Europe: 6500–3500 BC*, Thames & Hudson, London, 1982

Grant, John, *An Introduction to Viking Mythology*, Grange Books, London, 1995

Green, Miranda, *The Sun Gods of Ancient Europe*, Batsford, London, 1991

Green, Roger Lancelyn, *Myths of the Norsemen*, Penguin Books, Harmondsworth, 1970

Guerber, H. A., *Myths of the Norsemen*, Harrap, London, 1908

Hveberg, Harald (trans. Pat Shaw Iversen), *Of Gods and Giants*, Johan Grundt Tanum Forlag, with the Office of Cultural Relations, Norwegian Ministry of Foreign Affairs, Oslo, 1961

Ivanits, Linda J., *Russian Folk Belief*, M. E. Sharpe Inc., Armonk, New York, 1989

Jones, G. A., *A History of the Vikings*, Oxford University Press, Oxford, 1984

Jones, Gwyn (trans. and ed.), *Eirik the Red and Other Icelandic Sagas*, Oxford University Press, London, 1961

Kirby, W. F. (trans.), *Kalevala: The Land of Heroes*, 2 vols., J. M. Dent & Sons Ltd, London, 1907

Lönnrot, Elias, *Kalevala*, various translations

MacCulloch, John A. and Gray, Louis H., *The Mythology of All Races*, 13 vols., Cooper Square Publications Inc., New York, 1922

Novikov, N. V. (ed.), *Russkie shazki v zapisyakh i publikatsiyakh pervoi poloviny XIX veka*, Leningrad–Moscow, 1961

– *Russkie shazki v rannikh zapisyakh i publikatsiyakh XVI–XVIII veka*, Leningrad, 1971

Oinas, Felix J., *Essays on Russian Folklore and Mythology*, Slavica, Columbus, Ohio, 1985

Owen, G. R., *Rites and Religions of the Anglo-Saxons*, David & Charles, Newton Abbot, 1981

Oxenstierna, E. G., *The Norsemen*, Weidenfeld & Nicolson, London, 1965

Pears Encyclopaedia of Myths and Legends, *Vol. 2: Western & Northern Europe: Central & Southern Africa*, Pelham Books, London, 1978

Perkowski, Jan L., *Vampires of the Slavs*, Slavica, Cambridge, Massachusetts, 1976

– *The Darkling: Vampires of the Slavs*, Slavica, Columbus, Ohio, 1989

Popovic, Tatyana, *Prince Marko: The Hero of South Slavic Epic*, Syracuse University Press, Syracuse, New York, 1988

Potebnya, A. A., *O mificheskom gnachenii nekotorykh obryadov i poverii*, Moscow, 1865

Propp, V. I. (ed.), *Byliny*, Leningrad, 1957

Sawyer, P. H., *The Age of the Vikings*, Edward Arnold, London, 1971

Simek, R., *Dictionary of Northern Mythology*, Boydell & Brewer, Woodbridge, 1993

Sturluson, Snorri, (trans. Jean I. Young), *The Prose Edda*, Bowes & Bowes, Cambridge, 1954

Todd, M., *The Early Germans*, Blackwell, Oxford, 1992

Turville-Petre, E. O. G., *Myth and Religion of the North*, Wiedenfeld & Nicolson, London, 1964

Vries, J. de, *Heroic Song and Heroic Legend*, Oxford University Press, Oxford, 1964